FORTUNE AND FAITH IN OLD CHICAGO

FORTUNE AND FAITH IN OLD CHICAGO

A DUAL BIOGRAPHY OF
MAYOR AUGUSTUS GARRETT
AND
SEMINARY FOUNDER
ELIZA CLARK GARRETT

Charles H. Cosgrove

Southern Illinois University Press • Carbondale

To Geoffrey,
with best
wishes &
thanks for all
you do to
promote Chicago
history and
culture,
Charlie

Southern Illinois University Press
www.siupress.com

23 22 21 20   4 3 2 1

Publication of this volume has been made possible in part through a
generous contribution by Garrett-Evangelical Theological Seminary.

Jacket illustrations: oil paintings of Augustus Garrett and Eliza Garrett,
by C. V. Bond (posthumous, 1856); both images courtesy of Garrett-
Evangelical Theological Seminary.

Library of Congress Cataloging-in-Publication Data
Names: Cosgrove, Charles H., author.
Title: Fortune and faith in old Chicago : a dual biography of Mayor
Augustus Garrett and seminary founder Eliza Clark Garrett /
Charles H. Cosgrove.
Description: Carbondale : Southern Illinois University Press, [2020]
| Includes bibliographical references and index.
Identifiers: LCCN 2019023445 (print) | LCCN 2019023446 (ebook)
| ISBN 9780809337941 (cloth) | ISBN 9780809337958 (ebook)
Subjects: LCSH: Garrett, Augustus, 1801–1848. | Garrett, Eliza Clark,
1805–1855. | Garrett Biblical Institute—History. | Mayors—Illinois—
Chicago—Biography. | Women philanthropists—Illinois—Chicago—
Biography. | Chicago (Ill.)—Politics and government—19th century.
| Chicago (Ill.)—History—19th century.
Classification: LCC F548.25 .C67 2020 (print) | LCC F548.25 (ebook)
| DDC 977.3/11030922 [B]—dc23
LC record available at https://lccn.loc.gov/2019023445
LC ebook record available at https://lccn.loc.gov/2019023446

To Lallene J. Rector
with gratitude
for your leadership and grace

CONTENTS

ILLUSTRATIONS

A NOTE TO THE READER

*P*unctuation and spelling were far from standard in postrevolutionary America. Where old correspondence departs from current norms, I have added some punctuation and "corrected" some spellings for the sake of clarity. An interest in referring to people in ways that reflect gender equality has led me to call the Garretts by their first names. Exceptions are certain sections where I describe Augustus's business and political affairs. In these contexts, I often refer to him as "Garrett" in accord with the custom of the day. But in narrating Eliza's more public activities, I have not adopted the nineteenth-century convention of calling her "Mrs. Garrett" but have used her first name instead. I might have called her "Garrett," but that would have risked confusing her with her husband.

PROLOGUE

*T*his is the story of two adventurous people of the postrevolutionary generation. Augustus and Eliza (née Clark) Garrett met and married in the Hudson Valley village of their youth. Eager to escape farm life, they headed west, lured by rumors of great opportunities in Cincinnati. Unsuccessful there, they went on to New Orleans, then Natchitoches, and finally, all but completely disheartened by failure and personal tragedy, they risked their futures on a remote trading post called "Chicago" near the sleepy mouth of a prairie river.

Augustus amassed great wealth in Chicago, first as an auctioneer during the great land speculation of 1835, then as an investor in real estate and a commission agent for firms trading in goods between New York City and Chicago. He also served twice as mayor of Chicago. In the decades preceding the Civil War and before the rise of professional machine politics, he was among the handful of leading businessmen who took turns running the city as aldermen and chief executives, men who converted the "little log and clapboard village" into a booming commercial center.[1]

Only two of these early Chicago leaders have been treated in full biographies—John Wentworth, who also served as a congressman of the Fourth Congressional District of Illinois, and William B. Ogden, the city's first mayor, who was one of its most important developers as well as a pioneer in railroads. As for the other mayors and influential citizens of the city's early years—men such as Walter Newberry, Thomas Dyer, Benjamin Raymond, and Ira Miltimore—one finds at most only a handful of paragraphs devoted to this one or that, and almost nothing about the city's women. Primary sources are scarce, due in part to the destruction of so many personal and public papers in the Great Chicago Fire of 1871 but also to the failure of most families to preserve or send off to archives the relics of ancestors who had shaped the history and institutions of the city. As for the contributions of women in particular, antebellum culture

I

accorded women little place in public life. Their names and doings seldom appeared in the Chicago newspapers, and rarely was the correspondence of a woman preserved by her family or a library. As a result, even the most remarkable women of early Chicago are practically unknown.[2]

Eliza Garrett was one such woman. In most ways a dutiful nineteenth-century wife with little say or influence, limited in decision-making power even in her own home, she came into her own when her husband died, suddenly, in his forty-seventh year. This event made her something of a rarity in antebellum America—an independently wealthy woman. To preserve her inheritance, she gave up her house and lived like a church mouse, spending the next several years involved in various causes, including raising money for a preparatory school for the new Northwestern University and making plans to establish a "female college." In the end, Eliza decided to endow both a theological school and a women's college. Due to a contingency in the funding, the latter institution did not materialize; but the theological school was established, making Eliza the first woman in North America to found an institution of higher learning.[3]

The chapters to follow trace the lives of the Garretts from their courtship days in rural New York to their lives as public citizens in the fast-developing city of Chicago, where fortunes were made in the wake of Indian "removal," land speculators turned a frontier outpost into a metropolis, boosters bet that a canal would make Chicago the great commercial hub between the Eastern Seaboard and the Gulf of Mexico, citizen politicians managed city affairs in their spare time, and women struggled to have a say in more than household routines and tea parties. Augustus Garrett was a speculator, canal booster, and citizen-politician who made a name and a fortune for himself in the heady days of the young and rising city. Eliza Garrett was the wife who emerged from his shadow to make her own mark on history by giving away his estate.

CHAPTER I

NEWBURGH BEGINNINGS

*H*enry Hudson was probably the first European to visit Newburgh bay. In mid-September of 1609 his sailing ship, the *Half Moon*, making its way up the river that natives of the region called "Muhheakunnuk" and whites would eventually name "Hudson," paused in a small apron of the stream. There his navigator set down a brief description, remarking that it was "a very pleasant place to build a town on." A historian later imagined the scene more picturesquely—"sun streaming down on the over-hanging Highlands and the magnificent virgin forests which clothed the riverbanks with their gorgeous autumnal hues." Two hundred years after Hudson's visit to the spot, this bay was the main port for Newburgh (then written New Burgh). A town covering some thirty square miles was officially organized in 1788, and a village, huddled around the bay, was carved out of the town through legal incorporation in 1800—its chief claim to fame being that it had recently served as headquarters for Washington's Continental Army in the Revolutionary War.[1]

Leaving Newburgh on the North Road, one passed through the districts of north Orange County, where farmlands sloped rather steeply toward the Hudson River. Here stony fields struggled to produce barley and wheat, oats and peas; orchard trees sent their roots deep and wide to nourish the apples, pears, plums, and peaches that must fill the larder and the jar. There were sheep, hogs, and cows in pens and small barns, too, all for home consumption, not sale on the market. Yet here and there one spied bits of industry—the occasional brewery, gristmill, tannery, brick factory, and sawmill by which farming men tried to improve their lot. In Middle Hope of this district, north of Balmville, Augustus Garrett and Eliza Clark grew up.[2]

By the 1830s Middle Hope was a respectable hamlet consisting of a post office, two taverns, a school, a Methodist chapel, and a dozen houses. But when Eliza was born there on March 5, 1805, Middle Hope was a mere crossroads. Her parents' farm lay off the main road and somewhat to the north of Middle Hope, close to the county border. A mile or two farther on, in the little town of Marlborough in Ulster County, was a Presbyterian church. To this church, which stood on a bluff near the Hudson River, the Clark family journeyed most Sundays.[3]

She was the daughter of Benoni and Amy (Demott) Clark. Benoni's mother, Joanna Clark, was from Cornwall. For reasons not disclosed in the records, Benoni was adopted by his grandfather, Nathan Clark Jr., and for that reason carried the Clark surname. There may be a clue in the name "Benoni," a biblical word meaning "son of my sorrow." It appears with some frequency in the genealogies of New Englanders of the seventeenth and eighteenth centuries, more often than not as the name of children born under unfortunate circumstances—the death of the mother in childbirth, the death of the father before the birth of the child, a birth out of wedlock, or the death of the child soon after birth. Little is known of Benoni's parents, but it is possible that Joanna bore Benoni out of wedlock. This would explain why he carried the Clark surname. Joanna Clark eventually married a man named Samuel Stratton.[4]

Benoni, born in 1760, turned fifteen at the start of the Revolutionary War. No record indicates whether he served in any branch of the Continental Army, but he is listed as an ensign in an Orange County regiment of the New York militia in 1805 under Colonel Leonard Smith. Sometime after the war he married Amy Demott of nearby Balmville. They had five children, all born in Newburgh Township: Samuel, Isaac, Jeremiah, John, and Eliza.[5]

Amy Demott's lineage is somewhat cloudy. She was a granddaughter of Michael Demott and the daughter of either Isaac or James Demott, both of whom served in the Revolutionary War under a Samuel Clark. In the mid-eighteenth century, Michael Demott owned land in Balmville and kept a small tavern there. In 1786 Isaac and James were each granted parts of some four hundred forested acres of the German patent in Balmville.[6]

Balmville took its name from a tree, which stood beside the North Road on Isaac's property, west of his father's tavern. The tree was an eastern cottonwood that locals mistakenly identified as a species of poplar known as balm of Gilead. Various legends were passed down about the origin and antiquity of the Balmville tree. Science, however, would eventually establish that the tree—at least the one well known as "the Balmville tree" in the early nineteenth century—began growing in 1699. By the time Eliza came along a hundred years later, everyone knew the tree on her maternal family's land. It was thought to have medicinal properties, and its fame made it a destination for locals and villagers on Sunday walks. One can picture the Demott family picnicking there in the 1820s with Augustus Garrett the suitor on hand, full of mirth as he tried to charm his way into the family.[7]

Almost everyone in the districts outside Newburgh Village farmed, despite the poor conditions for cultivation. The average family produced little for outside sale, and there was little market for cash crops anyway. This made it difficult for a man to make a profit in hopes of increasing

The Balmville tree. From Barclay, "Balmville," between pages 48 and 49.

his landholdings or even making the transition from renting to owning. By 1800, when Benoni was forty years old, he still owned no land and possessed personal property valued at only $250.[8]

To understand Eliza, it is necessary to see her first in the world of her childhood and adolescence. Farm life affected women of the early 1800s in different ways. In Eliza's case, rural living placed frustrating limits on her cultural experience but also hardened her to plain living. As a result, she was eager to fly away to far-off cities with Augustus but also accepting of the hardships that went with his failures in those places.

In the young Eliza's world, farmhouses were small. Some Newburgh domiciles were built of stone; most were one-story wooden structures with just two or three rooms, like the one in central Massachusetts visited by Asa Sheldon around 1800. The house had "two rooms on the base and was one story in height" with "two glass windows in front and a board one in the rear that could be taken down at pleasure." The hearth was made of rough stone, and in the center of the room was a pine post that supported the attic floor. (Over the years, the family had carved out peels of kindling from this post, so that it had been whittled down to rather unsafe dimensions.) The Samuel Fowler house in Middle Hope may have been one of the nicer homes in the Middle Hope district. A surviving photograph shows a single-story edifice with four small windows flanking a middle front door and what appears to be a small loft or attic.[9]

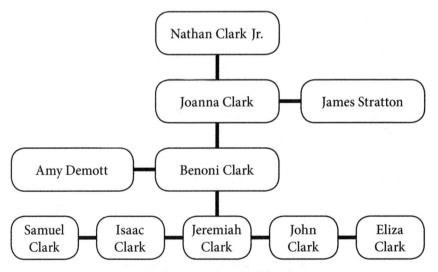

Eliza Clark Garrett's partial family tree.

Until the small domestic revolution that commenced around 1830, all cooking, dining, and work took place in the room with the fireplace, which most people called the "hall." In a two-room house, the only other room—a "parlor" or "chamber"—was for sleeping but also for entertaining guests since it contained what was usually the household's most expensive piece of furniture: the parental bed. Other members of the household often slept in this room, too, or in the hall, or in the garret beneath the eaves. A two- or three-room house had little in the way of furniture. Its interior walls were usually unadorned and unpainted, the floor dirty. Almost no one owned a broom. Outside, the yard was devoid of trees, weedy and slovenly, cluttered with odds and ends.[10]

The Clark family was not so remotely situated as some country dwellers, but distance and housework restricted Eliza's and her mother's contact with others. Farm-life's routines were divided by gender. The female sphere extended from the house and hearth to the garden and yard. The world of men reached from barn and workshop to fields and pastures, as well as woodlands, country lanes, and taverns. Eliza and her mother spent their days cooking and cleaning, cutting and carrying firewood, hauling water, washing and ironing, sewing and mending, cultivating the garden, tending chickens, canning fruits and vegetables, making soap and candles, curing meat—an endless "dull round of chores," as one woman put it. The seasonal rhythm of men's work gave them more time for leisure, for hunting in spring and fall and lounging about in taverns in the winter months. There was no break in women's work, even on Sundays and holidays, when they still had to feed chickens, collect wood, haul water, cook meals, and care for children. When a commission of the U.S. Department of Agriculture looked into the lives of rural women in the early 1860s, its report concluded that "a farmer's wife, as a too general rule, is a laboring drudge. . . . It is perhaps safe to say, that on three farms out of four the wife works harder, endures more, than any other on the place." The report also found that most husbands were cruel and insensitive to their wives.[11]

Apart from flour, which was ground at the mill, and store-bought salt, sugar, and spices, the Clark family produced everything it consumed, and most of the processing was done by Eliza and her mother—churning butter, curing and pickling meats; making vinegar, soap, and candles; slaughtering, plucking, and dressing chickens. They had no icebox, but in the winter, rooms with no fireplace were cold, and most houses had root cellars for long- and short-term storage. Into these caverns went apples, potatoes, beets, parsnips, turnips, carrots, and onions, as well as cheese and eggs. The day's meals included a large breakfast, a substantial noon meal, and the remains of dinner left covered on the table and eaten cold for supper. They had no cookstove. They prepared stews and porridges in a blackened iron pot over a large open hearth whose fire provided the principal heat for the farmhouse. Meat they fried in a pan set directly on the coals. Sometimes they roasted chicken in a small "tin kitchen" that stood on four legs in front of the fire. They baked bread in this tin box as well.[12]

Cotton fabrics were available in Newburgh dry-goods stores, and a family of means could bring store-bought cloth to a Newburgh tailor and have it cut or made up into clothing. But the loom and the woolwheel remained standard features of the rural home until the 1830s. Eliza and her mother spent many hours spinning yarn and weaving cloth, producing from their handmade textiles all the family's clothing—shirts and trousers, coats and capes, shifts and chemises, dresses, aprons, socks, gloves, caps, and scarves, everything except shoes and boots.[13]

Somehow Eliza managed to learn how to read and write, some of this training no doubt being acquired in Sunday school, where she was taught from the King James Bible. She probably did not attend a schoolhouse more than two hundred days all told, spread over several years. She may have had even less schooling since she was her mother's only daughter and was needed at home more than most girls. Like many literate people of her era, she spelled words inconsistently, produced run-on sentences (through lack of punctuation), and wrote in a somewhat inelegant hand. Nevertheless, her manner of expression as an adult was that of an educated person or at least someone whose speech had been refined by life among well-educated people and books. Her letters display only rare grammatical slips, no colloquial idioms or slang, no narrowness of vocabulary.[14]

* * *

Certain details of Eliza's religious upbringing bear directly on the most momentous events of her life and are worth clarifying at the outset. According to Reverend Jeremiah Porter, who was Eliza's pastor at the Presbyterian church in Chicago in the latter part of the 1830s, Eliza had belonged to a Presbyterian congregation in Newburgh before she moved west. Porter was correct in believing she arrived in Chicago a Presbyterian, but he was mistaken about the church to which the Clarks belonged. The Presbyterian church of Newburgh Village was four miles south of Middle

Hope. The Presbyterian church nearer to the Clark farm was in Marlborough, a town of Ulster County, just to the north and across the county border. This church stood on the east side of the North Road that ran through Balmville and Middle Hope before crossing into Ulster County on its way to points farther north. According to later histories—one of Ulster County and the other of the Samuel Clark family—Benoni and Amy Clark were members of this Marlborough Presbyterian church, and Eliza's maternal grandfather, Samuel Stratton, was one of its founders. These sources also say that Benoni and Amy rented a church pew and passed it on to their son Jeremiah Clark, Eliza's older brother. Jeremiah and his wife, Finetta, as well as Benoni and Amy, are buried in the church's graveyard.[15]

Nevertheless, some forty years after Eliza's death, a Chicago Methodist named Alvaro Field learned from correspondents in Newburgh of "an ancient tradition" that "Mrs. Garrett was at one time a probationer in the Methodist Church at Newburgh." According to Field, "her parents

Old First Presbyterian Church of Marlborough.
Courtesy of First Presbyterian Church of Marlboro.

lived in North Newburgh, and were prominent members of a Presbyterian Church two miles away," which is why "Eliza, the daughter, was so often attendant at the Methodist Church in town." The implication is that this Methodist church was closer to the Clark family farm than the Presbyterian church.[16]

There was in fact a Methodist "class" in Middle Hope that eventually established a Methodist chapel, Methodists having been active in Newburgh since the late eighteenth century. In 1786 Rev. Ezekiel Cooper preached the first Methodist sermon in the district in the barn of Samuel and Charlotte Fowler. Subsequently the Fowler residence became a regular preaching stop for Methodist circuit riders. A class was organized in Middle Hope around 1813 and met in a barn owned by Daniel Holmes (in the summer) and in the home of the Fowlers (in the winter). The Fowler–Holmes class was eventually organized into a congregation, and a church building was constructed in Middle Hope in 1822. This meeting place, called Asbury Chapel, was always supplied with circuit preachers.[17]

Field's statement that Eliza had been a probationer in the Methodist church implies that she had joined a class and was seeking Methodist church membership, which according to Methodist discipline was to be granted after a satisfactory probation of six months. Theorizing that she was a probationer makes it difficult, however, to explain why she came to Chicago not as a Methodist but as a Presbyterian. It also seems unlikely

Samuel Fowler house. From Ruttenber, "King's Highway," between pages 28 and 29.

2. *The Middlehope M. E. Church.*—The old original "Samuel Fowler's class" and the "Daniel Holmes' class," were organized into a church, Dec. 14, 1821, and Wm. Smith, Daniel Holmes, David Wyatt, Gilbert Holmes, and Daniel Merritt, were elected

 its first trustees. Arrangements were soon after made for erecting a church edifice, which was dedicated Dec. 29, 1822, under the title of "Asbury Chapel." ‡ It has always been supplied by circuit preachers, and is now associated with the M. E. church at Fostertown, the two churches forming the "North Newburgh circuit."

Asbury Chapel in Middle Hope. From Ruttenber, *History of the Town of Newburgh*, 233.

that someone like Eliza would have left the church of her parents for another denomination while still living in the same community. More likely, after the Methodist church of Middle Hope was organized in 1821 and Asbury Chapel was constructed in 1822, a teenaged Eliza occasionally attended meetings with friends.

It was an era of revivals among Methodists and Baptists, and even the more staid denominations were influenced in a revivalist direction. Reverend John Johnston, the well-educated minister of the First Presbyterian Church in Newburgh Village, held revivals in "The Square" during the winter of 1815–1816 and in a house in the New Mills district west of the village from the fall of 1824 through January of 1825. It appears that while these Presbyterian meetings occasioned the "sobs and tears" of sincere conviction, they were not as effective as the revivals put on by Baptists and Methodists, a fact noted by Johnston in his journal. He himself had experienced many revivals during his student days in western Pennsylvania at Jefferson College, where there was little formal study but much touring to attend church meetings. Occasionally, he and his fellow students assisted at revivals where people convulsed as if dying or suffering the throes of an epileptic fit, or they became immobile as if in a trance, only to awaken with complete memories of the prayers, hymns, and sermon. Generally, those seized by religious ecstasy would fall down. A minister fell in the pulpit. An elder fell while serving Communion. Johnston sometimes saw a dozen persons prostrate on the floor, so close to each other that he could have touched them all with the tip of his cane—"some praying, some silent, and others crying out in tones approaching shrieking." In later years he commented that a certain meeting contained "things . . . I did not then, nor do I now understand, nor do I think essential to true religion" but that were nonetheless marks of "genuine revival." He also testified that he himself had experienced revival of the "ordinary" mental form but not the bodily.[18]

The Marlborough Presbyterian church held revivals in 1811 and 1820. A few years later the Methodists held camp meetings. Freeborn Garrettson, then seventy-two, drew six thousand people to a Newburgh revival in 1824 (when Eliza was nineteen), and similar crowds came to hear him again in 1825. Details in a period account of the 1825 meeting give an idea of what was typical. The revival got under way on an August morning at 10:00 a.m. in tents set up in a pasture. The ground was wet from a rainstorm that had ended a severe drought, and that put people in a cheerful mood. From morning through afternoon and into the evening, they huddled in the hot tents, refreshed periodically by picnic lunches, suppers, and water carried in from a nearby spring. The emotional tone of the meeting intensified day by day. The sermons, always oratorical, became increasingly dramatic, the services of prayer and praise more fervent. At night people gathered in various "circles" for prayer and exhortation. The revival reached a climax on Thursday when Freeborn Garrettson spoke. All told, between sixty and a hundred people were converted. These transformations took place in the smaller gatherings between and after the preaching services. A correspondent for the *Methodist Magazine* reported that "in one of the praying circles there were fifty persons observed crying for mercy," in another tent "twenty persons were happily converted to God," and in still another "seven more were made to rejoice in pardoning mercy." This was a restrained account, since along with the singing, praying, and penitential tears, there was also a good deal of clapping, jumping, and collapsing on the grass or mud.[19]

The converts at camp meetings included those newly professing religion, as well as repentant backsliders. The fact that some six thousand persons attended the 1825 Newburgh camp meeting but only a hundred or so such "conversions" were recorded shows the extent to which the camp meetings were chiefly entertainment for many people. In rural areas, the revival was the greatest social event of the year, and people attended for all sorts of reasons. For some, the excitement had a spiritual quality, which they understood as the joy of religion. For others, spirituality did not enter into their fun. They went to be entertained by the spellbinding preachers, to mix with members of the opposite sex, and, in the case of men, to drink, play cards, and cause trouble.[20]

Members of the Clark family no doubt went to some of these revivals, but the evidence of Eliza's religious history suggests that she did not experience any emotionally earthshaking Methodist conversion or even a sober Presbyterian one. In fact, for personal and spiritual reasons, she did not join a church. Although she was a faithful church attender, she did not become a church communicant until many years later, in 1839, when she was thirty-four years old. Salient differences between Wesleyan and Calvinist doctrine at the time were factors in her decision, and a midlife conversion led her into the Methodist fold. Whether or not her personal journey would have been significantly different had she remained with the Presbyterians of Chicago, who held the same basic moral and social values as the Methodists there did, it was with the Chicago Methodists and under their influence that she embraced the cause of higher education and decided to devote the wealth she enjoyed in later life to schools of higher learning for both men and women.[21]

* * *

Augustus Garrett was born in Middle Hope on March 19, 1802, to John and Eustatia Garrett. The Garrett farm lay on the North Road just north of the Middle Hope crossroads, a stream, and "the old stone school house." The earliest surviving indication of where this schoolhouse stood is an 1875 map, which shows its successor at the southeast corner of the W. D. Barns farm on the west side of the road. Given the evidence of his letters and career, Augustus must have had a decent education, no doubt in that old stone schoolhouse near the Garrett farm.[22]

John Garrett, Augustus's father, was born in New York City in 1755. He was the son of a German sea skipper. Nothing is known about his mother. John was twenty-one when the Revolutionary War broke out, and he served as an artilleryman under Captain John Smith, being wounded twice—once in the leg and once in the arm. After the war he acquired a number of acres along the Hudson River in north Newburgh, either by purchasing them with his service pay or, more likely, being paid for his service with land. His wife, Eustatia—"Statia" to family and friends—was born in 1760 to Charles Morgan and Susannah Guion of Eastchester in Westchester County, New York. It is not known what year John and

Eustatia married or came to Newburgh, but his farm appears on the Newburgh tax rolls in 1785 and on the road list for 1786. The Garretts had at least eleven children besides Augustus, some of whose names appear on a grave marker in Newburgh's Old Town Cemetery. The personal losses registered on this monument are staggering but not uncommon for the times: seven of John and Eustatia's children were dead before Augustus reached his midtwenties. The oldest was thirty when he died, the youngest two months. Some of these deaths occurred in the South—in Baltimore and Savannah—after John and Eustatia had established themselves in Newburgh. Although it is not known what sent these Garrett children south—perhaps it was family connections—the migration of his siblings into slaveholding states would one day be the cause of Augustus's only direct dealings with commerce in human chattel.[23]

The religious identity of the Garrett family is somewhat vague. A Presbyterian minister presided over the marriage of Augustus's sister Rebecca in Baltimore in 1815, which does not necessarily signify that she identified with the Presbyterian church there. A connection with Methodism is suggested by a baptismal record from 1790 for Susannah Garrett, an older sister of Augustus who died very young. There was as yet no Methodist class in Middle Hope in 1790, but circuit riders had been stopping regularly at the Samuel Fowler house, which was just up the road from the Garretts. That house must have been the scene of Susannah's baptism. Statia might have belonged to a circle of the converted who met there when the circuit rider came through; or she may have taken advantage of his presence in order to have her baby baptized, without concerning herself with denominational identity. The baptismal records for the Newburgh circuit include no reference to Augustus or his other siblings.[24]

Since the estimated number of attendees at the Newburgh Methodist camp meetings in 1824 and 1825 equaled the whole population of the township, it is likely that the gregarious and fun-loving Augustus Garrett went to these revivals, if only because they were lively community events. It is also possible that a preacher caused him to weep and confess his sins, for despite his generally standoffish attitude toward religion, he sometimes became repentant at Methodist meetings, as two Chicagoans who knew him later testified. Yet his final expression of a religious preference was not for Methodism. According to Eliza, he told her on his deathbed that he wanted the funeral service of the Church of England. Given that neither he nor Eliza was a member of any Episcopal congregation, this dying request probably reflected a family connection with the Church of England. His paternal lineage was German, which does not suggest any link with Anglicans, but his maternal grandparents belonged to the Episcopal church of Eastchester.[25]

Augustus flirted with Methodism throughout his adult life but in the end was deliberate in rejecting his wife's Methodist church and her entreaties that he use his wealth, by then substantial, for Methodist causes. She honored his request for an Episcopal funeral service but ultimately subverted his larger wishes by assigning her part of his estate to the founding of a Methodist school of theology and a women's college to be organized by Methodists.[26]

At some point when Augustus was in his early twenties, John Garrett gave him a piece of land, preserving a life interest for himself and Statia. This meant that although Augustus could farm the parcel and would inherit it, the land would remain in the legal control of his father and mother until their deaths. The property lay about a mile south of the center of Middle Hope on the west side of the North Road, next to the farm of his sister Letitia and her husband, and about a mile north of Balmville, where Eliza's mother grew up. Augustus built a house, erected some outbuildings, and fenced the property. These improvements cost him about a thousand dollars.[27]

Having farmed with his father since boyhood, he now took up the work of his own place. It was tedious, time-consuming, and arduous labor with simple implements—hoe, shovel, rake, grain cradle, and plow. "I have followed that plow," a contemporary wrote in his journal, "more miles than any one man ever did or ever will [follow] any plow whatever in my *opinion*." In Augustus's day a man walked behind his draft animals when plowing; he sowed wheat and rye by hand, "broadcasting" the seed in wide arcs; he planted corn by hoeing up individual mounds and then secreting a few kernels into each hole made with a wooden peg; he hand-picked armies of worms from the leaves of his crops; he harvested wheat with a long-handled grain cradle, swath by swath, heap by heap; then he and his neighbors worked in teams to thresh each other's grain, also by hand. Farmers won plenty to eat from their efforts but ended up with little if any cash, and many fell into debt. These tough realities explain why Augustus hated farming. He was a gregarious young man, ever eager for company, full of ambition, and hungry for adventure. The lonely, monotonous routines of the field and barn did not suit him, and they were not financially rewarding.[28]

He found relief from his drudgery in public houses. Rural taverns were social centers where men gathered, shared news, drank liquor, and gambled with dice and cards. The walls of country inns were pasted with notices of sheriff's sales, community meetings, county court sessions, handwritten advertisements for goods, and personal messages. There was usually a room or two upstairs for traveling men to share a bed and its bugs. In such an establishment along the North Road—a smoky place, poorly lit, grimy, and rich with the aromas of the unbathed—the garrulous Augustus held forth. Around the blazing winter hearth he entertained little audiences of men with whimsical jokes and yarns, polishing the charm and wit that would later help him succeed as an auctioneer and a politician.[29]

He may have spent too many hours in taverns, for he had difficulty paying his debts. Or perhaps it was "lack of experience," as he later claimed, that led him to "fool away" his farm. Or did other pursuits—small entrepreneurial enterprises to which he devoted time and energy—cause him to neglect his chores? His heart was not in farming, in any case. He wanted to go into business and establish himself in a city. Stories of "the West" fired his imagination—not the leatherstocking tales of wilderness adventures but the reports of young cities on the make and the success-hungry men who were building them. Except for Missouri and half of Louisiana, all the western part of the United States still lay east of the Mississippi River, and in the latter part of the 1820s the most important adolescent city of the western states was Cincinnati. Augustus was thinking of going there.[30]

But marriage was also on his mind.

* * *

When Augustus courted Eliza, she was living with her parents on the Clark farm north of Middle Hope. Heirs of her great-uncle, Jehiel Clark, had a place near the center of Middle Hope not far from John Garrett's farm, and Augustus's own farm was about a mile farther south. Just south of there was Balmville, where Eliza's grandparents lived. These geographical proximities and the social networks of the communities along the North Road brought Augustus and Eliza together in the 1820s.[31]

Two different dates are reported for their marriage. Six years after Eliza's death, David W. Clark (no relation) wrote that Eliza and Augustus married in 1825. She would have been twenty that year, he twenty-four. But Alvaro Field, who probably knew the article by Clark, gives the year of their marriage as 1829. A Newburgh cemetery monument that lists their children records Imogine, born in 1830, as their first child. Charles was born in 1832 and John Augustus in 1833. If we assume 1825 to be the nuptial year, then no children were born to them in the first five years of their marriage, which seems doubtful. Of course, unchronicled miscarriages might account for this. All that can be said for sure is that Eliza and Augustus married in the latter part of the 1820s.[32]

Augustus wooed Eliza at a time when courtship and marriage were undergoing a profound change, shifting "away from the father-dominated family of the colonial era—with its emphasis on parental control, obedience, and restraint of emotions—toward a strikingly affectionate, self-consciously private family environment in which children became the center of indulgent attention and were expected to marry for reasons of romance and companionship rather than parental design and economic interest." European travelers to the United States in the early 1800s "praised the American marriage system because it permitted young people to select mates whom they loved and with whom they could enjoy a happy marriage." By the end of the eighteenth century, popular magazines were registering the ideal of romantic love, expressed in concepts that later social historians would characterize as the idealization of the loved one, belief in a "one and only" love, the notion of "love at first sight," and "glorification of personal sentiments." In one magazine piece, from 1794, a young man declared, "When I am not with her, her enchanting image pursues me; and when I retire to sleep, she fills my every idea; I slumber . . . I wake, and starting up in agony, wander round my chamber maniac-like." No doubt many young men and women of previous generations had enjoyed (or suffered) similar emotions. But to be tutored by popular literature in the cultivation and language of such feelings and to be encouraged to make them a weighty consideration in choosing a mate—that was something new.[33]

Some desired a communion of souls. That meant disclosing secrets as a solemn duty of true love. When it occurred to Edward Jarvis that he had never told his fiancée about the diary he kept, he confessed in that diary, "I am very sorry I did not tell her before. I have disclosed all my secrets (except this) to her and she has reciprocated the confidence. I will not be reserved on any other thing to her." Clayton Kingman sought the same communion with Emily Brooks, telling her, "I want you to be as open and confiding to *me*, as to *any one*, and I will be to you" He wanted them to be "more like one." Emily probably felt the same way, but it was more difficult for women to express their romantic passions to their fiancés. Literary women of the era devoted poems, novels, and discourses to the sentimental aspects of courtship, but surviving letters show that "prevailing gender relations did not allow [women] the power to articulate that ideal to specific men within particular relationships."[34]

It was not only educated city folk who learned the new language of love. Farmers near urban centers read popular magazines, and their children pored over the love stories just as eagerly as young people in the cities did. Moreover, despite the rationalism of Enlightenment culture, many people put trust in emotion, taking the view that the mind knows some things best, the heart others. That confidence in the heart was essential to revivalist religion, where listening to inner feelings was encouraged. Hence, it is not surprising that many people listened to their hearts in matters of love and marriage, too.

This did not mean, however, that romantic ardor was now the sole or even the primary consideration in choosing a mate. Romantic impulses had to compete with practical considerations and unsentimental parental advice, which tended to stress financial security and social status. Young men and women themselves were fully aware that marriage was the primary means of economic security for a woman. This consideration is made explicit in a letter from John Foster to Mary Appleton in 1824: "Could I, my dear Miss Appleton, could I have felt half as certain that you would be as safe in everything, as in my warm, constant, and undivided affection, I should not have so long restrained the expression of my wishes." In other words, he had not felt free to reveal his feelings until he had established himself in a profession.[35]

Young women were taught to prize, above all, the security a man could offer and not to lay too much store by the emotions he stirred. In 1825 a girl named Elizabeth Bradley copied into her commonplace book the words of a song that preached the follies of following the heart: "The lovers forsake us, the husbands remain." The song did not mean "lovers" in its later sexual sense. It meant that romantic attachments come and go, the bond of marriage being all that one can really count on. Whether or not Elizabeth herself agreed with this, some of her contemporaries did. In 1828 Edward Dickinson made clear to his fiancée, Emily Norcross, that he was more colonial than postrevolutionary in his view of marriage. "Let us prepare for a life of rational happiness," he wrote, telling her not to pine for "a life of *pleasure*, as some call it." He desired each of them to be "useful & successful" for the other. If she was looking for missives from him that sounded like the romantic novels and magazine articles she read, his advice must have struck her as dull stuff.[36]

Eliza Clark was in her early twenties when Augustus courted her. She was a pretty young woman, graceful and "divinely tall," one man recalled. Augustus was drawn to her as his opposite—steady where he was mercurial, careful where he was overconfident, always full of kindness where his good impulses flooded, then ebbed. Dogged in the pursuit of anything he wanted, Augustus courted Eliza when the cultural atmosphere was just getting dense with romantic ideals. In their world, letters were a primary mode of courtship since it was difficult for courting couples to find a time or place to be alone. The courtship epistles of Augustus and Eliza do not survive, but if his later business correspondence is a clue to his approach, he must have written Eliza long epistolary arguments setting forth the reasons why she should marry him. It must have been the sheer force of his personality that persuaded her in the end, not any practical considerations. His farm, which made him socially eligible to marry, was pretty much "fooled away" by the time he proposed to her. Not only that, he was full of talk about going west, something she was afraid to tell her parents.[37]

Born to the harsh realities and loneliness of farm life, many rural women of Eliza's generation may have wished to escape to the city. Almost the only ways to do that were to marry a man from the city or else marry a farmer with the wherewithal to make a city life for himself and his family. Whether or not Eliza was looking for such a man, she found him in Augustus. Yet Benoni and Amy's influence over her was considerable. We get a hint of this in what Jeremiah Porter recalled of how things stood with the Garretts when Augustus first arrived in Chicago. By that time, they had been married several years, but he had yet to succeed in business. Porter said that before the Clarks would "permit" her to join him, he had to prove himself. This permission was moral and emotional, of course, not legal; but it was nonetheless formidable.[38]

If Augustus's financial circumstances gave Eliza pause and caused her parents to doubt him, his compelling personality won her over. Yes, she liked the look of him—the wide-set eyes, strong nose, and long hair that curled and waved at the ends. But more persuasive were his intelligence, confidence, sense of humor, and restless ambition. She warmed to his eagerness for travel and adventure. The woman who loved that in a man must have had an adventurous streak herself.

CHAPTER 2

PROSECUTED AND PUT TO COST

*A*ugustus was eager to head west to Cincinnati in hopes of making something of himself in that promising city, but he had certain things to settle before leaving Newburgh. One was a matter connected with his nephew James Crow.[1]

James was the son of Augustus's sister Rebecca and her husband, Richard Crow, who had married in 1816 in Baltimore and settled on the ancestral plantation of Richard's father, John Crow. James was born in 1818. His mother died in 1823 and his father in 1830, at which point Augustus was made his legal guardian. Particulars about the size of the Crow plantation and its division through probate are not known. James had a living brother, Thomas, whose inheritance is not recorded. But a petition filed with the Baltimore City Orphans Court reveals that James inherited a slave, unnamed in the petition and referred to only as a "negro boy." Thus it came about that, in late summer of 1830, Augustus was faced with the question of what to do about this boy.[2]

In 1830 New York law on slavery was a complicated set of statutes, beginning with an act of 1799 that provided for gradual emancipation, the act to go into full effect not immediately but in thirty years—on July 4, 1827. This law banned "importation" of slaves into the state, except under certain conditions. Slave owners from other states who immigrated to New York with the intention of residing there permanently could bring only those slaves born after July 4, 1799, but before July 4, 1827. A subsequent act ordained that after March 31, 1817, these slaves became free but were bound to their masters, in the same manner as apprentices, until they attained a certain age—twenty-eight for males, twenty-five for females. By 1830 a change in the law ordained that this period of apprenticeship— really indentured servitude—terminated at the age of twenty-one for both males and females. Slave owners passing through the state were protected in their ownership of any slaves with them, but after nine months a slave still residing in New York was deemed legally free. Selling a slave was not permitted under any circumstance; nor could any slave imported after April 8, 1801, be legally transferred to another person for a term of service, a transaction that was also a kind of sale. Fugitive slaves from other states were to be returned to their masters. According to the later legislation, every person born *within* the state, "whether white or coloured," was free, and children born before March 17, 1817, to slaves within the state became indentured servants of the owner of their mother until they attained the specified age of twenty-eight for males, twenty-five for females. This term was limited to age twenty-one for those born after March 17, 1817, but before July 4, 1827. Masters of minors held in indentured service were required to provide them with at least two years of schooling. All slaves born before July 4, 1799, were declared free, effective July 4, 1827. So stood the law with its tangles of legislative compromise reflecting the divided hearts and interests of white New Yorkers.[3]

The bearing of all this on the young slave belonging to Augustus's nephew is as follows. If the master of a boy held in slavery moved to the state of New York in 1830, as James Crow did, the boy could expect one of three outcomes. His owner might sell him before going to New York in order to convert his value as property into cash. In the alternative, his master might carry him to New York, where he would be instantly converted from a slave into an indentured servant. This implied contract of servanthood could not be sold to another, and at some point in early adulthood, the servant would enjoy full freedom (although not full civil rights). Or, if the master claimed to be only a visitor to the state but remained longer than nine months, the slave boy would become free at that point. Augustus's orphaned nephew, James Crow, was now about to move to New York. This meant that some decision had to be made about the slave he owned. That decision was not up to James, who was still a minor; it was up to his guardian, Augustus, a native New Yorker. In 1830 the majority of New Yorkers opposed slavery, and for some of them it was a matter of principle not to benefit economically from the institution. Was Augustus Garrett such a man?

According to records of the federal census for 1810 and 1820, the John Garrett household in these years contained no slaves. The census records also show no slaves in Eliza's family. This was not exceptional. There were some ten thousand slaves in New York in 1820, when the state had a population of around a million people. Only 120 slaves were in Newburgh. Yet opinions about the national antislavery movement were divided, and there was strong opposition to abolition in some parts of the state, especially in Ulster County. One reason for the slow adoption of antislavery laws by the State of New York was the success of Ulsterites in blocking abolition efforts in the state assembly. A fifth of the population of Ulster County was slaves—among them future black abolitionist Sojourner Truth—and many Ulster slaveholders were farmers.[4]

If the Maryland slave boy belonging to Augustus's nephew hoped to secure his freedom as a result of being brought with the nephew into New York, he was disappointed. Augustus looked at the matter solely in pecuniary terms. The slave was an asset belonging to his nephew; in order to realize the value of that asset, Augustus engaged a lawyer to petition the Baltimore City Orphans Court as follows:

> The Petitioner Augustus Garrett, guardian of James Crow, respect-fully sheweth that a certain negro boy came to his hands as the prop-erty of said James Crow, which said negro can be sold advantageously for said Infant—that your Petitioner lives in the State of New York, with his said ward, and cannot take said slave into said state—he therefore prays an order for the sale of said Negro.[5]

The statement that the slave *cannot* be taken into the state of New York was conative, not legal, a veiled way of saying that Garrett did not want to lose the monetary value of the slave or take on the responsibility for him by bringing him to New York. The boy was put up for sale at one of the auction houses in Baltimore. If he had not already been separated from family members by prior sales, this transaction now severed him from his kin and from anyone else he cared for or who cared for him.

It would not be accurate to imagine that Augustus lived in a world so accustomed to slavery that he had never happened to reflect on its moral character or heard cogent arguments against it. In the taverns of New York, where Garrett spent a good deal of time, the question of slav-ery was one of the social and political topics that men took up, and it is likely that many people he knew or met in these settings were opposed to slavery. As a thinking man in a state that had recently shaken off the last of its own legal protections of the institution, he undoubtedly had his own opinions. Whatever they were in the abstract, in the concrete he was completely callous to the humanity of the boy he sent to the auction block in August of 1830.

It is a strange coincidence that the name of Augustus's nephew was, of all things, James "Jim" Crow and that the vaudeville song in which that name appears as a racial moniker debuted on a New York stage at about the same time. Around 1828 an actor named Thomas Rice, wearing black-face, sang and danced as "Jim Crow" in a grotesque stereotype of a hopping or jumping black man or boy. Owing to the popularity of the song, the term "Jim Crow" quickly became a derisive racial epithet.

* * *

Augustus did not learn about Cincinnati's meteoric rise from the Newburgh papers. The *Telegraph* and the *Gazette* took no note of Ohio River towns. It must have been in the public houses of north Newburgh, where men sat about jawing and drinking hard cider, that Augustus heard glowing rumors of Cincinnati and determined to make his career there.[6]

The first challenge was getting to the place. Augustus may have relied on advice from travelers he met in his rural haunts, or perhaps he went down to the town of Newburgh to seek out travel literature from a bookseller. Since construction and improvement of roads and waterways, including canals, were constantly under way in the new republic, up-to-date information was imperative and travel guides were widely available. Whatever his sources, Augustus knew that with the Erie Canal in operation, he could journey, by a combination of mostly water routes, from Newburgh to Cincinnati—traveling north on the Hudson to Albany, west on the canal to Lake Erie, east on Lake Erie to a northern Pennsylvania port, south by stagecoach and watercraft to Pittsburgh, then down the Ohio River to Cincinnati. The alternative was an overland trip by stagecoach—across the Allegheny Mountains—to Pittsburgh or Wheeling and from there to Cincinnati. A travel guide published in 1832 advised that families would probably prefer the water route as both less expensive and less arduous than overland travel.[7]

The Garretts were now a family of three, a baby named Imogine having been born to the couple in Newburgh in March of 1830. The trio journeyed to Cincinnati together. (Young Jim Crow, twelve at the time, remained with his grandparents on the north Newburgh farm.) Assuming that they traveled by steamship and canal boat, the trip took them at least two weeks. Upon arrival they found a bustling city of about twenty-seven thousand situated in a pretty valley of the Ohio River, flanked by majestic hills. Longfellow had not yet bestowed on Cincinnati the title "Queen of the West," but word had it that the town was full of opportunity for ambitious young men. In 1828 Englishwoman Frances Trollope brought her rudderless son Henry there after traveling across the Atlantic with the intention of establishing him and herself in the utopian village of Nashoba. When the Nashoba experience proved disappointing, Trollope investigated other options: "We heard on every side that of all places on 'the globe called earth,' Cincinnati was the most favourable for a young man to settle in."[8]

Boosterish Ohio papers were also full of news about "the tremendous commercial and industrial expansion of the Ohio Valley, especially in the river districts." Self-serving notions of Providence led many to bless this western expansion as the nation's divine destiny. In 1829 Edward Everett—a young Massachusetts congressman who would one day give the main address at the consecration of the National Cemetery at Gettysburg—was quoted as follows in the *Cincinnati Chronicle and Literary Gazette*:

View of Cincinnati, circa 1835, from the Kentucky side of the Ohio River. Painting by John Caspar Wild. © 2020 Museum of Fine Arts, Boston.

The growth of your western country is not merely the progress of the citizens, in a numerical multiplication. It is civilization personified and embodied, going forth to take possession of the land. It is the PRINCIPLE of our institutions, advancing not so much with the toilsome movements of human agency, but rather like the grand operation of sovereign Providence. It seems urged along its stupendous course, as the earth itself is propelled in its orbit, silent and calm like the moving planet, with a speed we cannot measure . . . scattering hamlets, and villages, and cities in its path—the abodes of civilized and prosperous millions.[9]

"Going forth to take possession of the land" meant laying claim to places occupied by Native peoples—Cherokee, Creek, Chickasaw, and Choctaw—and most white settlers wanted the Native population pushed westward. Everett made his remarks during the national debate over the Indian Removal Act, and his own opinions reflected something of the contradictions of white relations with indigenous peoples. Although Everett believed that national expansion was neither imperialistic nor rapacious but only the beautiful motion of a divine machine, irresistible and breathtaking in its course as it rolled westward planting "civilization" in fulfillment of what would eventually be called America's "manifest destiny," he also *opposed* the Indian Removal Act on humanitarian grounds and made speeches against it in Congress. Even some advocates of state appropriation of Indian lands were aware that their own principles of justice conflicted with their policy. Members of a Georgia legislative committee, reporting on that state's designs on lands occupied by Cherokee and other tribes, admitted that there was "more of *force* than of *justice*" in the state's claims but concluded that those claims "have been recognized and admitted by the whole civilized world" and that "under such circumstances force becomes right."[10]

Although Augustus could not have known it, his own future would be affected dramatically by national policy on the "Indian question," specifically the removal of Native peoples to western lands, which opened up huge tracts of new federal land that the government put on the market to facilitate white settlement in the North-West, as it was then known. Lands were sold and resold many times over, mostly through public bidding. It was an auctioneer's paradise, and Illinois was a primary arena. These events were still several years off when Augustus began plying the auctioneer's trade in Cincinnati; but the engines of Indian removal were in motion, and the failures in business that would lead Augustus to the right place and time to benefit from Indian removal were also under way.

The Indian question had been a primary issue in the election of 1828 in which Andrew Jackson and the newly formed Democratic Party defeated John Quincy Adams and his new Whig Party. At that time, Native peoples still occupied substantial tracts of land east of the Mississippi River. The westward edge of the exploding white population was moving into these regions, particularly in the Southeast. Two years into his presidency— with the support of most southern members of Congress and just enough votes from northern legislators—President Jackson succeeded in getting the Indian Removal Act passed. The legislation provided for an Indian Territory west of the Mississippi, and it authorized the Jackson adminis-tration to negotiate with tribes east of the river, the object being to achieve their transplantation farther west. Specifically, the Indians would cede their occupancy rights in exchange for money, the promise of a western territory, and transportation there. Although the resulting agreement was secured by treaty, the threat of force was implicit in the negotiations.

Garrett's specific opinions about Jacksonian Indian policy are not pre-served. In the latter part of the 1830s, he joined the Whigs, a party formed expressly to oppose Jackson. But Whigs came in different stripes, and just what sort of Whig Garrett made is unclear. A few years later he became a Democrat, but probably more for local and pragmatic reasons than na-tional or philosophical ones. The enthusiasm he expresses in letters of the 1840s about Jackson and James K. Polk, particularly respecting Polk's readiness to go to war with Mexico to hold onto recently annexed Texas, suggests that, at least retrospectively, he approved of Jackson's policy of western expansion, including moving Native peoples beyond the Missis-sippi. By then he also had a personal reason for applauding those actions.[11]

The city of Cincinnati was only marginally involved in the Indian re-moval project. In 1831 and 1832, the Seneca and Shawnee ceded one hun-dred thousand acres in Ohio in exchange for land in the Indian Territory. In the spring of 1831, the Garretts may have been among those Cincinna-tians who witnessed a group of Shawnee passing through Cincinnati on their arduous and death-shadowed journey west.[12]

* * *

Augustus was headed toward financial disaster, but he had no inkling of it. Instead, full of confidence, he went about establishing himself in business by the usual route taken in those days. He made connections. His first step was to visit one of the Presbyterian churches in town and explain to the minister that he was a newcomer, that his wife was a devoted Presbyterian, and that he hoped to start a business. Cincinnati had several Presbyterian churches when the Garretts arrived there, the largest being First and Second. Second Presbyterian, housed in a new building, may have had wealthier parishioners, but First Presbyterian Church, increased by recent revivals, had recently remodeled its building. Augustus would not have known which church boasted the more influential businessmen. He may have assumed it was the older First Presbyterian Church. If he made any inquiries, he heard that Second Presbyterian was in deep debt from its building project and had recently been served for foreclosure by the bank.[13]

It is nearly certain that Eliza attended one of the Presbyterian churches in Cincinnati since she was a committed Presbyterian and a faithful churchgoer both before and after her time in Cincinnati. Yet she did not become a communicant of any church until rather late in life. She was a reliable attender but not a member.[14]

It did not matter to Augustus whether Eliza joined a church or only attended. He was looking for men willing to help him make a start in business, and a prominent Protestant church was a place to find them. Since he had no money to speak of and no business expertise, he hoped to get into an occupation that called for little capital expenditure and no prior experience. Therefore, with the assistance of some Presbyterian businessmen, he became an auctioneer. The auction business required no apprenticeship and could be learned in a few weeks by a man of "memory, observation, and shrewdness."[15]

Auctioneering was not the most respectable career. The successful auctioneer was something of a showman, often with a taint of the carnival huckster. Shop owners and other small-scale merchants accused auctioneers of unfair practices, such as selling poorly made goods at inflated prices or undercutting smaller emporiums by dealing in volume. In the chain of bulk trade, from overseas through eastern ports and on to inland water towns like Cincinnati, the auctioneer represented the wholesalers in the local market. The businessman who sold a variety of wares from a small shop could not compete at scale. Cincinnati merchants more than once tried to have auctions outlawed and duties levied on foreign goods sold at auction.[16]

It also annoyed the small merchant that an auctioneer could go into business with little capital and therefore little risk. All Augustus had to do was acquire a municipal auctioneer's license, lease a storefront, and rent or purchase secondhand the basics of furniture—chairs, auctioneer's rostrum (or at least a table to serve for that), hammer, and bell. Then he went to the commercial landing and found importers who wished to auction off their bulk goods. With merchandise thus secured at no cost, he purchased newspaper ads or hired a boy, for pennies, to go around town posting broadsheets, ringing the bell, and shouting out auction times. At the appointed hour, the boy opened the doors to admit a small crowd, and the auctioneer stepped to his podium and began describing his first "lot."[17]

Augustus and his fellow auctioneers made their profits by charging commissions on the sale of others' goods. They were limited by Ohio law from charging more than a 6 percent commission for sales under a hundred dollars or more than an 8 percent commission for receipts over that amount. Precise statistics on what auctioneers were making by 1830 are not available, but the following information was collected by Benjamin Drake for the year 1826. There were, at that time, ten licensed auctioneers in Cincinnati, whose sales amounted to $233,800, returning each of them—if the returns were roughly equal and if the average fee was 7 percent—$1,637. Based on Cincinnati's population increase four years later, a rough estimate of the average commission on gross annual sales can be calculated at about $2,450 per auctioneer in 1830. Of course, the auction houses did not all achieve the same amount in sales, and each had overhead costs reducing its net.[18]

Augustus's chief expense was leasing space for his auction business. He might have secured a place for about $700 a year on Front Street, but none of the other auction houses were on Front. Most were on Main, where leases averaged about $1,100 a year. He could not afford newspaper advertisements. He had only the hired boy to paste broadsheets around town and to walk the streets crying out auction times. He faced fierce competition. The established, well-known auction houses were already popular hangouts, and they could take advantage of scale, extend credit, and successfully foreclose on delinquents. Garrett was a likable and entertaining fellow at his podium, but he was short on resources and business experience.[19]

Whatever Augustus earned as an auctioneer—and it is doubtful that he earned anything close to the average gross commissions of $2,450 a year—it was not enough. With lodging, board, and business rental costs amounting to at least $1,800 a year (about $42,000 in today's dollars), and sundry other personal and business expenses added to that, he fell into debt. By the time he left Cincinnati, he had incurred significant unpaid obligations, and his creditors had initiated legal actions. As he explained later, his Cincinnati losses were "great," and he was "sued and prosecuted and put to cost." One man who knew him claimed that Augustus owed $50,000. That figure sounds high, but whether or not people accurately remembered the amount, Augustus must have given them the impression that his Cincinnati debts were enormous.[20]

* * *

*A*part from occasional visits to Newburgh Village, Eliza had known only farm life. Now she resided in a growing city, the eighth largest in the United States. It was a heady experience. A European visitor in the early 1830s found "handsome brick houses, wide streets, and magnificent public buildings." There were also "brilliant shops, exquisites and dandies lounging about, and ladies attired in the last Parisian fashions."[21]

Alexis de Tocqueville was impressed, too, but saw chaos in the city's rapid growth—"great buildings, thatched cottages, streets encumbered with debris, houses under construction, no names on the streets, no

Cincinnati, Fourth Street West from Vine, circa 1835,
painting by John Caspar Wild. Courtesy of Alamy.

numbers on the houses, no outward luxury, but the image of industry and labour obvious at every step." The streets were a spectacle, busy with both commerce and free-roaming hogs. It was a city rule that garbage was to be deposited in the center of the street so as not to impede traffic, and down this center lane lumbered the scavenging swine. One paper, summing up street conditions in the 1830s, itemized mud, debris, stone, dogs, and hogs, living and dead.[22]

Housing was at a premium. With a population increase of 50 percent in just the previous four years, Cincinnati could barely accommodate all its residents and visitors, especially during the travel season. "The demand for houses greatly exceeded the supply," one writer observed. Many permanent residents unable to build or rent a house lived in hotels. Cincinnati boasted no establishments comparable to the fine hotels of New York and Baltimore. The best hotels—the Pearl Street House, Colonel Mack's Hotel, and perhaps one or two others—lacked eastern amenities, although they were clean and orderly. Refined travelers from eastern cities and Europe stayed in these places, although some visitors thought them little better than good public houses. The more affordable accommodations— in both hotels and boardinghouses, there being little difference between the two—were even plainer, full of people used to rough conditions and strangers sleeping two or more to a bed; many of the male lodgers were accustomed to dirty floors, lacked personal hygiene, had coarse manners, and caroused in the common rooms.[23]

Not a few local merchants preferred the ease of boarding at a hotel to cooking, washing, and otherwise managing a house of their own. Augustus and Eliza felt the same way. Since they could not afford to build or rent a house, it was just as well that they both liked hotels for their convenience and camaraderie. Their Cincinnati hotel was no plainer or rougher than their Hudson Valley farmhouse, nor much less commodious.[24]

For Eliza, the hotel was also superior to the farmstead in one especially important respect: the presence of other wives. Even in rural communities where farmhouses were in sight of each other, a woman typically saw only members of her own household every day of the week except Sunday and the occasional Saturday. Many a newlywed woman saw no other adult, including other adult family members, through most of the day. That had been Eliza's circumstance as a newlywed, and prior to that her only daily female companion had been her mother. Now, for the first time in her life, she had the daily company of female friends, which meant a

great deal to her. They were a welcome source of advice about caring for
an infant. Eliza was the youngest member of the Clark family, and she
had no extensive experience caring for babies and was a long way from
her own mother. The women of the hotel doted on Imogine and tutored
Eliza about teething, colic, clothing, bathing, temperature, air, and every
other thing that worried a young mother.[25]

Church services were much closer and easier to get to than back in New
York, where the distance from the Clark farm to Marlborough Presbyterian was at least a couple miles on difficult roads, often in foul weather.
Now Eliza could walk along plank sidewalks to a church just blocks away.
During their first few months in Cincinnati, Augustus accompanied her,
not out of conviction but in order to make friends with men who could
help him in business.

Whichever Presbyterian church Eliza attended in Cincinnati, she was
privy through the gossip mill, and perhaps directly from the pulpit, to a
dramatic moment in Presbyterian politics over slavery. In the early months
of 1831, disgruntled members of First Presbyterian Church began making
noises about "seceding" and forming their own congregation. They acted
the first week of April. At a meeting of the Cincinnati presbytery held at
New Richmond on April 5, 1831, representatives of this group presented a
petition "to be set apart from said church and with some others to organize into a church." On its face, the request was unremarkable. The city
was growing, and new churches formed periodically in all the denominations. But in this case, the petition was a protest against the proslavery
sermons of Reverend Joshua Wilson. Four days later, twenty members
of First Presbyterian—thirteen men and seven women—were officially
recognized as an independent congregation by the presbytery. Asa Mahan,
an active abolitionist, became the first minister of this newly constituted
Sixth Presbyterian Church.[26]

Reverend Mahan and his congregation were committed to the conviction that "not only is the Gospel the antagonist of sin, but it must
be applied to all *sin*," that is, not only to personal sins but also to social
wrongs that many churches were reluctant to treat as disciplinary matters,
considering them more political than moral. Sixth Presbyterian did not
make this distinction. Over the next decades, congregants were brought
before session not only for the usual transgressions, such as intemperance,
profanity, and breaking Sabbath, but also for such things as slaveholding and "enlisting in the United States army and going to Texas." The

last of these had to do with the United States' conflict with Mexico over Texas, ostensibly to defend white settlers there but ulteriorly to acquire and hold Texas itself, which eventually occurred in the mid-1840s. The Sixth Presbyterians were ready to expel members for fighting to preserve U.S. possession of Texas, not only because they regarded the annexation as unlawful but also because Mexico had outlawed slavery in Texas and the church feared U.S. control would bring it back. In the 1850s Sixth Presbyterian became a stop on the Underground Railway.[27]

There is no record of Eliza's opinions about the twenty abolitionists who formed Sixth Presbyterian Church in response to the proslavery preaching of Joshua Wilson or her view on another controversy provoked by the same minister a year later. The topic of this second altercation among the Presbyterians did not trouble her at the time, but it would later. Wilson was a champion of Old School Presbyterianism, and no matter which church Eliza happened to attend she no doubt heard the buzz about Wilson's public attack on Rev. Lyman Beecher. Wilson suspected Beecher, president of Cincinnati's Lane Seminary, of harboring New School heresies, such as rejecting the doctrine of infant damnation. This issue of the eternal fate of little souls vexed the hearts of many pious Protestants in the nineteenth century. Eliza would soon be one of them.

We do have a good idea of Augustus's sentiments on a number of subjects over which Sixth Presbyterian exercised moral discipline. He almost certainly had no objections to social dancing, card playing, or other such amusements. For most of his life, he was a drinker. Politically, he had no scruples about western expansion. He favored U.S. intervention in Texas. He was indifferent to the plight of the slave. He didn't give a hoot about doctrinal disputes.

The exit of the twenty parishioners from First Presbyterian was only the beginning of abolitionist activism in Cincinnati. Three years later Lane Seminary became the scene of antislavery radicalism. While its somewhat naive president, Lyman Beecher, was away on an eastern fund-raising trip, the seminary trustees, alarmed and worried about the reactions of Cincinnatians to the students' antislavery activities and public socializing with blacks, outlawed student meetings and dissolved the student societies. In response, a large contingent of the student body left the school and enrolled in nearby Oberlin College. The exit was called the "Lane Rebellion," one of many flinty sparks in the tinder of white abolition in the mid-1830s. Lane Seminary never fully recovered, and various members of the Beecher family, although none of them were sympathetic to slavery, suffered divisions over antislavery politics. One of them, Lyman's daughter Harriet, went on to write *Uncle Tom's Cabin*.[28]

* * *

The Garretts were gone from Cincinnati by the time of the Lane Rebellion. Augustus's failure in the auction business may have been one reason for their departure, but the most immediate cause was something else. Eliza was pregnant with their second child and in April gave birth to a boy. They named him Charles. The following month a Cincinnati paper reported an epidemic of cholera in Paris. In June it announced an outbreak in Canada. Dr. Daniel Drake, a Cincinnati physician and recently appointed chair of a city committee on cholera, began sounding warnings in letters to Cincinnati newspapers, urging people to prepare for the arrival of the disease by fleeing to the countryside. People did not flee, and at the end of September there was a reassuring report that cholera was abating in eastern cities. Yet Drake discovered fifteen new cases in Cincinnati from September 30 through October 7. All the sufferers died within hours of their first symptoms. Drake announced this alarming news in a letter published in the *Cincinnati Daily Gazette*, but the editor of that paper appended a comment challenging Drake's conclusions and reporting that the board of health and other leading physicians doubted that the deceased were victims of cholera. The newspaperman shared the worries of city officials that panic would affect business, especially if people began leaving the city.[29]

On October 11th, a sudden increase in cholera cases heightened anxieties. Advice from city doctors was confusing and conflicting. Drake, who had counseled an exodus to the countryside, now advised people to shut themselves up in their homes. "The whole atmosphere is poisonous," he told readers of the *Liberty Hall & Cincinnati Gazette*. The average Cincinnatian had the impression that almost everyone was coming down with the disease. The slightest abdominal twinge or the least feeling of lassitude sent the imagination flying.[30]

Augustus went bravely to his auction rooms; Eliza hunkered down at home with the children and studied the very precise directions published by Dr. Drake in a full-page newspaper notice. She was to watch for any sign in herself or her children of a stomach or bowel complaint. If that was detected, she had to act fast. "In this stage," the doctor said, the disease "is easily cured," but "all who neglect this stage are in danger of perishing." A sick child should be put to bed immediately, in a warm room, and made to drink hot tea of sage, balm, or thoroughwort. A warm poultice should be placed over the convulsing bowels; cold feet should be bathed in warm water. In addition, one was to administer a powder of calomel and opium. If these were not available, then a teaspoon of powdered rhubarb would do. Every hour a teaspoon of aromatic camphorated water should also be given. Eliza took the reasonableness of these measures for granted, but she wondered how she would ever manage to give tea to her nursing infant, if it came to that, much less powdered calomel and opium.[31]

The patient must also receive good nutrition, another reason why Dr. Drake no longer advised flight: the right sorts of food were not easily acquired while traveling. A cholera sufferer should eat only mutton, veal, poultry, eggs, milk, and "good ham," Drake said. One of his colleagues, Dr. John Henry, had different dietary recommendations, although he agreed about the importance of meat. According to Dr. Henry, the best diet consisted of Kentucky bacon, hominy, fruits, and vegetables.[32]

People were now in a panic. The theater closed; restaurants stopped serving food. The streets no longer teemed with traffic. People either stayed indoors or departed the city by land or water. Augustus and Eliza were uncertain what to do. Physicians advised staying indoors. The newspapers insinuated that anyone who left was a coward. One editor commented, "There has been a great deal of fleeing, most of it rather 'inglorious.'" Another paper called on Cincinnatians to face cholera like defenders of Troy and quoted from Alexander Pope's translation of the *Iliad*: "If I perish, let her see me fall / in arms at least, and fighting for her wall."[33]

The Garretts were not prepared to defend Troy. They left Cincinnati the third week of October, taking a steamboat down the Ohio toward New Orleans. A few days into their trip, Imogine began showing signs of cholera. She died aboard ship on October 25, somewhere below Evansville, Indiana.[34]

Almost everything they had been told about the disease, from its prevention to its remedies, was wrong. Medical science in 1832 had no accurate understanding of the cause or spread of cholera, much less any effective treatment. Cholera is contracted through ingestion of food or water that has been contaminated by the feces of an infected individual. Since cholera-causing bacteria are sensitive to acid, most of them die in the stomach's acid-rich environment. But if a person consumes food or water containing large amounts of the bacteria, some survive in the small intestine, where they quickly multiply and produce a toxin that causes a large volume of water and electrolytes to enter the bowels and exit as watery diarrhea. Sometimes there is vomiting. The result in serious cases is life-threatening dehydration within hours. The only effective treatment is immediate replenishment of the lost fluids and electrolytes. Otherwise dehydration leads to kidney failure, coma, and death. None of this was known in 1832. The field of medicine had yet to discover bacteria and their role in infectious diseases. It was widely believed that fevers were caused by "noxious miasmas" emanating from foul water, decaying garbage, and rotting carcasses—hence Dr. Drake's opinion that the whole atmosphere was poisoned.[35]

Most of the treatments recommended by Cincinnati physicians were of no value in combating the disease. Dr. Henry advised bathing the feet in a hot salt or mustard bath; applying hot bricks to the arms and legs, small of the back, and pit of the stomach; giving the patient plenty of warm tea once vomiting abated; and administering calomel and opium. The tea was an excellent idea since it replenished bodily fluids. The other remedies were worthless. Dr. Henry and Dr. Drake also bled their patients, for this procedure was thought to purge the body of poisonous elements carried through the blood. Whether this bleeding seriously weakened cholera victims or not, it certainly did not help them.[36]

In the middle of the crisis a layman hit on a very good preventative. Because he was also a black man, the editor who reported his suggestion felt a need to apologize for the source. Yet he passed on the opinion:

> There is an old saying that in an emergency "even the weak may give some help." Mr. Henry Boyd, a man of color, has suggested that the source of cholera is in the water, and that it may be removed by boiling all the water we use and letting it cool again before used. This is a very simple process which can produce evil to no one. Even our country friends of the market can boil and bottle their water, before they come to the city, and if the theory be well, bring it with them and incur no risk.[37]

* * *

$\mathcal{P}$aducah, Kentucky, was a river hamlet, fifty miles upriver from the junction of the Ohio and the Mississippi and situated at the point where the Tennessee River empties into the Ohio. The waters near the shore were treacherous, which perhaps discouraged early settlement. The land had been claimed by George Rogers Clark in 1795, and it was passed on to his brother William Clark when George died in 1818. William Clark was Meriwether Lewis's partner in the pair's famous western expedition of 1804. Clark eventually had a portion of his western Kentucky parcel platted as the town of Paducah, naming it for the chief of a tribe he believed to be "white Indians." But there were other claimants to the land, and a dispute over title eventually made its way through the courts. It would not be decided with finality until 1844 when the United States Supreme Court weighed in. Meanwhile, the town slowly populated. By 1821 a handful of white settlers had built a few dwellings. A plat recorded a decade later shows twelve blocks, but it is unlikely that they were fully occupied in 1832 when the steamboat carrying the Garretts stopped there and Augustus and Eliza carried the lifeless body of Imogine ashore.[38]

It is possible that the first town graveyard, located where city hall would later stand, had not been established, for the earliest inscription for anyone in that cemetery is 1841. According to what friends of the Garretts gathered, the couple buried Imogine "on the river's bank." Whatever the precise location of the grave, it was not marked in any permanent way. Nor is it likely that a minister presided over the interment, unless one happened to be traveling on the steamboat. Paducah had no churches. The boat did not tarry long.[39]

* * *

A week after burying Imogine, the Garretts were in New Orleans. Far from family and now also separated from their home and friends in Cincinnati, Eliza and Augustus suffered their grief without comforters. They must have been tormented by the thought that they were somehow to blame for Imogine's death, second-guessing every decision they had made, wondering aloud to each other about whether they should have left Cincinnati sooner or what other steps they might have taken to protect the child. For Eliza, these questions had a specifically religious coloring. As a Presbyterian, she believed that nothing happened apart from God's will, that every event was the outcome of divine design. So she was now confronted with the question of God's role in the death of Imogine. She understood that divine purposes were usually inscrutable, but if the death of Imogine was an act of God, was it also an act of divine discipline? Was she being punished for something? Was Augustus? Or could the death of their child be explained in a more reassuring way?

There were Presbyterian churches in New Orleans, and Eliza may have attended one. If so, she probably did not find meaningful support or counsel from the minister. No doubt there were ministers who could communicate sympathy to grief-stricken women, but in examining the diaries and correspondence of more than thirty northern Protestant women between 1800 and 1880, Karin Gedge found that they rarely mentioned being visited by a pastor or receiving personal spiritual counsel, and sometimes "poignantly remarked on the absence or failure of a pastor in a time of spiritual need." Clergy were generally inept at pastoral care for women. Harriet Martineau told of an American clergyman who confessed to her his sense of inadequacy when ministering to grieving women. He had paid an obligatory call to the home of a mother who had lost her infant. After "visiting and exhorting" her, he found her unmoved and in a worse state than when he arrived. Martineau commented, "How should it be otherwise? What should he know of the grief of a mother for her infant?" The mother needed sympathy, Martineau said, and the minister had no sympathy—or no way to communicate his sympathy to her. That he conceived his pastoral task as one of exhorting the grieving mother suggests that he offered only doctrine and advice.[40]

There was something more specific in the case of Eliza's grief. Her Calvinist faith taught that God destined persons for eternal salvation or damnation apart from any action or thought or intention on their part. This doctrine struck many people as abominable—especially in a post-Enlightenment age—but its logic flowed from a theological framework that most Calvinists otherwise found reasonable, at least in the abstract. Calvinists believed that the highest value in the universe was the divine glory. That glory was served by the absolute freedom of God in electing some to salvation and others to damnation, for this showed human beings that they had no claims on God. By making choices about the fate of souls before they came into existence, God ensured that the elect would know their "absolute dependence on Him" and would appreciate "His mercy toward them." Appeals to the idea of divine justice did not move the Calvinist from this opinion because Calvinists regarded all human beings as depraved and therefore deserving of wrath. Nor did appeals to the concept of divine love dissuade the Calvinist, because, unlike many other Christians, the Calvinist did not believe that God's glory and God's love of humanity were so perfectly unified that the one could not supersede the other.[41]

Confronted with the teaching that God's commitment to the divine glory was necessarily superior to God's affection for human beings and that this commitment satisfied itself in assigning some to eternal bliss and others to eternal horrors, Eliza and other earnest Presbyterians and Congregationalists looked for signs of their own election. Faith in Christ was such a sign but only when it was sincere and proved its authenticity through good works. Hence, devout Calvinists examined themselves to see whether they possessed sincere inward faith, and they made assessments of their daily behavior. The signs of election they discovered often seemed ambiguous but gave tolerable assurance, especially when reinforced by a tangible conversion experience at a revival meeting.

But what about one's children? Infancy, in Calvinist doctrine, remained a somewhat imprecise category but generally meant a period of life up to some age of accountability or moral understanding. The term certainly included babies and for some people may have encompassed toddlers and even those a bit older. What could one know about signs of election in infants and toddlers? In post-Enlightenment America, Calvinist opinion about the fate of those who die in infancy was evolving, and it appeared to some outside observers that Calvinists were in flight from their historical doctrine on the subject. An article published in March of 1832 in a Unitarian periodical, the *Christian Messenger*, noted the following contradiction between classical Calvinism and what the author judged was current ministerial opinion:

> We have been led to these remarks by a sermon from a highly respectable clergyman of the Presbyterian Church, to which we listened some two or three weeks since. In that discourse the speaker plainly asserted the salvation of *all who die in their infancy*. . . . It is now deemed almost incredible by many that the doctrine taught by the gentleman just mentioned should ever have been disbelieved or questioned. Indeed, a learned and popular divine of Boston, has affirmed, that in an extensive acquaintance with his brethren, the Congregational clergy, he never heard the doctrine of *infant damnation* taught, or knew it to be believed. Be that as it may, no man will deny that it is plainly, irresistibly implied in the Presbyterian Confession of Faith, and the Saybrook Platform, and is necessarily connected with all systems which embrace the Calvinistic principles.[42]

In fact, opinions on the subject were divided among clergy within the Calvinist branches of Protestantism. Some affirmed that all who die in infancy are saved—or at least those of devout parents are. Others asserted the apparently more traditional view that only the inscrutable class of the elect who die in infancy are saved. All infants come into the world with Adam's sin, they reasoned; therefore, God is not unjust to punish any he chooses, these being the nonelect. Evidently, those leaning toward New School Calvinism were less likely to press any version of the damnation-of-infants doctrine. Not only that, even some who publicly professed the harsh view wavered in their private opinions on the topic. Non-Calvinists were eager to show that classical Calvinism taught the doctrine, despite what some divines within the Reformed branch of Protestantism claimed. And what were the ordinary faithful to think? They worried, of course.[43]

The question of the infant's status in the eyes of God became a burning issue in the presbytery of Cincinnati. As previously mentioned, in the months before Eliza and Augustus left the city, Joshua Wilson—the same minister whose sermons defending slavery caused a contingent of his congregation to walk out and form Sixth Presbyterian in 1831—was busy denouncing Rev. Lyman Beecher for propagating New School views. That was in 1832. A year later, in the spring of 1833, Wilson opposed the ordination of Lyman's son George, demanding to know, among other things, whether George affirmed the depravity of infants at birth.[44]

* * *

New Orleans, the nation's fifth-largest city, was an auspicious place for the ambitious Augustus. But cholera was there, too, along with yellow fever. A New Orleans newspaper described conditions at the time of the Garretts' arrival:

> The Cholera or Cold Plague, together with the Yellow Fever, is raging to so great an extent, that coffins cannot be made fast enough to put the dead into. The Yellow Fever is very bad, and persons are taken off with Cholera in *two hours*. . . . Business is completely prostrated, stores shut up, and one half of the people have fled from town. Last night upwards of seventy coffins were at the grave yard, and none to bury them, and in consequence had to remain overnight. The grave yards are now full, and they are burying them outside of the yards.

People fought the disease by dosing themselves with brandy and port, slathering their meat in garlic, filling their dwellings with camphor vapors, and burning pitch and tar in the streets. Clouds of smoke enveloped whole city blocks. In the end, one in seven died.[45]

It may seem surprising that the Garretts remained in New Orleans once they discovered that cholera and yellow fever were raging there. But they did. This can be explained by the circumstances of Imogine's death. It had been impossible to escape the "miasmas" lurking on the crowded ship; and when Imogine fell ill, it had been equally impossible to carry out most of Dr. Drake's prescriptions for treatment. Hence, Eliza and Augustus were no doubt reluctant to board another steamship with baby Charles, thinking it safer to take up residence in New Orleans, perhaps on the outskirts of town.[46]

They did not remain longer than a few months. Augustus learned that a Louisiana town called Natchitoches—pronounced Nack-uh-tush—was on the verge of becoming a major port in the Mississippi River system. In river terms, the place was almost four hundred miles upstream from New Orleans. Steamships reached it by way of the Red River, a tributary of the Mississippi. From the Red, boats traveling upriver made a brief passage on the Cane River, a short channel on which Natchitoches lay. Augustus decided to make a trip to Natchitoches to ascertain whether he could establish a more profitable auction business there.[47]

The bright hopes of Natchitoches were connected with a curious feature of the Red River. A huge log jam, which locals termed the "Great Raft," made that river impassible above Natchitoches. Thomas Freeman and Peter Curtis, sent by President Thomas Jefferson to explore the Louisiana Purchase, brought back a description of the massive obstruction—tree trunks so thick in the water that they damned up the river "for its whole width, from the bottom to about three feet higher than the surface of the water." This raft stretched a hundred and forty miles upstream and was so dense and immobile that "large bushes, weeds and grass" had grown up on it. One could walk across it "in every direction." This enormous blockage meant that Natchitoches was the last stop for northern steamboats and for that reason an interior destination port.[48]

His investigations of business opportunities in Natchitoches led Augustus to move his family there. The Cane River city was an ethnically diverse community of French Creole, Spanish, Native Americans, blacks, and a growing contingent of Anglo-American settlers like the Garretts. The downtown was stretched out along one long street at the foot of a bluff. There was no Presbyterian church—or Baptist or Methodist—in this Roman Catholic parish. Hence, a churchly means of entrée into the social graces of the business class did not present itself for Augustus. Yet he must have managed to rent an auction room and talk his way into brokering a share of the growing trade in goods entering and exiting the city.[49]

Then Charles died. He was only ten months old. Augustus and Eliza were inconsolable. They had been in Louisiana just four months, but now, in their grief, they decided to return to New York. They left Natchitoches as soon as Augustus could scrape together travel money for the steamboat, stagecoach, food, and lodging. It took a month to make the grim trip home.[50]

Back in Newburgh, Eliza gave birth to another son, two weeks before Christmas. They named him John Augustus after his father and his grandfather (who had passed away in June). John Augustus did not live out the day.[51]

CHAPTER 3

THE GREAT FAIRY LAND OF FORTUNES

*E*asterners journeyed to Chicago by horse, wagon, stagecoach, railway, and water. In 1836 twenty-one-year-old John Wentworth traveled from Sandwich, New Hampshire, to Michigan City, Indiana, by stage, rail, and steamer, then completed the remaining miles to Chicago on foot, trudging behind the wagon that held his carpetbag. He carried a jug of whisky to bathe his blistered feet. When he reached the bogs outside Chicago, he chose to walk barefoot the rest of the way to spare his boots.[1]

Augustus came to Chicago by boat, journeying alone sometime in the good-weather months of 1834. He traveled thirteen hundred miles, he said, a figure that reflects the distance by the water route: up the Hudson River to Albany, west on the Erie Canal to Buffalo, south on Lake Erie to Detroit, north again into Lake Huron and up to the Canadian border, then west again into Lake Michigan and south to Chicago. According to period sources, that amounted to 1,367 miles. Years later Augustus would describe what this move to Chicago signified to him and Eliza:

> I left my country, the land that gave me birth, the land that my mother and father inherited for a long while. With all I left behind an aged Father & Mother and so did my wife, which caused her to weep for many salutary hours, to seek an asylum in a new country amongst strangers and settled at a distance of 1300 miles, and did not know when I arrived here that I should ever find a friend to nurse me if I got sick & if I died to have paid the last tribute of respect.[2]

His reference to anxiety about whether he would find "a friend to nurse me if I got sick" was not idle rhetoric. On the frontier, men separated from their families nursed each other in times of illness. Even young men rehearsed their health problems to each other, since every sickness might develop into a life-threatening condition. When Augustus learned that

43

one of his friends living seventy-five miles away was ill, the sacred duty of friendship prompted him to action:

> I was informed yesterday that you were dangerously ill, not expected to live. I engaged a buggy and a team of horses and started for your place today with the intention of seeing you this evening. I concluded however to go to the P.O. before I started. I hunted up Fuller and he went to the office and gave me your letter. You cant imagine how I felt when I opened that letter from you for fear that I would hear that you were in that situation [dying]. Seeing that you are better and will be out of it in a few days I have given up the journey, but in case you get worse again don't delay in letting me know it immediately. [A]lthough I am not a good nurse, I can do a great deal of good to be in the place where you are sick.[3]

When he wrote to his in-laws about his first journey to Chicago and his worry that he might fall ill with no one to care for him, he was recalling that he had in fact fallen ill and had lacked a friend to nurse him. Far from Eliza, sick, nearly penniless and debt-strapped, he had struggled with ailments during that first winter in Chicago, but "kind providence restored my health." He was determined to make good. Although his creditors in Cincinnati did not know his whereabouts, his sense of honor demanded that he pay his debts, and he intended to do so "to the last cent." It was also understood between him and the Clarks that, if he failed in Chicago, he would return to Newburgh, settle down on his old farm, and satisfy his entrepreneurial impulses by branching out into a supplemental business such as a mill. There were teeth in this agreement: Eliza would not join him in Chicago—Benoni would not permit her to join him—unless he achieved real success.[4]

Chicago was known to the average easterner as an insignificant "North-West" trading post on Lake Michigan and the scene of a brief but bloody battle of army troops against a group of Potawatomi during the War of 1812. Stories about the "Fort Dearborn Massacre" became part of the propaganda for relocating Indians west of the Mississippi. The Andrew Jackson administration, having already removed Native peoples from the Southeast, was working hard to push them out of other places, including the state of Illinois and the region called Wisconsin, which still belonged to the Michigan Territory. By 1833 many of the Sauk, Fox, and other Native peoples of Illinois and the Michigan Territory had already been driven west of the Mississippi as a result of the Black Hawk War of 1832. The final exodus was just a few years away. Along the westward roads and riverways, white citizens welcomed this news, and newspapers reported renewed plans for a long-envisioned canal that would link Chicago with the Illinois River at LaSalle. There was also talk of a railroad to do the same thing. It was already possible to travel by water from New York to Chicago, then go overland to the Illinois River, which connected to the Mississippi and thus to New Orleans. If the Chicago River could be linked by canal or railroad to the Illinois River—ninety-six miles away —goods would be conveyable by an efficient inland route from New York all the way to New Orleans. Easterners, mostly young men, began trickling into Chicago.

When Augustus arrived in the spring of 1834, the old Potawatomi village was long gone, and the few houses that Gurdon Hubbard saw when he first arrived in 1818 had become a small but bustling community. The settlement was hosted by the confluence of two rivers, one flowing across the prairies from the north, the other up from the south. Just west of Lake Michigan they joined to form the main stem of the Chicago River, which until recently had coursed in a leisurely hook eastward and southward along a large sandbar before hiccoughing into Lake Michigan near today's Madison Street. But the year prior, the Army Corps of Engineers had straightened the river mouth by cutting through the sandbar and extending solid piers out into the lake so that the river entered the water at a deeper point. There were now plans for a proper harbor.[5]

Fort Dearborn overlooked the river near the shoreline. Rebuilt on a smaller scale after being burned to the ground during a battle with the Potawatomi, the fort housed army personnel and their families, as well as a few settlers. To the west was a second small settlement, where the north and south branches of the river met at the forks called Wolf Point or simply the "Point." Miller Tavern stood just northwest of the forks; the Sauganash Hotel was catty-corner across the river to the southeast; and a few houses and taverns composed a little community west of the rivers. These traces on the west were the older part of the Chicago settlement. More recently, a string of homes and businesses had begun appearing on the south side of the main stem. Otherwise the scene was desolate of human habitation. Marshes covered most of the south and west sides. North of the river were woods, and beyond the settlement were tallgrass prairies and more woods.[6]

Wolf Point, circa 1833. Chicago History Museum, ICHi-005946; Justin Herriott, artist.

The growth of the town in its first boom year has been variously estimated. Theodore Andreas asserts that the population on January 1, 1834,
was "not far from 250." Bessie Pierce suggests a population of 1,800, although she does not specify at what point in the year the village reached
that mark. According to Eugen Seeger, by 1835 the settlement had swelled
to more than 3,000 people. The great influx began in the spring of 1834,
when the ice broke up and sailing ships, one of them carrying Augustus,
began to plow the lake again. It had been a particularly brutal winter for
the little village hunkered down in poorly insulated wood and log structures with temperatures plummeting to nearly thirty degrees below zero.
Chickens, pigs, and an ox froze solid in the streets, and almost no one
ventured outdoors except "an occasional Indian wrapped in his blanket
. . . or a muffled-up Frenchman, driving furiously in his cariole on the
river," which was covered with snow and ice. And wolves. They entered
the settlement after dusk, hungry and howling.[7]

   With the reopening of the harbor in March, sailing ships began to
arrive, far more in number than the entire previous year. By the end of
1834 the town could boast some 400 houses, 4 warehouses, 29 dry-goods

stores, 19 grocery stores, 5 hardware stores, 3 drugstores, 19 taverns, 26 wholesale businesses, and 17 law offices. Every incoming ship was loaded with people who had "caught the mania" and were "bound for Chicago, the great fairy land of fortunes."[8]

Chicago was not yet a *city* in 1834; it had only just voted itself a *town* in a state where "there was no social or business organization upon any settled principles" but only "a large crowd of strangers" looking for adventure. Such was how an early Illinois governor described the outpost. He went on: "We had no cities, no trade, no manufactures, and no punctuality in the payment of debts. We exported little or nothing." Into this blooming disorder the settlers poured, most of them men, most of them young. (Even a decade later, when the proportion of women had substantially increased, Chicago was still a young person's city, with only 9 percent of the population over forty and with males outnumbering females about three to two.) They boarded three to a bed in rustic hostels and "danced, smoked, and caroused until dawn" in the public houses. Augustus took up residence in one of the hostels, perhaps the Eagle Tavern or the larger Sauganash, where most of the lodgers owed the proprietor money and,

South Water Street in 1834, by William H. Gale.
Chicago History Museum, ICHi-032389, cropped.

when they did pay, were more likely to do so with a wagon, cord of wood, tomatoes, butter, or brandy than with money.[9]

Although Chicago was in many ways a welcoming place, full of booster-ish sentiment, those who already had a stake in commerce were protective of their interests. When Augustus's future business partner Nathaniel Brown arrived from Michigan on a schooner carrying a load of pine timber, he was told by local merchants that he was not free to sell it. When Brown attempted to purvey his timber anyway, the locals had him arrested, or at least threatened to do so. Brown appealed to Richard Hamilton of the Court of the County Commissioners, and Hamilton granted him a permit.[10]

Augustus needed more than a license; he needed connections to get established in what everyone in the know regarded as a lucrative business: land sales. He had no letter of introduction, which in many settings would have been de rigueur for passage into the good graces of the business class. In 1834, however, the well-educated and politically connected easterners of fussier manners and stiffer protocols were not yet in control of the village. Nor was Augustus's status as a rural farmer with limited education any impediment in frontier Chicago, where men of various strands of European descent and from different social backgrounds lived together on a basis of rough social equality. Even after the arrival in increasing numbers of more urbane and class-conscious easterners, influential citizens of Chicago championed frontier egalitarianism—at least for white men. The *Chicago Daily Journal* decided that Germans, Irish, Norwegians, and the "shrewd Yankee," together with the backwoods settlers (Illinois "Suckers" and Indiana "Hoosiers"), could and should find common cause under the banner of their shared humanity. Archibald Maclay, traveling secretary for the Baptist Bible Society, opined that ethnic diversity in Chicago was "unfriendly to the growth of prejudices," the latter being more character-istic of "olden communities." Hence, an unrefined and unconnected man like Augustus could introduce himself to anyone he wished.[11]

The first person he sought out was the minister of the Presbyterian church. The Presbyterians met in the loft of a building near Clark and Lake, and their pastor, Rev. Jeremiah Porter, kept a study on Lake Street. Augustus found Porter and introduced himself. He told the minister that he had come to Chicago saddled with debts but knew the auction trade and was ready to make a new start. He was also a married man, he said, although his wife would remain with her parents in Newburgh until he made a success. She was "a decided Christian," a Presbyterian, and would make an excellent parishioner in Porter's church. Porter was sympathetic and suggested that Augustus attend the Wednesday evening meeting, where he could be introduced to some "praying men" who could help him get established as an auctioneer.[12]

Among the members of Porter's church were rising businessmen, including postmaster John Bates, who operated his own auction business in a store on the west side of Dearborn between Lake and South Water. Bates had managed to get himself appointed an auctioneer of public lands when Chicago was first established as a town in 1833. U.S. law ordained that every township established by a federal land grant be divided into thirty-six sections, each a square mile, and that section sixteen be devoted "to the maintenance of public schools." In Chicago the boundaries of the school section, given according to their later names, were State Street to Halsted and Madison to Twelfth. The sale of this land was under the jurisdiction of the county and its commissioner, Richard Hamilton, who awarded Bates the right to auction land in the school section. In October of 1833 Bates sold lots and blocks of the school section, extending credit for one- to three-year terms at 10 percent interest. It is likely that his commission schedule was the same as the one that governed John Kinzie when he was a land auctioneer in 1831—2.5 percent commission on the first $200 and 1 percent on sales over $200.[13]

It was a favorable time for moneymaking in Chicago, thanks to the end of the Black Hawk War, the beginning of federally funded harbor construction in 1833, the chartering of the canal in 1834, the steady market in lands ceded by the Indians, and the hordes of newcomers pouring into town. Augustus arrived just in time to participate in the land craze, and his introduction to the "praying men" of the city's small business class— especially his new friendship with auctioneer Bates—made it possible for him to profit by this timing. Augustus had barely funds sufficient to pay a few weeks' room and board in a tavern, much less money to prepay a lease for an auction room. But with assistance from Bates and other churchmen, he was able to open an auction room in a small store on Water Street in preparation for the traffic in lands that were about to go on the market to finance the Illinois and Michigan canal.[14]

In the 1834–1835 session of the Illinois legislature, a bill was passed to fund the canal on bonds backed by the canal lands gifted to the state by the federal government. The Federal Land Law of 1800 provided for the appointment of two officers in district land offices: the register of documents and the receiver of public monies. They were each paid a salary and commission on sales. Lands were sold at auction at the government land offices, and what did not sell was sold the following day at the government price, $1.25 per acre in the 1830s. On May 28, 1835, Edmund Taylor, receiver of public monies, opened an office for canal lands on the second floor of Thomas Church's store on Lake Street. Sales continued through September 30, and there is reason to believe that some of the government sales were handled by Bates in his auction house, perhaps also by Garrett down the street. In any case, land sold by the government moved swiftly into a secondary market in the auction houses, and Bates and Garrett were the immediate beneficiaries. In his auction room on South Water Street, Garrett was so successful that, by July, he was able to rent space in the Bates building, a large three-story brick edifice on the west side of Dearborn near South Water—No. 1 Dearborn Street, "close to Cox and Duncan's clothing store, just opposite to which were Mr. Greenleaf's auction rooms."[15]

Garrett described his business as an "auction and commission house." This meant that he received goods on consignment, sometimes giving the consigner "a liberal advance." He also offered insurance on consigned goods. Hence, although transactions in land were his most profitable ventures, he was also disposing of other goods, both local products and eastern imports.[16]

By October of 1835, when he made an accounting of his sales, Augustus discovered that he had transacted $1,800,000 of business for the year thus far. In many cases the same property was sold more than once. A speculator would buy land at auction and sell it to a buyer who later put it up for sale. Or if a man failed to sell what he purchased at auction, he would bring it back to the auctioneer and "pay a dollar" to have it put up for auction again. Harriet Martineau happened to be visiting the town in the summer of 1836, when the place was alive with land fever and thick with speculators. Every merchant, it seemed, was using his profits to buy land with the intention of selling as soon as the price went up. "As the gentlemen of our party walked the streets," Martineau recalled, "storekeepers hailed them from their doors, with offers of farms, and all manner of land-lots, advising them to speculate before the price of land rose higher." Garrett marketed town lots on the basis of this inflationary curve. Selling some lots in Milwaukee, he urged prospective buyers to consider "the chance of realizing $18,000 or $20,000 on a Lot that will cost a few hundred."[17]

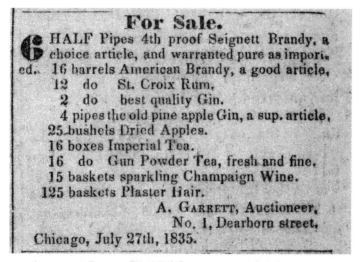

Augustus Garrett Auction and Commission House newspaper
ad, July 27, 1835. Chicago History Museum, ICHi-176175B, cropped.

Augustus Garrett "For Sale" newspaper ad, July 27, 1835.
Chicago History Museum, ICHi-176176B, cropped.

Assuming that he earned only a 1 percent commission on his auction
sales in this period, he would have netted $18,000, an extraordinary sum
in 1835. In fact, he made more than that, since his commission was 2.5
percent on the first $200 of any sale, and it appears that there was also a
fee of a dollar per auction paid by the seller. If we set his average earnings
arbitrarily at 1.5 percent, the net rises to $27,000. He had expenses—rent,
a clerk—and also debts from his Cincinnati fiasco, which he was now beginning to pay off. Yet even after paying overhead and a first installment
on his debts, he may have had as much left over as $10,000, no small sum

in an era when an Irish live-in domestic was given room and board plus $100 a year, a teacher in a New York State academy earned about $350 a year, and the clerk of a United States senator was paid between $1,000 and $1,400 a year. In addition to profits in the thousands of dollars just from his auction fees, he was also making money in his commission store. With his excess of cash, he began speculating in land.[18]

These triumphs in business emboldened Augustus to send for Eliza. Since he needed her parents' agreement, he probably wrote specifically to Benoni and Amy, addressing them affectionately as "Father and Mother" and rehearsing his successes and new financial situation. They gave their blessing. The next step was for him to travel to Newburgh to get her or else to send her money and instructions for travel on her own. The latter is more likely. In his 1884 history of Chicago, Theodore Andreas says that Augustus "sent on for his wife, whom he had left with her parents." Whatever the historian's source for this information, several considerations suggest that he was right in saying that Augustus sent for her instead of going back to New York to get her. On August 6 he and Eliza signed a deed for three Chicago lots, purchased from one James Campbell. The deed was made out in Chicago, which places Eliza there at the beginning of August. We know from a notice Augustus published in a newspaper that he was engaged in auctioning land from May 28 through September 30. He would not have traveled to New York during the auction season. In 1835 a trip to Newburgh and back took forty days or more and could not be undertaken until spring, when lake traffic resumed. But given that business activity and competition were heating up in Chicago at a rapid pace in 1835, Augustus had good reason not to be away from the city for five or six weeks that spring when government land was put up for auction: it was no doubt during that period of auctions that he brokered a good deal of the $1,800,000 revealed in his October accounting. Hence, he probably did "send" for Eliza, as Andreas says, instead of going to get her. She must have journeyed to Chicago between March 1st, when boat traffic resumed, and the first week of August, when she signed the real-estate deed.[19]

Augustus was perfectly confident that Eliza would be able to make her way to Chicago. He was also sure that she would be content once she arrived in her new home. She accepted all things with equanimity, was less perturbable and more even-keeled than he. She was also kindhearted, reliable, practical, and demanded almost nothing for herself. She had been through terrible misfortunes with him and had proven resilient. Her strength of character and loyalty to him were clear from the fact that she was coming to him, leaving her family behind after all her losses when she might have stayed put and demanded that he return to her. He could scarcely wait to show her his auction room, his stack of deeds for western lands, and his account ledger at the bank, and to introduce her to his friends and their wives in this town where everyone knew him and respected him.

* * *

Sometime in the spring or summer of 1835, Eliza stood on the deck of a long steam-powered paddleboat at one of the busy docks in Newburgh bay. As the steamer moved out into the stream, she saw, perhaps for the first time, the whole town of Newburgh rising in tiers toward the bluffs. The boat steamed northward, and Eliza kept her eyes trained on the embankment, catching glimpses of the familiar farmlands where she had grown up, the little port town of Marlborough, and the Presbyterian church, so close to the river, briefly visible through the trees.[20]

Eliza's journey was marked by breathtaking scenery and occasional little hardships, including overnight sojourns in dubious hotels and sweltering days in a horse-drawn boat that moved westward on the Erie Canal at a ponderous pace. Canal boats occasionally ran aground with shuddering jolts. The draft animals sometimes collapsed from the heat and the effort. When Eliza reached Buffalo, she traveled the rest of the way by sailing ship through the Great Lakes, probably arriving in Chicago near

The village of Newburgh in 1842. Author's collection.

dusk. (Chicagoans who went to the piers to watch the lake vessels arrive recalled later how grand and beautiful the ships looked as they sailed at eventide into the new Chicago harbor, their majestic lights swaying from the masts.) The boat docked at the pier or, more likely, dropped anchor offshore, requiring that the passengers and goods be ferried in on smaller craft. This was necessary because sandbars were always forming at Chicago: the northern side of the pier was continually silting in, and erosion on the southern side caused eddies.[21]

Augustus met her in a hired carriage and brought her to his hotel. The ride gave her a view of the city, whose population was now approaching three thousand people. On the south bank of the river, on a little rise near the harbor, stood Fort Dearborn, a large log building surrounded by a double stockade. As Augustus directed the carriage westward onto Lake Street, Eliza noted little shacks, newly thrown up; and when they arrived at Dearborn Street, he had the driver stop so he could point out the handsome three-story brick building where he conducted his auction and commission business. At this intersection, Chicago looked like a busy burg, but to the north, across the river, it was all oak wood, a reminder that the wilderness was still at the town's doorstep. Further on, at Clark Street, a large edifice was under construction—the Saloon Building, designed to be four stories tall with a large public hall. At LaSalle stood the four-story brick building of commission-merchant Gurdon Hubbard, and at the end of Lake Street, near the south bend of the river, was the Sauganash Hotel. Augustus and Eliza would make that lodging house their home for the next nine years.[22]

The Sauganash, said to have been named after Billy Caldwell, a.k.a. "the Sauganash," was built by Mark Beaubien sometime between 1829 and 1831 as an attachment to his log cabin. The new hostel was a two-story frame house with blue shutters. Beaubien moved his living quarters into the hotel and turned his log cabin into a barroom and office. The Sauganash was later expanded by an addition on the east that held a kitchen and more rooms upstairs. There was also a large barn on the grounds, and the whole property was fenced to keep in the cows and chickens. The hotel's precise location was given by John Caton as "80 feet south of the S.E. corner of Lake and Market Streets," which meant that it stood on the east side of the south branch just below the place where the north and south streams joined to form the main stem. When Beaubien operated the Sauganash, it was the chief community-gathering place. A visitor to the establishment in the winter of 1834—some months before Augustus's arrival—recalled that the whole household would gather around a fire in the log barroom. The loneliness of the prairie outpost and the bitterness of the cold made the fire-bright log house a jolly place, with Beaubien performing on his violin and the guests dancing. There being no white women around, the men danced with each other or with the occasional Indian woman (to the shock of visiting easterners). In 1833 the Sauganash hosted the election of the first trustees of Chicago shortly after its incorporation as a town.[23]

Beaubien left the Sauganash sometime in 1834, and the hotel remained empty until January of 1835, when a man named George Davis fixed it up and advertised its accommodations as the best in town. It is likely that Augustus moved in about this time. A few months later, when Eliza arrived, Davis was probably still operating the Sauganash; but in January of 1836, John and Harriet Murphy assumed management and renamed the establishment the United States Hotel. It appears that toward the end of 1836, the owner of the building had decided to tear it down and put the large lot to some more profitable use, but the hotel's residents kept off the demolition crew. That owner may have been Augustus Garrett, who

The Sauganash Hotel as it looked in the mid-1830s.
Chicago History Museum, ICHi-059715, cropped; C. E. Petford, artist.

purchased the place at some point in 1836. His vision of what he could earn by leasing new buildings on the site may have momentarily overcome his sentimental attachment to the Sauganash. Or perhaps he was one of the residents who held off the demolition men, subsequently purchasing the hotel precisely in order to save it from destruction.[24]

At Garrett's direction, the Murphys took down the old log cabin. Then, in September of 1837, they left the Sauganash and opened a new hotel on the west side of the river, taking the name "United States Hotel" with them. Garrett then let the Sauganash to a pair of theater managers named Harry Isherwood and Alexander Mackenzie. They set up the "Chicago theater" and declared an intention to remain through the winter. They converted the hotel dining room into a playhouse with seating (rough boards) for two or three hundred and "a few chairs" in front "for the ladies and their escorts." Isherwood painted some "pretty scenes," and the small company put on three plays: *The Idiot Witness, The Stranger,* and *The Carpenter of Rouen.* Typically, there was a drama and a farce, but the entertainments also included song, comedy, and dance—"illumined by candles and oil lamps" from early evening to midnight. This first Chicago theater was short-lived. It closed after only six weeks, and the hotel stood empty until a man named Seymour took over its management. At some point—probably in the spring or early summer of 1840—Augustus refurbished the hotel and brought the Murphys back as managers.[25]

Although Charles Latrobe called the Sauganash "a vile, two-storied barrack" in which "all was in a state of most appalling confusion, filth, and racket," others thought it a decent, attractive establishment. It tried to be that. "A pretentious white two-story building, with bright blue wood shutters" is how Juliette Kinzie described the hotel; it was "the admiration of all the little circle at Wolf Point." Joseph Balestier, writing in 1840 about Chicago lodging in 1835, said that "the Sauganash was esteemed the best," and Judge John Caton called it "a fashionable boarding-house" where "quite a number of young married persons had rooms." Apparently, there were not many young couples in Chicago at the time, for John Wentworth, in a letter to his sister, remarked on there being so few married couples in Chicago in 1837 that he was able to visit them all on a single New Year's Day. In view of Caton's comment, most of them must have been at the Sauganash.[26]

Renderings of the hotel show a long two-story building with an additional section jutting from the center on the east (which held a kitchen and additional rooms) and Mark Beaubien's original cabin (the bar and office) attached to the northern end. Judging from the number of second-story windows, there may well have been as many as fifteen or sixteen rooms upstairs and perhaps a few more downstairs as well. Augustus probably acquired several rooms for himself and Eliza. In 1844, while still living at the hotel, she was able to receive callers on New Year's Day, which implies that she had a sitting room. Perhaps Augustus also had a study. After he became the owner of the building in 1836, he probably had a set of rooms connected and remodeled into a suite.[27]

At the end of August 1835, residents of the Sauganash witnessed one of the most dramatic events of Chicago's early history. Thousands of Potawatomi were in the city, and Eliza must have been among the women who looked out from the second-story parlor windows of the Sauganash to watch the Potawatomi's farewell war-dance, for Judge Caton remembered these women and their varied reactions to the scene when the mass of warriors—leaping, crouching, and whirling as they processed—reached the yard just beneath the Sauganash's windows.[28]

The dancing Potawatomi men were at once triumphant and bitter in their dance. Their forebears had come into Illinois in the eighteenth century, under pressure from the Iroquois, an eastern people who migrated west in response to the rise of European settlement. In 1812 some of the Potawatomi living in the Fort Dearborn area attacked a group of U.S. soldiers who, with their families, were evacuating the fort. This event, memorialized in skewed white memory as the Fort Dearborn Massacre, fixed local Chicago opinion against the tribe. A decentralized people, the Potawatomi lived along various waterways and lakes in Illinois and Wisconsin, hunting the districts surrounding their settlements. In the eyes of the federal government, they, like other Native peoples, had no right of ownership to these lands, only a right of residence and use of resources, since the North-West was now under the control of the United States. In the key Supreme Court ruling on the subject, Chief Justice John Marshall set forth a doctrine of "discovery and conquest," which accorded the federal government title to lands that Americans had taken by force, leaving Indian nations only a right of presence. Although an individual Native person could acquire title to land in the ordinary ways, in the eyes of U.S. law no Native tribe enjoyed sovereignty over the lands they fished and hunted.[29]

By 1830 many Indians had already left the North-West, and those who remained were vastly outnumbered by white settlers. When the Indian Removal Act was signed by President Jackson in May of that year, the die was cast. The Potawatomi understood that the federal government would no longer permit them to occupy lands east of the Mississippi. Fearing "uncompensated removal," they supported leaders who enjoyed good working relations with whites, and they remained largely uninvolved in the Black Hawk War of 1832.[30]

After the Black Hawk revolt, the Jackson administration made plans for the removal of the Potawatomi into Iowa, which necessitated a treaty by which the Potawatomi and other Native peoples in the North-West would give up their rights of occupancy in exchange for what the law called "consideration," that is, some form of payment. In 1833 such a treaty was secured in Chicago between the federal government, represented by George Porter, governor of the Michigan Territory, and several chiefs and other representatives of the Potawatomi. According to one portrait, Porter plied the Native leaders with whisky during the weeklong parley, and at least two Indian negotiators were drunk when the agreement was finally made. Yet the Potawatomi appear to have been thoughtful bargainers— remarkably so, given the constraints of the situation confronting them. In exchange for their lands, the terms of the treaty gave them an equal number of acres west of the Mississippi, along with debt cancellation, goods, a nearly million-dollar immediate monetary payment, and annuities.[31]

In August of 1835, five thousand Potawatomi arrived in Chicago for a government payout and their leave-taking. At the end of the month, a large group of Indian men staged the war dance recalled by Caton. Looking back on it, he described, with all the prejudices of his ethnicity and class, what he had observed:

> The morning was very warm, and the perspiration was pouring from them almost in streams. Their eyes were wild and blood-shot. Their countenances had assumed an expression of all the worst passions which can find a place in the breast of a savage. . . . Their muscles stood out in great hard knots, as if wrought to a tension that must burst them. Their tomahawks and clubs were thrown and brandished about in every direction, with the most terrible ferocity . . . and with every step and gesture they uttered the most frightful yells, in every imaginable key and note, though generally the highest and shrillest possible. The dance, which was ever continued, consisted of leaps and spasmodic steps, now forward and now back or sideways, with the whole body distorted into every imaginable unnatural position, most generally

stooping forward, with the head and face thrown up, the back arched down, first one foot thrown far forward and then withdrawn, and the other similarly thrust out, frequently squatting quite to the ground, and all with a movement almost as quick as lightning.

The dance, performed in a parade, proceeded along the north side of the main stem of the river, then crossed to the west and moved south through the prairie along the west side of the south branch before crossing back east, directly in front of the Sauganash. The Indians continued with stylized war-steps toward the hotel, eight hundred of them, brandishing weapons, "a raging sea of dusky, painted, naked fiends," Caton said, until their front ranks stood right under the parlor windows. Some of the women retreated in horror. Others remained, transfixed.[32]

Several white observers besides Caton—no Potawatomi accounts survive—saw the scene in similar terms, treating the ceremonial dance as if it were proof of Native savagery and a justification for Indian removal. A week later a caravan of forty army wagons, with the Potawatomi men walking alongside, carried off the children and material goods of the tribe to their new lands beyond the Mississippi. One government expedition referred to the land as "too poor for snakes to live upon," and Potawatomi scouts who went to examine the place also found it barren and treeless. It is uncertain which parts of the five million acres the government agents or the Indian scouts meant, but the region was mostly prairie and lacked the vast woods and familiar large game that were thick in the ceded lands of northeastern Illinois and Wisconsin. To the Potawatomi, the new environment seemed alien and empty.[33]

Augustus had a vested interest in Jacksonian policies toward indigenous tribes because the lands traded by the Potawatomi and other Native peoples were now being sold by the federal government to white settlers and eastern speculators. Augustus was a broker in these transactions and also a speculator. In short, his growing fortune was immediately dependent on removal of the Indians. Over the next few years he purchased various properties, not only in Chicago, but in other places too, including 328 acres in Eliza's name, at the after-auction government sale price, in a paper town of the Des Plaines River valley.[34]

Eliza's pastor, Jeremiah Porter, was even better acquainted with the recent history that led to the August departure of the Potawatomi. As a missionary stationed first at Sault Ste. Marie and later at Chicago, Porter had considerable firsthand experience of Native peoples and had observed government dealings with them. Writing in his journal about the initial successes of Native forces against the army in the Black Hawk War of 1832, Porter opined that God brought "ten thousand" white soldiers out to the frontier in order "to slay them and to show that he is a God that judgeth in the earth." His information about the number of army regulars engaged against Black Hawk, and the white casualties, was flawed, but his sentiments were clear. At the end of August, after the Indian rebellion had been put down completely, Porter sneered at the "millions of dollars expended" and the "ten thousand American soldiers" sent into battle to kill perhaps "two hundred starving Indians." He accused the government of using the army to frighten Indians into making treaties. In a letter composed in Chicago the following summer, he offered a theological gloss on this policy, calling it "the mystery of iniquity." That September he observed to a correspondent that Indians "sell their fatherlands to the grasping whites, and retire for a resting place beyond the Mississippi," adding, "but woe to those who make haste to be rich. The Lord will not forget, and do you not forget to pray for us, that vengeance come not suddenly."[35]

The prevailing opinion among white settlers was that the Indians were savages, their removal was necessary, and the terms of the treaty were very "liberal." Porter's opposing views put him at odds with leading men of his congregation, particularly those who were profiting from the new economic conditions that followed the treaty. Under direct or veiled pressure, Porter left his Chicago charge in September or October of 1835. The only thorough study of the early history of First Presbyterian Church, an unpublished book written in 1932 by Gordon Riegler, concludes that Porter's New School views on the atonement, his opposition to the liquor trade, and his "pro-Indian" views caused an irreparable rift. His letters also hint that the elders wanted a more polished minister and were complaining that Porter was spending too much time nurturing other mission posts. Whether these were the real reasons or only pretenses fomented by his opponents is uncertain. We would have a clearer picture if the Chicago section of his journals had survived. Porter went on to Peoria, Illinois, and soon was in trouble again, this time expressly for his outspoken antislavery opinions.[36]

Eliza Garrett, observing the Potawatomi's protest dance against the great white land grab (of which she and her husband were beneficiaries), was told that the Potawatomi were given as many acres west of the

Mississippi as they gave up east of it, along with goods and payments in the millions of dollars. But she probably also knew the opinions of her pastor about the fundamental injustice of United States government policy toward Indians; she certainly had heard church talk about his opinions. If her conscience bothered her, she probably concluded that the United States' appropriation of lands in the North-West and her husband's growing prosperity in consequence were matters over which she had no control and was not expected to hold an opinion, much less raise an objection. Women had no public say in such things, and, privately, most held the views of their men. That said, we do not know Eliza's opinions—whether she sympathized more with her pastor's views or her husband's.

With other young married couples living at the Sauganash in the latter part of the 1830s, the hotel was a cheerful place for Eliza. She had plenty of time to socialize, with no children to care for, no hearth to tend, no cooking or wash to do, no laundering or other chores. She became friends with Harriet Murphy, who ran the hotel most of the years the Garretts lived there, and she got to know a few other wives who lived for periods at the Sauganash, including Mary Gurnee, who became a close friend. She and Mary did a bit of flower gardening in the large yard to the east of the hotel. The yard lay between the lodge and the barn, where horses were kept. Long-term guests each had control of a plot, "where they marked and shaped, planted and cared for the various figures which their various farms assumed." John Wentworth, one of the unmarried men at the hotel, a future U.S. congressman, and a good friend of Augustus, grew not only flowers but a bit of cabbage in his corner of this garden.[37]

Along with the friends at the Sauganash, Eliza's primary social world was the circle of women at First Presbyterian Church. The congregation was now assembling in a new building near the corner of Lake Street and Clark. The meetinghouse was a plain wooden structure, about forty feet long and twenty-five wide. Parishioners sat on benches of pine, and in spring, when water filled a ditch out front, the men used some of these benches to bridge the muddy gap. West-siders had trouble attending in any season. Seventeen Presbyterians lived together in a single house beyond the river. To get to church, they had to "go skipping from one log to another, across the swamps and bogs of the muddy prairies." Often the men of the party carried the women "across the black and treacherous holes." They crossed the river over a floating bridge. Eliza, ensconced in the Sauganash, was spared these trials, but she, too, had to pick her way through muddy streets, lifting her heavy skirts and making use of whatever boards had been laid down for pedestrians.[38]

Between Sunday services and Wednesday evening prayer meetings, Eliza and other service-minded women of the church visited the needy and the sick, brought comfort and food to those in the poorhouse and the jail, and raised money for charitable causes. Eliza was also an eager collaborator in other churchly enterprises. The women of First Presbyterian had established a Dorcas society at least as early as 1835, and an interdenominational Ladies Benevolent Association was organized by the churchwomen of the city in 1843. Eliza was a member and leader of both groups.[39]

Dorcas societies were women's charitable associations, organized in chapters with female officers, although legal necessities required oversight by boards of men. They operated as sewing circles that put on occasional fairs to support the work of the church, aid the families of home missionaries, and distribute charity to needy people. Historical recollections from early Chicago Presbyterians tell of annual fairs and fancywork being offered for sale at the Tremont House and on passenger steamers traveling between Chicago and Buffalo. It was common in the mid-nineteenth century for the members to collect donations of tea, sugar, and the like from local grocers, bringing these as gifts when they made initial visits to the dwellings of the poor in order to assess need. After these reconnaissance missions, they returned at a later date with clothing, mostly handmade articles. Most of the work of the Dorcas women took place in the parlors of members, where they sewed endlessly and assembled for periodic business meetings.[40]

Eliza Garrett was one of the organizers of Chicago's Presbyterian Dorcas Society and helped put on its first fair in 1835 or 1836. The fair was a church fund-raiser, hosted by a Mrs. James Boyer, whose house was the largest in Chicago. Eliza and Augustus hosted the second fair. Lacking a house, they opened the doors of Augustus's auction rooms, and Augustus, always the able promoter, publicized the fair with handbills and sent around his mounted crier, "Colonel George," to announce the event at the appointed hour.[41]

Meanwhile, across the river to the north, a devout Episcopalian named Juliette Kinzie was helping to found St. James Episcopal Church in a leafy neighborhood that soon became a small upper-class enclave. It happens that Kinzie thought very little of Dorcas societies, and she composed a somewhat disparaging novel about one. The story, set in rural Connecticut, features a young woman named Catherine, who is brought from an initial enthusiasm for fake and ineffectual religion, represented by her evangelical friends in a Dorcas society, to a moment of crisis in which she discovers the more authentic and benevolent religion of the Anglican faith. Kinzie looked with a jaundiced eye on Methodists, Baptists, and Presbyterians, and her novel is a gentle satire of what she took to be their showy religious sentiment, intolerant religious doctrines and discipline, and inept Christian charity.[42]

Whatever her Chicago impressions of Dorcas societies may have been —and there were probably few differences between a Connecticut Dorcas society and a Chicago one, inasmuch as the Dorcas women of Chicago were for the most part transplanted easterners—Kinzie writes as an outsider with no sympathy for the religious piety spawned by the Second Great Awakening and the Holiness movement. There is no complexity or nuancing in her portrait of revivalist religion. The revivalists come off as self-righteous, thoughtless people, and the Episcopalians as good and merciful folk. In Kinzie's eyes it is a virtue that "the English Church" does not know "experimental" religion, as one of her characters puts it, or "change of heart" and the "evidence" that gives a person "assurance."[43]

Experimental in this period meant "experiential," the powerful sense of being possessed by divine love, sometimes with fainting or physical agitation, the outer signs of the inner transformation. In the revivalist milieu, these emotions and bodily effects gave a person assurance of salvation. The external effects were on display at revival meetings, and those affected often testified about them. It was only natural that others, those still seeking experiential assurance, made efforts to imitate the prayers, the inner disposition, even the motions of body that they saw and heard about—in the hopes of being caught up in the same rivers of emotion and kindled by the same inner fires. Juliette Kinzie saw all that as phoniness. The earnest people engaged in the effort saw it as *seeking*.

Eliza Garrett was such a seeker, longing for assurance but not finding it. She had never been swept away. No matter what prayers she said or what receptivity she cultivated, no fire came. Therefore, although she was busy in the work of the Presbyterian Dorcas Society, faithfully attended worship services and prayer meetings, and was highly regarded by her pastor, she could not bring herself to apply for church membership. The session of First Presbyterian Church kept very meticulous records. From the organization of the church in 1833 through the succeeding decades, it recorded in its minutes the names of all persons who became communicants, stating whether they were received on the basis of a letter from another congregation or a satisfactory examination of their religious experience. These session records have been preserved intact for the 1830s and 1840s without any gaps. The name of Eliza Garrett does not appear in them.[44]

In light of this surprising fact, it is worth looking more closely at the way Rev. Porter describes Eliza's participation in his congregation. "I found Mrs. Eliza Garrett a valuable accession to our circle of noble women," he wrote in 1859, and to be "all that Mr. Garrett had represented her." Twenty-five years later, when Alvaro Field asked him about the Garretts, he phrased his answer in similar terms: "I found her a very valuable accession to our noble band of Christian women." In neither description did he say that she joined the church. Hence, Field was correct when he contended that although she "joined the Presbyterian women in their benevolent and society work," "there is the best evidence that she never was a member of that Church in Chicago."[45]

Her reasons can be guessed by a process of elimination. First Presbyterian Church of Chicago required that members adhere to a personal moral code, and the church session investigated and disciplined offenders. During the church's first decade in Chicago, individual members appear in the minutes on suspicion of using foul language, engaging in "unchristian conversation," selling spirituous liquors, frequenting the theater, dancing at public balls, committing adultery, and other infractions. Because of churchly discipline of these sorts, some young men postponed joining a church until they were married, settled down, and had renounced whisky. But desire for freedom from moral codes would not have been a reason for Eliza to have resisted church membership. The moral code of First Presbyterian Church of Chicago was no different from the one she grew up with as the child of devout Presbyterian parents. Moreover, had she been in rebellion against the code as a young married woman, she would not have made a good impression on Porter, who took such things very seriously.[46]

Certain considerations of social standing also caused some families to postpone church membership. City churches typically sold or rented pews as a means of financing a new building or otherwise supporting their ministries. Although churches also reserved free seats, these were not socially desirable, and it was expected that communicants would not make use of them but would instead rent their seating as an obligation of membership. The pew-rental system in antebellum Presbyterian churches discouraged at least some of the poor from joining. "The dearness of pew-rent," wrote one American, "turns poverty out of doors. Poor people have a sense of shame; and I know many a one, who, because he cannot go to Heaven decently, will not go at all." There is, however, no hint in the session books or trustee minutes that First Presbyterian of Chicago was selling or renting rights to its pews (mere board benches, after all), and, in any case, Augustus could certainly have afforded a pew for Eliza.[47]

In the era of the Second Great Awakening, many Presbyterians were influenced by revivalist religion. Although the *Manual of Communicants of the First Presbyterian Church of Chicago* did not mention a conversion experience as a requisite for membership, session minutes from the 1830s show that testimony about one's religious experiences, as signs of one's true conversion, was in fact demanded. Those who had already been ad-mitted to a Presbyterian church elsewhere could show a letter of good standing, but those with no letter had to be examined by the session, which consisted of a group of four elders, together with the pastor. Thus, on August 31, 1835, two men from Presbyterian churches back east appeared before the session in Rev. Porter's study. Lacking letters, they submitted to examination. "After giving account of their religious experiences," the clerk's minutes report, the "session voted to receive them." Not everyone who aspired to church membership felt prepared to do that, and in this era of revivalist religion those who could not find the experiential signs in themselves sometimes questioned their own salvation. In an earlier period, there had been special membership provisions for doubters of this type in Presbyterian and Congregationalist churches (a so-called Half-Way Covenant). But this was not an option for Eliza. Hence, her failure to join the Presbyterian church in Chicago, where she was otherwise an active participant in congregational life, would have been interpreted by her friends in the congregation as an indication that she was still seeking the experiential signs that assured one of salvation. Some of those friends were probably also in the same situation.[48]

Eliza had no letter from the Marlborough Presbyterian church back in New York or from any Presbyterian church in Cincinnati. She had been a Presbyterian her whole life but had never joined a church. The reason must be that she had never undergone a palpable conversion, at least not one that resembled what she had heard others describe. Nor did she have inner feelings that might count as marks of spiritual regeneration, at least not any she trusted.

Perhaps there was something in her psychological makeup that kept her emotions in check when she thought about God, attended prayer meetings, or listened to even the most powerful preaching. Since religious experience was certified by feeling, honest souls who lacked what they could count as authentic religious affections were reluctant to make public claims about their own salvation. It was a terrible predicament for the most sincere, and Eliza was, if anything, sincere. As much as she wished to belong to the church fully, she could not bring herself to go before the church session and lie about a conversion experience that she had never had or about inner stirrings that she did not feel.[49]

There was also something else. By the time Eliza arrived in Chicago, she had lost three children within the span of just three years. The death of a child was not uncommon in antebellum America. Almost every family lost one or more children to accident or disease, and they understood loss as the common lot. They suffered terrible grief nonetheless, and Eliza more than most because she had lost all her children. Whether from an inability to have more children or simply from fear of losing another child, she had no more children after John Augustus, who had died within hours of birth.

She searched for a religious interpretation of her losses. All serious Christians in her era did so, and there were certain generic ways of framing experiences of loss and making sense of them. A contemporary of Eliza named Phoebe Worrall Palmer went through such a process of searching when she, too, lost three children. She also left a record of her thoughts and feelings. Two strands of self-questioning intertwine in that record— self-doubt when she did not have assuring religious experiences and even more painful self-judgment when she lost each child.[50]

Noting the special emphasis on emotional signs of conversion in revivalist religion of the period, Phoebe Palmer's biographer comments that "the psychologist could no doubt find much to account for in Phoebe's 'block' and her resulting near obsession with emotion—or its absence—in religious experience." She would go to the "mourner's bench" seeking the experience of "exciting influences" that others found; she would make great efforts to work herself into "a state of extreme anguish before God," only to fail, believing that the problem was her inability to "feel the burden of sin upon my conscience, to the degree which I had heard others express." When each of her children died, she interpreted the death as divine discipline directed at *her*. After losing her first two, she spoke of them as "treasure given and then recalled, giving us two angel children in heaven and leaving us childless on earth." She decided that she "needed" this misery, "or it would not have been given." Surely it had happened, she believed, because she was not sincerely devoted to God. "God takes our treasure to heaven," she said, "that our hearts may be there also." A daughter was born a few years later, then another. Fearing that God might take another child, Phoebe tried to cultivate a chastened attitude. When the second of these daughters perished in a nursery fire, Phoebe was beside herself but worked out that God was trying to teach her "some great lesson that might not otherwise be learned." She pledged to devote to God the time she would have devoted to her child.[51]

For most devout Christians of antebellum America, a death was an act of God. Phoebe Palmer interpreted the deaths of her children as divine discipline, chastenings, as God drawing her heart away from attachment to the things of the world—even if those things were her own children. God was treating her lack of faith and true devotion, she concluded, by doling out parental discipline. Therefore, she felt that she herself was at fault for the deaths of her children, that they had been sacrificed for her. A psychologist might say that since rage against God was unthinkable for someone like Phoebe, she turned her anger inward ("retroflection") but also sublimated it through her religion.

It would be unwarranted to assume that Eliza Garrett's response to loss was the same as Phoebe Palmer's. Yet general similarities of circumstance and religious belief stand out, justifying the inference that Eliza experienced some of the same conflicting emotions that Phoebe did and interpreted them in a similar way. We have one compelling clue in her response to the death of her husband, which occurred in 1848, when he was not yet fifty and Eliza was only forty-three. In a letter to her friends Leonidas and Melinda Hamline several weeks after Augustus's funeral, she wrote as follows:

I cannot describe to you my feelings, you cannot realize what they are unless you could be placed in a similar situation, which the good Lord forbid should ever be either of your lots. I feel that I am indeed afflicted but I know that it is my benevolent Father that has done it and that as he has said that he afflicteth not willingly the children of men but for their good. I am constrained to believe that it is for my good that he has thus afflicted me. I wish to be benefitted by this dispensation.[52]

That the death of a loved one was a "dispensation" of God, God's own doing for a mysterious purpose, was the common Christian belief, the same belief embraced without question by Phoebe Palmer. If Eliza held this opinion as a Methodist when Augustus died, she certainly did so as a Presbyterian back in the 1830s, since Calvinists taught the doctrine more emphatically than Methodists did. Eliza must have asked why God had taken her children. Anger toward God would have been a natural, inevitable reaction. Conversion narratives show antebellum America women confessing anger at God for controlling their existence and for demanding a personal holiness and pure faith they could not achieve. A nineteenth-century Christian woman of devout character was also likely to interpret bitterness toward God as a fault in herself, as Phoebe Palmer did, proof that something essential was lacking in her faith. The two tendencies—anger toward self and anger at God—were not incompatible. Hence, Eliza, who by all accounts was a sincere person who wanted her inner disposition to be right, may well have suffered both, anger at God for taking her children and religious self-doubts that had plagued her since childhood. For whatever exact combination of reasons, she never underwent a definite conversion experience and felt that she lacked the inner signs of regeneration. Therefore, she could not go before the elders of her church in Chicago to seek membership.[53]

Women like Eliza Garrett and Phoebe Palmer received little comfort from their pastors, for it was the pastors who taught them to interpret every tragedy as an act of divine discipline. What care ministers gave was usually didactic and admonitory, for the clergy regarded mourning and melancholy as signs of resistance to God's providential will. Even if a minister made himself approachable by adopting an "affable and affective" manner, this was designed for interrogative purposes, "to lay open every wound to the very bottom" so that the right cure could be administered, the cure being essentially to move the will to acceptance of God's decree.[54]

Some in the vanguard of the women's movement commented on ineffective or nonexistent pastoral care for women in their day. Speaking to the Syracuse Women's Rights Convention in 1852, Abigail Price argued the case for the ordination of women on the grounds that the clergyman, because of his gender and particular experience, was incapable of providing adequate spiritual care to women. "In order rightly to appreciate the wants of others," Price said, "we must know and realize the trials of their situation, the struggles they may encounter, the burthens, the toils, the temptations that beset their different relations." She emphasized that no amount of formal education could prepare a man to know a woman's experience. "No one can demonstrate by college lore the weight of a mother's responsibility." Not even "the kindest father" could know. "Man may prepare sound and logical discourses; he may clearly define the mother's duty; he may talk eloquently about her responsibility"; but the mother, upon hearing him, will think to herself, "*You* cannot *know* of what you are talking."[55]

Most devout women believed that their minister was the only one with answers to their questions when they suffered loss. At the same time, they were often reluctant to approach him—hesitant to encroach on his time, burdened with feelings of awkwardness in speaking to a man about personal matters, sometimes paralyzed by a sense of their own unworthiness. It would not be surprising if Eliza often felt unworthy, unforgiven, beyond the reach of revivals, an object of mysterious divine discipline. Yet she remained devoted to the church and hoped for an "experience," all the while perpetually mourning her three children, far from her parental home. Uncertain about the state of her soul and haunted by her losses, she threw her unconverted self into service to others.

CHAPTER 4

CRASH AND CONVERSION

$\mathcal{T}$he impulse to buy real estate at an auction is ignited when "the common passion is artfully inflamed by a skillful orator." So said Joseph Balestier, looking back on the speculative frenzy of 1835 and 1836 in Chicago. Augustus Garrett was the most artful auctioneer in Chicago during the land craze and his auction room "the most popular resort of the speculating crowd," when Chicago was "only one great town market" and "the plats of towns, for a hundred miles around, were carried there to be disposed of at auction." People recalled his crier, a black man named George White decked out "fantastically" in a red army uniform, carrying a scarlet flag, and mounted on a white horse with bright-red housings. Every day "Colonel George" paraded the streets at a certain hour, "making all his movements with military precision," ringing a bell, and crying "auction!" as he named some of the merchandise or land to be sold that evening. At the appointed hour, the Colonel posted himself as doorman and admitted the eager crowd. This bit of minstrelish advertising said something not only about Garrett's instincts for showmanship but also his readiness to profit from racial humor.[1]

Alvaro Field recalled the Garrett establishment. As young men, Field and his friends amused themselves "through the long winter evenings . . . at an auction-room on the corner of Dearborn and South Water Streets" where "a jolly man, full of wit and curious pranks . . . kept throngs in giddy merriment as he cried off his goods with his euphonious, 'Going, going, gone!'" Augustus held his audience in thrall with homey humor and the occasional gag. According to one memory, in the months when the Methodist minister Peter Borein was holding emotional revivals, Augustus would hold up a handkerchief for sale and exclaim, "You will want this if you go to hear Borein preach." It was a paltry joke but brought a roar of laughter, for many of those present—including Augustus himself—had been reduced to tears at Borein meetings. Another time, perhaps in a

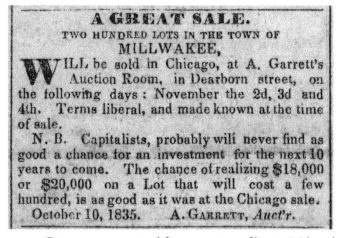

A GREAT SALE.

TWO HUNDRED LOTS IN THE TOWN OF

MILLWAKEE,

WILL be sold in Chicago, at A. Garrett's Auction Room, in Dearborn street, on the following days : November the 2d, 3d and 4th. Terms liberal, and made known at the time of sale.

N. B. Capitalists, probably will never find as good a chance for an investment for the next 10 years to come. The chance of realizing $18,000 or $20,000 on a Lot that will cost a few hundred, is as good as it was at the Chicago sale. October 10, 1835.   A. GARRETT, *Auct'r.*

Augustus Garrett newspaper ad for an auction of lots in Milwaukee, Oct. 10, 1835. Chicago History Museum, ICHi-176179B, cropped.

slow moment between lots, a "fastidious young gentleman" remarked to Augustus that he had seen a magician "break eggs into a man's hat and conjure birds from it, leaving the hat as clean as a whistle." Garrett bet the man five dollars that he could perform the same feat. He sent someone to fetch eggs, broke them into the gentleman's hat, stirred them, called forth birds, and declared, "I thought I could but I see I cannot." He paid the man the five dollars and told him to get a new hat.[2]

A more revealing recollection suggests that Augustus opined that business was almost necessarily dishonest because one inevitably dealt with dishonest people and had to contend with them on similar terms. One day an Indiana Hoosier came into his store, took out a knife, and was about to carve into a piece of furniture to see whether it was really mahogany, as advertised. Garrett told him, "Put up your knife and mind your own business." Then: "I have thought of joining the Church and being a good and honest man, but I will be damned if I can do business with you Hoosiers and do that too."[3]

New towns were being laid out all over Illinois where only a handful of white settlers lived. Maps showed rectangular lots and neat grids of streets with imagined churches and civic buildings. The walls of the Garrett auction room were plastered with them, and speculators were gobbling up the parcels, then regurgitating them by resale into the hands of other speculators. The trade in land also brought multitudes of new settlers.

Heady with the prospect of a sharp upturn in economic growth, the state legislature provided eight million dollars for improvements, financed by bonds—half of the money to go for railroad links and road improvements, the other half to complete the canal from Chicago to Peru. Everyone was confident that land values would swell. Therefore, Augustus plowed his earnings into real estate, some of which he sold as soon as the price rose, using the proceeds to purchase more acres, as well as lots and buildings in Chicago and tracts in far-flung places elsewhere.[4]

Augustus made some of his profits from a partnership with a man named Nathaniel Brown, a newcomer eloquent in schemes for land development in the Michigan Territory. Brown came to Chicago in April of 1835 with a load of Michigan pine on a schooner and was soon keeping company with Garrett, whom he remembered as "an exceedingly active and energetic young man" who was "selling dry goods, town lots and various other things which could be handled with very little capital at auction." In fact, they were both young men with little capital. Garrett proposed they form a partnership. Brown, cautious and also reluctant to cut Garrett in on all of his Michigan enterprises, agreed to a shared business venture concerning a large piece of Michigan land that Brown already owned.[5]

The land, situated in Ionia County west of Grand Rapids, was at the head of steamboat navigation on Grand River. The idea was to lay out a town, sell the lots, and erect a sawmill on the river to profit from the demand for wood when Ionia began to grow. Garrett and Brown engaged a Chicago surveyor to create a provisional plat based on the government map, then hired Chicago attorneys Giles Spring and Grant Goodrich to make out deeds. Brown went back to Michigan to see about building the sawmill, and Garrett began auctioning off lots.[6]

Augustus used the proceeds of the Ionia sales to purchase real estate in Chicago, and Brown, upon returning, discovered he was part owner of "several large blocks in the village" and "about three thousand acres of land in the Chicago land district, all of which was in the immediate vicinity of Chicago." Thanks to this success, Brown agreed to a general partnership. The firm purchased the Bates building, which Garrett was already renting, and a four-story brick edifice at the corner of LaSalle and South Water. By the winter of 1836, their profits were streaming into the Bank of Illinois at the rate of seven hundred dollars a day.[7]

The two men then brought in Nathaniel's brother Daniel, and "Garrett, Brown & Brother" quickly became one of the best-known auction, real estate, and merchandise businesses in the West, operating three large concerns out of three locations—the Bates building on Dearborn, the four-story brick building at LaSalle and South Water, and another store on Lake Street. As part of this expansion, Garrett and Brown formed a second company, bringing in a man named Oliver Thompson to enhance the import side of the business. Garrett, Thompson, Brown & Company sold various goods from New York suppliers—fabrics, fur and silk hats, men's and women's shoes and boots, tea and coffee, brandy and gin. Everything was transported up the Hudson River, across New York State on the Erie Canal, and through the waterways of the Great Lakes.[8]

Garrett and the Browns also speculated in land in various parts of northern Illinois, Wisconsin, Michigan, and Indiana, at one point owning as much as nine thousand acres, most of it in the form of so-called paper towns, the sort of thing their fellow Chicagoan Joseph Balestier described as "suppositious" settlements set out on paper "in the most approved rectangular

COPARTNERSHIP.

NOTICE is hereby given, that Augustus Garrett, Oliver H. Thompson, Daniel B. Brown and Nathaniel J. Brown, have this day formed a copartnership for the purpose of buying and selling Real Estate, and conducting a General Land Agency Business. Also, a general Auction, Commission, and Mercantile business, under the name and style of Garrett, Thompson, Brown & Co. They may at all times be found at their Store in Lake street or at their Auction and Commission Room in Dearborn street, where they will receive goods on consignment and make liberal advances on property left on sale. Insurance effected if required.   AUGUSTUS GARRETT,
                                OLIVER H. THOMPSON,
                                DANIEL B. BROWN,
                                NATHANIEL J. BROWN.
Chicago, November 27th 1835.

N. B.—All those having unsettled accounts with Augustus Garrett, or the late firm of Garrett & Brown, are respectfully requested to call and have the same adjusted.   A. GARRETT,
Nov. 27.   N. J. BROWN.

Garrett, Thompson, Brown, and Brown newspaper
announcement of their copartnership, Nov. 27, 1835.
Chicago History Museum, ICHi-176177B, cropped

E. PLATT & co.

Chicago Jan. 1, 1836.   31 4t

For Sale.

BY Garrett. Thompson, Brown, & Co. at their Auction and Commission Room on Dearbon street,

    30 Chests Y H. Tea,
    25 "   O. H. do.
    20 Catty Boxes Y. H. Tea,
    50 Bags Coffee.
Chicago, Dec. 22 1835.   1*31.

For Sale.

AT the Auction and Commission Room of the subscribers in Dearbon street,

    7 Pieces Blue Broad Cloth,
    5 "   Black   do.
    6 "   Olive. do,
    4 "   Steel Mixed. do.
    10 "   Imported Flannels,
  1000 Yards unbleached Sheeting,
  2000 "   "   Shirting
   75 Pieces Calicoes, various qualities,
  200 "   Cotton Thread,
  150 "   Ribbons, various kinds,
   7 Cases Silk Hats,
   2 " Fur do.
   3 Pieces Fancy Ribbed Kerseymere,
  12 " Sattinet,
  10 " Mole Skin.
  14 " Velvet Cord.

    GARRETT THOMPSON, BROWN, & Co.
Chicago, Dec. 22, 1835·   31.

For Sale,

AT the Auction and Commission Room of the subscribers.

  10 Cases fine Calf Boots,
  15 "   "   "   Men's Shoes,
   7 " Ladies Morrocco Shoes,
  15 " Mens Cow hide Boots,
  20 "   "   "   Shoes,
  100 Pair Ladies Prunell Shoes.

    GARRETT. THOMPSON, BROWN, & Co.
Chicago, Dec. 22, 1835.

For Sale.

AT the Auction and Commission Room of the subscribers, a general assortment of

Section of a Garrett, Thompson, Brown & Company Auction and Commission House newspaper ad, Dec. 22, 1835.
Chicago History Museum, ICHi-176178B, cropped.

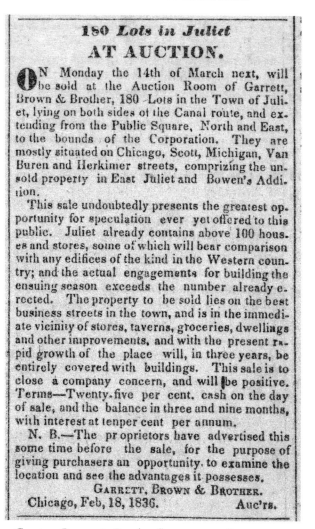

180 *Lots in Juliet*
AT AUCTION.

ON Monday the 14th of March next, will be sold at the Auction Room of Garrett, Brown & Brother, 180 Lots in the Town of Juliet, lying on both sides of the Canal route, and extending from the Public Square, North and East, to the bounds of the Corporation. They are mostly situated on Chicago, Scott, Michigan, Van Buren and Herkimer streets, comprizing the unsold property in East Juliet and Bowen's Addition.

This sale undoubtedly presents the greatest opportunity for speculation ever yet offered to this public. Juliet already contains above 100 houses and stores, some of which will bear comparison with any edifices of the kind in the Western country; and the actual engagements for building the ensuing season exceeds the number already erected. The property to be sold lies on the best business streets in the town, and is in the immediate vicinity of stores, taverns, groceries, dwellings and other improvements, and with the present rapid growth of the place will, in three years, be entirely covered with buildings. This sale is to close a company concern, and will be positive. Terms—Twenty-five per cent. cash on the day of sale, and the balance in three and nine months, with interest at tenper cent per annum.

N. B.—The proprietors have advertised this some time before the sale, for the purpose of giving purchasers an opportunity to examine the location and see the advantages it possesses.

GARRETT, BROWN & BROTHER.
Chicago, Feb, 18, 1836.   Auc'rs.

Garrett, Brown & Brother "AT AUCTION" newspaper ad for lots in Juliet (now Joliet), Illinois, Feb. 18, 1836. Chicago History Museum, ICHi-176180B, cropped.

fashion, emblazoned in glaring colors, and exhibiting the public spirit of the proprietor in the multitude of their public squares, church lots, and school lot reservations"—all imaginary, sometimes with "a fictitious streamlet seen to wind its romantic course through the heart of an ideal city."[9]

Some of the places where Garrett and Brown sold lots attracted a few citizens and limped along as small hamlets. Others never materialized and were eventually bought up as farmland. Augustus auctioned parcels

Auction broadside for Garrett, Brown & Brother, dated
May 21 (probably 1836). Chicago History Museum, ICHi-014152.

in Kankakee City, Vienna, Juliet, Enterprise, Peru, Dresden, and Bailey-
town, all of which lay in Illinois, and he continued to sell the company's
lots in Ionia, Michigan. All these towns had been recently platted, but
only about half of them went on to become populated towns. Kankakee
City, Enterprise, Dresden, and Ionia fizzled out, although some of these
names ended up as the monikers of other towns that did develop. The fate
of Ionia is an example and illustrates the vagaries of the land frenzy. To
establish Ionia, Garrett and Brown formed a partnership with Michigan
locals J. C. Hugunin and J. P. Place, who were to run a general store, a
lumber business, and a construction company to build houses in Ionia.
The plan went nowhere. According to what Brown told his biographer, the
federal land agents in Ionia County decided to establish a town of their
own by that name, and this second Ionia usurped Garrett and Brown's
town. Whether this is exactly what happened, the Ionia of Garrett and
Brown perished and was much later replatted as "Prairie Creek," another
settlement that failed to take root. Meanwhile a different town of Ionia
grew up nearby.[10]

It is an index of Garrett's and Brown's financial clout that when they
got into a dispute with the Chicago branch of the Bank of Illinois, they
were able to bring that institution to near insolvency. The tale of this
dispute also illustrates the complicated monetary realities of the era.

In addition to barter, Chicagoans exchanged goods and services using various forms of currency. These included gold and silver coins (specie) and banknotes (backed by specie), of which there was great variety, since every governmentally authorized bank had its own notes, as did legally chartered commercial banks. Insurance companies also printed currency. There were also notes printed by large concerns (which in appearance resembled banknotes), scrip given out by merchants, and "shinplaster" notes in small denominations printed by people offering professional services. Then there were various personal or business notes representing loans, which also functioned as a form of currency. Banks discounted the value of these loan-notes when accepting or cashing them.[11]

Garrett and Brown had an account at the Chicago branch of the Bank of Illinois, which leased space from them in their four-story building at LaSalle and Water. They also kept their commission store and auction house in this building. The dispute had nothing to do with the bank's lease, however, but concerned monetary transactions between the firm and the bank. A series of escalating frictions began when the bank's cashier instructed the teller to reject the firm's notes. Evidently, these were notes for short-term bank loans whose surety was in doubt, which reduced their fungible value. Garrett, Brown & Brother had received these notes from customers and had presented them at the bank for discount at 36 percent of face value. The bank agreed to discount the notes but required that Garrett and his partners first negotiate shorter terms with the borrowers, which proved unfeasible. According to Garrett and the Browns, the bank also claimed that the firm lacked sufficient cash on deposit, using this phony assertion as a pretext to retaliate for an earlier withdrawal of cash that depleted its supply of specie. Garrett and the Browns also regarded it as a punishment that when they cashed a small check and asked to be paid in New York Safety Fund or Michigan State notes, the cashier refused to pay them in anything except twenty-five-cent pieces.[12]

The bank's behavior so irritated Garrett and Brown that they demanded the full return of their sizable deposits—some twenty thousand dollars—which the bank refused to refund in specie but instead paid in Bank of Illinois notes redeemable for specie only at their other branches. Evidently, the bank interpreted the law requiring it to refund deposits with specie, if specie was demanded, to mean that any of its branches could pay that specie. Hence, if the Chicago branch had insufficient specie or did not want to pay with its own specie, it could pay with notes issued by another branch. But other branches could do the same, demurring from giving out specie on the grounds that only the mother bank at Springfield was required to pay in hard cash. Moreover, the mother bank could impose a two-month waiting period. Thus, as Garrett and Brown explained to readers of the *Chicago American*, "if a check for $1000 is presented . . . the owner is paid as follows: $200 redeemable at Springfield, $200 redeemable at Galena, $200 redeemable at Alton . . . and if it should be necessary to turn them into real capital, *specie*, he goes to Springfield and is required to wait the sixty days." At this rate it took months and a good deal of traveling to cash Bank of Illinois checks for specie.[13]

The bank did not back down but threatened not to do business with anyone who took a loan from Garrett, Brown & Brother, and it spread disparaging rumors about the firm. When the firm's withdrawal of twenty thousand dollars failed to alter the bank's policy, Garrett and Brown went around town buying up the bank's notes and presenting them for redemption. According to Brown—in a statement that contradicted claims he and Garrett published in the newspapers about the bank avoiding the payment of notes in specie by simply giving out paper from other branches—the bank began running out of specie and had to send to the parent bank in Springfield for coin. At this point the bank officers "sued for peace and amicable relations were again established."[14]

Garrett and Brown made their side of the conflict public by publishing two notices, dated March 1 and March 10, 1836, in the *Chicago American*. The bank did not respond in kind and must have suffered in public opinion. In the Jacksonian era, rank-and-file Democrats did not trust banks, and a few years later the *Chicago Democrat* would charge that the Bank of Illinois had been making a fortune in pork speculation while denying loans to local businesses. The claim was a distortion, but in an era of little regulation, the bank no doubt did show favoritism. The bank's conflict with Garrett, Brown & Brother, however, probably had more to do with the fact that the latter operated as a rival bank, making loans and functioning as "agent of the bank of Washtenaw whose notes they redeemed in specie or land-office money."[15]

Despite national worry about inflation of land values and overextension of credit, the economic boom in Chicago was still in full swing in the summer of 1836. On the Fourth of July, the first shovelful of earth was dug at Canalport to inaugurate construction of the Illinois and Michigan canal, with old settlers Gurdon S. Hubbard and John Beaubien officiating. Crowds gathered from the city and surrounding districts. Troops from Fort Dearborn put on a parade. A freshwater spring was doctored with whisky, sugar, and lemons as a punch bowl. And after the ceremonies, the revelers headed into Chicago, where a leading butcher mounted a large steer and toured the streets, escorted by a brass band and military men. Each time they passed Garrett's store, Augustus dispensed liquor from his warehouse. He also donated a tall eight-day clock, which soldiers set up in the street and used for target practice.[16]

A year later the general mood of the city was quite different. A precipitous economic downturn, later dubbed the Panic of 1837, led to a financial depression. Chicago was not the center of this crisis, but many Chicagoans held notes of highly leveraged speculators, and a lack of cash and credit also affected business generally. One cause of the national slump was the Jackson administration's directive in July of 1836 that the Treasury Department issue what came to be known as the Specie Circular. This executive order required that all purchases of government land be made in gold and silver. The purpose was to curb the speculation believed to be causing exorbitant inflation in the price of land. Beginning in August, federal land offices no longer accepted paper currency from buyers. This greatly increased demand for gold and silver coin in the western and southern regions where the government was putting millions of acres on the market. That in turn caused a significant drain on the specie reserves of eastern banks and a corresponding movement of gold and silver into the banks and land offices in the states and territories where public lands were being sold. Deleterious effects on eastern businesses were almost immediate.[17]

Another federal monetary decision also contributed to the economic collapse. In January of 1837, a previous congressional act went into effect that redistributed to the states the huge sums of money pouring into federal coffers from government land sales. The law also increased the number of federal deposit banks and required a more equal distribution of federal monies among state and federal banks holding federal funds. These provisions and the continuation of Jacksonian monetary principles by the Van Buren administration (which assumed power in March) set several trends in motion. Reserves of federal money began to move in many directions as they were redistributed through the banking network, and the federal deposits of some banks, particularly the New York institutions, which were already experiencing a drain on their cash reserves as a result of the Specie Circular, were further compromised. Specie in the vaults of New York banks dropped by 33 percent in only four or five months.[18]

Writing just two years after these events, an anonymous correspondent for the *New-Yorker* commented that "the monetary affairs of the whole country were convulsed—millions upon millions of coins were *in transitu* in every direction, and consequently withdrawn from useful employment." Hence money for investment or other business purposes was not available in sufficient supply in many places where it was needed and was piling up in places where people had no immediate use for it. Meanwhile, a similar decline was under way in England, where bullion reserves held by the Bank of England were dropping at the steady rate of 6 percent a month, flowing into America, where specie was the required currency of investment. Since the bullion was purchased with paper money, the Bank of England raised its discount rate, which slowed investment at home and abroad. Concerned about instability in America, the bank also directed its Liverpool branch to cease providing discounted loans to borrowers engaged in American commerce.[19]

As the American economy slowed and borrowers defaulted, it was not only well-funded eastern investors who suffered losses. Many ordinary citizens with little or no experience in real estate had been dealing in land. In a backward look in 1840, Balestier remarked sententiously to the Chicago Lyceum, "The farmer forsook the plow, and became a speculator upon the soil, instead of a producer from beneath the sod." In other words, farmers had been giving up farming or had bought up more lands than they could cultivate, simply for investment purposes, and no doubt often on contract or through bank or government loans. "Everywhere we went on our way home," recalled one traveler to the region, "American farmers offered their land for sale at speculative prices." People were eager to make a living without working, Balestier moralized. "The mechanic laid aside his tools and decided to grow rich without labor. The lawyer sold his books and invested the proceeds in lands. The physician 'threw physic to the dogs,' and wrote promissory notes instead of prescriptions." Many people financed these ventures on credit and were heavily leveraged. When the downturn came, the paper representing these loans—notes that had often been resold one or more times—depreciated dramatically. Borrowers could not pay their notes and were unable to sell their lands at the former inflated prices. Almost every form of business slowed as demand for goods and services diminished. According to Brown's biographer, it was this sharp economic downturn that caused Garrett and the Browns to part company and chart separate paths to financial recovery. Yet announcements in the newspaper suggest that they may have dissolved their partnerships before the crash, indeed as early as March of 1836.[20]

The Garretts' personal expenses were minimal. They lived in a hotel, had no children to support, and were not ostentatious or lavish. Augustus had learned hard lessons in Cincinnati and did not want to overextend himself through debt. To the degree that he offered credit to purchasers of lots he sold at auction, his practice was to give short-term notes. For example, in selling lots in Juliet, Illinois, in March of 1836, he required a 25 percent down payment in cash and the balance to be repaid in installments over a three- or nine-month term at 10 percent interest. He must have purchased most of his real estate with cash, since he was able to retain the bulk of his estate during the economic slump while others lost their mortgaged properties.[21]

He did suffer significant losses in the market value of his real estate, although not a drop to anything like pennies on the dollar. According to his own estimate, made during a later economic downturn in 1845, "the Western country" was at that time "not worth more than 50 cents on the dollar," which, he said, was "quite as bad as it was in 1837." He was not inclined to sell property at a loss, and his policy was to convert almost all his business profits into real estate. Consequently, he was relatively cash-strapped most of the time, at least for a man of his means. As he explained it, even though he had "accumulated a large amount of property," he could not "dispose of it in a new country for cash at any time & all times without a great sacrifice." He covered daily expenses with income from his rental properties.[22]

* * *

One evening in March of 1839, Augustus went, without Eliza, to hear Peter Borein, the spellbinding minister who was holding revival meetings at Clark Street Methodist Church.

The first Methodist mission to the city had collapsed when both congregants and minister fled during the Black Hawk War. A second congregation was established in late 1834 and was still in existence three years later when, at the 1837 Annual Conference of the Methodist Episcopal Church, the thirty-five-year-old Borein was appointed to "the Chicago station." He found the congregation meeting in "a small framed building, erected near Col. Hamilton's" on Clark Street just north of the river. The church's membership rolls had shrunk as a result of the financial crisis of 1837, when many citizens had fled the city. Most of Chicago's remaining population lived on the south side in any case, so Borein persuaded the congregation to relocate. In the summer of 1838 the building was moved on scows across the river to a lot at Clark and Washington. There a group of churchmen tore off the back wall and tacked on an addition, doubling the length of the sanctuary. Soon the congregation began to grow.[23]

Peter Ruble Borein—his last name was pronounced "Borin"—was born in eastern Tennessee in 1809. At the age of nineteen he was converted at a camp meeting and decided to become a gospel preacher. Not long after, he moved to Illinois, where a Congregationalist minister took an interest in him and advised him to attend Jacksonville College. Two years later he entered the Methodist ministry as a circuit rider, dropping his college studies at the urging of friends who believed him so naturally gifted that he needed no further schooling. He was an enormously popular preacher and ran into difficulty only when he made his antislavery views known to unsympathetic audiences in southern Illinois.[24]

The earliest Methodist meetinghouse in Chicago, circa 1832, on the west side of the north branch of the Chicago River, across from Elijah Wentworth's two-story tavern. Detail from Justin Herriott's 1902 painting. Chicago History Museum, ICHi-005946, detail of figure 3.1.

Grant Goodrich described Borein as "the handsomest man I ever saw" and said his voice was "like running waters." Alvaro Field called him "a born dramatist." He spoke vividly and with heart-searing detail. Sometimes he would collapse to his knees in tears in the middle of a sermon, overcome by emotion. According to one anecdote, "three young bloods" at a camp meeting, probably there only to socialize, paused to listen to Borein. After a few moments, they were all wiping their eyes, each one accusing the other: "What the hell are you crying about?" Borein was famous for causing tears. Goodrich, who sometimes choked up just telling a story about Borein, thought it was not only his words but also something rapturous in his expression that set him apart from the average minister. Preaching put Borein in a kind of ecstasy, and he would lead his spellbound hearers from scene to vivid scene, through melancholic depths and euphoric heights. Then he would close and give an altar call, often with a gospel hymn, singing out the first line, and a "Negro" man named Pete, whose voice was "tuned by divine love," would answer. The two of them, the white preacher and the black layman would sing, in call and response, and the beauty of Pete's voice would melt the hearts of the congregation. The revival meetings at Clark Street Church in the winter of 1838–1839 produced hundreds of converts.[25]

After hearing Borein two evenings in a row, Augustus took Eliza to the revival, and both decided to join the church. According to her former Presbyterian minister, Jeremiah Porter, Eliza went over to the Methodists because of Augustus—"that theirs might not be a divided house." This implies that she became a Methodist only because of her husband's decision. But the church receiving book and the testimony of early Chicago Methodists tell a different story. The receiving book shows both their names among those taken in during the March revivals, and members of Clark Street Church who knew Eliza said she was "converted" at those meetings. The testimony of Goodrich is especially significant. He was a member of Clark Street Church in 1839 and knew the Garretts personally, serving as Augustus's lawyer for many years and as Eliza's lawyer and sometime confidant after Augustus's death. Moreover, Goodrich's wife was a member of First Presbyterian Church and must have known Eliza quite well. According to Goodrich, "in the winter of 1839 Augustus Garrett ... and his wife Eliza were converted to God under the faithful ministry of brother Borein and united with the Methodist church."[26]

It is easier to understand Eliza's entrance into the world of the Methodists (after thirty-three years among the Presbyterians) if we consider her religious predicament. It was not any deficit of Christian belief or commitment that prevented her from joining a church but a lack of inner experience answering to the way her Calvinist religious tradition—as influenced by revivalist religion in the early nineteenth century—defined the marks of inner spiritual regeneration. Uncertain whether she was truly converted and doubtful that she could pass the inquiry into her experience by the minister and church session, she was never able to bring herself to take the necessary steps toward membership in a Presbyterian church.[27]

Eliza would have been welcome to join Clark Street Church with or without an end to her self-doubts. Methodists did not demand evidence of conversion as a condition of church membership. Anyone who truly sought salvation was welcome to join the church. The process began with admission to a "class." After attending at least two or three class meetings, a person was granted class membership "on trial." This period of probation lasted six months and required faithful attendance and conformity to Methodist rules of conduct. Did Eliza undergo a conversion *experience* at the Borein revival? Not everyone who entered a class and joined the church was converted in the nineteenth-century sense. The Methodists distinguished "seekers" from "believers." By *believers* they meant regenerated persons, that is, persons whose hearts had been converted and who had experienced the confirming inner witness of the Holy Spirit. But the church did not limit membership to the converted. Sincerity in seeking, not conversion, was the sole requirement. Hence, the church did not condition membership on a convincing recital of personal experiences in front of clergy or church officers or even before one's class, which was a setting where people did disclose their experiences, including their inner struggles. When Eliza went into her assigned class in March of 1839, she must have told the class whether she regarded herself as a seeker or a believer. But her path to membership in the church depended only on evidence of her Christian sincerity in the way she lived.[28]

The whole subject was a point of some confusion and controversy among evangelicals of the era. Presbyterians and Baptists looked askance at Methodist membership policies. When a Methodist revival in Cincinnati, held just a year after the Borein meetings in Chicago, swelled the ranks of the city's Methodist churches, representatives of other Protestant faiths cast doubt on the genuineness of the conversions, and local reports to that effect were republished in periodicals around the country.

Charles Elliott, editor of the *Western Christian Advocate* (a Methodist weekly), responded. "In some of the notices" of the revival, he observed, "it was carefully noted, when referring to the great accessions to the Methodist Episcopal Church, that many of those admitted into her pale were received without the requisite of having experienced religion." This gave the impression that "irreligious persons who are unfit members of any Church, are cordially received among the Methodists." That was not true, Elliott explained. Reception into a Methodist church began with probation, and any who lived contrary to the church's moral code were not received into full communion. Moreover, the General Rules of the church required of probationers "a decision to flee from the wrath to come, and to be saved from their sins." Methodists judged the sincerity of the decision by a person's behavior. Hence the church did not require an inner experience. Indeed, it distinguished but also accepted into its ranks those still seeking salvation, along with those who were regenerated. Church membership records marked the seeker with an S and the regenerated with a B for believer. Both categories of persons could be full members of the church.[29]

Although the receiving book of First Methodist Episcopal Church of Chicago shows Eliza's admission as a member of the church, the membership records that might have been coded with this system of S or B do not survive. In later years Methodists who knew Eliza spoke of her "conversion" at the Borein revival. Yet she was admitted to membership not after the typical trial period of six months but instead after more than a year. According to Methodist discipline, the probationary period could be extended but only by a month or two, and that extension was granted only when a decision about the candidate's admittance could not be made, due to uncertainty about the person's sincerity. The thirteen months that elapsed between Eliza's entrance into a class and her "full connection" cannot be explained by this rule and must have been caused by something else, most likely her own decision to delay full membership because she felt a lingering loyalty to the Presbyterian church and strong personal ties to the people there, especially after Augustus quit attending Clark Street Church.[30]

Little more than a decade after becoming a Methodist, Eliza used the Garrett estate to endow the first Methodist theological school in the West. Hence, Methodists who left recollections of her had a hagiographic interest in portraying her in a particular light. Speaking to the school's graduates a few years after her death, John Dempster memorialized Eliza's "beautiful character," "great heart," her name "never born to die" and called her a "Godlike woman." Eliza certainly did have a great heart and admirable traits of character, but all the recorded memories of her came from people interested in telling a grand story in which she played a saintly role. At least one of them decided that her saintly character did not evolve until she had been converted by the Methodists. According to Alvaro Field—a Methodist minister and onetime member of the Methodist class to which Eliza belonged—the Garretts were "gay, worldly people" before the Borein revival. As Field tells Eliza's story, she "was raised in one of the finest Presbyterian families" and as a teenager or young woman became a "probationer" in the Methodist church of north Newburgh. Field's Methodist readers would have inferred from this that Eliza sought church membership but was not received after her trial period because she failed to conform her lifestyle to the moral code of the Methodists or in some other way did not appear to be sincere. Field acknowledges that Eliza was active in the women's work of First Presbyterian Church of Chicago, but according to him, it was only after her conversion under Borein that "she became a noble, consistent Christian" and "remained a faithful member of the church." When Augustus "returned to the world," Field said, Eliza did not follow him back into their old lifestyle. Although she resided in "the best house in the city" and traveled "in the highest circles," she remained a "quiet, reliable, noble Christian woman" and ended her life "in holy triumph."[31]

Field either believed or found it convenient to imagine that Eliza the Presbyterian had been a "gay, worldly" person, absorbed in the pleasures of a life with her rich husband until she changed her ways as a result of her conversion at a Methodist revival. Besides "living in the best house," which was not an accurate description of Eliza's lodging in Chicago, what *worldly* meant in Field's eyes was defined by the Methodist book of discipline, which specified the following as unacceptable behaviors for a Christian: taking God's name in vain, working on Sunday, drinking spirituous liquors, buying or selling human beings, fighting, engaging in unlawful business practices, speaking ill of others, wearing gold jewelry and expensive clothes, and engaging in amusements that do not encourage piety. We can rule out most of these in Eliza's case, except adornment. Whether refinement in dress was still so frowned upon by the 1830s is uncertain. In a previous generation plainness of attire had been the norm in American

Methodism. In Northampton County, Virginia, in 1801 a young couple who converted during a revival "came out in plain Methodist dress to become members of the Methodist Episcopal Church." In these earlier days, itinerant ministers made it a habit to excoriate jewelry-bedecked women for their "pridefulness," and Methodists, like Quakers, continued to be associated in the public mind with simplicity of dress and lack of ornament. A generation later some non-Methodists still expected this of Methodists. For example, sometime in the 1850s, when a Presbyterian banker and his wife entertained the visiting Methodist bishop Matthew Simpson and his wife, Ellen, whom they had never met, they expected their visitors to display austerity of dress and were surprised when Ellen showed up wearing "a black silk dress embellished with ruffles, lace, and jewelry, her hair done in the currently fashionable style." But when the female author of a book on the virtues of the Presbyterian faith, published in 1852, advocated for a moderate position on dress, she noted that even the Methodists were no longer enforcing such rules.[32]

Surviving images of Eliza include a photograph from the early 1850s and two posthumous renderings based on the photograph. In these pictures she is well dressed but not lavishly clad, and, unlike the glamorous dresses of the Regency era, her outfits completely cover her arms and shoulders up to her neck. As for the possibility that she spent her days as a Presbyterian enjoying worldly amusements, that does not comport with the recollection of her by Jeremiah Porter, the Presbyterian minister who first welcomed her to his congregation in Chicago in 1835. Nor does it fit what Methodist minister Selah Cogshall remembered. He described Augustus as "a drinker, a profane swearer, and a rogue" but said that Eliza, before her conversion, was "very much *unlike* her husband in moral character and life." It is likely, therefore, that Field's remark about Eliza's worldly past was simply an inference drawn from his consideration of the Garrett wealth and his Methodist notion of conversion. He had been just a boy in the years when Eliza was a Presbyterian, and it served his interest to give Methodism full credit for her saintliness after she joined Clark Street Church, where he first met her.[33]

What about Augustus, who entered a class at Clark Street Church but dropped out before the conclusion of his trial period? It was a melodramatic era. Borein was famous for bringing tears, and Augustus was an emotional man. H. W. Frink recalls how shortly after the Borein meetings, Augustus went with Eliza to a revival at Poplar Creek and spoke to the assembly "with streaming eyes." At the Clark Street revival, too, he wept as he sat on a pine bench listening to the heart-stirring raptures of Borein.[34]

Borein had first accosted Augustus on the street. Augustus told him he wanted to join the church and become "a good and honest man," but he was "afraid" to go to the meetings. Eventually he did go—"he couldn't stand it any longer," one observer said—and attended an evening service. He sat down on a board bench in the center of the little church. The meeting concluded around nine or ten, but people stayed for another hour to talk, pray, and sing hymns. Borein spoke to Augustus. At his auction house the next day, Augustus held up a handkerchief and joked that anyone who went to the meetings at the Methodist church would need to buy one because "they will make you cry like hell." That night Augustus returned, and this time he rose to speak. He told his life story, confessed his failings, charted his regrets. He was eloquent in his homey way and sincere. Tears streamed down his face, and the mass of souls crammed into the small church seemed moved by the cadence of his voice—"like the oaks in the forest, swayed back and forth by the wind," as Cogshall picturesquely put it.[35]

Augustus told the congregation, "My wife is with me in this movement. She will be here tomorrow night." The next evening she was at his side. Cogshall recalled her appearance. She was "a handsome woman," he said, "lady-like and graceful in her movements, and divinely tall." She did not look like her later portraits, he said, which were "simply caricatures."[36]

If Eliza seemed composed, it was a mask. Borein's sermon, the sight of her husband's tears, and the intense turmoil in her own heart worked a profound effect. Now—when a church was ready to receive her without inquiry into her religious experience, without putting her in front of clergy or elders, without even demanding that she exclude herself if she detected no inner tokens of spiritual change—the long-sought experience came, the overwhelming wave of divine love, dissolving every pain, including that greatest pain. She thought about them almost every day. Imogine, Charles, and John Augustus. It was her duty to call them to mind, since otherwise they would be utterly forgotten. She lived in a melancholy age that encouraged thoughts of death, nostalgic yearnings, heart-softening sorrows. Therefore, although Borein said nothing about lost children, everything he said was about her lost children because she was once again in church, listening to a minister demand that she think about what really mattered; and what really mattered to her was them, taken in the bud of their lives by a severe God for reasons undecipherable. When the overwhelming surge of divine love came over her, it resolved that question without answering it, and afterward she felt a deep, still peace. She felt converted.[37]

CHAPTER 5

THE POLITICIAN

*A*n imagined dialogue "between a Whig and a Democrat," published in the *Morning Democrat* during the city elections of 1840, declared that Augustus Garrett, then running for alderman as a Democrat, had once been a Whig. In fact, he had been a Whig as recently as the previous election. According to a newspaper account of an 1836 rally of Cook County Whigs held in the Presbyterian church in Chicago, the Whigs—in addition to denouncing the Democratic presidential candidate Martin Van Buren and embracing William Henry Harrison, "a western man" and one of several Whigs who ran against Van Buren that year—appointed a "vigilance" committee to oversee the upcoming election. The nine-member group included Augustus Garrett.[1]

It appears, then, that Garrett arrived in Chicago a Whig and became active in local Whig politics. He voted for Harrison in 1836, when Harrison lost to Van Buren, but had changed his party affiliation by the 1840 election, when Harrison defeated Van Buren to become the ninth president of the United States. What did Garrett object to in Harrison's 1840 agenda that had not bothered him in 1836? A new national bank? Perhaps. Plans for internal improvements, which Harrison championed and Van Buren did not? Garrett was in fact an ardent advocate of public-works funding by the federal government. Protective tariffs? Concerns about tariffs are not mentioned in his surviving business correspondence. Likely his change of party affiliation was more personal and locally pragmatic than philosophical. John Wentworth, editor of the *Chicago Democrat*, was his close friend, and Democrats dominated Chicago politics throughout the 1840s. When Augustus threw his hat in the political ring by running for alderman in 1840, he did not want to be one of the losing Whigs, so he changed his party.[2]

This shift, then, had nothing to do with any political revolution in his thinking. He was motivated by a craving for public status and popularity, and not because his philosophy of municipal governance aligned more with that of the Democrats. In fact, four years later he told Wentworth, "I will be damned if I will vote the Whig ticket again," revealing by the very denial that, even after becoming a Democrat, his attitude toward the Whigs as a national party was not entirely settled.[3]

But he now loved Andrew Jackson, telling Wentworth in another letter that Jackson was "the Greatest Man that ever existed in this government." He did not elaborate. It cannot have been Jackson's fiscal policies that impressed Augustus, since those policies were widely acknowledged to be a chief cause of the Panic of 1837, which had adversely affected Chicago businesses. More likely, Augustus approved of Jackson's commitment to western expansion through Indian removal. In Illinois that policy had made Garrett's fortune possible.[4]

If we look for clues to what ultimately solidified Garrett's loyalty to the national Democratic Party, one issue stands out: Texas. The Whigs rejected John Tyler—who had become president when Harrison died after only thirty-two days in office—and ran Henry Clay against James Polk in 1844. Tyler, the ousted Whig, and Polk, the Democrat, were both ardent advocates of "annexation," the incorporation of the Republic of Texas into the domain of the United States. Annexation, once unpopular with both Whigs and Democrats, was now a Democratic cause. Tyler signed a treaty of annexation in April of 1844. Although it failed to win approval by the Senate, annexation was finally achieved in February of 1845 shortly before Polk's inauguration. Mexico asserted its right to Texas; the Polk administration was ready to go to war to defend its new territory; and the Whigs, who had opposed annexation, now also opposed war to defend the results of annexation.

Whig opposition to annexation angered Garrett. Throughout the history of the Texas question, he had been a staunch supporter of both independence and annexation for Texas. While there may appear to be a contradiction between these two positions, they were in fact closely linked in the ideology of Anglo-Saxon superiority, as speeches in the halls of Congress made plain. Senator and future president James Buchanan declared that "Anglo-Saxon blood could never be subdued by anything that claimed Mexican origin." Senator Levi Woodbury expressed outrage that "the men of the true Saxon race" had ever been subjected, under Mexican rule, to being "humiliated and enslaved to Moors, Indians, and mongrels." In a climate of highly charged racist animosity toward nonwhite and mestizo culture, political sovereignty for Texas the "republic" meant independence for white settlers in Texas from nonwhite Mexican rule. Annexation meant the same thing, namely, that the white population's freedom from nonwhite rule would be ensured through incorporation into the white-ruled United States of America.[5]

Not surprisingly, the extension of chattel slavery was wrapped up with the Texas question. Southern Democrats dreamed of dividing Texas into additional slave states, thus increasing their power in the Senate. Garrett may not have been stirred in one direction or the other by the slavery question. Although he opposed slavery abstractly, as did most Chicagoans, he was content to leave it alone. What moved him was the specter, purveyed by the newspapers, of white people in Texas suffering a Mexican invasion. Eliza felt the same way. "My wife would be willing to pull up stakes & go there & help the Texians than to see Texas invaded again," Garrett wrote his business partner, adding that he intended to do something himself "to relieve the oppressed & should you hear of my removal to that place you must not be surprised." Whatever the reasons for Garrett's initial entrance into local Democratic politics, the Texas question solidified his loyalty to the national Democratic Party.[6]

Garrett won his aldermanic bid in 1840, and his most public activities as a member of the Chicago Common Council that year concerned the so-called bridge wars. This conflict already had a long history. In the early years of the town's growth, the only bridge capable of sustaining wagons pulled by draft animals was the Dearborn Street drawbridge, a privately owned service that required six men for its operation and tended to malfunction. By 1837 there was general agreement that something had to be done about the bridge, and the new city charter gave the Chicago Common Council authority in the matter.[7]

What the council ought to do was a subject of intense dispute. A number of north-side businessmen had investments in new warehouses on their side of the river. South-siders interested in the grain market saw this as a threat. Their friends, who included Garrett, sympathized. As a result, strong opposition to a new bridge developed on the south side. As one Chicagoan later recalled, south-siders "menaced" the north side "with having no bridge at all," as would "'sarve 'em right' for certain freshly remembered warehouse schemes on the north bank of the river." These bridge-opposing south-siders had an ally in captains of river vessels, who did not like to wait for the drawbridge to be raised and favored replacing the Dearborn Street bridge with a ferry. Walter Newberry and William

Ogden, who represented the eastern financier Arthur Bronson, were two of the affected north-siders. They favored a new bridge instead of a ferry because farmers, arriving in Chicago from the south in "Hoosier wagons"—as many as five hundred a night during the harvest seasons—required a sturdy bridge if they were to convey their corn, wheat, and other grains safely across the river. As Ogden explained to Bronson, "Hoosier ox teams with wheat & c. wont come over the river on a ferry if they can avoid it." And those Hoosiers could avoid risky ferry-crossings by trading with south-side businessmen. Hence, the latter saw an opportunity to block north-side efforts to corner the grain market with their big warehouses. The south-siders hoped to preserve the grain business for themselves, but that could be achieved only if the Dearborn Street bridge were destroyed and replaced by a ferry instead of a sturdier bridge.[8]

By the time Garrett joined the city council, a number of options had already been contemplated. Many people thought that the farther the bridge was placed to the east, toward the harbor, the greater the inconvenience it would pose to river traffic. So they argued for a bridge at Wells Street or Dearborn, the site of the old bridge, but not farther east at Clark. On February 25, 1839, the council approved a span at Wells, authorizing "inhabitants of the city . . . to construct a Free Bridge by their own voluntary contributions across the Main Chicago River at Wells Street." That decision made, the council began entertaining proposals for dismantling and removing the Dearborn Street bridge, eventually issuing an order that summer to demolish the bridge and replace it with a ferry. A group of south-siders, exuberant at this news but worried that the aldermen might change their mind, "gathered upon the river before daylight, the next morning, and going to work with a will, in a very short time, chopped the bridge to pieces."[9]

The bridge smashers were confident that no bridge would be built at Wells, and they were right. Sufficient voluntary subscriptions for the Wells bridge never materialized. Naturally, the north-side warehouse men were not ready to give up, and in November Ogden lobbied for a bridge at Clark Street, assuring Mayor Raymond that he could raise subscriptions for bonds. About the same time, Ogden and Newberry also donated a tract of land to the Catholic diocese, and some viewed this as an effort "to influence votes on the bridge question." Catholic members of the council were grateful (a cathedral was subsequently built on the donated tract), and they supported the bridge project. The coincidence of these two things

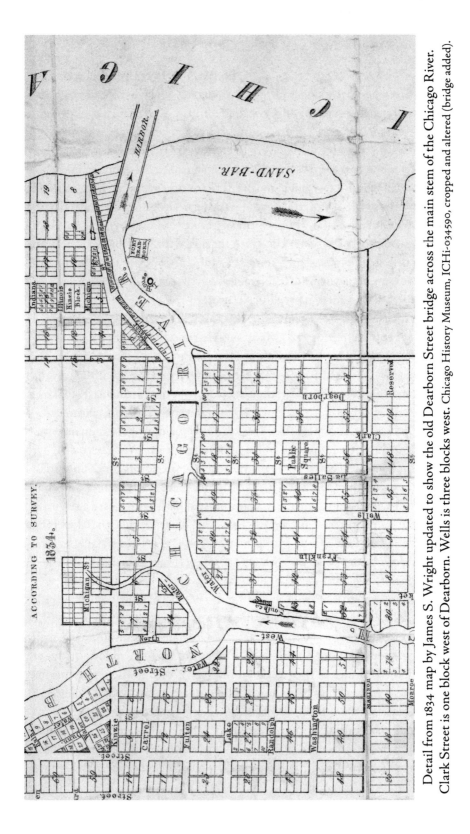

Detail from 1834 map by James S. Wright updated to show the old Dearborn Street bridge across the main stem of the Chicago River. Clark Street is one block west of Dearborn. Wells is three blocks west. Chicago History Museum, ICHi-034590, cropped and altered (bridge added).

is suspicious, but there is too little information about the inner political wrangling over the bridge question to determine whether there was any backroom quid pro quo. The vote was close, in any case. At its meeting on December 2nd, 1839, a divided council deadlocked on the question; Mayor Raymond, who was not a Catholic, cast the tie-breaking vote in favor of the bridge.[10]

The council ordered the creation of three thousand dollars in city stock and authorized the mayor to make contracts with subscribers. In other words, the subscribers not only bought the bonds, but they were also given responsibility for the construction. Ogden ended up purchasing nearly all the bonds—there being almost no willingness among other north-siders to put up money—and the mayor released the funds to him in the form of city scrip. By February 1840 he had drawn up plans for a bridge of his own design. The timber was on the way, and a contract had been signed with the builders.[11]

The bridge at Clark Street, then, was very much Ogden's personal project, which he carried out for the sake of his and Bronson's warehouses. But he still had to face vocal opponents, including Augustus Garrett. Although Garrett had no direct pecuniary interest in the grain trade, he was a popular south-sider with friends who had grain interests. His penchant for efficiency no doubt convinced him that if there were to be a bridge at all, it should be as far west as feasible so as not to impede river traffic. Yet he was motivated by personal animosity as well. He regarded Ogden as dishonest and may have resented Ogden's patrician bearing and status as a north-side elite.

Garrett and Ogden were both elected to the Chicago Common Council in March of 1840 when the bridge wars were still in full swing. Ogden, who had already served as Chicago's first mayor, sought a seat on the council to protect his interest in the bridge. Garrett ran as a champion of the opposition. The issue at this point was not whether to build a bridge, which had been decided, but where to build it, which had also been decided but remained contested. Some still supported a location at Wells Street, others the site of the old bridge at Dearborn. Still others favored Clark Street, the approved site where the council-authorized bridge was about to be constructed now that winter was abating.

On April 6 a new council received citizen petitions against the construction of the Clark Street bridge. Garrett was the bearer of a petition signed by Third Ward citizens that opposed construction of any bridge across the river and "instructed" the two Third Ward aldermen to vote accordingly or resign from the council. Additional words, marked by a caret (∧), were inserted above the statement against the bridge and read, "unless they change it to Wells Street." Thirty-five signatures followed. Since Garrett was a Second Ward alderman, his involvement with this Third Ward petition seems odd but can be explained by the inference that the Third Ward aldermen were supporters of the Clark Street bridge. Otherwise there would have been no need for the petitioners to "instruct" them to vote in accord with the petition or "resign their seats." In fact, one of these aldermen was Ira Miltimore, chairman of the Committee on Streets and Bridges, which had submitted a report in support of a bridge at Clark.[12]

That same evening a petition signed by seventeen men of the Fourth Ward was also submitted in favor of changing the bridge site to Wells Street. And another petition, not connected with any particular ward, was also presented in favor of Wells. This last set of petitioners—a whopping one hundred and fifty of them—stated reasons for their view, arguing that a bridge at Clark would impede more river traffic than a bridge at Wells and that, if the bridge were moved to Wells, it would be better subscribed.[13]

At the council meeting the following week, Garrett presented a motion to move the bridge to Dearborn Street; the motion was tabled. Garrett asked that it be referred to the Committee on Streets and Bridges, and that was denied. At the same meeting, several citizens of the Third Ward—men whose names had appeared on the petition protesting any bridge except one at Wells—lodged a petition alleging that the added words in the Third Ward petition had been inserted after the signatures had been

Third Ward petition with added words ("unless they change it to Wells Street"), Apr. 6, 1840. Photo by C. H. Cosgrove.

obtained, the implication being that the addition was unauthorized. It is unlikely that all thirty-six original signers actually objected to the addition since only six names appeared on the second petition.[14]

Miltimore, a south-sider, had no business interest in the bridge, and his committee's report implied that certain stated south-side objections to the bridge or its location were flimsy masks for other motives. The report pointed out that it was more expensive to operate a ferry than to build and maintain a bridge and, with respect to obstruction of river traffic, the delay and dangers resultant from "600 to 1500 or 2000 daily ferry crossings" were much more serious than any inconvenience posed by a bridge. The report also noted that the bridge would occasion delays for river traffic only seasonally and that these holdups would last just a few minutes and only a handful of times a day.[15]

There was some exaggerated rhetoric in the report. Would bridge adjustments to accommodate river vessels really occur only a few times a day? And how could there be as many as 1,500 or 2,000 ferry crossings a day when there were only 913 minutes of daylight on the longest day of summer? The council overlooked these improbabilities and proceeded in accord with the recommendations of Miltimore's committee. The first piles for the Clark Street bridge were driven on April 18, provoking immediate protest by south-siders, including Garrett. On April 20 he brought another citizens' petition to the council, this one advocating that the bridge site be changed from Clark to "the extreme end of the piers" as a safeguard against British invasion from Canada. Alluding to recent reports, the petition stated that Great Britain was preparing to wage war "with some foreign nation in order to secure peace at home" as a means of quelling threats of civil war in its manufacturing districts, imminent revolt in its West India colonies, and revolution in its provinces, including "the Canadas." The petition further stated that the foreign nation against whom Queen Victoria intended to wage this war was the United States and that she had already ordered twenty thousand troops into Canada. An invasion could be expected within six months, and Chicago, "the emporium of the west," was a likely military target. Therefore, the proposed Clark Street bridge should be moved to piers' end, essentially the mouth of the harbor, so that, in addition to facilitating commercial traffic across the river, it could obstruct the mouth of the river, blocking the entrance of British warships and canoes of northern Indians allied with the British. The council mockingly referred the report "to the President of the United States."[16]

There were very small kernels of truth in the alarms raised by the petition. In April the *Chicago American* published two articles about a threat of war with Britain over the border dispute in the Northeast. None of these news articles contained any hint of the claims made by the Chicago petitioners that the British government intended to start a war with the United States in order to drum up nationalistic sentiment among its disgruntled home and colonial populations. While it was reasonable to infer that a war with Britain over boundaries with Lower Canada could lead to a British invasion of Michigan and Wisconsin and that British warships might visit Chicago, the claim that the placement of a *bridge* at the mouth of the river would provide a defense was fatuous, a mere smokescreen for other motives.[17]

Miltimore and his committee concluded that although Dearborn was the best location, the bridge should be built at Clark Street because the monies were already subscribed and materials had been contracted. Ogden, who preferred Clark, was ready to accept a bridge at Dearborn or Wells. As for Garrett, he supported at different times the westernmost option (Wells) and the easternmost option (the piers). The only consistency in his shifting position was opposition to Ogden's preference for Clark.[18]

The bridge wars revealed several things about early Chicago. The city, divided into north and south by the main stem of the river, was also divided by north and south sectional interests. The minority group in this conflict quietly used the levers of government, probably exercised bribery behind the scenes, and effected their interests through their considerable power of finance. The majority, the south-siders, petitioned ineffectively, failed to back their stated interests with financing, and at one point expressed their views as a mob, smashing a bridge without municipal authorization. Some of the bridge's opponents were motivated by business interests, others by spite or resentment. With the possible exception of George Merrill, owner of a dry-goods store, none of the signers of the preposterous petition calling for a bridge at the piers to protect against a British invasion had any direct interests in the grain business, and they were not the south side's chief businessmen. Caleb Morgan was a cabinet maker, Charles Peck a saddler and harness maker, George Prescott a clerk. The other names do not even appear in the directories and must have been those of laborers and store clerks, and Garrett, who carried the petition to the council, was an auctioneer and dealer in real estate. Not only that, south-side opposition to the Clark Street bridge continued after it was built. Even when the city provided a sturdy bridge across the south branch, so that grain coming from the west could reach the south side, "aldermen from the south and west sides of the city joined hands in an attempt to obtain removal of the Clark Street bridge which Ogden had built." If the petitioners were not guided by mercantile self-interest, they were likely motivated by sheer sectional rivalry tinctured with class resentment toward social elites north of the river.[19]

Garrett's animosity toward Ogden continued unabated. That summer he used his political influence to injure Ogden's chances of election to the Illinois Senate. "I had the pleasure of defeating [Ogden] in getting to the Senate," he told John Seaman, his New York business partner. This act brought his personal dislike of Ogden into the open: "Since that time he has been a personal enemy both public and private." Garrett's former business partner, Nathaniel Brown, also recalled Ogden's run for the state senate. Brown had a store in Lemont and recalled Ogden's appearance in town to kick off his campaign by speaking from the steps of Brown's store. After the speech a man named Patrick Ballingall, a young Chicago lawyer, got up and called out, "Boys, don't vote for William B. Ogden. He's a rich man and a 'landgrabber who don't sympathize with a working man. If you send him to the Legislature, he won't represent your interests. I'm the man for you to vote for, because you can depend on me to do what is right by you."[20]

Garrett was a representative to the Democratic convention in Springfield that April. He later wrote that in publicly opposing Ogden's senate bid, he had "done it out of pure motives, knowing him to be dishonest and not worthy of the office." This allegation was not unfounded. According to Ogden's biographer, Ogden violated his self-avowed ethics of "honesty, integrity, and fair play" at times "when it served his purposes." Yet Augustus operated similarly. Although he peppered his letters with self-righteous declarations that display a sparkling sense of his own honor and integrity, he also engaged in unscrupulous business and political practices, justifying his ethically dubious actions on the grounds that the dishonesty of others left him no choice. "I love to cheat a cheat," he told Seaman.[21]

His hostility toward Ogden, and toward Ogden's real estate client Arthur Bronson, was further stoked by subsequent incidents. In a letter of December 1843, he brought up the two men in the course of allaying the worries of his New York business partner about certain reports the latter had heard:

Wm. B. Ogden, who is one of the most unpopular men in the city was formerly Mayor of the city and the tool of Arthur Bronson, is no doubt the individual who with the assistance of Arthur Bronson has no doubt made this attempt [to undermine or discredit Garrett in some way]. While I was in the city [New York], Bronson offered me a bribe of $500 (which you overheard yourself after he had the politeness to ask you to leave the room in order to keep you from hearing), if I would let him refer to me in relation to the Lake House property (belonging to him), if I would let him say it was worth so much. You know very well my feelings on such subjects and that I told you at the time that I considered it an insult. That is the manner in which W. B. Ogden has acted for Bronson.[22]

The Lake House was a failing hotel owned by John Kinzie, who had put it up as collateral for a loan from Bronson. Unable to pay the loan when the note came due, Kinzie negotiated an extension. Then, in May of 1841, the Illinois legislature passed an appraisal law, which "provided that no real or personal property could be sold to pay overdue debts unless it was sold for two thirds of its 'cash value' as judged by three householders of the county." The act, which the legislature made retroactive, was meant to protect farmers from losing their lands through indebtedness in a de-pressed economy, but the law applied to real estate generally and required that in any suit in which property had to be sold to pay a debt, the plaintiff, the defendant, and an officer of the court were each to choose one of the three householders who would act as citizen appraisers. In a collapsed real estate market, citizen appraisers tended to value property at its prior value, not its current market value. This meant that if citizen appraisal of the Lake House came in considerably above the current market value, the hotel was unlikely to find a buyer willing to pay at least two-thirds of that valuation. In that case, it could not be sold, and payment to Bronson would be indefinitely delayed. Therefore, it was in Bronson's interest that appraisal of the Lake House be based on current market values, not the inflated ones of the speculation years. It appears from Garrett's account that Bronson asked Garrett either to serve as his chosen citizen appraiser for the Lake House or to use his friendships and reputation to influence the appraisal process. Whatever the proposal, Bronson specified a value and offered Garrett a bribe to endorse that value. Garrett summed up his umbrage in his account to Seaman. "All the wealth that all the Bronsons have," he declared, "cannot bribe me to do one of those dishonest and dishonorable acts that I know both of these men have practiced."[23]

Ogden and Garrett must have crossed paths often enough during Augustus's early years in Chicago. They would have met in the Sauganash Hotel, where Ogden was a resident in 1835. By 1840 they were members of the same party and had many associates in common. Yet they did not become friends. Tensions between the two men may have developed as early as 1836, when Garrett and Brown were conducting their war with the Chicago branch of the Illinois State Bank. The bank president was north-sider John Kinzie; its directors included Gurdon Hubbard, R. J. Hamilton, and George Dole; and the cashier who gave Garrett and Brown so much trouble was W. H. Brown. These five men, all prestigious citizens, were Ogden's neighbors in the wealthy north-side enclave where they had built mansions and their families formed the nucleus of refined north-side society. Ogden and bank president Kinzie were also connected as fellow parishioners of St. James Episcopal Church. Kinzie, Hubbard, Hamilton, and Dole had also supported Ogden's brother-in-law Charles Butler and Ogden's business partner Arthur Bronson in their plan to construct the Illinois and Michigan canal with private capital. No doubt these Ogden friends had unfavorable things to say about Garrett, and in addition to whatever opinions Ogden imbibed from them, he probably considered Garrett a comical boor.[24]

As for Ogden's own feelings, he makes no mention of rivals, much less of enemies, in his letters to Bronson, Butler, and other correspondents during the period of the bridge wars. He may not have taken the conflicts personally. He was apparently a more even-keeled and self-confident man than Garrett, who seems to have believed that intrigues were always evolving against him. As is often the case in socially asymmetrical relations, while Garrett fumed and boiled about Ogden, Ogden took little note of Garrett.

* * *

Garrett did not seek reelection to the Chicago Common Council in 1841, but in 1842 he ran for mayor, on the Democratic ticket, and lost to Whig candidate Benjamin Raymond. Mayoral terms in this era were for one year, commencing in March. The following February the party's mayoral choice was Thomas Dyer, a friend of Garrett, but ill health and a death in his family led Dyer to withdraw and depart the city to attend to his relations. The Democrats were in disarray and sorely divided. Garrett wrote to the absent Dyer, outlining the political news of the city. He did not intend to run again himself, he said, and had been trying to decide whom to back or persuade to run. Hiram Pearsons, campaigning for the nomination "like a crazy man," had "salted every man he could," even selling a piece of property for a thousand dollars to do so. He had the north-siders "so worked up" they would either form their own party or have their own mayor. Initially, Garrett thought the Democrats should put up Mark Skinner, but Skinner would neither spend his own money nor work, so Garrett contemplated Dyer's own partner in the meat-packing business, a man named Elisha Wadsworth. Wadsworth agreed to run for First Ward alderman, not mayor. Other Democrats were approached but were "not willing to risk it." That increased party pressure on Garrett himself, but he continued to resist ("you know how I feel on that subject") until a friend persuaded him otherwise: "I could not honorably back out provided my friends insisted on it and that I did not belong to myself but to my party and that I had better go it."[25]

Garrett prevailed by a wide margin, winning 671 votes to Whig candidate Thomas Church's 381. The abolitionist Liberty Party's candidate garnered only 45. In his inaugural address to the Chicago Common Council on March 13, Garrett declared that the principle of his party was "the greatest good for the greatest number." This expression, which began cropping up in political speech in the 1840s, was a favorite phrase of the Democrats in making their case that Whigs favored the interests of the upper classes. According to Garrett, the application of the principle to Chicago governance required a policy of strict financial austerity to deal with municipal debt. He commended the outgoing council for reducing salaries and expenditures and urged the new council "to practice, if possible, a more rigid economy" so that "our taxes can be diminished to the lowest point." Combined taxation was "already too burthensome," he said, and reducing that burden would be the council's most important task.[26]

At that time the municipal tax rate was only half of 1 percent, and the county tax (also 0.5 percent) and state land tax (even less at 0.2 percent) lay outside the council's control. There was also a land tax, jointly imposed by the state and the county. The council had no control over it either. Hence, there was little room in these areas for substantial tax reduction by Garrett and the aldermen. But the city had the power to impose special assessments. Garrett must have been thinking of these when he spoke of tax reduction as a mayoral priority.[27]

Garrett was not alone in advocating strict economy. Raymond, the outgoing Whig mayor, had made the same assertions in his own inaugural address the year before, speaking of city debt, the severity of the times, and the need to economize. Nor was Garrett alone in regarding city, county, and state taxes as onerous. People in postrevolutionary America tended to see taxes as an infringement on property rights and a relic of Old World government. They also tended to look no farther than the ends of their own noses when judging the merits of a tax. Although the democratic power of near-universal white-male suffrage created pressure on state and national legislatures to invest in banks, canals, and other stimulative enterprises, those same democratic dynamics also produced opposing currents. In New York, farmers of the Hudson Valley and Long Island opposed any increase in taxes to finance the Erie Canal because they believed it would benefit upstate land owners but not themselves. In Illinois, too, residents who did not live near the proposed Illinois and Michigan canal route opposed any general taxes to support the canal. In both states a solution was found through "benefit taxation." New York counties along the canal route agreed to pay a tax surcharge, and in Illinois a similar ad valorem system of taxation was adopted as a condition of getting canal legislation passed in 1837 and 1839.[28]

The debt produced by the state's borrowing to finance the canal became insurmountable as the Panic of 1837 turned into a depression. By 1840 the state was in debt some fourteen million dollars for its canal and railroad projects and had yet to see the completion of either, except for one track running from Springfield to the Illinois River. Most of the Illinois canal tax was going toward covering interest on canal debt. When Governor Ford entered office in 1842, he judged that "the good money in the State, in the hands of the people, did not exceed one year's interest on the public debt." The Illinois State Bank collapsed in spring of 1842. The state was headed toward default, but successive Illinois legislatures in 1842 and 1843 refused to raise taxes—in fact, elected to decrease them—fearing that an increase in taxes would depopulate the state as Illinoisans moved elsewhere, thus exacerbating the debt problem.[29]

In March of 1842, a commissioner was appointed in Chicago to administer a new national bankruptcy law. By September forty Chicago merchants had applied, and the number would only increase. That fall the state outlawed the payment of state taxes with state banknotes. Henceforth, all taxes would have to be paid in specie, that is, gold and silver. This caused not only an immediate depreciation in the value of state bank paper but a hardship for citizens, which was only made worse by the tax increase legislated that same year to defray interest costs on the canal loans. By December people were "scarcely able to pay" in specie, and in February, just before Garrett was elected mayor, the governor cut the state tax rate in half, from thirty cents per hundred dollars of assessed value to fifteen cents. In line with this same relief policy, the legislature suspended the special interest-fund tax of ten cents and returned the state land tax to twenty cents. Of course, these measures only increased the state debt.[30]

In Chicago, too, municipal debt grew in the years leading up to Garrett's term as mayor, despite efforts to control expenses. At the close of 1841 the city's floating indebtedness was $12,388. A year later it was $16,372, an amount that exceeded its tax revenues for that year by 78 percent. One way the city incurred debt was to finance its affairs through the issuing of warrants—written orders specifying payment to named recipients, on demand or at a maturity date. Until 1843 these warrants had served as a form of transferable currency, but that March, just before Garrett took office, the state legislature made warrants nontransferable. Henceforth fewer persons and businesses were willing to be paid with warrants, which added to the strain on the city's finances.[31]

It was in this fiscal environment that Garrett proposed austerity and tax reduction, including adjustments in salaries for city officeholders and consolidation of certain offices. He asked the council to negotiate debt service to pay only the interest, until city finances were on a sounder footing. He opposed any expenditure to "ornament" the city, urging that the present goal should be the elimination of the city's debt within three years. After applauding the current system of common schools, he raised the question of whether music belonged in the curriculum. The immediate question was whether to pay a certain Mr. Gilbert sixteen dollars a month to teach the subject, but in the background was the sorry condition of the school fund brought on by poor management under a former school commissioner.[32]

Public nuisances were another topic. Garrett observed that the city had been lax about enforcing its own ordinances, including prohibiting overly exuberant citizens from firing cannons on Independence Day. He expressed opposition to any schemes by Chicagoans to bring slaves into Illinois; he favored the donation of lots for each of the city's churches; he encouraged places of business to close on Sunday; and he praised the city's temperance societies. Perhaps as much as a quarter of the citizenry

Oil painting of Augustus Garrett, by C. V. Bond (posthumous, 1856).
Courtesy of Garrett-Evangelical Theological Seminary.

belonged to these sobriety organizations. Although never a member himself and no abstainer, except for brief periods of self-reformation, Garrett was politic in applauding the positive moral influence of the temperance societies and commended them for eschewing partisanship in the recent election. He closed his speech with a peroration on the bright future of the city.[33]

The reference to slavery in Garrett's inaugural address is one of only a few hints about his views on the topic. Having recently heard rumors that certain parties in Chicago were contracting with associates in a Mississippi River town to bring slaves into the state, he summoned Chicagoans to "take all legal and honorable means to suppress anything of the kind that may operate abroad so injuriously to our reputations." He could count on public agreement with this policy. State, county, and municipal officials in Illinois were lax about the enforcement of both federal and state laws concerning fugitive slaves, as well as the state's own odious "Black Code," which was extremely prejudicial to those of African descent. Just a few months after Garrett's inaugural address, one of his fellow Illinoisans, H. H. Kellogg, described to a London abolitionist conference the status of the slavery question in Illinois, surveying the harsh law on the subject but remarking that "these laws are not all enforced." Although the state had plenty of proslavery citizens, especially in its southern districts, Chicago was an antislavery town. This did not mean that all were *abolitionists*, a term that referred to the demand for an immediate legal end to slavery in all the states and territories, which many antislavery whites regarded as politically impossible. Moreover, abolitionists were also divided between those who renounced political action on principle, as morally sullying, and activists who sought to pursue their ends through electoral politics. Opposition to slavery assumed gradations, and abolitionism was one span of tones on this spectrum.[34]

In Chicago, a home to stations on the Underground Railway, antislavery sentiment existed not only among Whigs but also among Democrats, most of whom hailed from New York. George Manierre, who managed the *Chicago Democrat* for several years in the 1840s, was a founder of the Chicago Anti-Slavery Society. His son recalled that their house on Michigan Avenue was a stop on the Underground Railway for slaves fleeing to Canada. William Ogden and his brother Mahlon were other staunchly antislavery Democrats, and Mahlon Ogden would be remembered for his role in securing the freedom of a black man put up for auction in November of 1842.[35]

That odious auction occurred just five months before Garrett's election. Edwin Heathcock, "a colored man," got into a quarrel with a white man—who was either his employer or a fellow laborer—while the two men were working in a field on the north side. Following the altercation, the white man went to Sheriff Samuel Lowe and reported Heathcock as a runaway slave. Heathcock told the sheriff this was untrue, but he could not produce papers proving his status as a freeman. The sheriff brought him before Judge I. C. Kercheval, who treated Heathcock as a free Negro who lacked papers. The judge sentenced him to be sold for one month of labor, in effect, a short term of indentured service. Sheriff Lowe was to hold an auction, and he placed Heathcock in the county jail for a period of six weeks, the time required for public notification of the auction.[36]

Heathcock's predicament quickly became known to the city's most ardent antislavery citizens, many of whom were Presbyterians and Methodists. Zebina Eastman, whose press published the antislavery paper *Western Citizen*, later told how Calvin DeWolf came to his shop late on the Saturday before the Monday auction. DeWolf, who was then reading law with Grant Goodrich and would later help organize the Chicago chapter of the Anti-Slavery Society, wanted Zebina to print up a handbill publicizing the Heathcock case so that residents would know that a slave auction was about to take place in their city under the color of law. At midnight, Eastman recalled, "we . . . sallied up Clark street, along the line to be traversed by the church goers on the morrow" and "posted these bills on the fences around the public square, up past the long, low Presbyterian church on the right, the equally low Methodist on the left . . . and on the board fences . . . on both sides of Clark street, so that the sober, if not the solid, men should have full notice of the Monday morning sale as they went to and fro to church, for the people of Chicago at that time were famous church goers." Throughout the following day, the handbills received sprays of tobacco juice and piercings from people disgusted by the event it announced. The sight of Heathcock's name must have stirred a special ire among Methodists since Heathcock was a member of their church. By the time of the auction, a crowd of sullen men and women had gathered at the site of the impending sale.[37]

What happened next has been told and retold in books on early Chicago as a testament to the city's proud antislavery stance in antebellum days. No doubt some white authors have been drawn to the story as a morality tale starring a white man who intervened on behalf of a persecuted black man. No account from Heathcock's own point of view survives. In any case, as Eastman tells it, the sheriff put Heathcock on a block near the log jail at LaSalle and Randolph and invited bids for one month of Heathcock's labor, the purchase money to be paid to the city for its expenses in jailing Heathcock for the past six weeks. The crowd remained silent. The sheriff repeated the invitation for bids. There were still no offers. So it went. At some point, one of the crowd asked whether the purchaser would be expected to return Heathcock at the end of the month. That is, would Heathcock be free after his month of work or only back in the hands of the sheriff for some further legal process? The sheriff answered that there would be no further obligation but noted that since nothing had been bid, he would have no choice but return Heathcock to jail. At this point a voice from an upstairs window of the courthouse called out a bid of twenty-five cents. The offer was from Mahlon Ogden. The sheriff declared the auction finished. Ogden came down to the street, handed the sheriff a quarter, and told Heathcock, "Edwin, you are my man. I have purchased you for twenty-five cents. Go where you like." At that the crowd broke into cheers, and the judge apologized, saying he had only been doing his duty.[38]

It may seem surprising that with an audience full of antislavery citizens, it took so long for someone to offer a token amount to secure Heathcock's freedom. But antislavery conviction led many to oppose purchasing slaves to give them their freedom on the grounds that doing so stained the conscience of the purchasers by involving them in the sinful institution and its commerce. This sentiment was especially strong among Protestants influenced by the Holiness movement, including many Methodists and Presbyterians. Mahlon Ogden, an Episcopalian, was not encumbered by Holiness scruples.[39]

There is no record of Garrett having witnessed the auction or having commented on it. His remarks in his inaugural address show that he regarded slavery as a disgraceful institution. The fact that in one election the abolitionist Liberty Party briefly joined with Whigs to support his Democratic candidacy shows that he was publicly known to be opposed to slavery. Yet he himself had once sold a slave (inherited by his Maryland nephew) rather than take the trouble to emancipate him. The simplest explanation of the contradiction is that he opposed slavery on principle but was not willing to lose money over that principle or suffer inconvenience because of it.[40]

Yet he came to regret selling his nephew's slave. That sale was made in the summer of 1830 just before the Garretts left for Cincinnati. By 1833 they were in New Orleans, where for the first time in their lives they witnessed slave auctions. The New Orleans market in human chattel was immense. Entire streets were taken up by auction blocks and holding pens, and the auction houses trafficked in the slave commerce as well. Half-naked men and women were exhibited like cattle to buyers "who inspected them like livestock" and purchased "a son but not the mother, a father but not the wife." It is difficult to imagine that Eliza was not horrified or Augustus not moved to reconsider his callous attitude toward slavery. His later involvement with Clark Street Methodist Church in Chicago is a further indicator. Those who joined the church were expected to follow the moral strictures set forth in the Methodist discipline and to confess their sins to their assigned classes. This included the sin of "buying and selling of men, women, and children," which means that Augustus, who was quite sincere when he underwent a religious conversion, must have confessed to members of his Methodist class that he had once sold a slave. He now saw this act as a stain on his life record. His remorse did not lead him into any kind of antislavery activism. It simply made him one of the many Chicagoans who thought slavery morally wrong, wanted it confined to the southern states, and hoped it would wither away in time, a common if naïve idea of the era that was especially attractive to men who had business interests that might be affected by any rupture in the social fabric.[41]

The Chicago city charter provided that a mayor be elected every year, and it gave him little authority beyond his own vote on the city council. Chicago had yet to develop its machine politics of later years, and no mayor served successive terms until John Wentworth in 1848 (although Garrett himself almost did). It was no foregone conclusion, then, that Garrett would get what he wanted. But the Democrats enjoyed a majority on the council, and unless members had very strong feelings to the contrary, they tended to defer to the mayor. Moreover, the prior council under a Whig mayor had operated under the same economizing philosophy that Garrett proposed. Over the course of Garrett's tenure, the floating liabilities went down by 30 percent, chiefly because the city continued to retire debt while not taking on any new long-term debt. The effective city tax rate also decreased dramatically from 6 percent to 0.6 percent, and the city collected less in tax revenues, although only 5 percent less, than under the previous administration. This difference between effective tax rate and tax revenues must have been the result of fewer special assessments and a reduction in the municipal tax on real estate. The music teacher's contract was not renewed.[42]

The routine work of the mayor and the Chicago Common Council in this era was reflected in the council's standing committees. In addition to those on finance, claims, police, fire protection, water, and printing, the council regularly heard reports from committees on streets and bridges, wharves and public grounds, and schools. Of these, the reports requiring the most attention were those of the Committee on Streets and Bridges. Its members had been a busy trio during the bridge wars, and bridges remained a near-constant concern. So did sidewalks.[43]

The subject of sidewalks reveals just how rough a place the burgeoning city was. Laid out practically on a swamp, the soggy, boggy town endured deep mud in rainy seasons and was a patchwork of ruts the rest of the year. Animals could tromp through almost everything, but pedestrians wanted clean, passable walkways. An ordinance of 1839 empowered the city to order the owners or occupants of any lot fronting a city street to construct "good substantial sidewalks adjoining to, and along the whole front of each lot or part of lot, of stone, brick, or wood" within thirty days of being notified. Where owners failed to comply, the street commissioner was authorized to lay the sidewalk and charge the owners for the work. Yet sidewalks materialized slowly. It may be that the council was reluctant to issue a citywide order for sidewalk construction or, more likely, that the city did not have the wherewithal to build them all at once. Thus a piecemeal policy evolved. Over the next several years the council issued periodic directives to lot owners to construct walks, and bands of citizens also petitioned for them. The city performed all the construction, and the owners paid for it. By the time of Garrett's tenure in office, the standard was a plank sidewalk four feet wide.[44]

Assessing property owners on a given street for the cost of a sidewalk and imposing similar special assessments on those who benefited most directly from other city improvements were standard methods of financing public works. It is evident that for boosters like Garrett and his fellow mayors and aldermen, special assessments did not reflect a philosophy of government financing, for they did not apply the concept to projects such as the canal or the city harbor. The federal government ought to bear the cost of the harbor, they believed, even though it was Chicago that reaped the greatest benefit from it; and the state ought to build the canal, even though some citizens and towns profited much more directly than others did. The same logic might have been applied to sidewalks and the like since, even though a shop owner benefited from his storefront sidewalk more than others, customers and suppliers also benefited. Hence, a booster philosophy argued for public sharing of the expense of local improvements. Yet the 1837 charter limited what the city could raise in revenues from property taxes to no more than half a percent of assessed value. Hence, Garrett and his fellow mayors and aldermen imposed special assessments to get around this limitation and to avoid the alternative of borrowing and increasing the municipal debt. But they exercised this power sparingly.[45]

No public buildings were constructed or parks beautified during Garrett's term as mayor, nor was any money expended for "other useful and ornamental purposes." Improvements of that sort could be done with city surpluses, Garrett suggested, once the city had retired its debt, a few years hence. In the meantime the city funded only the most necessary things, such as bridge and ferry maintenance, and firefighting units, along with paying salaries to the city physician, street commissioner, attorney, collector, and staff of the municipal court. And it passed ordinances, which cost nothing.[46]

A spate of ordinances was recorded in mid-May to address issues of public health and related nuisances. One law prohibited the dumping of "dung, carrion, dead animal, offal, or other putrid or unwholesome substance," including "the contents of any privy," on the lakeshore, waterways, public grounds, or city lots. It also forbade the disposal of "rubbish, wood, glass, stone, shells, chips, or any filthy or other substance" into gutters of the streets or alleyways; proscribed the grazing or roaming of animals in the public parks; prohibited the posting of handbills and placards on houses, stores, signs, and fences; and outlawed the placing of casks, crates, barrels, planks, stoves, or wood on sidewalks. The specifications paint a vivid picture of the citizens' habits the law was trying to put a stop to.[47]

The nature of the council's business in the early 1840s shows the extent to which the most pressing needs of the city were basic infrastructure and order. The charter was less than a decade old, and elected officials struggled to make the growing city a commercially friendly place and give the rough frontier face of the town a more urbane and decorous look. Businessmen of means were thrilled by every new brick building, and in 1840 Joseph Balestier warmed their civic hearts by assuring them that those who lodged or supped in Chicago hotels could "indulge in all the luxuries of the East."[48]

Garrett and the council were confronted with a few extraordinary expenses, among them a hydrant and hose and a Clark Street sewer. Yet the ordinary expenses of the city were appreciably less than the year prior, only about $4,500. One of the mayor's greatest single-handed achievements was to negotiate a reduction of one of the city's loans from a New York bank during one of his business trips to New York.[49]

Yet it all bored Garrett to death—the council meetings about sidewalks and wharfing privileges, the municipal paperwork and correspondence, the citizens taking up his time with their requests and complaints. He received no salary and could exercise only minimal patronage. City government was not yet a money-garnering opportunity for Chicago politicians. In fact, the mayoralty cost Garrett valuable time away from his businesses, and he was annoyed that he was expected to be a public example of generosity by contributing to benevolences. On top of his business activities, city work left him exhausted and took a toll on his health. Contemplating a run for a second term, he wondered, "What is there then to be gained by it more than to impair my health and pay out of my own individual pocket from $500 to $1000 a year to support paupers?"[50]

What was to be gained was *honor*. Public esteem was the meaning of both political office and business for Garrett, as for many men of his age. He craved a reputation for greatness. Explaining to his business partner John Seaman why he had enemies, he bragged, "I have gained ten times the honor that all the rest of the mayors have ever gained who have succeeded [sic] me. Again they have jealous [sic] because I have gained the victory over them again. I am accumulating too much property every [day] and all of the movements of this kind [attempts to undermine him] have tended to help me instead of setting me back."[51]

At the same time, Garett was an able mayor, not a visionary but a good manager. He wanted the city books to balance and the city streets to be clean and tidy. Although boosterish in outlook, he was, in his middle age, essentially risk averse and fiscally conservative, making him well suited to governance at this debt-ridden moment in Chicago's history.

As the year 1843 drew to a close, Garrett told Seaman that "the whole city" was "in favor of my re-election, both parties—Whigs & Locos, Church and Anti-Church." "Locos" was short for Locofocos, a derogatory term for the radical wing of the Democratic Party. "Church" referred not to religious bodies but to Thomas Church, a Whig leader. Garrett was a popular south-sider and a moderate. Thus five weeks later he was able to tell Seaman that "five hundred people, both my friends and those who used to be my foes," had urged him to run again. Yet he feared another year in office would be bad for his health. Speaking of their joint business, he told Seaman that being an agent for three insurance companies was better than being mayor because "they will pay and I would get as much popularity from the agencies as I would from the Mayorship." Public service did not appeal to him. "I would rather do the labour of 40 agents than be elected mayor and be the humble servant of about 8000 people." But when the Democrats convened in the second week of February to nominate their slate of candidates for the March municipal election, Garrett was the unanimous choice. He told a correspondent that "at the earnest solicitation of my friends and in order to conciliate and keep up the strength of our party but altogether against my own feelings I have consented to run again for mayor." He could not resist the limelight.[52]

There was a wrinkle. In January, during a four-month tour of northern Illinois and the Wisconsin Territory, Garrett had stopped in Milwaukee. At some point during an evening of drinking with a man named Brown, whom Garrett had just met, Brown fell over dead. It was concluded that he suffered a stroke, but when Garrett's political opponents in Chicago got wind of the incident, they turned it into a scandal by accusing Garrett of urging Brown to drink himself to death. The hope was to turn members of the Washingtonian temperance society and other teetotalers against Garrett. Back in Chicago, Garrett wrote to Josiah Noonan, a business associate in Milwaukee who was also editor of the *Milwaukee Courier*:

> They have all sorts of reports in circulation here in relation to the death of Mr. Brown. The Washingtonians have used all sorts of means to make capital out of it. I have made Goodrich, as he is one of the Speakers, tell the Society here in a publick meeting there were other reports contradictory and that he would write to Mr. Lyon who belongs to a Washingtonian Society in your place and that Lyon's letter would be read in the next meeting. I want you to attend to this matter and not let any false reports come here again. I wish you would state in your paper, if you think best, the facts in relation to it. You can refer to the documents.[53]

An inquest exonerated Garrett of any wrongdoing. Garrett wrote again to Noonan, pressing him to publish, and circulate to other papers, the result of the coroner's proceedings and to mention, if he could, "the Honorable course I took both before and after the death of Mr. Brown." Noonan obliged:

> *Hon. Augustus Garrett*, of Chicago, has been most ungenerously and unjustly assailed by persons who make their zeal in the temperance cause a cloak to cover personal malignity. The story that he was in anywise instrumental in leading to the intemperate drinking which it is *supposed* hastened an attack of apoplexy which terminated in the

death of a stranger among us is *totally* and *unqualifiedly* false, as many of
our most respectable citizens, who are acquainted with the facts, have
already testified. How this story ever reached Southport and Chicago,
and entered into circulation in these places is a mystery.

The *Chicago Democrat* republished Noonan's editorial, although it did
not manage to get it into print before election day. Evidently, the editor,
John Wentworth's brother George, disliked Garrett and was reluctant
to help him. The rumors about the Milwaukee episode, uncontradicted
by any Chicago newspaper, probably hurt Garrett with some teetotaling
Protestants.[54]

The election started off well but ended badly, even though Garrett
won. At its February meeting, the Democratic convention's sixteen dele-
gates nominated Garrett unanimously, and George Wentworth, perhaps
on instructions from his brother or simply from party loyalty, extolled
Garrett in the pages of the *Chicago Democrat*. "He has proved himself
to be a faithful public officer," the paper said, "and never before have our
City Councils been more wisely conducted." The editorial went on to
enumerate a few of Garrett's accomplishments—"the right enforcement
of many ordinances of the city which have heretofore been a dead letter,
the introduction of economy in all the departments, the maintenance of
good order throughout the city, the payment of a part of the city debt and
reduction of the rate of interest to be paid on the balance, and thereby
a restoration of the public credit." The Whig rejoinder was that anyone
could have done those things, which seemed to admit that Garrett had
been a good mayor.[55]

The argument over who achieved the best results in city government,
Whigs or Democrats, reflected the fact that there was little if any difference in philosophy between the two parties at the level of city governance. The upcoming election was "more of a local than a political nature,"
former mayor Raymond said, claiming that the Whigs had chosen their
candidate, George Dole, not for partisan reasons but because he was
popular with both Whigs and Democrats. In fact, for the very reason
that Raymond stated, candidates were chosen almost solely for partisan
reasons, there being no substantial differences in municipal philosophy
between them.[56]

The reason for this homogeneity was a shared policy of boosterism and
the very limited powers of the mayor's office and the Common Council.

Chicago politicians and business leaders were all advocates of city growth, and their disagreements about how much debt the city should assume and what taxes should be levied owed less to differing political philosophies than to differing judgments of the moment about how to maximize economic efficiency. Although the *Chicago Democrat* could warn that if Whigs were elected to state offices, they would "carry out, *so far as this State is concerned*, their banking system, their protective tariff, their distribution act, and assumption of state debts by the General Government," these were not municipal issues. Hence, when the *Democrat* declared after Garrett's election that "federalism, in all its forms, is annihilated here," it was only asserting the symbolic significance of Democratic success in the city as a harbinger of Democratic supremacy in state and national politics. Most of the populace did not see that it affected the well-being of the city what position the mayor took on the annexation of Texas, a state bank, protective tariffs, state debt, etc.[57]

Yet one's correct position on these matters, as a Democrat or a Whig, gave one an aura of decency and good judgment in the eyes of one's party, and these same opinions lowered one's stature in the eyes of the other party. Illinois governor Ford was a Democrat through and through, yet he could see that loyalists of both parties, fueled by newspaper editorials, ended up feeling confident "that their political opponents, and particularly those of them that are elected to office, are a set of insufferable rogues, bent upon the enslavement of the people or the ruin of the country." And that is why party loyalists in Chicago voted for their own candidates. It was not because they wished to bring a different set of policies to the mayor's office and the Common Council but because they believed the other party's candidates were fools or scoundrels or both.

Garrett's friend William S. Brown traded in these terms at a political meeting when, speaking of the difference between Democrats and Whigs, he contended that their respective actions in office "showed the republicanism and liberality of the one and hypocrisy and selfishness of the other," adding that these differences of moral character "proved conclusively that upon the ascendancy and maintenance of the good old fashioned democratic doctrines of Jefferson, Jackson, and van Buren, depended the preservation and perpetuation of our republican institutions." But a year later, when the *Chicago Democrat* defended Garrett's record as mayor, it focused on the reduction of city debt, which had also been a priority of his Whig predecessor in 1842.[58]

The day before the election, Garrett arranged for wagons to carry Norwegian voters to the polls, ordered at least one keg of beer for the Fifth Ward, met with fellow Democratic election judge Andrew Nielsen and Fifth Warder Samuel Grier, whose house near the polling place was the destination for the beer, and wrote a letter to the *Express* defending himself and former mayor Raymond for having accepted municipal gifts of five-dollar burial plots for themselves and their wives in the new city cemetery, gifts that Garrett deemed it would have been discourteous to have refused. In the same letter he also defended the Whig Raymond against the *Express*'s gratuitous remark about Raymond having never gotten the cemetery fenced. Garrett objected, giving the Raymond administration credit for procuring the ground for the new city cemetery and clearing it, and he explained that Raymond was not at fault for not fencing the graveyard because he left office at a season of the year when that was impossible.[59]

Garrett defeated his Whig opponent, George Dole, by only seven votes. On Wednesday the city's outgoing Common Council accepted the election results, and on Thursday Garrett swore himself into office. By then, however, the election was under a cloud. Disappointed Whigs were circulating accusations about irregularities in the Third and Fifth Wards, and petitions were being submitted to the council calling for an inquiry.[60]

In his inaugural address, Garrett struck a nonpartisan note, natural for a winner. Noting Whig animosity toward him, he declared, "I am totally unconscious of ever willingly having given them any cause of ill feeling." He also referred to the controversy over the election and asked the newly elected city fathers to take action. "Gentlemen of the Common Council," he said, "rumors having been raised that illegal proceedings and fraud had been resorted to in the recent municipal elections, I recommend you to appoint a committee to examine into the truth of such rumors and to report at as early a day as possible." The following Tuesday, the new council authorized an inquiry into the election and appointed an investigating committee, which began taking depositions. The committee permitted Garrett and Dole to be represented by lawyers, who did most of the questioning; but Garrett and Dole were both present, and from time to time Garrett interrogated witnesses as ably as either attorney. In one of the oddities of the proceeding, it was Garrett's personal lawyer, Grant Goodrich, who represented candidate Dole.[61]

One issue concerned when the Fifth Ward polls were opened on election day. The polling place was Elihu Granger's house, where ballots were handed in to the election clerks and judges through a side window that looked out on Granger's yard. The Whigs claimed the polls had been opened early, that is, before 8:00 a.m., and that the clocks at the polling place (Granger's house) had been moved forward to disguise that fact. Depositions about this revealed the homey details of timekeeping in antebellum Chicago. Henry Clarke set his clock by E. G. Reynold's watch, who adjusted his watch to City Time (the time on a certain clock in Smith Sherwood's jewelry shop on Lake Street); the Tremont House went by the jeweler Isaac Speer; and John Sullivan set his clock by comparing it to Thomas Welsh's watch, which ran eight minutes ahead of City Time. Much of this investigation of time had to do with whether one Thomas Joyce—who had awakened earlier than usual, put his kettle on the fire, and then crossed the river to get breakfast meat from a butcher—had, on his return, voted around 7:30; and whether one Michael Kennedy, passing by the polls as votes were being received, was correct that it was too early for the polls to have been open; and whether John Sullivan, who heard Kennedy complain, was also correct in corroborating Kennedy's claim. All four judges and the two clerks who conducted the election at the Fifth Ward poll said they began receiving votes *after* 8:00 a.m. Granger, a candidate for alderman and the owner of the house where the poll was set up, said the same. So did his boarder, George Kirk, who fixed the time at about 8:20 by a watch set to Sherwood's time. Samuel Grier recalled Joyce coming into Granger's yard with a skewer of meat but not stopping to vote because he said "there was time enough." His kettle was on the stove at home, after all, and he was eager to get his breakfast cooked. Henry Clarke thought he took Joyce's vote between 8:30 and 9:00. Joyce's name appeared on the register as the thirty-fifth person to vote. He had voted for Garrett's Whig opponent.[62]

Efforts to establish the time when the poll opened even led to the deposing of Joel Ellis, the butcher who sold Joyce the skewer of meat. The investigating lawyers wanted to know at what hour Joyce had opened his shop. Ellis said it was before eight and that customer Joyce did not mention whether he had yet voted or not. It came out that ten minutes after selling Joyce his breakfast meat, Ellis left his store and went to the Washington Coffee House, arriving just in time for the bell that rang in the first table. The invariable custom was to sound the bell at 8:00 a.m.

or within minutes of that hour. The bell-ringer went by the grandfather clock in the dining room (regulated by Speer the jeweler's time), which stopped whenever someone sitting on the settee happened to bump one of its weights, a frequent occurrence. It was customary for the breakfast bell to be rung about eight or not long after eight, but never before eight. Little could be deduced from this about when Joyce voted since there was no reason to doubt that Joyce got his skewer of meat from Ellis sometime before eight. The only question was whether he voted on his way to get his meat or after he ate.[63]

The investigation did not establish anything definitive about when the polls opened in the Fifth Ward, but it did find that two clerks, one in the Third Ward and one in the Fifth, were not eligible to vote in Chicago, which made them ineligible to serve as election clerks. Age in the one case and length of residence in the other were the disqualifiers. There was also an allegation that the judges of the Fifth Ward had opened folded ballots before putting them in the box, the implication being that they did so in full view of those waiting to vote in order to intimidate them—that is, to pressure them to vote in a certain way or not to vote at all. Several witnesses had seen election judges open ballots. When asked about this, the judges admitted to opening some number of ballots but said it was only to ensure that certain voters had not submitted more than one vote.[64]

The Whigs further charged that the officials at the Fifth Ward poll received illegal votes, that is, votes from persons whose age or length of residency made them ineligible to vote in the ward. According to testimony, certain voters had been properly challenged when the clerks or judges had reason to doubt their eligibility. Some who were challenged did not contest their rejection. Others later swore in their votes, which meant that they could be prosecuted if it turned out they had voted illegally. During this part of the investigation, two names recurred—John McCarty and Daniel Driscol. Election judge George Brady said he challenged both of them and that they later swore their votes in. It was candidate Dole's contention that eight or more other voters had been illegal, invalidating the Fifth Ward results. This was never proven.[65]

Bribery, "treating" (giving out drinks), and other inducements to secure votes were expressly illegal according to Illinois law. Whigs claimed Garrett and his supporters had hired wagons to bring in voters. A keg of beer had been brought by wagon to Grier's house, they said, and drinks were dispensed to garner votes for Garrett. The most damning accusation was that Garrett had been paying Norwegians for their votes. Whigs found one Oren Overson, who admitted that Garrett had given him a dollar and a voting ticket with Garrett's name already filled in. Under questioning by Dole's lawyer, Overson said the dollar was not for his vote; and when Garrett himself took up the questioning, the Norwegian explained that he could not read English but could read the name "Garrett," and that the dollar was for splitting rails at some previous time.[66]

In the end, Garrett managed to defang the charge that he transported voters to the polls, treated them, and otherwise engaged in fraud. He put Dole's lawyer, Goodrich, Dole himself, and Alderman Murphy under oath and asked each of them whether in previous elections candidates of various parties had used their influence to get votes, whether they or their supporters had paid for teams or expended money to treat, and whether they had knowledge "of any fraud or illegal proceedings on the part of myself at this last election." Goodrich admitted that candidates in past elections had used their influence to secure votes and that they and their supporters had provided teams. As a "cold water man," Goodrich said, he was unfamiliar with treating but knew of no fraud committed by Garrett. Dole agreed that candidates had typically used their influence to get votes and said he was familiar with candidates' friends hiring teams and treating. He conceded that he, too, knew of no fraud on Garrett's part. Alderman Murphy acknowledged that candidates and their supporters usually treated, and he admitted that he himself had once paid for a team. He, too, knew of no instance where Garrett engaged in any fraud or other illegal activity.[67]

Other rumors circulated against Garrett and his supporters. It was claimed that a meeting had taken place at the Sauganash or at John L. Gray's house to plan an early opening of the Fifth Ward poll so "the Norwegians" could vote before everyone else. Garrett, Nielsen, and Grier admitted that they had met at the Sauganash the evening before the election but denied having arranged to open the polls early. George Brady, Grier, Lisle Smith, and maybe Granger were at John Gray's that night. Brady told the investigating committee that he suggested they open the polls right at eight or just after so that the Norwegians could vote before others arrived. Grier explained that threats had been made against the Norwegians by men who wanted to prevent them from voting and that he himself had been threatened. The group at Gray's agreed that they would open the polls right at eight so that the Norwegians could vote before other voters arrived and before men got liquored up. As for treating, Nielsen said that a "Dutchman" brought a half barrel of beer to Grier's. He did not know who paid for it. Brady also recalled the cask and said that Grier offered him and other friends some. Grier said he paid for the keg himself with "my own good money" and that from time to time he would treat his friends.[68]

The Chicago Common Council referred certain legal questions to its Committee on the Judiciary, composed of two Whigs and one Democrat—Buckner S. Morris, Asher Rossiter, and George Davis. Morris and Rossiter concluded that, as a matter of law, an election conducted by ineligible clerks was null and void; the lone Democrat, George Davis, argued that the clerks in question, having been appointed, had authority de facto under the legitimate authority of their superiors, the election judges. The majority also found that whether the purpose was nefarious or benign, the opening of ballots by election judges was a violation of law. If accepted by the council, the majority report was enough to vacate the results in the Third and Fifth Wards. Davis issued a minority opinion contending that there was no legal basis to set aside the election. Thus, the two Whigs on the judiciary committee took Dole's side, and the sole Democrat took Garrett's.[69]

On Saturday evening, March 16, the Common Council met to hear the report of the Committee on Elections and to decide what action to take. Earlier that day Garrett had heard from Samuel Hoard, a clerk of the circuit court, that Davis had turned against Garrett and "sold himself over to the Whigs." Garrett went to see Davis and learned that, despite the legal opinion Davis had submitted, he was now agreeing with his two colleagues on the judiciary committee that the election results in the Fifth Ward were invalid because election judges had opened some of the ballots and the clerk was not a legal voter in the ward. Garrett discounted these problems as mere technicalities and called Davis a "scoundrel" for making claims "about frauds and illegal voting."[70]

In a letter to his close friend and confidant James Malony, Garrett bragged that in all forty pages of testimony there was not one word about any fraud on his part (or Dole's or anyone else's). Then he made a self-damning admission. "I attended to that matter myself," he says. "It was attended to with a little trouble and Salt."[71]

Garrett may have been justified in calling the use of ineligible clerks a technicality, cause for a fine but not grounds for nullifying the election results. The opening of ballots was another matter. Not only was it against the law for election judges to open ballots during voting, doing so in public view might well intimidate voters, suppressing the vote for one or more candidates, whether that was intended or not. At the very least, the misbehavior of the election judges warranted a special election in the Fifth Ward. As for the testimony about fraud, Garrett's statement that he took care of that with "salt" meant that he paid off some of those who were deposed by the investigating committee. Given the righteous indignation of his tone in narrating these events to a trusted confidant, it is possible that he used money to ensure that certain Whigs he did not trust would not make false allegations. More likely, however, he thought himself so unfairly injured by certain accusations that he felt justified in making bribes to suppress all negative testimony about himself, both the false and the factual. He probably did pay for votes, in various fashions, including giving Oren Overson a dollar.[72]

It was not to save his election that Garrett salted witnesses. He cared only about his reputation and quickly devised a plan to recoup his honor, the execution of which he recounted to Malony in a blow-by-blow description of the Saturday evening council meeting. The meeting was held in the Saloon Building with Garrett, still mayor, presiding. "The room was so crowded they were on top of each other to see what was to take place," Garrett told Malony. Forty pages of depositions were read aloud, and Garrett thought this reading "had a tendency to raise me in the estimation of every person in the room." Then Alderman Morris—a member of the majority of two on the judiciary committee who had already found the election to be invalid—offered a resolution that the results in the Fifth Ward be thrown out. Garrett let him make a speech, after which Garrett stood and made his own short speech.[73]

Garrett's speech contained a magnanimous gesture, calculated to impress, and its grandeur caused him a flush of elation. He later recalled to Malony how at that moment, when he rose to speak, he felt "as good as if I were in heaven." After a few kind remarks about Dole, he announced, to the astonishment of the new Whig majority on the council, that "in case they wished to gain the election on those grounds after fraud had been alleged . . . I cordially and respectfully resigned my seat." The room was stunned into silence, filled "with awe and such feeling you never saw before." There were cries of "Don't you do it, keep your seat. They are all a damned set of scoundrels. If you resign, we will be damned if we don't elect you again, etc., etc." Garrett then calmly tendered his resignation.

The Saloon Building, where the Chicago city council met.
Chicago History Museum, ICHi-037030, cropped.

The council was in "perfect confusion," caught completely by surprise and unsure about what to do next. Garrett instructed them to appoint one of their members to chair the meeting. They chose Morris, and no sooner had Morris taken his place in the chairman's seat than the crowd of onlookers erupted in hisses. One would have thought there were "a thousand geese in the room." People objected to Morris taking over the meeting and cried out, "Turn him out! Pitch him out of the window! Kick him downstairs!" With the whole room in an uproar, one of the aldermen moved to adjourn, and the rest promptly concurred.[74]

That same evening two citizens' committees visited Garrett and urged him to run again. He told them he had no intention of doing so. Then, still in the grips of euphoria about his performance at the council meeting, he set down his account in the letter to Malony.[75]

The council held another special meeting a week later, on Saturday the 23rd. Again the Saloon Building was crowded. The majority and minority judiciary reports were read. When a resolution to accept the majority opinion was to be voted on, Alderman Morris objected to the aldermen from the disputed wards participating in the vote. They were allowed to vote, however, and a tie resulted. The council decided that Miltimore, acting as chair, could break the tie, even though he had already voted as alderman. Miltimore demurred and called for another vote. Again a tie. Fourth Ward alderman John Murphy stood up and resigned; the aldermen Granger, Brown, Davis, Poussard followed suit. Miltimore then turned the chair over to Alderman Chapin, who carried on with the six remaining aldermen. They declared Dole elected, but Dole refused. They then ordered a new aldermanic election in the Third and Fifth Wards and a new general mayoral election.[76]

George Wentworth neglected to publish the story of Garrett's resignation, which irked Garrett since he had been hoping for a newspaper account of his grand gesture. There were other perceived slights. When Garrett's inaugural address was published, George refused to give Garrett's clerk extra copies of the paper for Garrett to send to family and friends, asking why he needed so many and whether he had paid for them. Nor would he let Garrett see copy in advance, and he was vague about whether he would meet with Garrett to discuss business. Garrett pulled his advertising from the paper and wrote an explanation to John Wentworth, George's brother.[77]

After his resignation, the Democrats insisted that he run again against Dole. When Dole withdrew, the Whigs persuaded Alson Sherman, a Democrat, to run with their support. The Democrats had no objection to Sherman except for his party disloyalty in going over to the Whigs. Fewer people voted this time, and the outcome was that Sherman, a well-liked fellow, won 51 percent of the vote; Garrett garnered 42 percent; and Henry Smith, the abolitionist candidate of the Liberty Party, received the remainder.[78]

After the special election, the *Daily Democrat* praised Sherman as a man who had "arisen to his present position by honesty, perseverance, and industry." Or was that George Wentworth's way of implying a slap at Garrett? Garrett explained to Seaman that since he had not wanted to run again, he had persuaded some of his friends "to manage secretly against me, and Sherman is elected."[79]

It is conceivable that Garrett let it be known among party leaders that he would be happy for Sherman to win, but it is also possible that he made statements of that sort to them out of fear he might lose. When it was all over, however, he felt relief. Several months prior he had written to Seaman, "I am busy all the day long and can't do any more," adding that "after 3 months I will get clear of the city business which will relieve me of about one half." Now he confided, "I have seen more real enjoyment since

Sherman's election than I have in the past 12 months." But nine months later, still out of office, he was telling Seaman, "My labors are greater than I can bear; they must not be so great hereafter for I can't stand it."[80]

Three months later he was a candidate for mayor again.

*   *   *

Not only did the Democrats nominate Garrett in the election of 1845, but, for a brief time, he had substantial Whig and even abolitionist support. On the Saturday before the election—with Garrett already the Democratic nominee—"the disaffected Whigs and Abolitionists called a mass meeting at the Court House" and endorsed him as their candidate. The Whigs then withdrew and held a second meeting at the Saloon Building with some mix of the same factions, and this time nominated John Kinzie. "Every Whig in town," Garrett told Malony, had supported him before his nomination, but when party leaders discovered divisions among the Democrats, the Whig leadership rallied and Garrett's strength with voters diminished. He guessed he would be defeated by a slim margin but told Malony he did not care a whit and would not spend a dime campaigning.[81]

He was surprised and gratified when he won, garnering nearly 51 percent of the vote in a three-way race in which Kinzie took 43 percent and the Liberty Party received 6 percent. He felt quite vindicated after the pall that had caused him to resign in 1844. He bragged to an associate that he had "licked out the Whigs, Abolitionists, and fag end of the Democratic party." In his inaugural address, he suggested that the people had elected him because "they entertained an undiminished confidence that my abilities and energies would be honestly, faithfully, and efficiently devoted to the promotion of the best interests of our already important and rapidly increasing city." He also spoke generously of Kinzie, calling him "deservedly one of the most popular and respected among our citizens." The rest of his inaugural address was a lengthy dissertation on a variety of subjects, from concerns about revenues and what to do about erosion of the harbor to contentions over wharfing privileges along the river and the newly built high school building.[82]

The Common Council was dominated nine to three by Democrats. Yet no sooner was he ensconced in his mayoral duties than a very public row with J. Young Scammon, an Ogden intimate, led him to another dramatic resignation, which he then took back. Details of the altercation do not survive, but it appears to have had something to do with a newly completed school building.[83]

The schoolhouse, a very large facility in the First Ward, had been proposed by the Committee on Schools, chaired by Ira Miltimore. First Ward alderman J. Young Scammon had championed the project, and the school was built during Mayor Sherman's term. The idea was for younger students to receive instruction on the lower floor, with the upper story being given over to high school instruction. During construction, however, when the rest of the city got a better notion of its size and cost, popular sentiment shifted. Although the edifice provided the city's very first high school, it was convenient only for students in the First Ward and cost a whopping $7,500. People branded the building "Miltimore's Folly," and its unpopularity may explain why Sherman did not run for office a second time.[84]

Garrett pointed out the chief points against the use of the building for a school and proposed that the city sell it for six thousand dollars and distribute the proceeds to four districts for smaller schools. He also joked that the school might be converted into an insane asylum to house those who had urged spending public money on it. It was a thoughtless remark, and Scammon, listening to it as a newly elected alderman, no doubt took offense. Bad feelings boiled over at a council meeting toward the end of April, words were exchanged, and Garrett, feeling mistreated, made his dramatic show of resigning. In the end, the Common Council decided not to sell the building, and the "big school-schoolhouse" lived on.[85]

So did Garrett's wisecrack. Although removed from the published version of his address, it survived anecdotally, thanks to Scammon, as Garrett's only opinion on schools, as though he had seriously proposed turning the school into a mental hospital and lacked any vision for education.[86]

In fact, schools were very much an interest of Garrett's administration in his second term. A June petition for a school was granted for District 4. A two-story building, constructed at the corner of LaSalle Street and Ohio, cost four thousand dollars and was occupied by January 1846. Yet funding for schools in the rapidly growing city was otherwise scarce. The city had been depending on the school fund and a school tax to finance schools. The school fund was nearly depleted, however, and the State of Illinois had recently made the school tax illegal through its legislation of taxation limits on municipalities. At his final council meeting, Garrett heard a petition from the Committee on Schools, which wanted the city to build a school in District 8 as soon as possible but lacked resources.

Meanwhile, frustration about inadequate provision of public schools in the growing city was leading citizens to petition to build their own schools.[87]

The recent Illinois tax law prevented the city from imposing any additional taxes for city repairs and improvements. Yet the city continued to impose special assessments for sidewalks on the grounds that these were not taxes, a theory that was tested and affirmed several years later by the Illinois Supreme Court. As for streets, the city paid for their construction and improvement through general taxes, including a citizen's labor requirement. The municipal charter gave the city the power to tax personal and real property for "lighting the city streets, supporting a night watch, making and repairing streets and bridges, and paying the operating expenses." The charter also required each male citizen to contribute three days' labor to build and maintain streets, and refusers had to pay the equivalent as a fine. An 1839 ordinance specified the fine as three dollars, applicable to males twenty-two through fifty-nine years of age. Garrett wanted this fine reduced but did not prevail. (The reduction was not made until the 1847 revision of the charter, which specified the fine as fifty cents a day and made it applicable to a person only for streets in his own ward.)[88]

Besides schools, many other matters demanded Garrett's and the council's attention at their weekly meetings, requiring him to call special sessions throughout the year to get everything done. A brick-making business was taking sand from City Cemetery on the theory that it was not public ground. People were cutting holes in the river ice, whether for fishing or refrigeration, causing the council to pass an ordinance to control the practice and ensure public safety. The city had not yet constructed a waterworks to bring lake water into the city but now ordered the construction of aqueducts to siphon river water, assessing the cost to property owners who also had to pay to run pipes from an aqueduct to their property. The owners protested the primary assessment.[89]

In his inaugural Garrett had complained of the previous administration's expenditure of $2,918 on lakeshore protection, suggesting that the city might as well have spent the equivalent by throwing salt into the lake to make an inland sea. He also thought the United States Congress should be paying for any harbor improvements to protect the lakeshore, inasmuch as "our harbor is used as a great national highway." Now he changed his tune. Michigan Avenue, which at that time nearly abutted the beach, was under constant threat from the lake. In July the council authorized five residents to take action against encroachment by the lake waters, and the city approved a loan to construct a breakwater. After bids were taken for the breakwater, Garrett signed a city contract with Benjamin Tibbits to build the structure—a five-hundred-foot extension of the existing breakwater (which was in front of the public square). The specifications given by the Committee on Streets and Bridges called for the barrier to be a crib six feet wide, built of oak timbers, iron spikes, and stone, which would rise one or two feet above the lake surface and be reinforced by pilings set within the outside timbers of the crib at intervals of fifteen feet. By November 22nd Tibbits and his crew, who were by then glad to be done with the chilly waters of Lake Michigan, had completed the work at a cost of $1,700. The city imposed special assessments on lakefront property owners to pay back the loan. The owners protested with petitions and lawsuits, and the following year the city began refunding the monies collected.[90]

Water was not the only thing making encroachments on city property. Discarded wood, barrels, and bricks, as well as various household and business articles impeded traffic on streets and sidewalks. Garbage and dead animals were dumped in vacant lots and alleyways. The stench of rotting flesh and other offal led one paper to dub Chicago "a City of pestiferous odour." There was also a problem of mud and stagnant water, which became favorite dump sites for discarded animal carcasses. The city had not yet dealt with its geographical location in a lowland—part swamp, part tentatively dry land. In March the Common Council debated whether to fill a slough at the foot of Wabash Street and enacted an ordinance to ensure uniform slope to sidewalks as an aid to drainage.[91]

Garrett also pressed the council to take public health more seriously. The city's board of health had been meeting only sporadically, and the council had been largely ignoring its reports. As mayor, Garrett chaired the board and saw to it both that the board reports were heeded and the city health ordinances enforced. He also urged the construction of a new hospital, or "pest house," and the council immediately appointed a special committee to make a report on the subject. Bids to build the hospital were taken in early April, and the structure was up and ready for interior plastering by April 25.[92]

The hospital was called a pest house because persons with communicable diseases such as small pox were quarantined there. In fact, it was a recent report of a few cases of small pox that prompted Garrett to make city health his first priority. Just weeks into office he issued a proclamation encouraging vaccination:

PROCLAMATION

Whereas there have been two recent cases of Small Pox in our city, removed to the pest house, and three more cases believed to be small pox; and whereas, in my opinion, it will generally spread throughout the city unless every precaution is used by our citizens generally, to guard against. . . . I would therefore earnestly recommend *every person* that has not been vaccinated for a number of years to get vaccinated *immediately, without delay.* . . . The poor, who are unable to pay for vaccination, will be vaccinated gratis by Dr. Smith, by calling at his office, 134 Lake Street. —AUGUSTUS GARRETT, Mayor. Chicago, March 28, 1845.[93]

Cemeteries situated near the lake also posed health risks, although most of the concern about them had to do with respect for the dead, not sanitation problems resulting from corpses being buried in city land with a high water table. Public meetings about cemetery conditions had been held in 1842 after heavy rains brought ruptured coffins to the surface. The newspapers expressed the public's outrage against the spectacle of "bones bleaching on the lakeshore," and former mayor Benjamin Raymond was criticized for not seeing to it that the cemetery was fenced. During his first term as mayor, Garrett's Common Council had the fence erected, and Garrett had meant to do more, mentioning in his second inaugural the "depredations by the disinterment of bodies . . . in the grossest violation of private feeling as well as public decency." He was referring to grave robbing. In his second term, when erosion was damaging a different, older cemetery, Garrett insisted on an ordinance requiring the city sexton to notify the mayor whenever shifting sand or some other cause exposed coffins in "the Old Burying Ground."[94]

There were moments of levity. Among various matters in connection with animals, living and dead, the council was asked to deal with a problem of wild geese on the city walkways and thoroughfares. A group of petitioners demanded action:

To the Honorable, the Members of the Common Council of the City of Chicago, Ill.

As you have begun the good work of removing nuisances, we would call your attention to what your Petitioners consider one of the greatest.

We find of late a number of Flocks of Geese parading the streets and using especially the sidewalks for a common Highway. And, as the old Proverb holds true, that they eat all before them and poison all behind them, and moreover are the Nastiest of all Creatures. We would pray your honorable Body that they receive from your hands no Quarter, but that you dispose of them in a summary manner. And as in duty bound, we with all good Citizens will ever pray till said nuisance be removed.

Faced with fifteen earnest signers, the council responded immediately with a tongue-in-cheek ordinance requiring that the owner of any goose collected by the pound keeper pay a fine of twelve cents for said goose, plus pound fees. If there were owners of geese, theirs were not the wild geese trooping down the town streets.[95]

The old canard of the bridge wars about threats of a British invasion came back in a new version toward the end of Garrett's term. The United States and Great Britain had been governing the Oregon Territory in an uneasy and ill-defined partnership. Expansionist talk by the incoming Polk administration provoked fears of war with Britain. Chicagoans worried that the British would invade from Canada and take control of their city. That prospect may not have been likely, but war with Britain was not inconceivable. Less than a generation ago—when Garrett was in his teens—the two nations had engaged in a full-fledged military conflict. Although most of the military clashes in the War of 1812 were confined to the seas and southern states, the British had made an incursion from Canada into New York State toward the end of the hostilities, getting as far as Plattsburgh on Lake Champlain, where U.S. forces met and defeated them. John Wentworth recalled that the British had also surprised American troops at Mackinaw toward the end of that war, and he gave a speech to the House of Representatives during the national debate about Oregon, demanding action to strengthen the fortifications of Mackinaw. Otherwise, there would be "no hope for our Lake Michigan towns."[96]

By January of 1846 concerns about British invasion from the north were still resonant, perhaps heightened by worries that the conflict with Mexico made the nation even more vulnerable to British invasion from the north. Garrett called a citizens' meeting at the courthouse on January 8 "to take into consideration the best method of defending our city in case of war." The meeting was cancelled for what may have been a lack of real concern, but then a few days later Wentworth wrote from Washington, expressing fears of a British incursion from Canada.[97]

As his term in office ended, Garrett had the satisfaction of knowing that, for a second time, he had proven a capable city executive. He had helped reduce the crushing municipal debt by continuing to pare city expenditures and by renegotiating terms with the city's New York creditors; he had overseen the addition of needed infrastructure and public schools; and he had taken city health in hand. By mid-March he was happily out of office and free from public duties.

Yet by summer he was engaged in public matters again, this time as a private citizen. Newspapers in Chicago were reporting "barbaric scenes ... of daily occurrence on the frontier of Texas." When the Polk administration asked governors to raise troops to enforce U.S. interests in its border dispute with Mexico, Garrett responded by subscribing "an unlimited amount" of money for uniforms to clothe the first Chicago company. Apparently, the federal government had not allocated funds for uniforms or even equipment, although there was an assumption that citizens who paid for such things would eventually be reimbursed. A second Chicago company was formed through subscription as well, and when the governor requested yet another company from Chicago, Garrett advanced more money to equip them. He succeeded in recruiting fifty-eight men, but that number fell short of the full requirement of "sixty-four privates, eight non-commissioned [officers], three commissioned officers, and two musicians."[98]

Garrett had once declared to Seaman that he intended "to do something to relieve the oppressed"—meaning he wanted to help defend what was then the Republic of Texas against repossession by Mexico. He had even told Seaman not to be surprised to hear that he had gone off to war. But now, in the summer of 1846 and out of office, he did not contemplate joining a fighting unit. He was forty-five years old and in dubious health, worse than he knew.[99]

CHAPTER 6

THEIR SEPARATE SPHERES

"You know I don't want it extensively large . . . say large enough for thirty persons." Augustus was writing about his dining set in a letter to his cousin John Seaman on December 28, 1843. The Garretts were "going to housekeeping" in the spring.[1]

It was Eliza's idea. Now that her husband was a well-known politician, people expected her to entertain. For example, on New Year's Day, just three days away, Governor Ford would visit Chicago, and Mayor Garrett would receive him. But where? In the Garretts' little parlor at the Sauganash? Were they not to have a supper with other guests? Where was that to take place? Surely not in the Sauganash dining hall with other boarders traipsing in and out? Eliza felt embarrassed. She was the wife of the city's chief executive and could not even entertain properly. In the end, Augustus took the governor and Thomas Dyer on a carriage ride. Eliza was not included.[2]

Eliza had been pressing for a house for some time. Augustus kept promising and putting her off. He was too busy, he would say, and he was cash poor. A solid, well-built house with all the architectural fineries—the sort of place the other businessmen of Chicago had built for themselves—would be expensive. If he constructed a house in the current market, he would have to sell depressed real estate at a loss in order to finance the project. Yet he was now doing just that. And he would not even benefit as a purchaser from fallen real estate values because he already owned the lot he planned to build on.[3]

Contemplating his house, Augustus could not help but think of the man he regarded as his nemesis—William Ogden. When Ogden first settled in Chicago, he, too, took up residence in the Sauganash, but only briefly. Soon he was constructing an elegant home on the north side, bringing in an eastern architect who arrived with plans and finishing materials—windows, stair railings, and trimmings. The completed structure was a large double house with a broad pillared veranda, facing Ontario Street and surrounded by maple, cottonwood, ash, cherry, birch, and hickory trees. Ogden had a greenhouse for table flowers and fruit houses for grapes, peaches, apricots, and figs. All in all the mansion cost him ten thousand dollars. The Garretts heard about this house but may never have laid eyes on it. They were implicitly excluded from genteel social life on the north side, and Augustus likely regarded Ogden and the other north-siders as snobs.[4]

The Garrett house was to be on Franklin Street. Garrett owned a lot on the east side of a triangular block, whose shape was the result of the curve of the river as it joined the main stem, causing South Water Street to cut across the block hypotenuse-like. Thus, the Garrett house would stand just northeast of the Sauganash, between Lake and South Water, and within easy walking distance of the Methodist church at Clark and Washington and the Garrett & Seaman building at 147 South Water.[5]

They built a brick house with stone finishings at 12 Franklin. Garrett ordered the stone and some "fashionable railings" from Seaman in New York. He also asked Seaman whether he could have the latter's old doors now that Seaman had replaced them with new mahogany doors in his Manhattan house. Garrett did not need anything so lavish as mahogany doors, he explained, and hoped to save money by building his house to fit Seaman's doors. He also told Seaman "to keep on the lookout if you can purchase some articles second handed such as are not soiled." Did he mean furniture, rugs, and curtains? Perhaps "second handed" applied to the dinnerware he instructed Seaman to buy: "a set of silver plated castors, some butter knives and salt spoons, mustard spoons, and also a dining and tea set of knives and forks of the most fashionable kind (if you get silver forks a dozen will be enough)."[6]

Eliza had no say in choosing even the tableware, as is clear from the way Augustus thought out loud in his letter and allowed Seaman discretion in the purchases. "Perhaps the forks had better be silver," Augustus mused, telling Seaman, "I will leave that for you to judge, but not German silver." He wanted his cousin to purchase the articles "wherever you can get them cheap on account of my influence." He then remembered washbasins and chamber pots for the bedrooms. "You may get me also four ewers and basins together with chambers of a good fashionable quality. Let them be tolerably nice." Augustus did not want to purchase "extravagant articles" until he had considered all the possibilities for more economical expenditures. He consented to adding a greenhouse so that Eliza could have cut-flowers year-round.[7]

She was eager for her bedding and linens to be sent from New York. Those precious personal articles, which she and her mother had sewn and embroidered before she married, had been stowed away in her parents' house for the last fourteen years. Augustus wrote to his brother-in-law, Frederick Flaglor, asking him to ship Eliza's things. Although Frederick was at least six years his senior, Augustus assumed his usual imperious air in giving other people instructions. "I want you to go to New Burgh and purchase a dry goods box and pack up Eliza's bedding and linens," he wrote. Frederick was to "line the box on the bottom and the sides with some of the coarse things," then "send it to John H. Seaman, New York, and he will send it immediately to us with some of the merchants' goods." The box would go to Seaman by boat, and Frederick was to "find someone on the boat to NY that you can put the box in charge of," or "you can get the captain to." Then he was to "go to Aunt Drake's and inform them that you have sent a box for John to forward to me."[8]

Aunt Drake was Susannah Drake, wife of New York physician Charles Drake and sister of Eustatia Morgan, Augustus's mother. John Seaman had married the Drakes' daughter Anne, making John and Augustus cousins by marriage. Augustus occasionally sent greetings to Aunt Drake, jokingly proposing in one epistle that he "would very much like to have her for my financier" and would take her advice "in any of my business transactions."[9]

They were in their new home by the second week of April and now turned their attention to papering the walls and furnishing the rooms. They purchased a horsehair sofa. Augustus's nephew Thomas, now living in Chicago and working as a furniture maker, was busy crafting tables and chairs. They "fixed up" a guest room and hoped the Seamans would pay them a visit. It was a sore point. The Garretts made trips to New York almost every year. The Seamans had never come to Chicago. Now that he could host the Seamans in his own large home, Augustus believed they would come and wrote to John about it: "I expect before this reaches New York to see John and wife here and if you have not as yet started I want you to immediately: if you wait to get ready you will never come." They did not come, but they sent the Garretts a pair of ottomans as a housewarming present.[10]

Augustus went to New York twice that summer on business, and he and Eliza made a New York trip in the fall. In addition to seeing the Seamans, they visited Aunt Drake, who persuaded them to take an orphan into their care. It seems she had rescued the youngster from the New York House of Refuge and—probably because she found him a handful—asked the Garretts to take him to Chicago. Back in Illinois, a week or so later, Augustus wrote Seaman an amusing letter about how the experiment had worked out. Master Edward Francis Heath, Esq., as Augustus referred to him, fell sick on the trip back. He and Eliza nursed him all the way home, hired "four doctors" to look at him, put him in a first-class seat, took him into their own stateroom on the steamship, and got up every hour of the night to give him medicine.[11]

The boy was better by the time they got home. They purchased him a new suit of clothes, decking him out "from head to toe," and gave him a servant's role in the house. He had "but one failing." He sweated. Especially at night. They made him a bed on the sofa, and he sweated the hair of the sofa. They put him in the garret, and he sweated even more there, soaking the bed. At this point, Augustus's narrative became fantastic. The boy perspired so much, he wrote, that copious droplets seeped onto the floor and streaked the walls below. "It run down on our newly papered walls and it had a tendency to change the color. I don't think it done much injury, for it made a beautiful color itself. It was similar to what is called Chrome Yellow, and if it had went all around the room it would have made a very handsome border." He went on. "My wife awoke me and says, 'What is that dripping so on the carpet?' I listened and heard it drop, drop, drop. I knew it was Master Edward Francis Heath Esq.'s sweat, but I concluded to let her find it out herself. When it come morning she soon discovered what was the matter. So next night Sir Master Edward Francis Heath Esq. had his bed put in the little building in the yard. It did not seem to suit his Royal Highness. He got up in the morning and commenced blackening my boot, got one half done and then eloped." For three days Augustus searched high and low for Edward, learning eventually that the boy had hopped a wagon to Dixon. Augustus concluded his account by suggesting that next time Aunt Drake got a boy from the House of Refuge, she should be careful not to select one who sweated too much.[12]

* * *

The winter holidays found Eliza in cheerful spirits. She spent December purchasing gifts for friends, family, and the wives of Augustus's business associates. After Christmas and through New Year's Day, she received calls, and sometimes her parlor and front room were both full of visitors and dense with the scent of hyacinths. Gifts came in, among them a lovely birdcage and two canaries. She named one "Katie" after a friend, and Augustus named the other "Robe" after James R. Malony.[13]

Augustus was in a cheery mood, too, enjoying the fact that he had no more burdensome mayoral duties and was being flattered by his party: everyone wanted him to run again. Even in complaining to John Seaman about the latter's wordy letters, he used a lighthearted tone, calling him "St. John" after the biblical letter-writer. Eliza heard him dictating in the parlor to his clerk: "John F. Seaman, Esq. Dear Sir, I have received I presume all of St. John's Epistles to Augustus and they have been carefully examined." He finished by suggesting that if John had planted a hyacinth when he started his last letter, it would have bloomed before he finished writing.[14]

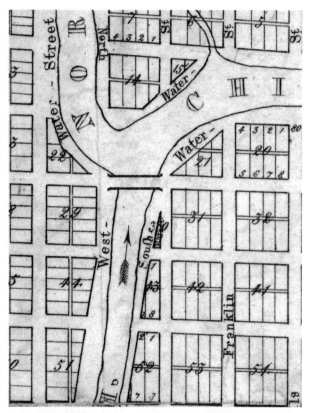

Detail from 1834 map by James S. Wright showing blocks 21 and 31 of the Old Town at Wolf Point, where the north and south branches of the Chicago River join the main stem (bridge added). Chicago History Museum, ICHi-034590, altered detail from figure 5.1.

Yet there were worries. On New Year's Day they had received a troubling letter from Eliza's father. It concerned the farm that Augustus's father had given him many years ago. In conveying title, John Garrett had retained a life interest for himself and Augustus's mother. Augustus had improved the farm and operated it but fell into debt and had to sell, realizing practically nothing for the farm because it was encumbered by the parental life-interest, which diminished its value. Eliza's father, Benoni Clark, subsequently purchased the farm as a kindness to Augustus but only after Augustus and Eliza had gone to Chicago. Over the years there had been talk of Augustus buying back the farm, but he had always begged off. Benoni eventually sold it to Eliza's brother Sam, who borrowed money to purchase it, securing a loan that required only interest payments for the term of the loan, the principal falling due when the term was up. Sam failed to keep up his interest payments, and the Clarks asked Augustus for help. At Eliza's urging, he had begun sending money each month to cover this expense. Now the Clarks wanted him to unburden the family by taking the farm off their hands.[15]

For two weeks, Eliza and Augustus talked about what to do. They were both angry with her brother Sam. Nearly a year ago he had made matters worse by persuading Eliza's father to purchase his failing mill, which Sam had also acquired on credit and run into the ground. In that case, Augustus had written to Jeremiah, Eliza's older brother, stating his opinion about Sam's actions and using the occasion to express his own inflated sense of self-righteousness. He told "Jerry" that what Sam had done was "such an ungenerous, unfeeling, unjust, unchristianlike, unnatural, unkind of transaction that I dare not give way to my feelings to write freely on the subject." But he did write freely. "God knows my own heart. Rather than to have done such a thing with an aged father, I would rather been stripped of everything I had in the world & worked on my knees for six cents a day, nearly enough for me to purchase me one meal a day of the worst kind." Augustus then framed the matter in theological terms. "The all wise providence," he opined, had caused Sam to lose his worldly goods "in consequence of his cheating others," and "his own heart will tell him what he has lost." Augustus "always knew" that Sam "never would prosper, that he would only flourish for a season; & so it has turned out. Only I think he has not got to the end of it yet, and the noble act you have done in putting a stop to it will always make you prosper. It cannot be otherwise. I would write more on the subject but I cannot give vent to my feelings."[16]

Thus was the moral high-mindedness of Augustus when it did not cost him any money. But now, faced with the most recent chapter of this family drama, he was resisting Eliza's pressure to do what seemed obvious to her—buy the farm to relieve her father, who was innocent of all the troublemaking. She understood that Augustus did not have cash reserves anywhere near $2,000, but she saw no alternative. She also felt helpless. She had no power over any of the money that Augustus had made over the years or the properties he had acquired, including those he had put in her name. She could do nothing for her father except try to persuade her husband to do something for him.

As for Augustus, although he had claimed he would rather labor on his knees for six cents a day than injure an aged father, he now cast the plight of Benoni solely in financial terms and the adverse effects on himself. He probably did not show Eliza the letter he wrote to her parents explaining this. If he had bought the farm for $2,000 nine years ago as they had wished, he told them, and had borrowed the money to do it, the interest and principal over those nine years would have amounted to $4,160 for a farm he did not want. That burden would have ruined him in Chicago for any recovery after his losses in Cincinnati, and "you would always have been sorry" to have caused that. As for buying the farm now, "it has not been so convenient," he explained, "for me to pay at any time as you have anticipated, although I have accumulated a large amount of property. You cannot dispose of it in a new country for cash at any time & all times without a great sacrifice, and I don't believe that you would have been willing to see me sell property worth $10,000 to pay $2000 and then could not enjoy the $2000, after I paid it." He was certain "your affections are different from that towards us." Nor would they want him to borrow money, when loans cost 12 percent interest. He then told them what he would do. "I have a place," he said, "within three miles of this city that is worth at least $3000. I was offered $1500 for it a few days since & I understand that the man still wants it. I will sell it for the money and pay it to you for the farm, provided you will deed it to my wife." He then added melodramatically that if he could not sell the property he had just mentioned, he would "sell our furniture to raise it."[17]

It was an odd letter and revealed Augustus torn between his image of himself as a generous man and the avarice that made him slow to sell property at a loss even in a family emergency. There was no need to have gone into such detail about the finances of the thing, but he had felt compelled to explain why he was sending them only $1,500. He wanted them to know the sacrifice it cost him. But to the Clarks, farmers used to living close to the bone, their wealthy son-in-law's emphasis on the loss to him when they were the ones in need must have sounded hollow and unfeeling.

From a financial standpoint, however, everything he said was factually true, even if a bigger man would have kept his money difficulties to himself. He was often short on cash, and both Eliza's and his own relations periodically asked for financial help. He was not always able to help immediately. Less than a year ago, he had written to his sister to assure her that he would send money he had promised. "After I get through some affairs," he explained, "I will help you out of debt but I have so many things to do that I cant do everything at once." In other words, since he could not simply write a check but would have to sell property, he could not act immediately. At that time, he had also been worried that he would have to begin sending money to his mother as well, if she did not start getting her widow's pension for her husband's service in the Revolutionary War. Now, nine months later, economic conditions in Chicago were bad, comparable in some ways to the terrible year of 1837, with businesses and banks failing almost every day. Notes owed to Garrett & Seaman, and some on which they were guarantors, fell due without payment from insolvent creditors. While Augustus was deciding how to handle the request from the Clarks, he and Seaman were negotiating settlement of a bad debt with a Chicago store that ended up costing them $2,000. In fact, it was only three months ago that a cash-strapped Augustus had left his horse and buggy with a Galena merchant, asking him to sell it for him because he was "very much in want of money." And as for the land and buildings he owned, Chicago real estate values had in fact plummeted and now typically fetched only half their original purchase price. Hence, he was not exaggerating when he told the Clarks that the buyer to which he referred was willing to pay only $1,500 for a property originally worth $3,000. Nor was he exaggerating when he said that money could not be borrowed at less than 12 percent. Just a month earlier he had written to the State Bank of Indiana at Michigan City, hoping to get short-term business loans there for less than the standard 12 percent rate in Chicago.[18]

Augustus's suggestion that, as a last resort, he would sell their furniture was partly a noble gesture and partly a selfish wish. He and Eliza were both tired of maintaining a house. Now, a year after building it, they were thinking about selling and taking up residence in a hotel in New York

City. There they could enjoy a decent urban life and be just a short trip from their family on the Hudson.[19]

* * *

A move to New York would require renegotiation or termination of Augustus's business arrangement with John Seaman, which depended on Augustus's presence in Chicago. The business partnership had seemed attractive to Augustus when he was trying to weather the national depression into which the country descended after the Panic of 1837. Recovery had been slow. By January of 1840 nearly 90 percent of banks had suspended operations or gone under. In 1841 nine states defaulted, and Illinois was almost one of them. In June of 1842, when outgoing secretary of the U.S. Navy, James Kirk Paulding, traveled up the Illinois River, he found people everywhere "complaining of hard times." Farmers no longer had markets for their cash crops and livestock. "All wish to sell and no one cares to buy," Paulding noted. As he continued north past Peru, he saw the effects of the collapsed land market. Some newly minted hamlets had a few residents, others "nothing but a name and a lithographic map to demonstrate their existence." People "had been precipitated from the summit of hope to the lowest abyss of debt and depression." In Chicago the hotels were almost empty, and city residents were struggling to find purchasers for their goods and services.[20]

Augustus had soldiered on after ending his partnership with Nathaniel Brown. Having invested almost all his earnings in land and other real estate, he was rich in real property and nearly debt-free, but cash-poor. This meant that when the economy collapsed, his losses were mostly on paper. Yet he was not in a position to take advantage of the drop in land prices, as Ogden and Bronson had done, because, unlike them, he had no way to finance real estate endeavors except to borrow money, which he was loath to do.

Yet he was compelled to secure business loans. After the Panic of 1837, auctioneering was no longer a vibrant business, and many who rented space in his buildings could not pay. Augustus had turned his energies toward developing a general commission business, but trade was slow, and he was not always able to remain solvent. To hang on to his real estate until conditions improved, he borrowed modest sums of money, and he and Eliza lived frugally. Until 1845, when they finally built their house, they lived at the Sauganash, their room and board being paid as offsets to what the manager owed on the lease, and they did without luxuries. This was the period when Augustus was "often short of change," "was wont to send back to his laundress to be rewashed the shirts he could not redeem," and sold his horse and buggy in Galena to raise a bit of cash.[21]

By the time of the Galena trip, things should have been looking up. A year earlier he had started three new businesses, all of them partnerships with Seaman. Their enterprises began with marine and fire insurance. Seaman's idea had been to form partnerships as joint agents of the Atlantic and the National Insurance Companies, which Seaman already represented, and to sell insurance in Chicago. They came to an agreement in the fall of 1843. Several months later, they entered into a second partnership to take advantage of Augustus's commission business in Chicago. The plan was to serve as consignment merchants. Augustus would take orders in Chicago for New York merchandise that John would ship west through the waterways, and John would take orders in New York for goods of the North-West that Augustus would ship east by the same routes.[22]

The arrangement was almost scuttled when John heard rumors that Augustus was not the prosperous businessman he claimed to be but rather was broke, with legal judgments against him in three states. Garrett said these were malicious lies of his competitors, whose purpose was to induce his creditors to call in their loans. He suspected that Ogden and Bronson were in the background somewhere, spreading falsehoods about him. Whatever the sources of the rumors, they had caused a certain Mr. Hallett to believe that Garrett was insolvent and that he had made phony representations about the collateral behind certain loans Hallett had made to him. Hallett sued for return of the principal on his promissory notes, and Garrett was compelled to swear out an affidavit of surety, stating that he was worth $70,000. He assured Seaman that this affidavit was on file with the state supreme court.[23]

Seaman's worries were allayed and the partnership proceeded, but from the beginning there had been frictions between the two men. John began purchasing goods in New York without first asking Augustus whether there was a ready market for them in Chicago. "I think it best," Augustus wrote tactfully, "not to purchase any more goods on our account without first consulting me on the subject, unless you hit upon some *extra* bargains, as I can at all times give you any information you may wish." John obliged by writing him long repetitive letters full of minutiae that began to grate on Augustus. He needled John in a wry response. "I left Chicago on the

4th of January. I went to every important town, traveling between ten and twelve hundred miles. I arrived at home day before yesterday and found I had quite as long a journey to undertake, nothing [less] than to travel through nine of your long letters." Although the two men were the same age, Augustus often spoke to John as if he were a junior partner. "There is one fault in your communications," Augustus informed him. "You occupy a great deal of time in explaining many things when a boy seven years old could comprehend the most of the explanations." There was more. "For God's sake in all letters hereafter do not mention Furs, Beeswax, or Ginseng again. Should I be so successful as to get as many skins as you have mentioned furs in your different letters, I could clothe the whole Russian Army with furs and retire with a fortune off the profits of the same." As regards beeswax, "you have mentioned it as many times as there are bees in a bee hive. I have read it so often that I can hear a continual buzzing in my ears." And "were the Chinese as numerous as you have written ginseng in your former letters I am sure Great Britain never could have succeeded in conquering them. I do not know the precise number of the Chinese nation, but there is one thing I do know—that you have mentioned ginseng as many times as there are Chinese."[24]

He adopted a more deferential tone with John Brouwer, president of the National Insurance Company, but he did not hesitate to instruct Brouwer about how the fire insurance business operated in Chicago. The National had a policy of not insuring leased properties, probably because they assumed that lessees tended not to take care of their properties with the same care exercised by owners. Garrett asked Brouwer to reconsider that policy, telling him that most real estate in Chicago was leased and that "some of our best men wish to be insured but are debarred on account of them being on leased premises." Other insurance companies in Chicago did insure leased properties, Augustus mentioned, and he himself had inadvertently written some $650 in such policies but hoped Brouwer would see the advantage to the company. He also requested greater authority to write policies according to his own judgment of risks, rather than have to seek prior approval from the home office. Seeking permission in advance caused delay—all communications with New York had to be done by mail—which cost the company lost business when other insurance firms acted more quickly.[25]

Augustus also had to allay Brouwer's worry that proprietors might take out insurance policies and then burn their buildings. Augustus explained that buildings in Chicago were in such demand that people moved them from one location to another. Indeed, there was hardly a day that one did not see a building being rolled on logs down the street. A man had no reason to torch his building for lack of buyers, but many Chicago merchants were unwilling to insure their stock without insuring their buildings.[26]

As for the new Garrett & Seaman General Agency and Commission Store, Garrett soon realized that there was no reason why it could not service dry-goods stores along the riverways of northern Illinois. His initial inspiration may have been a payment from Bracken & Tuller, a Chicago store unable to make good on its note. The firm gave Garrett merchandise in lieu of cash, and Augustus took this merchandise to Dixon on the Rock River, where he purchased a store. He then formed a partnership with an associate named G. G. Stearns and John's younger brother Willett Seaman, who had been working in Chicago as a clerk for Bracken & Tuller. These two would operate the Dixon store as an agent of Garrett & Seaman, and since Rock River was a tributary of the Mississippi River, this new Garrett, Seaman & Stearns outfit could, in theory, supply not only Dixon and surrounding farmers but other river towns along the waterways.[27]

Augustus also sought to expand the Garrett-Seaman insurance business. The Chicago insurance market was rather saturated, so he made long excursions by horse and buggy to towns throughout northern Illinois and southern Wisconsin. At one point, frustrated that business was lagging and feeling himself overworked, he told Seaman that he was going to "purchase a horse, saddle, and bridle and employ a competent person to go to almost every town in the State and Territory and give them letters to some competent person in each town to give him information in relation to every merchant." Augustus guessed this would take a good two and a half months at a cost of $200. He was probably not factoring in the cost of the horse, since it could be sold upon return, but only the expenses of hosteling for the horse and the clerk. It shows the breadth of Augustus's professional network that he thought he could get letters of introduction to businessmen or city officials in all those places, some familiar to him from his own travels, others not. He does not reveal whether he found a clerk willing to slog through the cold and snow of Wisconsin and downstate Illinois on a horse, drumming up insurance business, but he probably did. Times were tough.[28]

JOHN MURPHY, United States Hotel; the subscriber would respectfully announce to his old friends and the public generally, that he has returned to his old and popular stand, where he hopes, by unremitted attention to the comfort and welfare of his guests, to receive that share of their patronage that his exertions may merit. The house has been thoroughly renovated, cleansed, and painted, with a good yard and barn attached, the rooms are airy, pleasant, and agreeable; his bar will be supplied with the choicest wines and liquors, his table with all the substantials and delicacies of the season, his servants attentive and obedient, and he pledges himself that nothing shall be wanting to render their stay pleasant and comfortable. Chicago, Jan. 1, 1844.

L. M. OSTERHOUDT, Sauganash Hotel, corner of Lake and Market sts., Chicago, Ill.; farmers will find the best accommodation for their teams.

D. L. ROBERTS, Chicago Temperance House, LaSalle Street, nearly opposite the [State] bank building, Chicago, Ill.

SKINNER & SMITH, Mansion House, 84 and 86 Lake Street, Chicago, Ill.; baggage taken to and from steamboats free of charge.

THOMAS & WHEELOCK, the Washington Coffee-House, Lake Street, third door east of the Tremont House; this entirely new and splendid house has been fitted up by the proprietors in the most modern and approved style; the bill of fare will embrace every variety to be procured in this and eastern markets; hot meals can be had at all hours; fresh oysters kept constantly on hand. The proprietors pledge themselves that nothing shall be wanting on their part to give their customers entire satisfaction.

INSURANCE COMPANIES.

A. GARRETT, agent, Marine and Inland Insurance, agency of the Atlantic Mutual Insurance Company of the city of New York in the City of Chicago; cash capital, $100,000; with notes subscribed on the Mutual plan for $350,000; total, $450,000. Persons wishing to participate in the profits of this company, are informed that the company is now prepared to make insurance on marine and inland risks, on terms favorable to the applicants, who are assured that the company will be disposed to settle claims with such promptness and liberality as to warrant a large share of the public patronage; the board of trustees have endeavored to furnish the insured the means both of safety and profit, and they trust that when the plan for accomplishing this is investigated it will be found satisfactory. Under the charter of the company the excess of certificates of earnings over $500,000 can be paid off successively, which is a result that will be looked for in a reasonable time. Trustees: Walter R. Jones, Josiah L. Hale, George Griswold, Jonathan Goodhue, Elisha Riggs, Henry Parish, Thomas Tileston, Henry Coit, Charles H. Russell, E. D. Hurlbut, Jos. W. Alsop, jr., John C. Green, William S. Wetmore, Augustin Averil, Samuel T. Jones, Lowell Holbrook, P. A. Hargous, Edward H. Gillilan, Meyer Gana, Wm. C. Pickersgill, Geo. T. Elliot, James McCall, Ramsay Crooks, Edwin Bartlett, Caleb Barstow, A. P. Pillot, A. LeMoyne, Leonardo S. Suarez, Christopher R. Robert, Richard T. Haines, Leory M. Wiley, Edmund Laffan, Daniel S. Miller, S. T. Nicoll, William F. Havemeyer, Josiah Lane, Joshua J. Henry, William Sturgis, jr., Reuel Smith, A. A. Low; Walter R. Jones, president; Joshua L. Hale, vice-president. December, 1843.

Augustus Garrett insurance ad in 1843 Fergus/Norris city directory.
Chicago History Museum, Fergus' Historical Series, ICHi-176173, cropped.

A. GARRETT, agent, Fire and Marine Insurance, agency of the National Insurance Company of the City of New York in the City of Chicago. The above-named company have established an agency in the City of Chicago where they are prepared to insure against loss or damage by fire, and also against loss or damage on goods and merchandize in the course of transportation on the lakes, canal, or railroad. Directors: William G. Ward, John Bower, Stephen Holt, Philip W. Engs, Wm. S. Slocum, Wm. W. Campbell, John F. Mackie, Marcus Spring, Jacob Miller, John Newhouse, Samuel S. Doughty, John F. Butterworth; John Brouwer, president; James W. Savage, Secretary. December, 1843.

GARRETT & SEAMAN, general agency and commission store, in the four-story brick building on South-Water Street, 2d door from Clark Street. The undersigned give notice that they have formed a partnership, to commence on the 1st of May, 1844, under the name and style of Garrett & Seaman, for the transaction of a general agency and commission business, both in Chicago and New York. They will attend to the purchase and sale of merchandise and the sale of wheat, and all kinds of produce in the city of New York; Mr. Seaman is a resident of the city of New York, and well acquainted with the business of purchasing and selling merchandise and produce, and will at all times give his personal attention to any and all kinds of business entrusted to his care; the house in Chicago will be ready to supply country merchants with all kinds of merchandise at New-York prices, adding transportation only. N. B.—Constantly on hand, marble mantels, tombs, monuments, head-stones, table tops, etc.; they will on application furnish articles in the above line at short notice. December, 1843.

G. S. HUBBARD, agent, Ætna Insurance Company of Hartford, Conn.; this well-known company is now prepared to take risks against fire in the City of Chicago and its vicinity at low premiums.

GEORGE SMITH & CO., bankers and insurance brokers, (bank building), LaSalle Street, Chicago, Ill.

E. S. & J. WADSWORTH, agents, Hartford Fire-Insurance Company, 113 Lake Street, Chicago.

JEWELLERS, ETC.

V. FALLER, clock and watch maker, Dearborn Street, near the Tremont House, Chicago, Ill.

S. J. SHERWOOD, 144 Lake Street, Chicago, Ill., general dealer in gold and silver watches, clocks, jewelry, gold safety-chains, gold fob-chains, gold spectacles, thimbles, pencil cases, breast pins, finger rings, silver spoons, music boxes, card cases, pocket brushes, needles; watches and clocks repaired and warranted; cash paid for old silver.

LAND AGENTS.

HENRY W. CLARKE, general land-agent, office on Clark Street, opposite City Saloon, Chicago, Ill. Will promptly attend to the payment of taxes in Illinois and Wisconsin; redemption of land sold for taxes, etc., etc.

OGDEN & JONES, northwestern land-agency, general land-agents for the northwestern states and territories, office on Kinzie Street, east of North Dearborn, Chicago, Ill. William B. Ogden, William E. Jones.

Augustus Garrett insurance ad and Garrett & Seaman General Agency and Commission Store ad in 1843 Fergus/Norris city directory. Chicago History Museum, Fergus' Historical Series, ICHi-176174, cropped.

He also tried other strategies. One was to offer insurance agencies to well-established businessmen in other cities in exchange for their business and their influence. He made such an appeal to one Alfred G. Courtenius. Garrett would provide him a "book of instructions" and some canceled policies as examples. In exchange, Courtenius would take insurance from Garrett on his spring and fall merchandise and would give letters to other merchants in his city, offering them a discount of 5 percent at Garrett & Seaman in New York when they "went East to purchase their goods." Businessmen paid for this kind of "influence," whether in cash or comparable reciprocation. In fact, Garrett's own arrangement with Seaman entailed a $1,500 yearly payment to Seaman for his influence. How this fit into their partnership is unclear, but it is likely that when they wrote up terms, Seaman made the argument that his influence in New York, a city thirty times the size of Chicago, was more valuable than Garrett's influence in his hometown.[29]

By November of 1844, Garrett and Seaman were representing three insurance companies—the National, the Atlantic, and the Mercantile—with sales commissions of about $5,000 a year between them. Their general agency and commission store, however, was not doing well. It was partly the times, partly themselves. The two men did not see eye to eye on many matters, most having to do with clients and associates. On top of that, Garrett was often frustrated by what he regarded as a lack of business acumen in Seaman. ("It is singular that you can't comprehend more than you do.") Seaman probably thought Augustus a braggart and know-it-all.[30]

The premise of the import-export business was that Garrett and Seaman need not take any capital risk. They did not own the merchandise or pay insurance on it. Those risks and costs belonged to the sellers. Garrett and Seaman simply took a commission on the various orders and sold insurance on the goods in transit. To facilitate sales, they also guaranteed the notes of some of the buyers or accepted joint risk with sellers on buyers' notes.[31]

As 1844 concluded, Seaman wrote optimistically that he expected they would clear $16,000 in profit for the year. Garrett doubted they would clear $8,000. The problem was debt that was uncollectable or only partially collectable. The western country was about to "burst up," he said. It was already happening. Over the last eighteen months, with demand for goods increasing as stores were established all over the North-West, eastern companies, sensing a boom, had eagerly extended credit to store owners who, in the end, could not pay or had never meant to pay. There were now "at least three stores where one is needed," and even honest men were acting badly because "honest men cannot compete in the same town with those who never intend to pay." Augustus said he would be happy to take fifty cents on the dollar for the paper he and Seaman held.[32]

The news worsened. O'Donaghue & Marshall, a mercantile business with a reputation for excellent credit, collapsed. It seems that Garrett and Seaman had guaranteed one of the business's notes for $2,000 and would now have to sell other notes at a discount to raise cash to pay the debt. Over the course of several weeks, Garrett was able to work out an arrangement whereby he would take control of the company's stock of goods, auction it off, and pay the creditors sixty cents on the dollar. The loss meant that when their books were balanced for 1844, they would show a profit of only $5,000 for the year, less than a third of the $16,000 John had sunnily predicted.[33]

Augustus was tired of the partnership. His health was bad. He was weary of endless correspondence and paperwork. He and John were at odds over Garrett's business relations with friends in the North-West. He worried about money to pay his personal expenses. "Unless I find easier times," he wrote just days before he learned that O'Donaghue and Marshall would not be able to pay their note, "I will sell some property here in less than 6 months if it don't bring ¼ of its value." In the months since building and furnishing his house, he had been unable to replenish his savings. "This being rich without money is not what it's cracked up to be," he told John, and "I will go through another year and unless my health is better I shall retire and let you carry it through." He penned these words two days after receiving the letter from his father-in-law asking him to buy the farm.[34]

While contemplating an exit from his business partnership with Seaman, he was also lobbying for a position in government that paid a salary. With Democrat James K. Polk elected president and John Wentworth reelected to Congress, Garrett thought he could get a political appointment. Back in November he had hinted at this to Wentworth and in one letter had spoken frankly: "I will inform you that it is John Kinzie's office." He added, "It is expected by everyone that Dyer and myself is to have something. Let me say to you that valuable offices are of value to you and I think a Hint to the Wise is enough." Thomas Dyer was an influential Chicago businessmen and Democratic Party leader; John H. Kinzie, son of an original Chicago settler and fur trader, was the outgoing Whig register of the U.S. land office in Chicago, a post that paid $3,000 a year. A few weeks later Augustus wrote again, reminding Wentworth that he had supported him in his congressional election, which obligated Wentworth to give him something in return. "I have a claim on you for the receivership at this place," he said, telling Wentworth to "hold onto those two offices"—the receivership and postmaster—until he had se-cured them for Garrett and Dyer. Nothing happened, but in February he was still hoping for a position. In March he wrote to his best friend, Robe Malony, telling him that their mutual friend Dyer was a "dog" for not using his influence to help him get the land-register appointment. Malony would probably hear soon that Dyer got the receivership and a man named Jackson the register.[35]

In April he wrote to Polk himself, requesting that the new president "not make immediate appointments" to the offices of receiver and postmaster:

> Believing from your inaugural that you wish to be the President of the People, not to subserve the interest of a few political demagogues, has induced me to write you a few lines to defer the matter for the present. I am inclined to think that the interest and wishes of the citizens of Chicago should be looked to as well as the influence of our Senators from the Southern part of our state, who are living some three hundred miles from our city, and have scarce ever seen our flourishing city.

Augustus signed his letter as authoritatively as he could—"A. Garrett. Dem. Mayor of the City of Chicago." Not surprisingly, the president did not respond to this unsolicited advice, and in the end Augustus received no appointment. Dyer got the receivership, Jackson the register, and a man named Hart Stewart was reappointed postmaster.[36]

Besides his business woes, in March and April he was worried about Malony. Robe was sick in bed in St. Louis, and those who reported on his condition were doubtful he would recover. Augustus wrote to encourage him. He believed divine providence would see Robe through and advised, "Go to bed early. Don't you allow yourself to get excited on any occasion, and pour down the Sassaparilla without fail in large quantities." He was deeply attached to the younger man, "the best friend I have on earth," he told George Wilde. To Seaman he confided that if Robe died, "there will be no one alive on earth that I care a straw about." He was speaking hyperbolically, of course, since he had a wife and other friends and family that he did care about. But he felt closer to Robe than to any other person. Many nineteenth-century men formed similar friendships with each other, intimacies they felt to be deeper than those they shared with their wives.[37]

Garrett dissolved his partnership with Seaman in the fall of 1845, closing the commission store in Chicago and giving up the insurance agencies. Robe survived.[38]

* * *

The house at 12 Franklin had two rooms for receiving guests and a dining room that could seat thirty people. In March of 1845, the governor and Democratic members of the state legislature dined at Eliza's long table after passing the revenue bills to fund the canal and avoid defaulting on the state's debt.[39]

An event like this, the appearance of a politician or business associate of her husband at her dinner table, was one of the few intersections between Augustus's world and her own. They did enjoy the occasional outing together. They were friends with Walter and Mary Gurnee, and when Walter became treasurer of the new racing track, they made a visit to the races. From time to time they went to a ball. They traveled to New York every year. Otherwise, Augustus was so absorbed in his business and city work that he had no time for family life.[40]

Politics and business—Augustus's two all-consuming preoccupations —were the exclusive territory of men, and he rarely discussed them with Eliza. Nor did he take interest in her affairs, whether the running of the house, social entertaining, church, or her activities in the various organizations to which she belonged. He did not mind a comment or two on these subjects, especially a humorous anecdote, but if she talked too much and too seriously about them—if she sought his opinion, for example, or simply wanted to describe, say, her church work to him—he called it "blowing." "My wife is making preparations to receive calls," he told Seaman. "She now and then asks me a question but I tell her that I have nothing to do with her affairs, that she must attend to hers and that I will attend to mine. She blows me a little and all the satisfaction I can get is to blow her back again and so it goes."[41]

Eliza belonged to one of the sewing circles that provided clothing and the occasional basket of household goods to needy families. She was elected treasurer of the new Ladies Benevolent Association, one of the rare efforts of the city's churches to combine forces for a worthy cause. There were divisions from the start. Protestants and Catholics were suspicious of each other. The north-side Episcopalians, ruled by the dominating Juliette Kinzie, looked askance on the revivalist Baptists and Methodists. Eliza came home from the meetings with stories about quarrels. Augustus found these anecdotes amusing enough to mention in a letter to her brother Jerry. "Eliza was elected treasurer of the Ladies Benevolent Association," he said, "but there were so many different religions mixed up in it that she afeared there would be a bust in it." He went on to paraphrase her description of the meetings: "the Methodists complain of the Presbyterians & the Presbyterians of the Baptists & they of the Episcopalians & they of the Catholics & so it goes." She had no patience for petty squabbles and resigned. Soon after, the organization disbanded.[42]

The Ladies Benevolent Association was as close as any Chicago women's group came to achieving public status. Eliza and her female friends belonged to a sphere of activities that the men of the city generally ignored and treated as trivial. Of the various community societies listed by J. W. Norris in his 1844 city directory, not one was a women's organization. Even the female seminary, which educated young women to be schoolteachers, was run by men. In fact, only a handful of women were even listed in the school's directory. All female proprietors of businesses were milliners, dressmakers, and boardinghouse operators. The only other female income earners were teachers and laundresses.[43]

An English visitor commented on the separation of men's and women's spheres in America. The American male was not as "domestic" as the Englishman, he said. "Business and politics engross the thoughts of the men. They live in their Stores and Counting houses, and associate with their wives as little as may be." The prevailing ideology of separate domains was mostly white and urban. It was also to some extent more prescriptive than actual even in white urban settings. Eliza, for example, was able to handle real estate matters for her friends the Hamlines, telling Melinda Hamline in one letter that "the deed for the land will be ready for you as soon as the notes and obligations I gave to sell the property to you arrives [sic]" and adding her judgment that "if you wish to sell the property . . . you can get $5600 for it." It is true that she gave this counsel after Augustus's death and was only taking his place as advisor to the Hamlines. Yet her expertise showed that a wife might learn something of her husband's business. In fact, the Hamlines ran the *Ladies' Repository* together, with Melinda serving as editor.[44]

Nevertheless, the professions belonged almost exclusively to men. Almost all businesses small and large were owned and operated by men; almost all property belonged to men; and almost every organization was run by men or had all-male boards, including most women's organizations. Not only that, urban workplaces where men like Augustus spent their time tended to be gender-exclusive domains, and when husband and wife did not both belong to a church, which was the case with the Garretts for most of their lives, the separation of spheres was even more pronounced.[45]

Following his 1839 conversion during the Borein revival meetings, Augustus never communicated at Clark Street Methodist Church. His dramatic, tear-soaked conversion was an evanescent turn to religion, given up in a few weeks' time. After that he underwent periodic "reforms," which always made Eliza hopeful that he would return to the church. One of his reforms was preceded by a turn to Bible reading. He became voluble with scripture and lectured his friends. John Seaman got a pen-full a few days before Christmas in December of 1844. Augustus was angry about things Seaman had said about Robe. After tearing up two intemperate letters to his cousin, he finally wrote a missive he was willing to send. He wanted to set the record straight about Robe and gave Seaman a piece of his mind. "I will now correct your errors," he began. A page later he subjected Seaman to a lesson in theology and spiritual introspection: "Man is depraved and is prone to evil. You must admit that you have through the course of your life, if you look back, done wrong. You say that you was brought up Christian and in the same sentence you say that you never forgive a wrong. A Christian that can't use the Lord's Prayer is one of Joe Bower's Christians." (He was referring to the writings of Joseph Bower, which charged Christians with hypocrisy.) Then he quoted the lines about forgiveness from the Lord's Prayer, remarking that a Christian cannot simply skip over them—as Seaman was doing in refusing to forgive Robe—and he had a scriptural argument against selective use of the Bible: "for he says in plain language that who addeth or taketh away from the prophecy of this Book, his name will be taken from the Lamb's Book of Life."[46]

Two months later Augustus renounced drink. "This being 22d February," he told Robe, "I have resolved never, never to drink another drop of Ardent Spirits." The date was Washington's birthday, and Augustus made a point of emphasizing that he had no intention of ever joining the

Washingtonian temperance society. But he did "profess religion" again, later that year, and returned to Clark Street Church. For a brief period he was a devoted congregant and accompanied Eliza to church services and prayer meetings. The prayer meetings were held in the basement of the new brick church, and Eliza witnessed his "simple childlike recitals that would melt the whole congregation to tears." But it didn't last. He started drinking again, and that was the end of his churchgoing, although not of his personal belief in God, his acceptance of the Bible as holy revelation, or his belief in Jesus as his savior. These remained axiomatic for him—as they did for many non-churchgoing men of his age—along with a sense of his own fidelity to Christian morality (church rules against drinking and swearing excepted). "Although I am not religious," he told Seaman, "I have a hope of not being excluded from that place where God has designed for all just men."[47]

Eliza was faithful. She belonged to a small group, a Methodist "class," led by a layman named David Bradley. Bradley's class met every Sunday afternoon at four o'clock, sometimes at the Bradleys, sometimes at the Garretts or the home of another class member. In accordance with Methodist rituals, the meetings opened with a hymn, and Eliza and the other members knelt while Brother Bradley prayed for them, mentioning each by name. Then he confessed his own spiritual condition, rehearsing his experiences of the preceding week. A participant in one of these early-nineteenth-century Methodist classes describes how the class leader would recall "his joys and his sorrows, his hopes and his fears; his conflicts with the world, the flesh, and the devil; his fightings without and his fears within; his dread of hell, or his hope of heaven; his pious longings and secret prayers for the prosperity of the church at large and for those of his brothers and sisters in class particular." Then each class member would do the same, receiving from the leader some appropriate advice, encouragement, or exhortation. One effect of these practices was that class members became extremely close. They were intimates who knew each other's deepest thoughts. Hence, when a member of Bradley's class described Eliza as "a quiet, reliable, noble Christian woman," his words were more than superficial courtesy.[48]

Maintaining one's standing through the Methodist trial period for membership required a certain standard of conduct spelled out in the Methodist *Doctrines and Discipline*, which gave a list of prohibited behaviors, as well as positive expectations: showing kindness and mercy, "giving food to the hungry," "clothing the naked," visiting and aiding the sick and those in prison, and performing other good works set forth in the Gospels. This was not just pious talk. Communicants like Eliza were devoted to charitable activities.[49]

Yet she was unable, as a married woman, to carry out any acts of charity on her own if they involved monetary donations. While her husband could offer to match every five dollars given to the church for a building program, as he once did, she could not. Nor could she give to other benevolent endeavors. As a matter of law and social convention, she had no authority in matters of money. And when she tried to talk Augustus into giving to worthy causes, perhaps some great project of mercy or public good, he made vague promises but did not follow through.[50]

Then he died.

* * *

Eliza had known Augustus to complain about his health. In the spring of 1842, when he was only in his early forties, he told a correspondent that he planned to go south for the winter but only if his health permitted it. He believed he had a weak heart. Sometimes his work left him exhausted, especially when he traveled. He told Seaman that he would not run for mayor again because it required "more than a person in my health is able to perform." After he resigned from his contested term, he told Seaman he felt healthier and was gaining a pound a day. In another letter he announced that he had figured out the cause of his ill health: "I happened to discover what was the matter with me. I have in previous years been bled freely, and I required bleeding as I had been habituated to it ever since. I have been gaining rapidly and weigh 175 pounds, and in the gain cannot make any of my vests meet." This sense of well-being after bleeding was probably a placebo effect, although high blood pressure might have caused symptoms that were temporarily relieved by the periodic bloodlettings.[51]

They were still living in their house at 12 Franklin Street. Augustus had given up his store and was conducting real estate business from home. He went out from time to time to hobnob with friends or take care of a business matter. He was either passing near the Sherman House or seeing someone there when he collapsed on November 24, 1848. His friends were afraid to move him farther than the nearest bed, and he lay in the Sherman House for several days, weakening by the hour.[52]

The physician summoned to his bedside concluded he would not recover. The doctor probably bled him, too, which was standard procedure
and something Augustus would have requested. He did not improve. Eliza
sat with him. When he was alert, his mind wandered. He knew he was
dying, he told her, and talked "on the subject of Death" and "the vanity
of this world and how little we knew what a day would bring forth." The
end came on Thursday, November 30, 1848, at half past ten in the evening.
He was forty-six.[53]

Doctors attributed the cause to "congestion of the brain," a vague
term used by nineteenth-century physicians for a variety of conditions,
including stroke. The newspapers printed glowing obituaries, describing
Augustus's career in politics and business, and noting his general popularity. They also lauded his charity, asserting in inflated terms what
his close friends and Eliza knew was untrue—that he was "possessed of
generous impulses" and "liberal of his wealth, bestowing in charities and
in donations to excite to deeds of benevolence, large sums of the fortune
which he had accumulated."[54]

The following morning, Eliza awoke to her loss. The house was very
silent, the world outside, too, blanketed by snow. It had snowed storm-
ily in the night. Ships still braving the lakes had a rough time, and one
ice-encrusted schooner arrived with missing sails.[55]

John Link, the clerk who worked for Augustus out of the house on
Franklin, a young man of twenty-two whom they had come to regard as a
son, drove Eliza to Clark Street Methodist Church, where she explained to
her minister, Rev. Hooper Crews, that Augustus had requested a Church
of England service. His mother had been Anglican. Eliza hoped the rector
of the Episcopal church could conduct the rites but do so in Clark Street
Church. Later that day Crews approached Rev. William Barlow of Trinity
Episcopal Church and arranged for the two of them to lead an Anglican
funeral service at Clark Street.[56]

Friends came to see her. She was gracious to all her sympathizers,
hiding her pain and choosing her words carefully when her Methodist
friends searched for positive things to say about Augustus. In their eyes,
he was a lapsed convert who had "returned to the world," a man of "vicious
habits," devoted to money and dead to religion. But Eliza saw him as a
man who believed in God but could not reconcile himself to institution-
alized religion, who lived as a Christian in his own way, was deeply loyal
to his friends, and had always been devoted to her. He had told her on

his deathbed that he was not afraid to die, though he knew he had failed to live as he had wanted. Time had run out on him.[57]

Early Sunday morning, a mass of mourners gathered for the funeral at the Methodist church. The sanctuary was packed. Newspapers judged the funeral the largest the city had ever seen. Current mayor James Woodworth and several ex-mayors attended, afterward joining other mourners in a slow procession to City Cemetery, where the body of Augustus was laid to rest not far from the curling November breakers of Lake Michigan. The *Chicago Daily Democrat* published the following account:

> The funeral of the late ex-Mayor Garrett on Sunday last, was the largest ever seen in this city. At an early hour the Methodist Church, in which the funeral services were performed, was crowded to excess. The funeral service of the Episcopal Church was read by Rev. Barlow, Elder Crews of the Methodist Episcopal Church repeating the responses.—The impressive service seemed to effect [sic] the immense concourse with devotional feelings.—The Mayor, several ex-Mayors, the Common Council of the city and the family of the deceased attended as mourners in the procession, which was a very long one.[58]

Letters poured in, including condolences from Leonidas and Melinda Hamline. Eliza had entertained the Hamlines in her home when they last visited Chicago. She now wrote to them, thanking them for their "very kind and sympathizing letter." She felt perfectly free to tell them how she felt. "Affliction has indeed come upon me suddenly. Death has taken from me my Husband + Protector + almost I may say my only Earthly relative." Looking back, she lamented that Augustus had not used his wealth for any worthy cause, charitable or religious: "I had prayed and hoped that he would live to do some little goode in the world before he should have been called to give up his account." She was also coming to terms with what his will disclosed—that he had left nothing to any church or any benevolent or civic organization, and that his bequest to her was only a life estate, tying her hands. "God's ways are not our ways," she wrote. "I feel to say thy will O Lord be done." But she felt lost without Augustus and poured out her heart to her two friends.

> Dear Friends
>
> . . . I cannot describe to you my feelings & you cannot realize what they are unless you could be placed in a similar situation,

Last page of a letter of Eliza Garrett to Leonidas and Melinda Hamline,
Jan. 29, 1849. Styberg Library of Garrett-Evangelical Theological Seminary.

which the good Lord forbid should ever be either of your lots.
I feel that I am indeed afflicted but I know that it is my benevolent Father that has done it and that as he has said that he
afflicteth not willingly the children of men but for their good,
I am constrained to believe that it is for my good that he has
thus afflicted me. I wish to be benefitted by this dispensation,
although I feel alone in the World so far as earthly friends are
concerned. Still I feel that I have a kinde Father in Heaven who
has said that not a sparrow falls without his notice and who is
ever willing to hear and answer my feeble petitions. I have found

comfort and consolation in believing and trusting in my Savior. This World is fast losing its charms for me. I feel like striving more earnestly to lay up treasure in Heaven. My dear Friends, I have often thought of your kinde admonitions and feel that they have been a greate help to me in striving to live a Christian. Your visit with us I look upon as a great Blessing [to] me. As a family we all have reverted to it with pleasure. Even now I feel thankful to my Heavenly Father for allowing me the privilege of entertaining such kinde Friends. I hope to see you again in our city. Although I have not a place where I can entertain you, yet I have a heart to welcome you. I have been staying since Mr. G's death with a Friend. I have made no calculations in regard to the future, only the present is mine. I hope to hear from you as soon as it is convenient. Pray for me.

Respectfully and affectionately your friende,
Eliza Garrett[59]

CHAPTER 7

THE FOUNDER

$\mathcal{A}$fter Augustus died, Eliza moved in with a friend. In September of 1849, her mother, Amy Clark, died at the age of eighty. "Since I last wrote to you," Eliza told Melinda Hamline in an October letter, "I have been called to pass through another very heavy affliction. My only surviving Parent my Mother has been called to the World of spirits. She was a Christian for many years and has left a good evidence that my loss is her everlasting gain. This is a great consolation to me. I think I feel perfectly resigned to her Death, that is, if I am a proper judge of my own heart."[1]

She was now living with the Gurnee family. Walter and Mary Gurnee had known the Garretts for more than twenty years, back to the late 1830s when both couples boarded at the Sauganash Hotel. They became good friends, and their fortunes advanced in similar ways. Like Augustus, Walter became a wealthy man. He started out as a partner in a store that sold groceries, hardware, and leather goods. In the latter part of the 1840s, he built a tannery. He was also active in municipal government as treasurer and mayor.[2]

The Gurnee mansion stood on Michigan Avenue near Adams Street. Thirteen people occupied the Gurnee house. In addition to eight Gurnees and Eliza, there were Mary's sister and husband, along with two domestic servants. The house, which was not far from the lake and faced the beach, stood on an eighty-eight-foot lot and was several stories tall. From her upstairs room, Eliza could look out at the vast inland sea and observe the steady construction of the Illinois Central Railroad, now being erected on offshore pilings just four hundred feet from Michigan Avenue.[3]

Melinda Hamline wanted Eliza to move into a Methodist household. Eliza responded tactfully: "If I really believe that I would be religiously benefitted I would do so if I could find anyone willing to accommodate me. The family that I have been staying with for the last year are olde and tryed friends. They gave me a home out of friendship entirely [and] they

Chicago from the lake in 1866, showing the Illinois Central
railway on pilings and the mansions on Michigan Avenue. The
Gurnee house may be represented in the far distance. Jevne and
Almini lithograph. Chicago History Museum, ICHi-062074, cropped.

have made sacrifices for my comfort. I do not know whether I could be
as happy in any other family. I love them very much."[4]

* * *

The Gurnee house, enlivened by children, gave Eliza a family life she had
not enjoyed in many years. In 1849 there were six younger Gurnees,
ranging in age from nine-year-old Delia to baby Grace. Eliza became especially close to Delia and her six-year-old sister, Mary-Evelyn. Between life at
the Gurnee home, her involvements with Clark Street Church, and "a great
many correspondents," she led a rewarding and mostly contented existence.[5]

Yet one thing troubled her. "I feel the necessity of a deeper worke of
grace in my heart," she told Melinda. "I try to Pray for it as well as I know
how." She meant something very specific, what Methodists called "entire
sanctification," or sometimes called "full baptism of the Holy Spirit," "the
blessing," or "divine love." The terms designated a definite experience and a
completion of one's conversion—freedom from sin and full consecration to
God. Although this was a doctrine of "perfection" and may have produced

arrogance in some, those who sought entire sanctification tended to be highly introspective, self-critical people who continued to find fault in themselves after the experience and regarded their sanctification as a source of personal assurance, not pride. Leonidas Hamline, for example, confessed in a letter to his wife, "I have not served as I ought," but "I have to remember that I was truly converted on the 5th of October, 1828, in Villanova, New York. I was wholly sanctified in New Albany, Indiana, in March, 1842."[6]

He knew the latter date more specifically as March 22nd. Traditionally described, the "blessing" took a palpable form. Mary Apess compared it to "electric fire" going all through her. Jarena Lee felt "as if lightening had darted through me." Leonidas Hamline sensed a divine hand pressing on his forehead and sending holy energy through him. He told Walter Palmer that "for a few minutes the deep of God's love swallowed him up." Zilpha Elaw fell to the floor. So did Julia Foote. Because the blessing was experienced as a definite moment of change, a sensible event and not a slow process, it was customary to mark it, just as one dated one's conversion.[7]

The Methodists held ten weeks of evening revival meetings to start the new year of 1850, and Eliza attended many of the services in hopes of experiencing entire sanctification. "We have been holding a series of meetings in Clark Street Church during the Winter," she wrote to Melinda in March. "They commenced on the first of January [and] have been kept up every evening until this week." More than a hundred people joined the Methodist Church or were won over for other denominations in town. Others sought sanctification. "Some few profess to have experienced this much to be desired blessing," she wrote, adding, "I am sorry to say that I am not of the happy number."[8]

Eliza underwent this personal disappointment in a period when Methodists were debating the nature of the experience itself. Phoebe Palmer had recently challenged the assumption that a "sensible" experience was essential. Some people were sanctified in that way, she said, but the essential thing was to claim the blessing by faith and believe one had received it. She and her husband Walter Palmer had been traveling the Holiness circuit, leading eager seekers into the deeper work of grace. Their approach was called the "Palmer method."

The Hamlines and the Palmers were close friends, yet Bishop Hamline and other Methodist ministers were initially dubious about Palmer's claim that sanctification could be had by faith alone without, as they understood her to be saying, the inner witness of the Spirit. Palmer answered that faith must indeed be accompanied by an inner awareness of complete consecration. Thus, the distinctions between Palmer's teaching and the standard Holiness doctrine became fuzzy. Contributing to this fuzziness were different estimations of what constituted genuineness in affect during the moment of sanctification. Urbane dislike for the highly demonstrative emotionalism of the camp meetings made Palmer's method attractive to a certain class of city Methodists, especially the well-educated.[9]

Leonidas and Melinda Hamline were enthusiastic supporters of the Palmers' Holiness efforts, and over time Bishop Hamline became more sympathetic to Phoebe Palmer's insistence that sensible emotions of joy were not necessary proofs of entire sanctification. It is likely that Melinda influenced him. She, too, had been a long-disappointed seeker, attending numerous revivals in the 1830s where others had "stepped into the pool and were made whole," while she came away empty. Then in the winter of 1842–1843, during an intense period of searching, she read Phoebe Palmer's series of articles "Is There Not a Shorter Way?" in the *Christian Advocate and Journal*. Deeply impressed, she renewed her seeking. At a prayer meeting she felt a sense of peace and did what Palmer had instructed—she claimed the experience of entire sanctification without palpable proofs. In the years that followed, lacking any of the "powerful manifestations" that others described, she endured perpetual temptations to doubt that there had been any real change in herself but was resolved to believe and not demand "signs and wonders." Henceforth, she became a champion of Palmer's "shorter way."[10]

Given her own experience, Melinda was an empathetic spiritual adviser to Eliza, who, after her disappointment following the winter revival meetings of 1850, was consoling herself that "although I have not experienced this greatest of all blessing still I have some of the comforts and sweets of Religion and am fully determined to press my way on to know more of that love which passeth knowledge." Melinda sent her books by writers of the Holiness movement. She probably also counseled her that a palpable experience at a revival meeting was not essential. One needed only claim "the blessing" through sincere faith.[11]

Over the course of the next several months, the books and letters from Melinda helped resolve Eliza's struggles. Grant Goodrich noticed a change in her, which he termed "an increase in her faith." She spoke of it herself, and by 1852 she was no longer lamenting her lack of "the blessing" when describing her religious sentiments to Melinda or reporting on revivals at Clark Street Church.[12]

* * *

*A*ugustus Garrett's will provided for Eliza and some of his relatives but made no charitable bequests. Augustus never intended to do anything philanthropic with his wealth, even though he sometimes made vague statements about knowing that he should. "He knew his duty but he did not do it," as Goodrich phrased it:

> [Garrett] repeatedly expressed his conviction that with his activity of mind and restless energy, he could never live a christian unless he devoted his energies and wealth to founding and building institutions for the Church. "He knew his duty, but he did it not," and as a consequence he lost his religion and the offered crown of glory. In December, 1848, he was summoned into the presence of his Judge, and his widow was left to perform the great work which he had refused to do.[13]

Goodrich had more than once urged Augustus to make donations to worthy Methodist causes. Augustus mentioned one such effort in a letter to Robe Malony written in March of 1844. In response to entreaties from Goodrich about helping a struggling seminary—that is, a small college for young men—Augustus had enlisted Malony and another associate named "Col. Mahony." Now, in his letter, Garrett told Malony that he and Mahony should ask that their names be removed from the subscription list because Goodrich had led them to believe that they were buying stock but now claimed the monies were a *donation*:

> I want you and Col. Mahony to each write me a letter, each a separate letter, requesting me to take your name off the subscription list for the Rockford Seminary for the following reasons. First that the members of the Methodiste, Mr. Goodrich in particular, has persecuted me as well as yourselves falsely and scandalously & Second that when you subscribed you were under the impression that you was subscribing for stock instead of giving it as a donation. Thirdly that the amount descried [sic] to cancel the debt [of] the Seminary is considerably less than the amount they wished to raise. I do not intend to pay my subscription, neither do I want my friends to that I induced to subscribe. I am not going to lend my aid to build up a church that will avail themselves of every opportunity they can get to injure me. I don't mind the amt of the money so much as I do

the principle. Nothing more at present. Show this letter to the Col. Write your letters a little different.

Yours & C.
A. Garrett[14]

Augustus was confused about the name of the school. There *was* a Rockford Seminary, but it had been organized by the Presbyterians. The Methodists had a Rock River Seminary at Mt. Morris. Its first building was constructed in 1839, and over the next few years the institution remained encumbered with debt. When Rev. Daniel J. Pinckney became the new principal of the school in August of 1842, he enlisted Chicago Methodists to help him raise funds for the seminary. One of these Methodists, namely Goodrich, solicited a subscription from Garrett, who agreed, thinking he was purchasing stock. His assumption was not unwarranted. One method of funding educational institutions was to secure subscriptions in the form of stock through arrangements whereby the subscribers retained their interest in the initial face value of the stock and the institution invested or loaned monies from the stock, reaping some or all the profits and dividends. But Goodrich had meant a gift for the school, not an investment, and he assumed Garrett understood that.[15]

When Augustus announced that he wanted his money back, Goodrich and Pinckney accused him of reneging. That wounded Augustus's sense of honor, and he charged Goodrich and the rest of the Methodists with misusing him. The rift did not lead him to dismiss Goodrich as his attorney, however; and a year later, in the flush of a second religious conversion, he was providing funds to finish the basement of a new building for Clark Street Church.[16]

Methodist friends of the Garretts had always hoped that Augustus would engage in some kind of benefaction during his lifetime or would include a charitable bequest in his will. Augustus always made encouraging pronouncements when people inquired about whether he had any philanthropic plans. And when Eliza urged him to do some great thing with his wealth, he gave her the impression he was contemplating it.

He wasn't. In his will, he sought to prevent Eliza from donating his real estate—which was the bulk of his wealth—to Methodist causes. He divided his estate between her and certain of his family members, differentiating between his male and female heirs in the mode of inheritance when it came to his real property. To his male heirs, Charles Flaglor and

James and Thomas Crow, he gave what the law calls "fee simple" (or "fee absolute"), that is, full and unrestricted ownership of their portions. But to his three female heirs—Eliza and his two sisters—he bequeathed what is called a "life estate," that is, a right to possess and use, as well as earn proceeds from, inherited real estate during one's own lifetime but not the right to sell it or give it away or pass it on as one's own estate. Upon their deaths, these properties would go to male heirs.[17]

Thus, Augustus had done everything he could to ensure that Eliza's allotted share in his real estate would eventually pass from her to his nephews, barring her from bequeathing any portion of it to the Methodist Church or to any other person or organization. There was a way around this, however. Her attorney and friend, Grant Goodrich, explained that she could assert her right of dower.

Dower was a privilege established in English common law whereby a wife could renounce her husband's will and inherit from him under a different legal custom. Traditionally, the right of dower was one-third of a husband's estate, but in Illinois, thanks to a recent statute, a wife was entitled to half if she and her husband had no living children. This was exactly Eliza's situation, and two months after Augustus's death, when the estate was submitted to probate, she "renounced the benefits" of Augustus's will and "asserted her rights of dower, whereby she became entitled to one-half of the estate." She and the heirs then agreed to a partition, and a bill was filed with the Cook County Circuit Court in 1851. By this instrument she came into full legal possession of her share, which paved the way for her to devise a will of her own and bequeath her inheritance to any persons or institutions she chose.[18]

It was a momentous decision. She had gone against Augustus's wishes and taken charge of half his wealth. Now she planned to use it for worthy causes. She was already at least marginally involved in Methodist efforts to establish schools of lower and higher education. The charter for "North-Western University"—or Northwestern University, as it was later called—was signed by the governor on January 21, 1851. The university organizers met six months later to move the project forward. They sought a land grant from Congress, but nothing came of it, and they were therefore entirely dependent on private subscriptions. During this time, the organizers were also at work to provide a local stream of students by creating both preparatory and primary schools located in Chicago. A member of the university committee—probably Goodrich—asked Eliza to approach the Hamlines about a subscription for the primary school, which it was hoped could be in operation by fall of 1853. Eliza was serving as the Hamlines' real estate agent in Chicago, making sure their taxes were paid and informing them about the value of their property if they wished to sell it. She wrote to Melinda Hamline in February of 1852:

> The committee of M. E. University are making an effort to raise suffi-cient funds to put up a building in this place as a primary department in connection with the contemplated University. It is important that this school be put in operation as soon as possible. It is thought that 10,000 dollars will be sufficient to accomplish the object. They have not yet attained the amount necessary. I have been requested to lay the object before you and say to the Bishop and yourself that if you feel disposed to subscribe something for that purpose it will be gratefully received by the committee and friends of the institution.

She went on to suggest that if they subscribed for a thousand dollars, they could pay it in yearly installments of two hundred dollars. Thus far, the committee had obtained four subscriptions in this amount, one of them no doubt from her.[19]

She was happy that she could now support such endeavors not only with her time but also with money; but on a March morning shortly before dawn, less than two weeks after her letter to the Hamlines, a fire broke out in the yard between the Sauganash Hotel and its barn. Soon nearly the entire block was reduced to ashes, including the hotel, its outbuild-ings, three clothing stores, a fruit store, a barbershop, and a grocery. All the lots on which these edifices stood belonged to Eliza, and some of the buildings were hers. The fire marshal suspected arson, but nothing was proven. Fortunately, the buildings were insured, but settling the claims, rebuilding, and finding new lessees was a protracted matter. John Link assisted Eliza with the business aspects, and Grant Goodrich represented her with the insurance companies and tenants.[20]

With philanthropic ideas developing in her mind, Eliza decided to take only four hundred dollars a year for her own expenses and regular chari-table contributions, which she intended to limit for several years until the estate recovered. She also decided to make out a will. Her thought was to establish some worthy institution, such as a school, supporting it with the revenues of her estate during her lifetime and passing on the bulk of the estate to the trustees of the institution as an endowment after her death.[21]

Her first step was to seek advice. In October of 1851 she wrote to Bishop Hamline and asked his opinion. Only a fragment of this correspondence is preserved, a quotation from the close of the bishop's response in which he encourages Eliza to trust God's guidance. These lines do not mention his specific advice, but one can imagine that Hamline suggested she leave her estate to an educational institution, since establishing Methodist universities was on his mind. It is also likely that Eliza asked the Hamlines what they thought about the idea that she devote her estate to founding or aiding a Methodist women's college, for that was on *her* mind. If she did broach this subject, she found a ready ear in Melinda Hamline, who was an ardent advocate of university education for women. Eliza also had the encouragement of John Link, who was sympathetic to the cause of women's higher education and would later assist a struggling women's college.[22]

Eliza did not act immediately but continued to ponder the matter of her will. A year passed before she brought up the subject with her lawyer,

Photograph of Eliza Garrett, 1850s. Courtesy of Garrett-Evangelical Theological Seminary.

Oil painting of Eliza Garrett, by C. V. Bond (posthumous, 1856).
Courtesy of Garrett-Evangelical Theological Seminary.

Grant Goodrich. Yet she was still not ready to frame the particulars.
According to Goodrich, Eliza approached him in 1852 and asked him to
canvass "persons whose judgment concerning the great interests of the
church he would deem worthy of special regard." Among the men he
consulted was Daniel Kidder, corresponding secretary of the Methodist
Sunday School Union. Kidder argued for a theological school, and a year
later, when he was in Chicago for a Sunday school conference in the fall

of 1853, he reiterated to Goodrich that a biblical institute for training ministers was "the grand desideratum of our educational enterprises in the West." Soon after, Goodrich and Eliza spoke again, and she told him that she intended to devote, in his words, "the largest portion of her property to benevolent purposes." He summarized to her the opinions he had collected and proposed a school for educating ministers. "Such a purpose had been for some time the subject of her thoughts," Goodrich said. She recognized that Methodist clergy exhibited "zeal and self-devotion," but most lacked sufficient education.[23]

Goodrich's conversation with Eliza took place in the latter part of September. Within days of their meeting, she consulted her pastor John Clark and Daniel Kidder in Goodrich's office. She also spoke to Hooper Crews, a former pastor who was coincidentally in Chicago at the time. Each of these men, Goodrich said, offered her the same advice. Someone, perhaps Kidder, also gave her Stephen Vail's newly published book advocating for ministerial education in the Methodist Church. Thus, in the span of about a week or two in September of 1853, several Methodist men whom Eliza highly esteemed urged her to devote her estate to the theological school that they wished to establish in the North-West. Goodrich interpreted this confluence of unified voices as a providential sign.[24]

Goodrich's account became the standard version of Eliza Garrett's path to founding Garrett Biblical Institute, giving the impression that she and the Methodist organizers of the school were of the same mind from start to finish. They were not. Although she was eventually persuaded to endow a theological school and was ready to do so enthusiastically, she also wanted to found a women's college and leaned toward dividing her estate equally in support of both ventures, something they opposed. Hence, her meetings with Goodrich, Kidder, Clark, and Crews left her torn between what they wanted and what she wanted. Nor was she silent about it. At her meeting with Goodrich and Kidder in Goodrich's law office, she told them that she wished to found a female college. Kidder would later recall suggesting to her that Methodists were already busy founding schools and colleges but had been slow to do anything about the most pressing need of the moment—ministerial training. What he did not admit was that these Methodist colleges and universities were for men, not women, the new North-Western University being an example of that.[25]

According to Goodrich, the "tenor" of Eliza's will was decided shortly after Kidder's departure, although the will itself was not drawn up until several weeks later. Meanwhile, Kidder, back in New York, penned a letter to Goodrich repeating his argument against a women's college. "While the demands are so great for a Biblical Inst.," he wrote, "they can hardly be considered urgent for the establishment of a Fem. college." This implies that Eliza had been quite emphatic about founding a female college and that Kidder wanted Goodrich to talk her out of it.[26]

As for Goodrich, whatever his initial feelings on the subject, he became convinced that Kidder was right. The estate should not be divided between two schools, jeopardizing the success of both. A theological school was the priority, he thought.[27]

Eliza's intention was to support a new school or schools right from their founding, out of her estate earnings, but the Garrett properties had not yet recovered from the devastating 1851 fire. All that could be done at the moment to further her plan was to compose her will. In early December of 1853 she met with Goodrich to work out the details. She now agreed that she ought to make a bequest for the planned theological school, but she still insisted on endowing a female college. Goodrich told her the consensus opinion of the seminary organizers was that it would be unwise to divide her resources between two schools. Then he suggested a way she could avoid jeopardizing the theological institute while still providing for the women's college. She accepted the compromise and, on December 2, signed the final version of a will in which she gave John Link, whom she thought of as a son, a full third of her estate, apportioned thirty-two thousand dollars to various other relatives and friends, and assigned the remainder of the estate, amounting to a little less than two-thirds, to the "Garrett Biblical Institute." She also directed that should the institute not need all the monies bequeathed to it, the excess be used to establish a female college:

> And in case at any time the said trust property, the rents, issues, and proceeds thereof, shall exceed the amount necessary to build, fit, furnish, endow and support said Biblical Institute as aforesaid, I direct and devote the surplus to accumulate, or otherwise to be invested for accumulation, for the purchase of a site and the erection, within the city of Chicago, or its vicinity, of a female college.[28]

Charles Stuart, writing in 1922, says that Eliza's final decision about her will was influenced by Goodrich and John Dempster, an organizer of a Methodist school in New Hampshire who visited Chicago, as well as by Peter Borein, the Methodist minister whose revivals brought about her conversion in 1839. Hearing the same advice from all three men, she is supposed to have declared, "The will of the Lord is clear. I have been directed by Him, though I knew it not." Stuart did not give his source, and the quotation sounds apocryphal. Goodrich was an influence but not Dempster. Eliza had already made out her will by the time Dempster passed through Chicago and was invited into local Methodist conversations about a theological school in the North-West.[29]

As for Borein, a bit of lore about him and his influence on Eliza's decision was passed down through the generations and found its way into some remarks by Northwestern University president Charles Little in 1906. In a retrospective on the seminary, Little described Borein as "a man of unusual eloquence and piety, but of imperfect education" who "often attributed this fact to the lack of a school in which men like himself might obtain a proper education for the ministry, and frequently said this in conversation with Mrs. Garrett." It seems unlikely, however, that Borein, who died just six months after Eliza joined Clark Street Church, had any conversations with her about ministerial education, much less confided his life regrets to her. He probably scarcely knew her. More likely, Borein made statements about his education to others, and it was understood that Eliza knew of them since they were repeated in later years as part of the stories about Borein and the founding of Garrett. The stories were somewhat misleading. Borein had more education than many ministers, including some college training, and he had managed to learn Greek and Latin. He was hardly an untutored bumpkin. Yet remembering him that way served the purposes of both sides in the debate about education for ministers. Those who opposed it pointed to Borein as the charismatic preacher whose spiritual gifts would have been ruined by academe. Those who favored it claimed he had always regretted that he dropped out of school and never received any formal ministerial training.[30]

Eliza's will provided for a female college to be supported by excess income from her estate not needed for the seminary. Not surprisingly, in the ensuing decades the seminary always needed all the revenues generated by the estate—and more. Hence, Frances Willard would one day comment, "Even good Mrs. Garrett, while she made mention in her will of doing something for women's education, conditioned this upon a contingency so remote that it is practically certain never to arrive." The organizers of Northwestern University, essentially the same men who founded the theological school, were largely uninterested in providing a college curriculum for women; some were even opposed to the idea. In fact, a decade later when Evanston women, including Melinda Hamline, solicited the Northwestern University Board of Trustees to form a female college as part of the university or to matriculate women into the men's college, the trustees hesitated, then did nothing.[31]

The idea of including a provision for a female college was, therefore, entirely Eliza's, and it had to swim upstream against a flood of contrary opinion, only to die without spawning on the rocks of Goodrich's careful wording. In the end, Eliza trusted that the Methodist men knew best.

In Methodist circles, people had been calling the envisioned school "Methodist Episcopal Biblical Institute" or "North-Western Methodist Biblical Institute." But the trustees decided to name the school "Garrett Biblical Institute." Eliza must have communicated to her brother Jeremiah and other New York friends and family that the school was named for Augustus, for a Newburgh tradition grew up that Augustus was the school's benefactor. Indeed, as late as 1903, when Newburgh historian Edward Ruttenber wrote his history of "the old Main Road"—the northern pike where Augustus's father John Garrett once had a farm—he spoke of Augustus as the "founder of the Garrett Biblical Institute." Ruttenber knew that Eliza had made the gift, but he devoted his words of tribute to her husband:

> Turn from the place of his residence on the old Main Road, turn from the stone on which his name is recorded [the Garrett marker in the Old Town Cemetery of Newburgh] to that higher monument that bears the name of Garrett—the Biblical Institute which bears his name—a living fountain 'whose waters make glad the city of our God,' and whose lustre rests on the cradling bed of its founder—the primitive farm house on the Old North Road."

Grant Goodrich and the other trustees had a different intention. They named the school "Garrett" to honor Eliza, not Augustus, and always spoke of her as the founder.[32]

Eliza also made bequests to individuals—to members of her family and to certain friends, including two of the Gurnee girls—Delia, who was thirteen when the will was composed, and Mary Evelyn, who was ten. All told she made eleven monetary bequests—five to females totaling fifteen thousand dollars and six to males totaling twelve thousand dollars. There was also something notable in the bequests to Delia and Mary Evelyn, who were under the age of twenty-one. The wording of their bequests contained unusual language, specifically the expression "to her separate use and control." Without this wording, the gifts to the girls would have been in their father's control and, unless placed in a trust, could have been used by Walter Gurnee in any way he saw fit. Eliza's intention, then, was to give Delia and Mary Evelyn money of their own, outside anyone else's control.[33]

She was very sensitive to the predicament of a woman who was completely dependent on a man for money. A married woman's legal status was that of a *feme covert*, without the right to own, manage, or sell property, including property she brought to the marriage. A single woman who was not under the legal guardianship of her father could exercise financial independence, but a married woman could not. Apart from a special legal arrangement, a wife could own nothing. This was Eliza's relation to money and property in her marriage to Augustus. Everything belonged solely to him, and even in death he had endeavored to deny Eliza any final say over his property by granting her only a life interest in his real estate. But Goodrich had shown her a way around that, and now, in her own will, she instructed him to write bequests to Delia and Mary Evelyn in words that would grant them sole control of the money she left them.[34]

Thus, in two particulars of her will—in the clause about the female college and the bequests to Delia and Mary Evelyn—she sought to do something for women's elevation and independence.

* * *

John Dempster, the eastern Methodist, appeared on the scene just three and a half weeks after Eliza signed her final testament. Dempster, onetime organizer of Latin American missions for the Methodist Church, had already established the first Methodist theological school in the United States at Concord, New Hampshire, in 1847. He was now stopping in Chicago on his way to Bloomington, where he was to meet with Methodists to discuss plans for a similar institute. Philo Judson persuaded Dempster to speak with the Methodists in Chicago before going on to Bloomington, and on the day after Christmas, Dempster addressed a meeting of "Friends of Biblical Learning" at Clark Street Church. In the discussion following his remarks, the Friends decided to establish a Biblical Institute Association and solicited Dempster's help. According to a handwritten document labeled "Dempster contract" and dating to a few days after this meeting, the arrangements for the school were as follows. A board of five directors was established, composed of Grant Goodrich, Orrington Lunt, John Evans, John Clark, and Philo Judson. Dempster agreed to serve as a professor and to recruit two other faculty. The directors promised to provide salaries and buildings, the latter to be constructed on newly purchased land for Northwestern University. Evans, Dempster, and Judson were given the task of drawing up articles of association to be modeled on those of the Methodist Biblical Institute at Concord, New Hampshire.[35]

These agreements were predicated on the commitments already made by Eliza four weeks prior. In other words, it was Eliza's decision to establish a theological school with the proceeds of her estate that created the circumstances in which Dempster, passing through Chicago, discovered that whatever tentative plans there may have been for a school in Bloomington had already been preempted by foundations laid in Chicago. As it happened, two of the directors of the Biblical Institute Association were executors of Eliza's will, and one of these was Goodrich, her personal attorney.

It was understood that during her lifetime Eliza would support the school with proceeds from her estate. Yet her properties were still encumbered by debt. For the time being, financial support for the institute would have to come from elsewhere. There was optimism, however, that within five years or so the Garrett estate would be generating income again, enabling Eliza to contribute most of the monies needed to operate the school. In other words, the organizers figured that if they could get the school off the ground, there would be sufficient financial resources as it grew, thanks to Eliza's commitment to fund the institute during her lifetime and posthumously, through her bequest.[36]

In July of 1854, construction of a building was begun on the wooded lakeshore grounds of the still-undeveloped campus of Northwestern University, and by January a three-story wooden structure was ready for the four students and three faculty of the first term. Dempster Hall, as it would eventually be named, was meant to serve until the organizers could erect substantial buildings of brick and stone. This all-purpose temporary

Eliza Garrett in an engraving by J. C. Buttre based
on a photograph. Author's collection.

edifice included recitation rooms, a chapel, a kitchen, and accommodations for thirty or more students. As the year 1854 came to a close, the interior walls were not yet plastered, and solicitations were still going out to Methodist friends to help furnish beds, heat stoves, tables, chairs, and washstands for the dormitory section of the building. Students were not charged tuition or rent, but they did pay two dollars a week for board, had to supply their own light and fuel, and could expect to spend thirty-five dollars for books over the course of their study.[37]

A dedication was held on New Year's Day of 1855, and Eliza went up with other members of Clark Street Church, including school organizers Grant Goodrich and Orrington Lunt. Traveling the road to Evanston was difficult in winter. The Chicago & Milwaukee Railroad had still not reached that place, so the group went by sleigh, mostly along the lakeshore. After a four-hour journey, they arrived at the plain, white wooden building in dense oak near the lakeshore at the north end of the university grounds. There they gathered in the chapel with faculty, students, trustees, and other well-wishers of the fledgling school to hear speeches by Professor Dempster and Dr. James Watson, editor of the Methodist periodical the *Northwestern Christian Advocate*. Eliza's cheeks flushed red when Watson mentioned her by name. She did not want to be praised. It made her feel uncomfortable.[38]

In June the school celebrated the completion of its first term, during which its ranks had swelled to sixteen students. Again the friends from Chicago made the twelve-mile journey north. This time the weather was mild. They set out at dawn and made stops along the way to pick wild-flowers and strawberries. Upon reaching the campus, they strolled the grounds, then attended a service in the chapel. Once again Dr. Watson was the featured speaker. He held the company in rapt attention for more

Dempster Hall. Courtesy of the Northwestern University Archives.

than two hours as he defended, with vivid illustrations that undoubtedly included the case of Peter Borein, the cause of ministerial education. Garrett Biblical Institute still had to justify its existence in the face of many Methodists who thought book learning tended to depress spiritual ardor. After the service, the company took their noon meal beneath the trees. Then they returned to the chapel to hear Bishop Matthew Simpson set forth arguments in favor of *university* education. "The light of letters and the discoveries of science would grow dim," he warned, "in the absence of our universities." Thus the day's celebrations reflected the intimate connection between the founding of Garrett Biblical Institute and the establishment of Northwestern University as a dual Methodist effort in the interest of higher learning.[39]

Eliza's plans to found a women's college were never realized, but Northwestern University soon began admitting women. It did not happen without a struggle and only after the school moved to hire a new president in 1870 who made the admission of women one of his conditions for accepting the position. Three years later and just eighteen years after opening, Garrett Biblical Institute—which had never had any official bar against admitting women—received its first female student, and in 1879 Garrett became the second school in the United States to grant a theological degree to a woman. Today, enlarged by mergers and clad in neo-Gothic architecture, the seminary still stands near the shore of Lake Michigan on the campus of Northwestern University, having graduated nearly ten thousand men and women.[40]

* * *

Eliza had occasionally suffered abdominal "attacks" and in late November 1855 was severely stricken. On Sunday she went to church. At noon the next day she began vomiting bile. Walter Gurnee brought in physicians, who diagnosed her condition as "bilious colic" caused by "an obstruction of the bowels."[41]

John Link remained at her side over the next few days. By Thursday she was so ill she guessed she must be dying and asked John whether she was "past recovery." He told her "she was very sick" and "they feared so." Then he wept bitterly. She told him not to weep; she was prepared to die.[42]

Grant Goodrich came. He found her serenely calm but extremely weak. He brought a copy of her will to which he had added a codicil, previously discussed, which stated that the school named in the will was the one the Illinois legislature had recently chartered as Garrett Biblical Institute. She directed him to make a mark for her below the codicil because she was too weak to sign. Then she lifted her hands and declared, "Bless the Lord O my soul," quoting the psalmist. She did not speak again and died at 3:00 p.m. on November 22nd, 1855. She was fifty years old.[43]

POSTSCRIPT

*L*ate on the night of October 8, 1871, after learning that a fire was burning out of control on Chicago's west side, Orrington Lunt went to his west-side office at 36 South Clinton and collected what he could carry from his safe. The fire had already leapt eastward across the south branch of the river and was raging furiously as it made its way in a northeasterly direction through the south side. But it was also creeping more directly north in Lunt's direction. He could see the bright glow and smoke; ashes wafted in the air around him.[1]

Lunt was an organizer of both Garrett Biblical Institute and Northwestern University. He had scouted out the Evanston land for the university grounds where the institute was given its home. A member of the boards of both institutions, he served as the institute's secretary, which is why the minutes of the board of trustees and other records were in the iron safe at his Chicago office on Clinton Street. With the fire practically at his heels, Lunt carried the minutes, cash book, and property deeds and abstracts, as well as records of Northwestern University, to his residence at 188 Michigan Avenue. It soon became clear that the fire was likely to consume the entire business section of the south side, perhaps as far as the lake, so Lunt took his family and what valuables and keepsakes he could carry, including the institute and university records, to another place of safety.[2]

What Lunt called the "great conflagration"—history would know it as the "Great Chicago Fire"—consumed Lunt's office on Clinton Street, melting his safe. It devoured his Michigan Avenue home. It destroyed all the buildings owned by lessees of the Chicago lots of Garrett Biblical Institute, as well as the school's own four-story commercial building at Lake and Market and its two adjacent stores.[3]

According to one researcher's examination of the pre-fire tract book—also saved from the great inferno—when Augustus died, he "owned 220 feet fronting on South Water, 480 on Lake, 220 on Randolph, and a few brick buildings—far more commercial property than anyone else in Chicago then possessed." He may have had additional holdings outside the taxable city limits, the author suggests. In fact, he had property in Wisconsin, and Eliza's name was on certain parcels in Will and LaSalle Counties. Records of the institute show that the estate also included forty-eight feet on Michigan Avenue just south of Twelfth Street.[4]

Augustus bequeathed some of the Lake Street property to his nephew, James Crow, and in the early 1850s Crow had brick buildings at numbers 225 and 227–231. When Eliza asserted her right of dower, the division of the estate had to be redone. Eliza came into possession of parcels on Michigan, Randolph, the Wisconsin land, and the prime real estate on Lake Street and South Water, which included the Sauganash Hotel and adjacent buildings. In 1851 fire destroyed the hotel and properties nearby. Eliza rebuilt the lots, and by 1853 they held a new set of brick buildings.[5]

In the 1849 tax rolls, the assessed valuation of the properties belonging to the estate of Augustus Garrett was recorded as $94,700. Since assessments in that period tended to be only 40–50 percent of actual value, the market value was probably around $200,000. Eliza inherited half the estate, which included half the real estate. Hence, her share of the real estate would have been $100,000 or about three million in today's dollars.[6]

The institute's inheritance from Eliza was essentially her share of Augustus's real estate. In 1856, when the school came into possession of this property, it is unclear what the value was. An article in a Methodist periodical edited by the Hamlines put the value at $100,000, much less than the figure of $300,000 given by Goodrich that same year in an address celebrating the school's official charter.[7]

The institute's trustees made leases with various businessmen of Chicago, charging 6 percent per annum of the assessed value of the property. These contracts required independent assessments by representatives engaged by the parties, producing the nearest thing to an accurate determination of the property's market value. In August of 1858, an accounting in a treasurer's report put the value of the institute's real estate at $284,500, and in December the treasurer reported that income from the properties amounted to a little more than $7000 a year and was likely to increase to $11,000 in the near future.[8]

In 1860 the newly organized Republican Party leased the institute's property at Lake and Market, site of the old Sauganash Hotel, and constructed a huge shed-like convention building made entirely of wood, a "wigwam," as such structures were called at the time. Abraham Lincoln was nominated for president there on May 18, 1860.[9]

It was no accident that the convention organizers negotiated with Garrett Biblical Institute for lease of a site for their convention hall. According to Methodist historian Alvaro Field, in 1860 all the Methodist ministers of northern Illinois save three supported the Republican Party and Lincoln. This included all the ministers who helped organize Garrett Biblical Institute and Northwestern University, as well as the lay founders of the school. Grant Goodrich was ardently antislavery. He knew Abraham Lincoln personally, had once invited him into a law partnership, and was an avid supporter of his nomination.[10]

Goodrich became frustrated when Lincoln showed what Goodrich regarded as excessive caution in furthering the cause of emancipation. Antislavery clergy in Chicago felt the same frustration and, in early September of 1862, signed a "memorial" urging Lincoln to act. John Dempster, now serving as a professor of theology, joined William W. Patton, a local Congregationalist minister, in carrying this memorial to Washington, DC. There they met with Lincoln privately, read the statement aloud to him, and heard his views. Dempster's account of the conversation with Lincoln was subsequently published in the *New York Times* and other leading papers, as was Lincoln's public reply to the memorial. (This reply later became prime material for historians seeking to establish Lincoln's evolution toward the Emancipation Proclamation, which he issued two weeks later.)[11]

Other antislavery activists belonging to the circle of Chicago and Evanston Methodists included Northwestern University founder John Evans. Evans was an organizer of the Republican Party in Illinois, an opponent of the Fugitive Slave Law and extension of slavery into the territories, and a supporter of the Thirteenth Amendment. Orrington Lunt, intimately connected with both schools from the beginning, was also an abolitionist— he used to sing in a quartet at abolition meetings—and a special friend to the African American Methodists of the city. He sold them a lot for their own church building, then donated half the money they owed him when the church fell into financial difficulty after many of the congregation fled to Canada in the wake of the Fugitive Slave Law.[12]

As already noted, the Garrett Biblical Institute owned the land on which the convention wigwam stood, leasing the parcel to the owner of the building. In the early months of the Civil War, the institute negotiated the purchase of the wigwam itself, then leased it to the firm of Broughton & Young, which converted it into a set of retail stores. Seventeen businesses moved in, and the property began generating substantial income. Then disaster struck. On Saturday evening, November 13, 1869, the building "departed in a volume of fire and a cloud of smoke." In reporting on this event, the *Chicago Tribune* commented that the pine structure, only nine years old, was "the grandest and at the same time the most dilapidated structure in the United States." The institute decided to build its own retail stores on the lot. By March a building committee was taking bids, and soon a new Garrett block and two adjacent stores were in operation. These enterprises were short-lived. A year later the Great Chicago Fire struck, sweeping through the buildings at the site and destroying the school's properties on Randolph as well. Only its parcels on Michigan Avenue were spared.[13]

The fire roared into City Cemetery, too, turning wooden markers to ash, ruining stone monuments, and cracking open vaults. The pillar erected to mark the graves of Augustus and Eliza might have been a victim of the stone-shattering heat had not Orrington Lunt removed the marker and the Garrett remains two years prior.

Although the Garretts are not listed by name in the old records of City Cemetery, lots 441 and 442 are listed for Garrett Biblical Institute and were almost certainly their graves. Today, the section of the old cemetery that contained these lots is in Lincoln Park just north of North Avenue and east of Clark, including the current parking lot for the Chicago History Museum. Eliza provided in her will that "sixty dollars a year be paid and laid out . . . in preserving and beautifying the lot in the cemetery in which my husband is buried." This would have been lot 441, and the adjacent lot 442 would have been owned by her as well. Upon her death, her quasi-property interest in these lots was transferred to the institute as part of her estate.[14]

City Cemetery (also known as Chicago Cemetery) was not the first burial ground in Chicago. Although no known Native American burial grounds have been found in the area of the original town, the early white settlers of the place interred their dead on the banks of the Chicago River. In 1835, when the village population stood at several thousand, two cemeteries were established near the shore of Lake Michigan, a Protestant cemetery to the north and a Catholic cemetery south of town. Some years later the city approved the establishment of a new cemetery, and in 1843 the Chicago Common Council ordered that there would be no more interments in older burial grounds.[15]

Late in his first term as mayor, Augustus had seen to the matter of fencing the cemetery; and in his address to the council at the beginning of his second ill-starred term, he referred to "depredations . . . committed, from time to time, by the disinterment of bodies from the cemetery, in the grossest violation of private feeling as well as of public decency." He went on to urge "the most constant vigilance to prevent such occurrences in the future, and the offering of large rewards for the detection of the offenders."[16]

In later years the grave robbers were students of Rush Medical College, who occasionally raided paupers' graves to collect bodies to aid their study of anatomy. But the college had not yet been established at the time of Garrett's inaugural address; hence, the object of the grave raiders' interest must have been jewelry and other valuables. In the 1850s Pinkerton detectives were hired to ferret out the grave violators. The Pinkertons arrested a student of the medical college and a man named Martin Quinian, city sexton, who had conspired with students in grave robbing. They were ironically referred to as "Resurrectionists," and an 1878 article in the *Tribune* published a tongue-in-cheek retrospective on them.[17]

Violation of graves was not the only problem faced by City Cemetery. The graveyard was situated on the north side of North Avenue between Clark and Dearborn Streets. Just to the east was a slough; not far beyond that lay the Lake Michigan shoreline. The high water-table caused many graves to take on water as soon as they were dug. Dr. John H. Rauch, an indefatigable defender of the city's health, worried about exhalations given off by the foul river and the cemetery itself. The city finally ordered the end to interments in City Cemetery in 1859 and, in 1860, entered into an agreement with a newly established cemetery called "Rose Hill" (later Rosehill) stipulating that a section of the grounds be reserved "as a burial place for such bodies as [the city] might direct to be there interred." Inexplicably, the order was not carried out, and human remains continued to enter City Cemetery until 1865. During the same period, however, exhumations and re-interments occurred, particularly of remains in the southernmost part of the cemetery.[18]

The problem reached a crisis with the Civil War, when bodies of cholera victims—Southern prisoners of war who had perished at Camp Douglas on the south side of the city—were buried in City Cemetery. Their graves were dug only three or four feet deep to avoid contact with the water table, but water from rain percolated through the cemetery plots and drained toward Lake Michigan, which was by then the chief source of the city's drinking water. Confronted with these health concerns, the city continued to dither until an unrelated lawsuit compelled it to act. The Illinois Supreme Court determined that twelve acres of land within the cemetery boundaries belonged to the heirs of Jacob Milliman. Rather than purchase the tract for the price demanded by the heirs, the city decided to vacate it. The bodies in what came to be called the "Milliman tract," including the remains of Confederate soldiers, were transferred to Oak Woods Cemetery in 1866 and 1867.[19]

Rosehill Cemetery refused Confederate remains but accepted other bodies from the old cemetery according to its prior agreement with the city. As early as 1860, Garrett Biblical Institute had inquired about purchasing lots in Rosehill for deceased students, at least one having died a little over a year before. The cemetery offered lots to the institute at a rate of one-third of assessed value, based on its policy of discounting the price to religious or benevolent associations. The trustees decided to consult family and friends of the Garretts about the transfer of their remains from City Cemetery to the more hospitable environs of Rosehill. Once permission had been secured, Orrington Lunt arranged for the removal and re-interment.[20]

The task was accomplished in the first week of October 1869. It entailed not only the careful unearthing and removal of the caskets but also the movement of the large monument to its new home, seven miles away. Lunt purchased a double lot at Rosehill—section F, lot 161—and arranged for the monument to be moved there first. Then, on October 6, 1869, he supervised the transfer of the remains. The burial at Rosehill was private. Lunt memorialized the event in a coda to a set of minutes of the institute's board of trustees, writing, "remains Mr. and Mrs. Garrett removed by O. Lunt Oct. 6, 1869, from Old Cemetery to Rosehill lot, buried in front of monument, Mrs. Garrett south side." Lunt would have mentioned Grant Goodrich and others had they assisted. He must have handled the somber duty by himself with the help of the sexton, grave diggers, and a horse-drawn wagon.[21]

The four-sided monument in Rosehill towers over two small grave markers bearing the names "Augustus" and "Eliza." At the time of Augustus's death, Eliza had directed that not only his name but the names of their three children be engraved on the faces of the pinnacle. He is memorialized on the northward panel:[22]

AUGUSTUS GARRETT

BORN

AT NEWBURGH NY

MAR. [19?] 1802[23]

DIED

AT CHICAGO IL

NOVEMBER 30 1848

The names of Charles and John are inscribed on the eastern face:

CHARLES GARRETT

BORN AT CINCINNATI

APRIL [___][24] 1832 DIED AT

NATCHITOCHES LA

FEBRUARY 9 1833

————

JOHN GARRETT

BORN AND DIED AT NEWBURGH

DECEMBER 11 1833

On the southern panel stands the name of Imogine, their firstborn:

IMOGINE GARRETT

DAUGHTER OF AUGUSTUS & ELIZA

GARRETT

BORN AT NEWBURGH

ORANGE CO NY

MAR. [7?][25] 1830

DIED AT PADUCAH KY

OCT 25 1832

When Lunt moved the pillar to Rosehill, he ordered that the monument, which had been situated in the City Cemetery so that Augustus's panel faced the nearby pathway, be configured so that Eliza's panel faced the path in front of the plot. Thus, at the top of the monument, facing west, the stone read:[26]

ELIZA CLARK

WIFE OF AUG

USTUS GARRETT

BORN AT NEWBURGH

ORANGE CO NY

MAR 5 1805

DIED AT CHICAGO

NOV 22 1855

ACKNOWLEDGMENTS

A number of libraries and repositories provided valuable documentary material for this book, including Styberg Library of Garrett-Evangelical Theological Seminary, Northwestern University Archives, Chicago History Museum, Presbyterian Historical Society, Newberry Library, Newburgh Free Library, and Illinois Regional Archives Depository at Northeastern Illinois University. I wish to offer a special thanks to several current and former librarians at the Styberg Library who assisted me with many aspects of information gathering— Library Director Jaeyeon Chung and staff members Mary-Carol Riehs, Daniel Smith, Kathleen Kordesh, and J. Lauren Mondala. These librarians secured numerous resources, helped me with challenging research questions, and assisted with photographs and images. Kevin Leonard at the Northwestern University Archives offered valuable and gracious assistance with the university records pertaining to Augustus Garrett and the founding of the two schools. The old records of three churches were made available to me, and I am grateful to Dianne Luhmann for assistance with the records of First Presbyterian Church of Chicago, to Reverend Laurie McNeill for access to the records of First Presbyterian Church of Marlboro, and to Mary-Carol Riehs for taking me through archives of First Methodist Church of Chicago. I am very appreciative of my faculty colleague Dr. Barry E. Bryant for his guidance in all matters Methodist and Wesleyan. I also extend heartfelt thanks for the support and encouragement of President Lallene J. Rector of Garrett-Evangelical Theological Seminary. The Seminary helped underwrite the project, and for that I extend my gratitude to the Board of Trustees.

Through the course of my research, I also received assistance from Janine Protzman of Poughkeepsie, New York, great-great-great-grandniece of Eliza Garrett by descent from Eliza's brother Jeremiah Clark. Thank you, Janine, for the many enjoyable conversations about your ancestor.

My editor at Southern Illinois University Press, Sylvia Frank Rodrigue, was extremely helpful and a pleasure to work with, as were the other staff at the press, including Jennifer Egan and Wayne Larsen. Robert Brown's meticulous copyediting saved me from many slips and unhappy formulations. Finally, I wish to acknowledge how much I was aided in the beginning of my work by Ila Fischer's fine article on Eliza Garrett, which appeared as a chapter in Rosemary Keller's book *Spirituality and Social Responsibility: Vocational Vision of Women in the United Methodist Tradition*. For a brief introduction to Eliza Garrett, one can do no better than Ila Fisher's account.

NOTES

AGLB Augustus Garrett Letter-Books. Northwestern
     University Archives

CCCPF Chicago City Council Proceedings Files. Illinois
     Regional Archives Depository at Ronald Williams
     Library of Northeastern Illinois University

CHM   Chicago History Museum

EGLC   Eliza Garrett Letter Collection. Styberg Library of
     Garrett-Evangelical Theological Seminary

WOLB William B. Ogden Letter-Books held by the
     Chicago History Museum

PROLOGUE

1. "Speech of General Henry Strong," in *Early Chicago: Reception to the Settlers of Old Chicago prior to 1840 by the Calumet Club of Chicago, Tuesday Evening, May 27, 1879* (Chicago: Calumet Club, 1879), 26–34, 31 ("little log and clapboard village").

2. Don E. Fehrenbacher, *Chicago Giant: A Biography of Long John Wentworth* (Madison, WI: American History Research Center, 1957); Jack Harpster, *The Railroad Tycoon Who Built Chicago: A Biography of William B. Ogden* (Carbondale: Southern Illinois University Press, 2009). There is not even a biography of Juliette Augusta McGill Kinzie, although she records the lives of herself and her husband, John H. Kinzie, up to the mid-1830s, just before Chicago received its charter, in *Wau-Bun: The "Early Day" in the North-West* (New York: Derby & Jackson, 1856).

3. On Eliza as the first woman in America to have founded an institution of higher learning, see [Davis W. Clark,] "Mrs. Garrett: Founder of the Garrett Biblical Institute," *Ladies' Repository* 18 (1858): 427–30, 427 ("the first female in our country who has attained that distinction"—of founding an institution of higher learning comparable to the colleges and universities of the day); Rima

Lunin Schultz and Adele Hast, eds., *Women Building Chicago, 1790–1990: A Biographical Dictionary* (Bloomington: Indiana University Press, 2001), 306 (first woman to found a theological seminary). Garrett Biblical Institute received its charter in 1853 and opened its doors in 1855 to applicants with a high school or college education, granting different degrees depending on prior educational qualifications. The claim that Eliza was the first female founder of an institution of higher education seems to hold for the non-European western hemisphere. As for other schools of higher learning founded by women in North America, Mount Holyoke was established by Mary Lyon in 1837 as a female "seminary" (essentially a high school for training missionaries and teachers) and did not become a college until 1891. Smith College was founded by philanthropist Sophia Smith in 1871. Cottey College was founded as a finishing school in 1884 by Virginia Alice Cottey Stockard. If one wishes to count royal charters in the colonies, then the earliest school established by a woman in North America would be the College of William and Mary, founded in 1693 when both William III and Mary II signed its charter.

I. NEWBURGH BEGINNINGS

1. Edward M. Ruttenber, *History of the Town of Newburgh* (Newburgh, NY: E. M. Ruttenber, 1859), 9 ("sun streaming down"), 10 ("a very pleasant place"); Horatio G. Spafford, ed., *A Gazetteer of the State of New York* (Albany, NY: B. D. Packard, 1824), 339 (town of Newburgh some thirty square miles).

2. Various period sources and later studies mention the produce of Newburgh. On the local industries of the farmlands in those days, see the brief summary for the mid-1830s in Marc C. Carnes, "From Merchant to Manufacturer: The Economics of Localism in Newburgh, 1845–1900," in *America's First River: The History and Culture of the Hudson River Valley*, ed. Thomas S. Wermuth, James M. Johnson, and Christopher Pryslopski (Poughkeepsie, NY: Hudson River Valley Institute, 2009), 113–31, 116.

3. A description of Middle Hope in 1836 speaks of a post office, two taverns, a Methodist chapel, and a dozen houses; see Thomas F. Gordon, *Gazetteer of the State of New York* (Philadelphia: T. K. and P. G. Collins, 1836), 605 (under "Newburgh"). A monument to the Garretts in Rosehill Cemetery in Chicago gives Eliza's birth year as 1805, month and day not legible; the date is given as March 5 in Davis W. Clark, "Mrs. Eliza Garrett," in *Our Excellent Women of the Methodist Church in England and America* (New York: J. C. Buttre, 1861), 201–9, 201, originally published as "Mrs. Garrett: Founder of the Garrett Biblical Institute," *Ladies' Repository* 18 (July 1858): 427–30. A letter from Augustus Garrett to Eliza's parents, January 15, 1845, gives the

Clark address as "Benony Clark, Middle Hope, Orange County" (AGLB II: 32); see also Nathaniel Bartlett Sylvester, *History of Ulster County, New York* (Philadelphia: Everts & Peck, 1860), 99 (Benoni Clark, Eliza's father, "resided at an early day within the present limits of Orange County, near the Ulster County Line"); Edgar W. Clark, *History and Genealogy of Samuel Clark, Sr., and His Descendants*, 2nd ed. (St. Louis: Nixon-Jones Printing, 1902), 29, 55; also Edward M. Ruttenber, "The King's Highway: Its Early Road Districts and the Residents or Owners of Lands Thereon," *Historical Papers* [of the Historical Society of Newburgh Bay and the Highlands] 10 (1903): 21–33, 27.

4. A careful analysis of the circumstances in naming a child Benoni among New Englanders of the seventeenth and eighteenth centuries is presented in Grace M. Pittman, "O My Son Benoni: A Personal Name as Marker of Family Circumstances," *NEXUS* 7 (1990): 17–21 (a journal of the New England Historic Genealogical Society). Joanna married Samuel Stratton Clark (Clark, *History and Genealogy of Samuel Clark, Sr.,* 29).

5. Hugh Hastings, comp. and ed., *Military Minutes of the Council of Appointment of the State of New York, 1783–1821,* vol. 1 (Albany, NY: James B. Lyon, 1901), 809; Clark, *History and Genealogy of Samuel Clark, Sr.,* 55–57 (the children of Benoni and Amy Clark); also Ruttenber, "King's Highway," 27. The Demott surname is spelled Dermott in Clark's *History* and in Sylvester, *History of Ulster County,* 99. But it is spelled Demott in all other sources, including Samuel W. Eager, *An Outline History of Orange County* (Newburgh, NY: S. T. Callahan, 1846–1847), 87.

6. Ruttenber, "King's Highway," 27 ("Amy DeMott, of the line of Michael DeMott, of Balmville"); Eager, *Outline History of Orange County,* 87 ("At Balmville Michael Demott lived as early as 1764 and kept tavern . . . and he had a number of children, among whom were William, Jacobus, and Isaac, who inherited the estate"); Edward M. Ruttenber, *History of the County of Orange, with a History of the Town of Newburgh* (Newburgh, NY: E. M. Ruttenber and Sons, 1875), 275 (Corp. Isaac Demott and Priv. James Demott listed as members of Capt. Samuel Clark's company in Col. Hasbrouk's regiment, June 8, 1778). According to Eager, Isaac inherited his father's estate, but a more exacting reconstruction by Barclay shows that Isaac and James Demott were granted portions of land in Balmville not owned by their father in 1786 and that these acres were bounties promised them in exchange for enlisting during the Revolutionary War. See David Barclay, "Balmville: From the First Settlement to 1860," *Historical Papers* [of the Historical Society of Newburgh Bay and the Highlands] 8 (1901): 45–58, 48. *Patent* is a term for an original land deed.

7. On the Balmville tree, see Barclay, "Balmville," 49–50. The location of Demott's small tavern east of the tree is noted by James Donnelly as quoted in Ruttenber, *History of the County of Orange*, 182. According to Barclay, the name Balmville was given to the place near the end of the eighteenth century (45). The earliest documented reference to Balmville that I have found is in an 1837 list of unincorporated towns. According to Ruttenber, the place was formerly known as Hampton and associated with Acker's Ferry (*History of the Town of Newburgh*, 128, 130). On Augustus's humor and gregariousness, see note 29 of chapter 1.

8. Eager, *Outline History of Orange County*, 18 (poor quality of land for farming); New York State Archives (Albany, New York), *Tax Assessment Rolls of Real and Personal Estates*, Series: B0950; reel 15, box 36, folder 18 (assessment of Benoni Clark's property)—image in Ancestry.com. Among the farmers who tried to improve their lot with supplemental businesses was Eliza's brother Jeremiah. In 1826 he and a man named William Seabring took over the DuBois mill in Marlborough. Apparently, the enterprise did not last more than a year or two. The mill is mentioned in Charles H. Cochrane, *The History of the Town of Marlborough, Ulster County, New York* (Poughkeepsie, NY: W. F. Boshart, 1887), 66. Cochrane states only that Clark and Seabring ran the mill in 1826.

9. Jack Larkin, *The Reshaping of Everyday Life, 1790–1840* (New York: Harper & Row, 1988), 112 (quoting Asa Sheldon's description of the Massachusetts house); Ruttenber, "King's Highway," photographic plate of the Fowler house between pages 28 and 29.

10. Larkin, *Reshaping of Everyday Life*, 122–48.

11. Larkin, *Reshaping of Everyday Life*, 17 (on the gendered division of labor on a farm); also Sarah F. McMahon, "Laying Foods By: Gender, Dietary Decisions, and the Technology of Food Preservation in New England Households, 1750–1850," in *Early American Technology: Making and Doing Things from the Colonial Era to 1850*, ed. Judith A. McGaw (Chapel Hill: University of North Carolina Press, 1994), 164–96, 166–71 (noting gender differences but also a practical blurring of distinctions); W. W. Hall, "The Health of Farmers' Families," in *The Report of the Commissioner of Agriculture for the Year 1862* (Washington, DC: Government Printing Office, 1863), 453–70, 462 ("a farmer's wife").

12. McMahon, "Laying Foods By," 171ff.; John C. Miller, *The First Frontier: Life in Colonial America* (New York: Dell, 1966), 183 ("Every farm family, no matter how self-sufficient, had to buy its salt, sugar, and spices"); Larkin, *Reshaping of Everyday Life*, 51 (no cookstove, the "tin kitchen"); Estelle

M. H. Merrill, "By an Old-Time Fireside," *New England Kitchen Magazine* 1, no. 3 (1894): 131–36, 133 (meats roasted and bread baked in the tin kitchen of colonial days).

13. An advertisement in the *Newburgh Gazette* (July 17, 1824) reads, "READY MADE CLOTHING . . . Those who bring their own cloth can depend on having it cut or made up fashionably, and on reasonable terms." According to a New York gazetteer published in 1824, Newburgh produced 21,788 yards of cloth that year (Spafford, *Gazetteer of the State of New York*, 339). Although it was an era of transition for the better-off in their acquisition of clothing, spinning and weaving would have been basic to women's work in the humble Clark household during Eliza's rural girlhood (1805–1825). According to Larkin, the loom and spinning wheel did not begin to disappear until the 1830s, when manufactured cloth became readily available in cities (*Reshaping of Everyday Life*, 50).

14. A report sponsored by the United States Department of Education in 1925 estimated that, in 1840, the average child received some 208 days of schooling altogether. See William T. Bawden, ed., *The National Crisis in Education: An Appeal to the People* (Washington, DC: Government Printing Office, 1920), 49. The average was undoubtedly lower in 1810–1820 when Eliza was of school age, especially in rural areas. For testimony about education in Sunday schools of the time, see [American Unitarian Association,] *First Annual Report of the Executive Committee of the American Unitarian Association* (Boston: Isaac R. Butts, 1826), 61. There are references in Eliza's correspondence to books, indicating that she engaged in private reading.

15. Alvaro D. Field, *Worthies and Workers, Both Ministers and Laymen, of the Rock River Conference* (Cincinnati: Cranston & Curts, 1896), 312–13 (testimony of Jeremiah Porter); also Jeremiah Porter, "The Earliest Religious History of Chicago" [An Address Read before the Chicago Historical Society in 1859], in *Fergus' Historical Series*, no. 14 (Chicago: Fergus, n.d.), 76. On the Clarks, Samuel Stratton, and the Marlborough Presbyterian church, see Sylvester, *History of Ulster County*, 99 (under "Biographical Sketches, Jeremiah Clark"); Clark, *History and Genealogy of Samuel Clark, Sr.*, 29, 55; Cochrane, *History of the Town of Marlborough*, 108. Benoni and Amy Clark are buried in the cemetery of the First Presbyterian Church of Marlborough. The oldest church session book postdates an 1868 fire in which all the church's documents were destroyed. It appears that the membership list of this book was initially compiled on the basis of then-current members. Eliza's brother Jeremiah and his wife, Finetta, are both listed but not Benoni and Amy, who were dead by then. Eliza had become a Methodist in Chicago in 1839 and by then was also dead.

16. Field, *Worthies and Workers*, 313. In his preface Field states that he collected biographical information about northern Illinois Methodists while conducting research for capsule biographies originally intended for his *Memorials of Methodism in the Bounds of the Rock River Conference*, published in 1886. Whether he contacted relatives of Eliza in New York in the early 1880s or only after writing *Memorials* is unknown. He did not contact Jeremiah Porter about Eliza's religious history until after the publication of *Memorials*, in 1887. It is also uncertain who would have known then—when he did inquire of Newburgh relatives—anything as specific as her attendance at Methodist meetings in the 1820s. Her brother Jeremiah, who remained in Marlborough his whole life, had died in 1877.

17. Ruttenber, *History of the Town of Newburgh*, 231–33; Ruttenber, "King's Highway," 29; C. M. Woolsey, *History of the Town of Marlborough, Ulster County, New York, from Its Earliest Discovery* (Albany, NY: J. B. Lyon, 1908), 377; also Rufus Emery et al., *A Record of the Inscriptions of the Old Town Burying Ground* (Newburgh, NY: Historical Society of Newburgh Bay and the Highlands, 1898), 150 ("Samuel Fowler and Charlotte Purdy Fowler were father and mother of Rev. Samuel Fowler. It was at their residence in Middle Hope that Methodism was cradled in Newburgh"). According to Ruttenber, Asbury Chapel eventually became part of the north Newburgh circuit (*History of the Town of Newburgh*, 233). There were additional Methodist Episcopal churches in these years, but they were in other neighboring towns, one to the west at Gardnertown, one in Rossville, and one in Fostertown, which was not organized until 1833. Therefore, it must have been Asbury Chapel that Eliza attended. The chapel was "three miles north of this village [i.e., Newburgh]" (see Ruttenber, *History of the Town of Newburgh*, 233n). Balmville lies directly in between, and that is the town from which Benoni Clark's mother, Amy, came.

18. James Carnahan, ed., *The Autobiography and Ministerial Life of the Rev. John Johnston* (New York: M. W. Dodd, 1856), 16–36 (his education), 43–58 (descriptions of revivals), 51 ("some praying"), 52 ("things . . . I did not then"), 108–15 (revivals held by Johnson, "sobs and tears"), 108; Ruttenber, *History of the County of Orange*, 281 (location of New Mills district).

19. J. Newton Kugler, *A Brief History of the First Presbyterian Church Marlborough, New York, 1764–1914* (Newburgh, NY: News, ca. 1914), 15 (describing revivals of the Marlborough Presbyterian church); John D. Moriarty, "Newburgh Campmeeting," *Methodist Magazine* 8, no. 11 (November 1825): 440–41 (describing the 1825 meeting; the quotations are from this article); Margaret Washington, *Sojourner Truth's America* (Urbana: University of

Illinois Press, 2009), 72 (referencing the Newburgh revivals held by the Methodists, including typical revivalist behavior, such as clapping, jumping, and falling down on the grass or mud).

20. Washington, *Sojourner Truth's America*, 72 (on the character of revival meetings).

21. Eliza's spiritual life is discussed in greater detail in subsequent chapters.

22. According to a notice of his death in the *Chicago Weekly Democrat* (December 1, 1848), Augustus was in his forty-seventh year when he died. In the parlance of the time, this meant that he had passed his forty-sixth birthday. In that case, he was born in 1802. The inscription on his monument in Rosehill Cemetery gives his birthday as March 19 (although what looks like a 9 is uncertain), and the faded last digit of the year of birth is consistent with a 2. According to Ruttenber, John Garrett's farm lay north of Newburgh on what was once called the King's Highway (later "the Old Main Road" or "old North Road"), being located north of the Jehiel Clark farm and also just north of the river that ran through Middle Hope near its "Stone School House" ("King's Highway," 23, 28). Ruttenber states that the Middle Hope schoolhouse survived until about 1830; it stood near the site of a second schoolhouse, which replaced it at the southeast corner of the D. D. Barnes farm ("King's Highway," 26), that school being shown on the 1875 map of Newburgh in Frederick W. Beers, *County Atlas of Orange, New York, 1875* (Chicago: Andreas, Baskin & Burr, 1875). Clark's *History and Genealogy of Samuel Clark, Sr.* refers to Jehiel Clark purchasing 140 acres of land near Balmville (57), which may well have been the case; but Ruttenber makes it clear that "the old Jehiel Clark place," which was occupied by his son Samuel Clark around 1850, was in Middle Hope (Ruttenber, "King's Highway," 23, 34, with 34 being the second-to-last page of the article numbered incorrectly by the printer).

23. Augustus's father, John Garrett, appears on a tax roll for 1785 and the North Road list for 1786 (Ruttenber, "King's Highway," 28). Some particulars about the history of John are given in a capsule biography of his grandson James C. Crow, in *History of McHenry County, Illinois* (Chicago: Interstate Publishing, 1885), 852. On the genealogy of Eustatia Morgan Garrett, see Debra Guiou(n) Stufflebean, *A French Huguenot Legacy: A Biography of the Guion Huguenots* (Morrisville, NC: LuLu Enterprises, 2011), 230–33. The details about John Garrett in this history are inaccurate, however. Information about John Garrett and his family is given on a monument in the Old Town Cemetery of Newburgh: John Garrett (born October 15, 1755; died June 7, 1833); his wife, Eustatia (born August 23, 1760; died January 1846); their

children—Charles D. (died October 5, 1782, at ten months), Susannah (died October 21, 1793, at the age of four), Esther (died October 17, 1793, at the age of two), Jessie (died in Baltimore, March 16, 1818, at the age of thirty), Thomas D. (died in Baltimore, April 29, 1818, at the age of twenty), Isaac (died in Savannah, August 17, 1818, at the age of eighteen), Rebecca Crow (died in Prince George's County, Maryland, October 20, 1823, at the age of twenty-seven). According to a civil case arising over his will, Augustus had a sister Letitia (who married Valentine Flaglor), as well as a sister Mary (who married a man named Banks) (Gay v. Parpart, 106 U.S. [1883] 679, 687). The federal census implies that, in 1820, the John Garrett household was composed of parents John and Eustatia and their children Augustus (about nineteen years old), a boy (in the age range of ten to fifteen), and Letitia (between the ages of sixteen and twenty-five). This unnamed brother of Augustus was probably a census taker's error in listing another son instead of the daughter Mary. A baptismal record referred to in note 24 (next) gives Eustatia's name as Statia. Augustus's sister Rebecca was married in Baltimore to a man from Maryland (see note 24). Whether they met in New York or Maryland is not known. On Garrett's sale of a slave, see chapter 2.

24. A Maryland marriage record and a newspaper mention Augustus's sister Rebecca marrying Richard B. Crow at the end of December 1815 in Baltimore: Robert W. Barnes, *Maryland Marriages, 1801–1820* (Baltimore: Genealogical Publishing, 1993), 40 (record number 20 BA–222, spelling Rebecca's surname "Garret"); Robert W. Barnes, *Marriages and Deaths from Baltimore Newspapers, 1796–1816* (Baltimore: Genealogical Publishing, 1978), 76 ("CROW, Richard B., and Miss Rebecca Garrett, all of Balto, were married last Tues. by Rev. Duncan"). The Rev. Duncan who presided must have been Rev. John M. Duncan of Baltimore, mentioned in a number of period sources as a Presbyterian clergyman. Newburgh baptismal records include a reference to the baptism of Susannah Garrett. See Augusta Leslie, "Record of Baptisms and Marriages Copied from and Compared with the Original Entries in Stewards' Book, Newburgh, N.Y., Circuit of the Methodist Episcopal Church," in *Historical Papers* [of the Historical Society of Newburgh and the Highlands] 8 (1901): 11 ("April 27, 1890, baptized Susanah Garratt [sic], the daughter of John Garrat [sic], and his wife Statia").

25. Ruttenber, *History of the Town of Newburgh*, 140 (population of Newburgh in 1825–1826), 168; Field, *Worthies and Workers*, 315 (recollection of Garrett professing religion in 1846; the context appears to be the Methodist church to which Field and Eliza Garrett belonged); an "Old Timer" of Chicago, writing in 1893 and quoted in a short typescript biography of Garrett (CHM),

said that Garrett often offered prayers of repentance at revival meetings; Augustus's request for a Church of England funeral comes from a letter (Eliza Garrett to Mr. and Mrs. Hamline, January 29, 1849 [EGLC]). Augustus's maternal grandmother, Susannah Morgan, who married Charles Morgan, was the daughter of Lewis Guion of Eastchester, Westchester County, New York. (The connections are mentioned in an extract from a legal document in the *New York Genealogical and Bibliographical Record* 53 [1922]: 329). It appears that she belonged to St. Paul's Episcopal Church in Eastchester, for her father, Lewis Guion, and her husband, Charles Morgan, are listed as pew renters of that church in Robert Bolton, *History of the Protestant Episcopal Church, in the County of Westchester* (New York: Stanford & Swords, 1855), 385. Therefore, Augustus's mother, Statia, grew up in the Episcopal church in Eastchester.

26. See chapters 6 and 7.

27. Augustus Garrett to Benoni and Amy Clark, January 15, 1845 (AGLB II: 30) (recounting the terms on which his father gave him the farm). The size of the farm is not recorded. It sold several years later for nine hundred dollars, its value diminished by his parents' life interest. Perhaps it would have been worth two thousand dollars had it been free and clear of any encumbrance. The location of Augustus Garrett's farm is based on correlating the following: an advertisement for a sheriff's sale of Fowler lands, which mentions the relation of the farms of Augustus Garrett and Valentine Flaglor (*Newburgh Telegraph*, June 28, 1831, 3); a description of farms circa 1850 (including mention of subsequent inhabitants) lying on the west side of the North Road from Balmville to Middle Hope, with reference to the location of Valentine and Letitia Flaglor's farm (Ruttenber, "King's Highway," 34); and F. W. Beers's 1875 map of Newburgh.

28. The quotation ("I have followed that plow") is cited in Larkin, *Reshaping of Everyday Life*, 15. The description of the details of farm life in rural New York in the early 1800s is based on various sources, including historical studies of the period and original contemporary sources. These are, more or less in the order of the topics mentioned (except for those in Larkin), as follows: D. B. Grigg, *The Agricultural Systems of the World: An Evolutionary Approach* (Cambridge: Cambridge University Press, 1974); Larkin, *Reshaping of Everyday Life*, 15–16, 23, 48–49; Richard Sisson, Christian K. Zacher, and Andrew R. L. Clayton, eds., *The American Midwest: An Interpretive Encyclopedia* (Bloomington: Indiana University Press, 2007), 1027; William T. Coggeshall, "The Advantages of Planting Grain with a Drill, Practically Considered," *New Jersey Farmer* 4, no. 6 (February 1859): 172; Paul K. Conkin, *A Revolution Down on the Farm: The Transformation of American Agriculture*

since 1929 (Lexington: University Press of Kentucky, 2009), 9; *New England Farmer*, June 14, 1823, 364; *American Farmer*, April 21, 1826, 33. The mechanical thresher was something of a novelty in the 1820s, and it is doubtful that Augustus had use of one. Tellingly, there are no references to Cyrus McCormick or to mechanical reapers in *New York Farmer and American Gardner's Magazine* for the years 1834–1836, when the McCormick reaper was still a local product manufactured and sold by McCormick on his Virginia farm. It was only after McCormick transferred his operations to Chicago that he met with commercial success, thanks to the appetite for innovation in regions of recent agricultural settlement. See Paul A. David, *Technical Choice, Innovation and Economic Growth: Essays on American and British Experience in the Nineteenth Century* (Cambridge: Cambridge University Press, 1975), 199–200; Douglas Harper, *Changing Works: Visions of a Lost Agriculture* (Chicago: University of Chicago Press, 2001), 34; *American Farmer*, December 4, 1829, 299; see also Craig Canine, *Dream Reaper: The Story of an Old-Fashioned Inventor in the High-Tech, High-Stakes World of Modern Agriculture* (Chicago: University of Chicago Press, 1995).

29. Anecdotes come down about how funny and entertaining Garrett was in his auction rooms (Field, *Worthies and Workers*, 129, 313–14); *Some Recollections of John V. Farwell: A Brief Description of His Early Life and Business Reminiscences* (Chicago: R. R. Donnelley & Sons, 1911), 52–53. His letters to his business partner also include very humorous passages.

30. Augustus describes his failure in farming in a letter to Eliza's parents in which he speaks of "the farm that I fooled away in my youthful days for lack of experience" (Augustus to Benoni and Amy Clark, January 15, 1845, in AGLB II: 30).

31. Compare information about Benoni and Jehiel Clark in Clark, *History and Genealogy of Samuel Clark, Sr.*, 55, 57. On the location of the Jehiel Clark farm, see note 22 above.

32. Clark, "Mrs. Eliza Garrett," 201 (giving the marriage year as 1825); Field, *Worthies and Workers*, 314 (1829 marriage year). Field refers to "ancient tradition at Newburgh" about Eliza's Methodist connections, which may suggest that he wrote to her relatives there; but he carried out his biographical investigations in the mid-1880s or perhaps even as late as the early 1890s, when Eliza's brother was already dead (see note 16). The year 1825 is also given in Matthew Simpson, ed., *Cyclopedia of Methodism*, 5th ed. (Philadelphia: Louis H. Everts, 1883), 390. But this short article probably relies on Clark.

33. Daniel B. Smith, "The Study of the Family in Early America: Trends, Problems, and Prospects," *William and Mary Quarterly*, 3rd ser., 39 (1982):

3–28, 18 ("away from the well-ordered"; Smith is summarizing converging conclusions by various researchers on the topic in the 1970s); Karen Lystra, *Searching the Heart: Women, Men, and Romantic Love in Nineteenth-Century America* (Oxford: Oxford University Press, 1989), 227ff. (change in courtship in the postrevolutionary era); Herman R. Lantz, Margaret Britton, Raymond Schmitt, and Eloise C. Snyder, "Pre-industrial Patterns in the Colonial Family in America," *American Sociological Review* 33 (1968): 413–26, 419 (quoting a study by Furstenburg: "praised the American marriage system"), 419–20 ("one and only," etc.), 419 ("When I am not with her").

34. Edward Jarvis quoted in E. Anthony Rotundo, *American Manhood: Transformations in Masculinity from the Revolution to the Modern Era* (New York: Basic Books, 1993), 111 ("I am very sorry"); Clayton Kingman in Rotundo, *American Manhood*, 111 ("I want you to be as open" and "more like one"); Catherine E. Kelly, *In the New England Fashion: Reshaping Women's Lives in the Nineteenth Century* (Ithaca, NY: Cornell University Press, 1999), 131n8 ("prevailing gender relations").

35. John Foster quoted in Lystra, *Searching the Heart*, 133.

36. Elizabeth Bradley quoted in Kelly, *In the New England Fashion*, 136; Edward Dickinson to Emily Norcross (parents of Emily Dickinson) as quoted in Richard B. Sewall, *The Life of Emily Dickinson*, vol. 1 (2 vols. in 1; Cambridge: Harvard University Press, [1974] 1994), 47 ("Let us prepare for a life").

37. A man who knew her when she was in her midthirties describes her as "handsome," "graceful in her movements," and "divinely tall." Selah Cogshall quoted in "The Reverend W. Selah Cogshall's Early Remembrances of Methodism in Chicago—The Great Revival in the Winter of 1839—Conversion of Mr. Garrett, Etc.," *Chicago Daily Tribune*, November 24, 1873, 5. On Augustus's having "fooled away" his farm, see note 30. Eliza's anxiety about telling her parents about Augustus's plans is clear from a letter (see note 38). Augustus's business letters show his humor and energy in argument as he builds a logical case to his recipients for seeing things from his point of view. One suspects that he courted Eliza with the same combination of charm and logic.

38. In view of what we know of patterns in the industrial age—that women and men began migrating to cities as soon as factories offered them jobs there—it is likely that many women of earlier eras also longed for a city life, especially given their experience of isolation on the farm (see note 11 of chapter 1 and note 25 of chapter 2). In an 1887 letter to Alvaro Field, Porter recalled his meeting with Augustus as follows: "Mr. Augustus Garrett came a stranger to my study in infant Chicago to tell me of his plans.

Having failed as an auctioneer in New Orleans and Cincinnati, he wished to start anew in Chicago, hoping, if now successful, *to induce the parents of his wife to permit her to join him* at Chicago" (Field, *Worthies and Workers*, 312; emphasis added).

2. PROSECUTED AND PUT TO COST

1. Friends' recollections of the Garretts have them leaving Newburgh and heading first to Cincinnati, then to New Orleans and Natchitoches, Louisiana, before moving to Chicago. The earliest testimony, on which others may be based, is that of Jeremiah Porter as preserved in Alvaro D. Field, *Worthies and Workers, Both Ministers and Laymen, of the Rock River Conference* (Cincinnati: Cranston & Curts, 1896), 312–13; also Jeremiah Porter, "The Earliest Religious History of Chicago" [An Address Read before the Chicago Historical Society in 1859] in *Fergus' Historical Series* no. 14 (Chicago: Fergus, n.d.), 76. In a letter to Eliza's parents, Augustus refers to his having failed at business in Cincinnati (Augustus Garrett to Benoni and Amy Clark, Chicago, January 15, 1845 [AGLB II: 31]).

2. For the family history of James Crow, see *History of McHenry County* (Chicago: Inter-State Publishing, 1885), 852; also the reference to his parents in chapter 1, note 24 of this book. On Augustus's role in the matter of James Crow's slave, see Petition of Augustus Garrett, Guardian of James Crow, filed 18 August 1830, Baltimore City Register of Wills (Petitions), MSA SC 4239–14–141 M11025, Schweninger Collection, Maryland State Archives.

3. 1799 act: chapter 62, "An Act for the Gradual Abolition of Slavery (29 March 1799)," in *Laws of the State of New York Passed at the Twenty-Second Session, Second Meeting, of the Legislature* (Albany, NY: Loring Andrews, 1799), 721–23. 1817 act: chapter 137, "An Act Relative to Slaves and Servants (March 31, 1817)," in *Laws of the State of New York Passed at the Fortieth Session of the Legislature*, vol. 4 (Albany, NY: Websters and Skinners, 1818), 136–44. See also part 1, chapter 20, title 7 and part 2, chapter 8, title 4, article 2 of the laws of the State of New York as excerpted in [New York Manumission Society], *Selections from the Revised Statutes of the State of New York, Containing All Laws of the State Relative to Slaves and the Law Relative to the Offences of Kidnapping, Which Several Laws Took Effect January 1, 1830* (New York: Vanderpool & Cole, 1830), 3–9.

4. David N. Gellman, *Emancipating New York: The Politics of Slavery and Freedom, 1777–1827* (Baton Rouge: Louisiana State University Press, 2006), 20, 49, 135 (slavery and Ulster County); *Newburgh Gazette*, August 21, 1824 (reporting that 10,092 slaves were living in the state of New York in 1820).

5. Quotation from Petition of Augustus Garrett, Guardian of James Crow (see citation in note 2).

6. Examination of many issues of the *Newburgh Telegraph* in the late 1820s and the *Newburgh Gazette* in the 1830s uncovered no references to Cincinnati as a place of growth and opportunity. Of course, the Newburgh papers had no reason to tout other cities.

7. *Niles' Weekly Register* 30 (July 1, 1826): 320 (a route from New York to Pittsburgh via Lake Erie and Chautauqua Lake with very little overland travel); Calvin Colton, *Manual for Emigrants to America* (London: F. Westley and A. H. Davis, 1932), 184–85 (the water route by way of the canal was longer but cheaper).

8. Memorial on the Garrett grave marker in Rosehill Cemetery, Chicago (giving the date and place of the birth of the Garretts' daughter, Imogine, as March 1830, Newburgh); Colton, *Manual for Emigrants to America*, 185 (implying at least two weeks and probably more of travel time by the water routes from New York to Cincinnati); Henry Wadsworth Longfellow, "Catawba Wine" (1850) ("To the Queen of the West / In her garlands dressed / On the banks of the Beautiful River"); Frances Trollope, *Domestic Manners of the Americans*, vol. 1 (London: Whittaker, Treacher, 1832), 68.

9. Daniel Aaron, *Cincinnati, Queen City of the West, 1819–1838* (Columbus: Ohio State University Press, 1992), 15 ("tremendous commercial"); Edward Everett in the *Cincinnati Chronicle and Literary Gazette*, July 18, 1829.

10. Everett's speech opposing passage of the Indian Removal Act was published in *Register of Debates in Congress, Comprising the Leading Debates and Incidents of the First Session of the Twenty-First Congress*, vol. 6 (Washington, DC: Gales and Seaton, 1830), 1058–79, especially 1068–74. He made a subsequent speech in 1831 calling for repeal of the act. The report of the Georgia legislative committee is quoted in Steve Inskeep, *Jacksonland: President Andrew Jackson, Cherokee Chief John Ross, and a Great American Land Grab* (New York: Penguin Books, 2015), 234.

11. Garrett's political opinions and affiliations are discussed in chapter 5.

12. Daniel F. Littlefield and James W. Parins, eds., *Encyclopedia of American Indian Removal*, vol. 1 (Santa Barbara, CA: Greenwood, 2011), 217–18.

13. The method by which Augustus made connections in Cincinnati is an inference from the approach he used in Chicago (see chapter 3). Information about the Presbyterian churches of Cincinnati circa 1830 is from Ezra H. Gillett, *History of the Presbyterian Church in the United States of America*, vol. 2 (Philadelphia: Presbyterian Publication Committee, 1864), 358 (recent revivals that had dramatically increased the size of First Presbyterian); Charles

T. Greve, *Centennial History of Cincinnati and Representative Citizens*, vol. 1 (Chicago: Biographical Publishing, 1904), 620–22 (early history of Presbyterian churches in Cincinnati), 622 (founding of Presbyterian churches in Cincinnati, there being three by 1830 and perhaps a Fourth Presbyterian); Aaron, *Cincinnati*, 192 (Second Presbyterian's new building; it was the wealthier congregation).

14. Presbyterians kept meticulous membership records, and the rolls for neither First Presbyterian Church of Cincinnati nor Second Presbyterian include either of the Garretts. Eliza is also not listed in the membership records of First Presbyterian Church of Chicago during the years she attended. Most revealing, it is clear that she had no letter of membership from either her Marlborough Presbyterian church nor any Cincinnati Presbyterian church with which to join First Presbyterian in Chicago. On the reasons why Eliza did not seek church membership, see chapter 3.

15. Alfred T. Andreas, *History of Chicago. From the Earliest Period to the Present Time*, vol. 1: *Ending with the Year 1857* (Chicago: A. T. Andreas, 1884), 621 (Garrett in auction business in Cincinnati); Nathaniel Whittock et al., *The Complete Book of Trades* (London: Thomas Tegg, 1842), 10 ("memory, observation, and shrewdness").

16. Goods were auctioned off in bulk in an eastern city, such as New York; from there they traveled to other destinations, where they were auctioned off again. Deals were made at the docks by both auctioneers and shop owners, the latter becoming irritated when they found that articles for sale in their shops were going for less next door under the auctioneer's hammer. See *Proceedings of the National Convention for the Protection of American Interests in the City of New-York, April 5, 1841* (New York: Greeley and McElrath, 1841), 10–12 (critique of the auction system and its connection with wholesale, cheap, poorly made foreign imports); [A Committee of New York Merchants], *An Examination of the Reasons Why the Present System of Auction Ought to Be Abolished* (Boston: Beals, Homer, 1828), 16 (on the claim that auctions promote the manufacture of poorly made goods), 18 (on the claim that auctioneers are men of low character, unscrupulous); Lewis E. Atherton, "Auctions as a Threat to American Business in the Eighteen Twenties and Thirties," *Bulletin of the Business Historical Society* 11 (1937): 104–7; *Journal of the House of Representatives of the United States, Being the Second Session of the Eighteenth Congress, Begun and Held at the City of Washington, Dec. 6, 1924* (Washington, DC: Gales & Seaton, 1824), 96 (Cincinnati merchants petitioned Congress on January 3, 1825, asking that duties be imposed on foreign goods sold at auction).

17. The fee for the yearly auctioneer's license was based on one's prior six months of sales, which meant that one probably paid only a registration charge when starting out. See *Charter and Code of Ordinances of the City of Cincinnati* (Cincinnati: Council of the City of Cincinnati, 1828), V.1.100, 100.4, 103. Period sources speak of "auction rooms," the pulpit, hammer, and bell. In Chicago, Garrett hired a man to go about town on a horse ringing a bell and announcing the auction's goods and times. See Field, *Worthies and Workers*, 314. It was common to use handbills, and one of the broadsheets from Garrett's Chicago days as an auctioneer survives (held by CHM).

18. Chapter 4 of *Acts of a General Nature, Ordered to Be Re-printed, at the First Session of the Eighteenth General Assembly of the State of Ohio*, vol. 18 (Columbus: P. H. Olsted, 1820), 10–11 (Ohio law regarding auctions); Benjamin Drake and E. D. Mansfield, *Cincinnati in 1826* (Cincinnati: Morgan, Lodge, and Fisher, 1927), 81 (number of auctioneers and their sales in 1826). If the increase in city auction sales tracked with the increase in city population from 1827 to 1830, then Drake's information about gross auction sales for the year 1826 permits a rough estimate of auction earnings for 1830, when there were still about the same number of auctioneers in the city. (Robinson and Fairbank, comps., *The Cincinnati Directory for the Year 1831* [Cincinnati: Robinson & Fairbank, 1831], speaks of nine auctioneers but actually lists eleven.) The population at the beginning of 1827 was about 16,230 according to Drake (*Cincinnati in 1826*, 57). According to the census, it was 24,831 in 1830, an increase of 8601, or a bit more than 50 percent. Using that percentage, we can work out the following very rough calculations: 1.5 × $233,800 (gross sales in 1826) = $350,700 (gross sales in 1830) ÷ 10 auctioneers = $35,070 average gross sales per auctioneer × 0.07 average commission = $2,455 average gross profit per auctioneer.

19. Information on leasing business space in Cincinnati in 1841 is given in Charles Cist, *Cincinnati in 1841: Its Early Annals and Future Prospects* (Cincinnati: by the author, 1841), 265–67. Four stores and two offices were leased by the proprietor of a building on Front Street for $3,950—an average of about $658 per unit, although store rental may have been costlier than office rental. That same year leases for stores on Main Street averaged $1,100 a year, and at the corner of Third and Main, a small office rented for $900 a year. It is possible that rents were much lower in 1830, but the 1841 figures are for a year not long after the real estate/economic crash of 1837, and costs *then* may have been lower. The Robinson and Fairbank city directory for Cincinnati in 1831 shows seven out of eleven auctioneers on Main Street and none on Front.

20. See note 19 above (on business leases); W. G. Lyford, *The Western Address Directory* [. . .] *Together with Historical, Topographical, and Statistical Sketches (for the Year 1837)* (Baltimore: Jos. Robinson, 1837), 349 (hotel rates for room and board were $1.25–1.50 per diem in Cincinnati when the author stayed there in 1837); [Selah Cogshall,] "The Reverend W. Selah Cogshall's Early Remembrances of Methodism in Chicago—The Great Revival in the Winter of 1839—Conversion of Mr. Garrett, Etc.," *Chicago Daily Tribune*, November 24, 1873, 5 (describing what Augustus owed as "$50,000 less than nothing"). The figure $1,800 is a low estimate for the combined hotel bill (at least $90 a month) and rental of a store (at $700 a year), and Augustus would have had other business and personal expenses as well. The calculation in current dollars (2018) is based on the following formula: 1830 dollar(s) × (2018 CPI ÷ 1830 CPI). Formula and information on the consumer price index (CPI) published by the Federal Reserve Bank of Minneapolis is available at https://www.minneapolisfed.org/community/teaching-aids/cpi-calculator-information (accessed June 2018). Augustus refers to his Cincinnati debts when he left Cincinnati in a letter to Benoni and Amy Clark, January 15, 1845 (AGLB II: 31) (including his reference to being "prosecuted and put to cost").

21. C. D. Arfwedson, *The United States and Canada, in 1832, 1833, and 1834*, vol. 2 (London: Richard Bentley, 1834), 128–29 ("handsome" and "brilliant," in an account of the author's visit to Cincinnati in February 1833); Karl Bernard, *Travels through North America, during the Years 1825 and 1826*, vol. 2 (2 vols. in 1; Philadelphia: Carey, Lee, and Carey, 1828), 136 (another mid-1820s European visitor who found Cincinnati to be a city laid out in a grid with mostly brick houses).

22. Alexis de Tocqueville quoted in George W. Pierson, *Tocqueville and Beaumont in America* (Oxford: Oxford University Press, 1938), 552–53; *Cincinnati Chronicle and Literary Gazette*, February 11, 1837 (street conditions and hogs) as paraphrased in Aaron, *Cincinnati*, 91.

23. Trollope, *Domestic Manners of the Americans*, vol. 1, 58 (on the housing problem, including "the demand for houses"). Period descriptions of Cincinnati hotels come from wealthier travelers who stayed at the best hotels in town. See William Bullock, *Sketch of a Journey through the Western States of North America from New Orleans, by the Mississippi, Ohio, City of Cincinnati, and Falls of Niagara, to New York, in 1827* (London: John Miller, 1827), xvi, 134 (describing dinners at Colonel Mack's Hotel); Frederick Hall, *Letters from the East and from the West* (Washington, DC: F. Taylor and Wm. M. Morrison, 1840; Applewood Books reprint), 106–7 (deprecating the Pearl Street House

as no better than a typical good public house, based on his experience of it in the summer of 1838). What the rest of the hotels were like can be guessed by considering the limits of what the average person could afford in hotel accommodations and what living conditions and personal habits were like in the 1820s and early 1830s, especially in the West (see Jack Larkin, *The Reshaping of Everyday Life, 1790–1840* [New York: Harper & Row, 1988], 127–32).

24. Bullock, *Sketch of a Journey through the Western States*, xvi, 134 (Cincinnati merchants who preferred hotels to housekeeping). As far as I can determine, Augustus and Eliza lived in hotels from at least 1830 to 1844, including years of wealth. They must have liked the convenience and the social life, for only a year after they finally built a house, Augustus remarked that "we are tired of housekeeping," meaning that both of them were tired of all the work entailed in maintaining a house, were maybe a bit lonely in it too, and were ready to go back to a hotel. Garrett to Benoni and Amy Clark, January 15, 1845 (AGLB II: 32).

25. A government study of the lives of farm women conducted in 1913 found a good deal of loneliness and boredom, especially on the plains but also in denser farming communities. See the United States Department of Agriculture, *Social and Labor Needs of Farm Women* (Report no. 103; Washington, DC: Government Printing Office, 1915), 11, 12, 16, passim. Even women who grew up on farms in rural Kentucky in the early twentieth century, where farmsteads were in sight of each other, told me that there was almost never any socializing during the week and that often it was only on Sunday that they saw friends and could socialize. It was different for the men, who worked together on each other's farms ("swapped work") and gathered at general stores when their farm work was slow. Circumstances in the 1820s cannot have been any less isolating for rural women. For an idea of opinions about infant care in the period, see Catherine E. Beecher, *A Treatise on Domestic Economy, for the Use of Young Ladies at Home and at School*, rev. ed. (Boston: Thomas H. Webb, 1843), 213–20 ("On the Care of Infants").

26. M. E. Thalheimer, "History of the Vine Street Congregational Church of Cincinnati," in *Papers of the Ohio Church History Society*, vol. 9, ed. Delavan L. Leonard (Oberlin, OH: Ohio Church History Society, 1898), 41–56, 45–46 (formation of the Sixth Presbyterian Church in response to proslavery preaching by Joshua Wilson); Church Record Book of the Sixth Presbyterian Church, 1831–1887, vol. 1, 31, Cincinnati Historical Society; Minutes of the Sixth Presbyterian Church, vol. 1, 32, Cincinnati Historical Society; "Editorial Correspondence," *Public*, March 29, 1902, 805–8, 807 ("seceded," with Asa Mahan as the first minister).

27. Acquisition of Texas occurred in 1845 when the Polk administration annexed the territory, sparking the Mexican War. On the moral principles and disciplinary cases of Sixth Presbyterian in the 1830s through 1860s, see Thalheimer, "History of the Vine Street Congregational Church," 49 (cases of church discipline), 51 (stop on Underground Railway); Church Record Book of the Sixth Presbyterian Church, 1831–1887, vol. 1, 31; Minutes of the Sixth Presbyterian Church, vol. 1, 32; "Editorial Correspondence," 807 (regarding Asa Mahan).

28. Joan D. Hedrick, *Harriet Beecher Stowe: A Life* (Oxford: Oxford University Press, 1994), 102–5.

29. The Garrett monuments in the Old Town Cemetery in Newburgh and Rosehill Cemetery in Chicago give information about Charles. On the cholera epidemic, see Ruth C. Carter, "Cincinnatians and Cholera: Attitudes toward the Epidemics of 1832 and 1849," *Queen City Heritage*, Fall 1992, 32–48, 33 (newspaper references to cholera in Paris and Canada in May and June 1832); *Cincinnati Daily Gazette*, June 18, 1832 (Drake's first warning letter on cholera); *Liberty Hall & Cincinnati Gazette*, July 5, 1832 (Drake's warning letter reprinted in another paper); *Liberty Hall & Cincinnati Gazette*, September 27, 1832 (reassuring news); *Cincinnati Daily Gazette*, October 8, 1932, 3 (Drake's report of fifteen cases of cholera and the editor's response).

30. *Liberty Hall & Cincinnati Gazette*, October 18, 1832 ("The whole atmosphere"); John F. Henry, "A Letter on the Cholera as It Occurred in Cincinnati, Ohio, in the Month of October, 1832," *Transylvania Journal of Medicine* 5, no. 4 (1832): 507–33, 521 (the author's impression that the whole population suffered from the disease to one degree or other).

31. *Cincinnati Chronicle*, October 13, 1832, extra edition (Drake's guide for treating cholera); reprinted in Carter, "Cincinnatians and Cholera," 34.

32. Drake in the *Liberty Hall & Cincinnati Gazette*, October 18, 1832; Henry, "Letter on the Cholera," 533.

33. Carter, "Cincinnatians and Cholera," 37 (theater closed, hotel restaurant not serving); *Liberty & Cincinnati Gazette*, November 8, 1832 (inglorious fleeing); *Cincinnati Daily Gazette*, October 15, 1832 (quoting Alexander Pope's translation).

34. The Garrett monument in the Old Town Cemetery in Newburgh lists the date and place of Imogine's death as October 25, 1832, Paducah, Kentucky. According to the earliest rehearsal of the Garretts' lives, the child died of cholera, which fits the circumstances of the Garretts' departure from Cincinnati in the midst of a cholera epidemic. See D. W. Clark, "Mrs. Eliza Garrett," in *Our Excellent Women of the Methodist Church in England and America* (New

York: J. C. Buttre, 1861; originally published in *Ladies' Repository* 18 [July 1858]: 201–9, 202) ("a daughter, four years old, who died a victim of cholera"). Steamboats traveled about ten miles an hour and a hundred miles a day in 1830. The distance by water from Cincinnati to Paducah was 456 miles. Hence it took four to five days for the Garretts to reach Paducah. Imogine must have shown symptoms around the third or fourth day, since people died of cholera within four to eight hours of showing signs of the disease. Calculation of the travel time from Cincinnati to Paducah is based on information in S. L. Kotar and J. E. Gessler, *The Steamboat Era: A History of Fulton's Folly on America's Rivers, 1807–1860* (Jefferson, NC: McFarland, 2009), 62.

35. Keya Chaudhuri and S. N. Chatterjee, *Cholera Toxins* (Berlin: Springer, 2009), 4 (describing the cause, progress, and treatment of cholera). "Noxious miasmas" is an oft-used phrase of the period.

36. Henry, "Letter on the Cholera," 525, 527.

37. *Liberty Hall & Cincinnati Gazette*, October 18, 1932 (Henry Boyd's advice); quoted in Carter, "Cincinnatians and Cholera," 36. This Henry Boyd was a carpenter who built up a prosperous business in Cincinnati and thereby won a place for himself in Carter G. Woodson, *Negro Makers of History* (Washington, DC: Associated Publishers, 1928). Woodson did not know about Boyd's percipient suggestion during the cholera epidemic.

38. On the early history and founding of the town, including the founding of churches, see John E. L. Robertson, *Paducah: 1830–1980, a Sesquicentennial History* (Paducah: by the author, [1980]), 1–17.

39. The City of Paducah website gives basic facts about the early cemeteries: www.paducahky.gov. When city hall was built in 1847, the human remains from that first cemetery were transferred to a new one, Oak Grove, to the west and beyond the town border. The earliest date on a monument in that later cemetery is 1841. On the burial of Imogine, see Clark, "Mrs. Eliza Garrett," 201 ("the melancholy task of burying on the river's bank their first-born"). Abel Stevens, probably relying on Clark, says the same. See Abel Stevens, *The Women of Methodism: Its Three Foundresses, Susanna Wesley, the Countess of Huntingdon, and Barbara Heck* (New York: Carlton & Porter, 1866), 282 ("They lost their first-born child by cholera, in its fourth year, while passing down the Mississippi, and were compelled to pause and leave it in a grave on the bank of the river").

40. Karin E. Gedge, *Without the Benefit of Clergy: Women and the Pastoral Relationship in Nineteenth-Century American Culture* (Oxford: Oxford University Press, 2003), 179 ("poignantly remarked"); Harriet Martineau, *Society in America*, vol. 2 (Paris: Baudry's European Library, 1837), 251–52.

41. The phrases "absolute dependence on Him" and "His mercy toward them" are not direct quotations but rather characterizations of how people spoke and wrote about the subject (typically capitalizing the pronoun when it applied to the Deity).

42. S. [J. T. Sawyer], "Salvation of Infants," *Christian Messenger* 1 (March 10, 1832): 149.

43. See Peter J. Thuesen, *Predestination: The American Career of a Contentious Doctrine* (Oxford: Oxford University Press, 2009), 176–79 (Presbyterian conflicts over damnation of infants, personal differences in what was professed publicly and believed privately). For period discussions, see N. L. Rice, *God Sovereign and Man Free: On the Doctrine of Foreordination and Man's Free Agency* (Philadelphia: Presbyterian Board of Publication, 1850), 120–22 (denying, against claims by Alexander Campbell, that Calvinism contemplates the damnation of those who die in infancy); Francis Hodgson, *An Examination of the System of New Divinity; or, New School Theology* (New York: George Lane, 1839), 324–27 (a Methodist's examination of current Reformed Protestant opinion; remarks on vagueness about the age range covered by the term *infant*). On infant damnation among Old Schoolers, see George L. Prentiss, "Infant Salvation and Its Theological Bearings," *Presbyterian Review* 4 (1883): 548–80, 558–61; Charles P. Krauth, *Infant Baptism and Infant Salvation in the Calvinist System: A Review of Dr. Hodge's Systematic Theology* (Philadelphia: Lutheran Book Store, 1874) (disputing Hodge's liberal view on the subject as a departure from the unified position of Calvin, the Westminster Confession, and the Reformed divines through the Second Helvetic Confession).

44. An account, quoting Harriet Beecher Stowe's firsthand recollection, is given in Nancy Koester, *Harriet Beecher Stowe: A Spiritual Life* (Grand Rapids, MI: Eerdmans, 2014), 62–64.

45. *Star and Adams*, November 5, 1832 ("The Cholera or Cold Plague"), as quoted in Kotar and Gessler, *Steamboat Era*, 238; Gayle Aiken, "The Medical History of New Orleans," in *Standard History of New Orleans, Louisiana*, ed. Henry Rightor (Chicago: Lewis, 1900), 203–25, 213 (one in seven died); Charles E. Rosenberg, *The Cholera Years: The United States in 1832, 1849, and 1866* (Chicago: University of Chicago Press, 1962), 38 (people's efforts to protect themselves from cholera).

46. Testimony about the Garretts by those who knew them indicates that Augustus went into the auction business in New Orleans, which means that they stayed in that city for at least some period of weeks or months. See Porter, "Earliest Religious History of Chicago," 76 (in business as an

auctioneer in Cincinnati and New Orleans); Field, *Worthies and Workers,* 314 (mentioning Cincinnati, New Orleans, and Nacogdoches, Texas [*sic*]).

47. On Natchitoches as the Garretts' next destination, see note 50. On the town: Louisiana Writers' Project, *Louisiana: A Guide to the State* (New York: Hastings House, 1941), 301 (Natchitoches believed to be on the way to becoming "the second largest city in Louisiana"); Wellington Williams, *The Traveller's and Tourist's Guide through the United States of America* (Philadelphia: Lippincott, Grambo, 1855), 174 (travel distance by steamboat from New Orleans to Natchitoches).

48. Richard Seale, "The Town of Natchitoches," in Philip Gould et al., *Natchitoches and Louisiana's Timeless Cane River* (Baton Rouge: Louisiana State University Press, 2002), 22 (the work of Shreve, quotations). A detailed account of the Great Raft, the bayou and river systems connected with it, and Shreve's removal project is given in Jacques D. Bagur, *A History of Navigation on Cypress Bayou and the Lakes* (Denton: University of North Texas Press, 2001), especially 105 (regarding the length of the Great Raft).

49. The cemetery memorials to the Garrett children imply that the family left Cincinnati in October of 1832 and were living in Natchitoches in early February of 1833. Natchitoches in the 1830s is described in William Darby and Theodore Dwight, *A New Gazetteer of the United States of America* (Hartford, CT: Edward Hopkins, 1833), 333.

50. Garrett monument in Rosehill Cemetery, Chicago (death of Charles on February 9, 1833, in Natchitoches, Louisiana). In 1830 it took sixteen days to go from New Orleans to Pittsburgh—eight days from New Orleans to Louisville and another eight days to Pittsburgh by steamboat. See "Steamboats in the West," *Hazard's Register of Pennsylvania* 5 (1830): 74–75, 75. The Garretts first had to go southeast on the Red River to connect with the Mississippi and then travel north to Pittsburgh; from there to Newburgh was nearly four hundred miles by stagecoach.

51. Garrett monument in the Old Town Cemetery of Newburgh (places and dates of death for John Garrett and John Augustus Garrett); Garrett monument in Rosehill Cemetery, Chicago (birth and death dates and place for John Augustus Garrett). Only the Newburgh monument gives the middle name of the Garretts' son.

3. THE GREAT FAIRY LAND OF FORTUNES

1. Don E. Fehrenbacher, *Chicago Giant: A Biography of Long John Wentworth* (Madison, WI: American History Research Center, 1957), 14–16; Alfred T. Andreas, *History of Chicago: From the Earliest Period to the Present*

Time, vol. 3: *From the Fire of 1871 until 1885* (Chicago: A. T. Andreas, 1886), 839 (quoting Wentworth regarding the jug of whisky for his feet); Donald L. Miller, *City of the Century: The Epic of Chicago and the Making of America* (New York: Simon & Schuster, 1996), 77.

2. Augustus Garrett to Benoni and Amy Clark, January 15, 1845 (AGLB II: 30) (commas added to this run-on sentence); John Hayward, *Appendix to Hayward's New England Gazetteer and Specimens of the Northern Register* ([Boston]: W. White, 1841), 23 (Albany to Buffalo = 363 miles; Buffalo to Chicago = 943); it was 61 miles on the Hudson from Newburgh to Albany. The total: 1,367 miles. One author's account of early Chicago puts Augustus's arrival there in the fall but seems to think the year was 1836, which casts doubt on the information. See H. G. Cutler, "Chicago prior to 1840, V.: The Body of the Town," *Magazine of Western History* 13, no. 3 (1891): 338–43, 343.

3. Augustus Garrett to James Malony, July 28, 1844 (AGLB I: 179) (about Malony's illness; punctuated added); Augustus Garrett to Benoni and Amy Clark, January 15, 1845 (AGLB II: 30) ("kind providence"). In letters to his cousin and business partner John Seaman, Garrett always reported his health; and the letters to friends written by William B. Ogden, another young Chicago entrepreneur, include frequent mention of his illnesses (Ogden letter-books, CHM).

4. Augustus to Benoni and Amy Clark, January 15, 1845 (AGLB II: 31) (describing that first winter in Chicago before Eliza joined him, he says that "kind providence restored my health," implying a serious illness; he also mentions paying his Cincinnati debts "to the last cent"). Rev. Jeremiah Porter summed up what Garrett told him, namely that "having failed as an auctioneer in New Orleans and Cincinnati, he wished to start anew in Chicago." Alvaro D. Field, *Worthies and Workers, Both Ministers and Laymen, of the Rock River Conference* (Cincinnati: Cranston & Curts, 1896), 312.

5. Miller, *City of the Century*, 48, 50 (what Hubbard saw in 1818); *War Department Annual Reports, 1913*, vol. 2: *Report of the Chief of Engineers, U.S. Army*, part 1 (Washington, DC: Government Printing Office, 1913), 1116.

6. See the map in Christopher R. Reed, *Black Chicago's First Century*, vol. 1: *1833–1900* (Columbia: University of Missouri Press, 2005), 46 (1830 map reproduced from Andreas showing wooded areas), 53 (quoting an old-timer about the marshes); Ann Durkin Keating, ed., *Chicago Neighborhoods and Suburbs: A Historical Guide* (Chicago: University of Chicago Press, 2008), 4 (late 1820s settlement with houses and taverns on west side at Wolf Point).

7. Alfred T. Andreas, *History of Chicago, From the Earliest Period to the Present Time*, vol. 1: *Ending with the Year 1857* (Chicago: A. T. Andreas, 1884),

128; Bessie Louise Pierce, *A History of Chicago*, vol. 1: *The Beginning of a City, 1673–1848* (New York: A. A. Knopf, 1937), 44; Eugen Seeger, *Chicago, the Wonder City* (Chicago: Geo. Gregory, 1893), 86 (population of 3265 by end of 1834); Charles F. Hoffman, *A Winter in the West: By a New-Yorker*, vol. 1 (New York: Harper & Bros., 1835), 242–43 (journal entry for Chicago, January 10, 1834, describing the cold and desolation of the scene, the occasional Indian or Frenchman on the river, the wolves).

8. Seeger, *Chicago, the Wonder City*, 85 (frame houses), 86 (numbers of vessels, houses, stores, etc.); Thomas Ford, *A History of Illinois from Its Commencement as a State in 1818 to 1847* (Chicago: S. C. Griggs, 1854), 181 (easterners who had "caught the mania" and were "bound for Chicago, the great fairy land of fortunes").

9. Ford, *History of Illinois*, 178 ("there was no social," etc.); Melvin G. Holli and Peter d'Alroy Jones, eds., *Ethnic Chicago: A Multicultural Portrait*, 4th ed. (Grand Rapids, MI: Eerdmans, 1995), 47 (where the young men lived and how they "danced"), 49–51 (Chicago, a town of young men in the 1830s); Pierce, *History of Chicago*, vol. 1, 172–73 (Chicago in 1843—youth, proportion of males to females); ledger of the Sauganash Hotel (CHM) (credit entries for lodgers revealing how guests paid their room and board in those years).

10. Howard L. Conard, *Nathaniel J. Brown: Biographical Sketch and Reminiscences of a Noted Pioneer* (Chicago: Palmer, 1892), 4–5 (Nathaniel Brown and his pinewood).

11. Pierce, *History of Chicago*, vol. 1, 186, n56 (quoting praise for ethnic diversity in Chicago from *Chicago Daily Journal* and Maclay in the *Daily Democrat*, November 29, 1847); Timothy R. Mahoney, *Provincial Lives: Middle-Class Experience in the Antebellum Middle West* (Cambridge: Cambridge University Press, 1999), 152–53 (on letters of introduction).

12. John S. Wright, *Chicago: Past, Present, Future*, 2nd ed. (Chicago: Horton & Leonard, 1870), 99–100† (describing the use of the loft of the Peck store; before the church constructed its edifice on South Water, it met in the front of the loft; and in the rear, separated by a curtain, were the sleeping quarters of Peck and Porter, as well as the latter's study, "until he erected his study on Lake street, about No. 150"). The account of Augustus's self-introduction to Porter is given in Jeremiah Porter, "The Earliest Religious History of Chicago" [An Address Read before the Chicago Historical Society in 1859] in *Fergus' Historical Series* no. 14 (collected with other articles; pagination not consecutive), 76; essentially the same story is told by Porter in a letter to Alvaro Field, quoted in Field, *Worthies and Workers*, 312–13. According to a church manual from 1840, the prayer meeting was held on Wednesday

evenings, a very traditional time for all Protestant churches: *Manual for Communicants of the First Presbyterian Church in Chicago, Compiled Jan. 1, 1840* (Chicago: Edward Rudd, 1840), 12. Copies of this manual are held by the library of the University of Illinois at Chicago and by the Newberry Library.

13. On the founders of First Presbyterian Church, most of whom were important businessmen, see Porter, "Earliest Religious History of Chicago," 58; Frederic C. Jaher, *The Urban Establishment: Upper Strata in Boston, New York, Charleston, Chicago, and Los Angeles* (Urbana: University of Illinois Press, 1982), 467 (listing, in addition to Bates, George W. Dole, William H. Brown, Philo Carpenter, and Philip F. W. Peck); also Philo A. Otis, *The First Presbyterian Church, 1833–1913*, rev. ed. (Chicago: Fleming H. Revell, 1913), 26n45 (mentioning Hiram Pearsons, who came in 1833 and was one of the original trustees of the church and had a large real estate business). On Bates and his auction business and building, see Andreas, *History of Chicago*, vol. 1, 151, who also notes that the building address, once the city got numbers (which occurred much later), was number 8 and number 10 (476). On the auctioning of public lands, see Malcolm J. Rohrbough, *The Land Office Business: The Settlement and Administration of American Public Lands, 1789–1837* (New York: Oxford University Press, 1968), 8 (the school section provision); J. Seymour Currey, "Chicago's First Public School House," *Fort Dearborn Magazine* 3, no. 8 (November 1922): 23, 29; Andreas, *History of Chicago*, vol. 1, 117, 133, 146 (auction commissions of Kinzie in 1831 and Bates in 1833; auction of school section plots).

14. Jaher, *Urban Establishment*, 457 (the economic boom after 1833); Andreas, *History of Chicago*, vol. 1, 122ff., 133ff. Given that Bates was town postmaster and an auctioneer of some influence, I infer that Bates was one of the men of First Presbyterian Church who, according to Porter, helped Augustus. Apparently, he did not see Garrett as a competitor to be foiled, for Garrett was soon renting substantial space in his building (see below). An act of February 16, 1831, of the Illinois Statutes required a license for auctioneering: *Revised Statutes of the State of Illinois* (Springfield, IL: William Walters, 1845), 461. On Garrett's first store on South Water, see the next note.

15. Ford, *History of the State of Illinois*, 180 (canal project funded by state loans backed by canal lands); Rohrbough, *Land Office Business*, 31ff. (officers for federal land offices), 43–45 (auctions followed by sales); Henry H. Hurlbut, *Chicago Antiquities* (Chicago: Fergus, 1881), 326 (receiver of public monies in Chicago); also Fremont O. Bennett, *Politics and Politicians of Chicago, Cook County, and Illinois* (Chicago: Blakely, 1886), 44. The receiver was appointed by President Jackson, according to John C. Power and S. A. Power, *History of the*

Early Settlers of Sangamon County, Illinois (Springfield, IL: Edwin A. Wilson, 1876), 707 column 2. On the land office in the store of Thomas Church, see Ulrich Danckers and Jane Meredith, *A Compendium of the Early History of Chicago to the Year 1835 When the Indians Left* (River Forest, IL: Early Chicago, 2000), 45. According to Everett Dick, the land officers typically did the direct selling, but "if an unusually large amount of land was to be sold . . . the land officers were allowed to hire an auctioneer." See Everett N. Dick, *The Lure of the Land: A Social History of the Public Lands from the Articles of Confederation to the New Deal* (Lincoln: University of Nebraska Press, 1970), 37. On the land craze in Chicago in 1835, see Andreas, *History of Chicago*, vol. 1, 133–34. Andreas mentions that, from June 15 to 30, auctions of public lands were held in Bates's building, which implies that the government sold the lands at auction, perhaps with the aid of local auctioneers. For example, back in 1831, John Kinzie acted as auctioneer for canal lands (Andreas, *History of Chicago*, vol. 1, 117). An 1835 ad in the *Chicago American*, November 21, 1835 (internally dated July 17), refers to a store on South Water just vacated by Garrett and taken over by another merchant. This implies that, in the beginning, Garrett did not rent space in the Bates building but started off in a different store. One of Garrett's own repeated 1835 ads, dated July 27, 1835, says that in July he had just begun renting the three-story store on Dearborn Street for his auction and commission business (this ad appeared on August 1, 1835, and in succeeding issues of the *American*). This must be the large brick building owned by Bates that the biographer of Nathaniel Brown says the firm of Garrett & Brown purchased (Conard, *Nathaniel J. Brown*, 6). Various sources situate Garrett's auction room in what must have been the Bates building on Dearborn near South Water. J. D. Bonnell recalled that "Dearborn street . . . was the 'lively' street, for Garrett's auction room was located there, on the west side of the street, close to Cox and Duncan's clothing store, just opposite to which were Mr. Greenleaf's auction rooms." See Andreas, *History of Chicago*, vol. 1, 137 (Bonnell excerpt starts on 136), 151 (on the west side of Dearborn between Lake and South Water); Field, *Worthies and Workers*, 314 (at the corner of Dearborn and South Water). Bates, the chief auctioneer of the city when Garrett arrived, must have assisted Augustus, probably by recommending him to Taylor.

16. An ad that ran in the *Chicago American* in the summer of 1835 calls his business an "auction and commission house" and mentions the possibility of "liberal advances."

17. *Chicago American*, October 31, 1835 (Garrett notice announcing $1,800,000 in sales based on an accounting at the end of the first ten months

of 1835); Harriet Martineau, *Society in America*, vol. 2 (Paris: Baudry's European Library, 1837), 260 (shopkeepers offering land to passers-by from their doorsteps); Andreas, *History of Chicago*, vol. 1, 137 (parcels of land sold over and over by speculators; fee per auction of a dollar paid by the seller—quoting J. D. Bonnell); *Chicago American*, February 27, 1836 (Garrett ad: "the chance of realizing $18,000").

18. Carol Groneman, "Working-Class Immigrant Women in Mid-Nineteenth-Century New York: The Irish Women's Experience," in *Industrial Wage Work*, ed. Nancy F. Cott (Munich: K. G. Saur, 1993), 145–63, 150 (compensation of a live-in domestic in 1830 in New York); Sevan G. Terzian and Nancy Beadie, "'Let the People Remember It': Academies and the Rise of Public High Schools, 1865–1890," in *Chartered Schools: Two Hundred Years of Independent Academies in the United States, 1727–1925*, ed. Nancy Beadie and Kim Tolley (London: Routledge, [2002], 2013), 251–83, 254 (what a teacher earned in New York State in 1840); United States Department of the Treasury, "Report from the Secretary of the Treasury in Compliance with a Resolution of the Senate, Relative to Increase of the Salaries of Clerks, 24th Congress, 1st Session, S. Doc. 355," in *Public Documents Printed by Order of the Senate of the United States, First Session of the Twenty-Fourth Congress*, vol. 5 (Washington, DC: Gales & Seaton, 1836), doc. p. 2 (pay range for a U.S. Senate clerk). On Garrett's speculation in land, see below.

19. In a surviving letter from a later year, Augustus addresses Amy and Benoni as "Father and Mother" (Augustus Garrett to Benoni and Amy Clark, January 15, 1845 [AGLB II: 29]). D. W. Clark, "Mrs. Garrett: Founder of the Biblical Institute," *Ladies' Repository* 18 (1858): 427–30, 427, reprinted in *Our Excellent Women of the Methodist Church in England and America* (New York: J. C. Buttre, 1861), 201–9, 202 (giving 1835 as the year of Eliza Garrett's arrival in Chicago); Porter, "Earliest Religious History of Chicago," 76 ("hoped, in time, to bring her here" and "soon his wife joined him"); Andreas, *History of Chicago*, vol. 1, 621 ("sent on for his wife"); Garrett Papers (CHM) (deed for lots signed in Chicago by Augustus and Eliza, August 6, 1835); Andreas, *History of Chicago*, vol. 1, 134 (government land office in Chicago was opened May 28, 1835, with sales continuing through September 30). According to John Wentworth, in 1835 a schooner carried goods from New York to Chicago in twenty days. See [John Wentworth,] "Speech of Hon. John Wentworth," in *Early Chicago: Reception to the Settlers of Chicago prior to 1840 by the Calumet Club of Chicago* (Chicago: Calumet Club, 1879), 45–62, 51. Of course, this must mean by steamer up the Hudson, then by barge on the Erie Canal, then by schooner from Buffalo through the Great Lakes to Chicago. According to

Pierce, travel from Buffalo to Chicago in 1833 was twenty-two days by water (*History of Chicago*, vol. 1, 76–77).

20. Steamboats were preferable to stagecoaches, the latter being a rough way to travel, especially for a woman, given the male characters she might meet along the way. See Amos A. Parker, *Trip to the West and Texas, Comprising a Journey of Eight Thousand Miles through New-York, Michigan, Illinois, Missouri, Louisiana and Texas, in the Autumn and Winter of 1834–5* (Concord, NH: White and Fisher, 1835), 21; Pierce, *History of Chicago*, vol. 1, 81. Eliza probably traveled alone. She had no sister to go with her, and it would have been a hardship for any farm family to lose someone's labor during the busy period of spring and summer. It was uncommon for a woman to travel without a male companion or at least without another woman. But any woman who accompanied Eliza would have had to make the return trip alone. Hence, Eliza probably had no travel mate.

21. Rachel Widmer Diary, Collection 19428, New York State Library, Albany (transcribed) (a woman's record, from the year before Eliza's journey, detailing experiences on the same water routes going west via the Hudson River and Erie Canal); Pierce, *History of Chicago*, vol. 1, 47, 92–93 (on problems with sandbars, etc.), 81 (the majestic ships with their lights).

22. The identification of locations of buildings on Lake Street in 1835 is based chiefly on Hurlbut, *Chicago Antiquities*. Bates describes Dearborn as a street that crossed the drawbridge into a stand of oaks (ad in the *Chicago Democrat*, July 15, 1834, which Hurlbut quotes in *Chicago Antiquities*, 536). In every direction beyond the town boundaries, and at a good number of places within them, the countryside was swamp, prairie, and woods. The Garretts' long tenure at the Sauganash Hotel is implied by direct and circumstantial evidence. John Caton remembered that young married couples lived at the Sauganash, and John Wentworth recalled that in those days very few married couples, young or old, lived in Chicago (see below). Together these two testimonies argue for the Sauganash as the likely place of residence for the Garretts, at least when Eliza arrived in 1835. Then there is the direct evidence. The earliest surviving pages of the Sauganash Hotel ledger, which are from 1838, carry entries for Augustus that imply his residence there. He already owned the hotel (as of 1836). The earliest Chicago directory, a reconstructed 1839 listing, shows Augustus as a lodger at the Sauganash, as do later directories. The 1840 federal census shows the names "A. Garrett" and "John Murphy" side by side in the Second Ward, implying the presence of both in the Sauganash, where Murphy was the manager. The Garretts did not move into a house until spring of 1844, soon grew tired of it, and by 1845

were thinking of moving back into a hotel (see chapter 2, notes 3 and 4, and chapter 6 on their move into a house).

23. Description of the Sauganash circa 1831 in James N. Hyde, *Early Medical Chicago: An Historical Sketch of the First Practitioners of Medicine in Chicago* (Chicago: W. B. Keen, Cooke, 1876), 13 (two-story building, blue shutters); a painting of Wolf Point done by Justin Herriott in 1902, presumably on the basis of old-timers' recollections, shows the hotel, the barn, some cows, and a fence; John D. Caton, "The Last of the Illinois and a Sketch of the Pottawatomies" (1870), in *Miscellanies*, ed. John D. Caton (Boston: Houghton, Osgood, 1880), 114–45, 142 (giving the location of Sauganash, which must be lot 4 in block 31 on James Thompson's 1830 plat); Hoffman, *Winter in the West*, vol. 1, 242 (journal entry for Chicago, January 10, 1834, mentioning the fire-warmed barroom, attached to the main house, as a gathering place); Hurlbut, *Chicago Antiquities*, 512 (various details about the building); Sauganash as site of the election of trustees: Andreas, *History of Chicago*, vol. 1, 633. Entertainments at the Sauganash: Andreas, *History of Chicago*, vol. 1, 633; Holli and Jones, *Ethnic Chicago*, 47.

24. Hurlbut, *Chicago Antiquities*, 507–14 (testimonies about the Sauganash from 1834 through the 1840s); Fehrenbacher, *Chicago Giant*, 18 (the saving of the Sauganash from destruction according to a letter of Wentworth to his sister, dated November 10, 1836). On Garrett's ownership of the Sauganash and the land on which it stood, see Craig Buettinger, "The Concept of Jacksonian Aristocracy: Chicago as a Test Case, 1833–1857" (PhD diss., Northwestern University, 1982), 50 (referring to Augustus Garrett purchasing the Sauganash in 1836, based on his search of a pre–Great Fire tract book in possession of the Chicago Title and Trust Company); the Sauganash lot—number 4 in block 31 on James Thompson's plat—also shows up in a tax assessment of Garrett's Chicago property made in February 1838, the record of which was preserved in the Augustus Garrett Papers (CHM); and the 1838 Sauganash Hotel ledger (CHM) carries entries for Augustus that imply his ownership of the hotel: in September 1840, John Wentworth's bill at the hotel is marked "by A Garrett order" (p. 7); an entry in Garrett's own bill for November 1840 indicates a payment "by Cash and rent of House."

25. Hurlbut, *Chicago Antiquities*, 511–14 (on the Murphys' various tenures as managers of Chicago hotels); *Chicago Daily Tribune*, October 17, 1937 (the theater group at the Sauganash); letter of Martha Freeman Mason to her friend Julia Boyd in New York, December 16, 1888, published in the *Chicago Daily Tribune*, October 17, 1937, E4 (mentioning the board seats and the few chairs up front); *Chicago Daily Tribune*, July 17, 1946, 16 ("illumined by

candles and oil lamps"). In May of 1839, Mackenzie was back, again asking for a license to open a theater (proceedings, Chicago City Council, Doc. 844, May 20, 1839).

26. Latrobe quoted in Milo M. Quaife, *Chicago and the Old Northwest, 1673–1835* (Chicago: University of Chicago Press, ca. 1913), 350 ("a vile, two-storied garret"); Juliette Kinzie in Mrs. [Juliette] John H. Kinzie, *Wau-Bun: The "Early Day" in the North-West* (New York: Derby & Jackson, 1856), 187 ("a pretentious"); Joseph N. Balestier quoted in Hurlbut, *Chicago Antiquities*, 508 ("the Sauganash was esteemed the best"); Caton, "Last of the Illinois," 142 ("a fashionable boarding-house"); Otis, *First Presbyterian Church*, 233 (John Wentworth anecdote). A list of businessmen of the city, made out in 1837 and published with additional information by Fergus in 1876, includes Augustus as a boarder at the Sauganash: Robert Fergus, comp., *Fergus' Directory of the City of Chicago, 1839* (Chicago: Fergus, 1876).

27. Augustus Garrett to John Seaman, December 28, 1843 (AGLB II: 46) (Eliza preparing to receive calls on New Year's Day, 1844).

28. Caton, "Last of the Illinois," 142.

29. Ann Durkin Keating, *Rising Up from Indian Country: The Battle of Fort Dearborn and the Birth of Chicago* (Chicago: University of Chicago Press, 2012), 235–44 (there was no "massacre"); Johnson v. McIntosh, 21 U.S. 543 (1823) (United States Supreme Court decision regarding Native rights to lands in federal control).

30. Keating, *Rising Up from Indian Country*, 225–28.

31. Miller, *City of the Century*, 61–63 (on the treaty and the claim that Governor Porter used alcohol to weaken the resolve of the Indian representatives); Keating, *Rising Up from Indian Country*, 229 (on the terms of the Chicago treaty and the Potawatomi as negotiators).

32. Caton, "Last of the Illinois," 141–45 (description of the Potawatomi war dance; the quotation).

33. Miller, *City of the Century*, 63 (on the final removal, with the quotation about land too poor for snakes); James A. Clifton, *The Prairie People: Continuity and Change in Potawatomi Indian Culture, 1665–1965*, expanded ed. (Iowa City: University of Iowa Press, 1998), 291; Kelli Mosteller, "Potawatomi Allotment in Kansas," in *Indigenous Communities and Settler Colonialism: Land Holding, Loss and Survival in an Interconnected World*, ed. Zoë Laidlaw and Alan Lester, 214–32, 218–19 (Basingstoke, UK: Palgrave Macmillan, 2015).

34. The two sales in Eliza's name are in Township 34N, range 10E, lot SE sect. 04 and lot NE sect. 04, these being acreage in present-day Manhattan Township. The date of purchase is June 22, 1835. This record is part of the

Illinois State Archives Depository and can be viewed online in the Illinois Public Domain Land Tract Sales Database. There are many listings for Augustus. He was also serving as land agent for his brother-in-law Valentine Flaglor. See William B. Ogden to G. H. Woodruff, January 19, 1841 (WOLB III: 142–43) (mentioning sale of land in Juliet [name changed to Joliet in 1845] around 1837 by Garrett or his assignee Flaglor to another party). Listings for Flaglor (Valentine Flaglor) in the Illinois State Archives Depository are from 1850. Valentine is either Augustus's brother-in-law or his nephew, the two having the same name.

35. Jeremiah Porter journal, summer of 1832 (CHM, original and microfilm); letters of July 8, 1833, and September 4, 1833 (American Home Missionary Society Collection) as quoted in Gordon A. Riegler, "Jeremiah Porter, a History of the First Presbyterian Church Chicago, and a Narrative of the Frontier" (typescript, 1932; held by the Newberry Library), 176, 178–179, 183–184. Porter believed that the U.S. government treated Indians abominably and that the white entrepreneurs exploited the government's land grab. This did not mean that he lacked prejudice toward Native peoples. When some of the Potawatomi who had come to Chicago for their final payment from the government went begging door to door, Porter thought that their faces, their "grimaces," looked "like the incarnation of evil." See Porter, "Earliest Religious History of Chicago," 71–73.

36. Andreas, *History of Chicago*, 303 (Porter leaving Chicago in September of 1835). In his "Earliest Religious History of Chicago," Porter says that he left Chicago for Peoria in fall of 1835 (63), and in a letter he refers to his leaving in terms that suggest it has already occurred (letter of November 4, 1835, in the American Home Missionary Society Collection; quoted by Riegler, "Jeremiah Porter," 210). Riegler, "Jeremiah Porter," 205–13 (on the reasons for Porter's departure from Chicago), 292–96 (on his antislavery preaching); Andreas, *History of Chicago*, vol. 1, 303 (also recounting Porter's antislavery activity); further, see Sidney Blumenthal, *A Self-Made Man: The Political Life of Abraham Lincoln, 1809–1849* (New York: Simon & Schuster, 2016), 169; Paul M. Angle, *"Here I Lived": A History of Lincoln's Springfield, 1821–1865* (Springfield, IL: Abraham Lincoln Association, 1935), 79–80. The CHM holds Porter's journals, but the pages for Chicago are missing, although excerpts were published by Porter in a magazine article in 1875 (*Chicago Times*, December 19, 1875).

37. The Garretts used a laundry service, no doubt because they were hotel residents, and did so even when Augustus was intermittently cash-poor (more than likely after the crash of 1837, for one); for one friend recalled that

"when short of change," Augustus "was wont to send back to his laundress to be rewashed the shirts he could not redeem." See [Henry Strong,] "Speech of Gen. Henry Strong," in *Early Chicago: Reception to the Settlers of Chicago prior to 1840 by the Calumet Club of Chicago, Tuesday Evening, May 27, 1879* (Chicago: Calumet Club, 1879), 26–34, 31. Walter Gurnee arrived in Chicago in 1836 ("Early Mayor Dead," *Chicago Tribune*, April 19, 1907, 7), and the 1840 census shows his name directly after that of Augustus Garrett, implying that he and his wife Mary lived in the Sauganash since that is where the Garretts were (and the hotel's manager, John Murphy, precedes Garrett's name in the same census). Putting Gurnee's arrival date together with this census date, and considering that the Sauganash was a preferred hotel of young married couples, one can infer that the Gurnees were there from 1836 through at least 1840. That Mary was a close friend of Eliza is shown by the fact that Eliza moved into the Gurnee home after Augustus's death (see chapter 7). With respect to the flower gardens, including Eliza's, see Hurlbut, *Chicago Antiquities*, 513 (referring to the gardens when Mrs. Murphy ran the Sauganash, which was in two different periods in the 1830s and 1840s). Hurlbut also mentions Wentworth's garden and his cabbage.

38. On the Murphys, see above; on the church building, etc., see Otis, *First Presbyterian Church, 1833–1913*, 24–25 (with quotations).

39. Porter cited in Field, *Worthies and Workers*, 313 (looking back on his years in Chicago and remembering that Eliza worked with the "noble women" of his congregation); Field himself in *Worthies and Workers*, 313 (Eliza joined the women of the Presbyterian church "in their benevolent and other society work"); Andreas, *History of Chicago*, vol. 1, 462 (showing Chicago had a poorhouse, for he mentions an injured canal worker who was taken to the poorhouse in 1838); Kathleen D. McCarthy, *Noblesse Oblige: Charity and Cultural Philanthropy in Chicago, 1849–1929* (Chicago: University of Chicago Press, 1982), 7 (referring to the organization of the first Dorcas Society of Chicago in 1835 and the Ladies Benevolent Association in 1843, although citing no sources); Thomas Carter, comp., and John C. Grant, ed., "An Historical Sketch," in *The Second Presbyterian Church: June 1st, 1842 to June 1st, 1892* (Chicago: Knight, Leonard, 1892), 100–2 (describing the origins and work of the Dorcas of First Presbyterian in 1835 or 1836); Augustus Garrett to Jeremiah Clark, April 8, 1844 (AGLB I: 132) (mentioning that Eliza belonged to the Ladies Benevolent Association and served as an officer).

40. Information about the mission of Dorcas societies is based on the purpose statements found in Dorcas constitutions from eastern cities, such as that of the Dorcas Society of Boston, established in 1819: *Constitution of*

the Dorcas Society Instituted in Boston, 1819 (Boston: n.p., 1829), 6; cf. Juliette Kinzie, who outlines the purpose of a Dorcas society in an unpublished novel and portrays its activities: [*The Dorcas Society*], 51 passim (full citation in note 43 below). Information about the Dorcas Society of Chicago is from Carter and Grant, "An Historical Sketch," 100–102 (rehearsing a few memories of the Dorcas women).

41. Carter and Grant, "Historical Sketch," 101 (the early fairs in the home of Mrs. James Boyer and the Garrett auction rooms).

42. Juliette Augusta Magill Kinzie, [*The Dorcas Society*], unpublished, undated, handwritten manuscript, lacking title and first chapter (CHM). It is likely, although uncertain, that she composed the book sometime during her period of novel writing in Chicago, where she lived from the early 1830s until her death in 1870. Kinzie's published books have received some attention from scholars, but this unpublished novel has never been studied.

43. Kinzie, [*The Dorcas Society*], 140 (a character's comment on the Church of England).

44. Minutes of the Session, First Presbyterian Church of Chicago, held by the Newberry Library.

45. Porter, "Earliest Religious History of Chicago," 76; Field, *Worthies and Workers*, 313 (letter from Porter quoted by Field, and Field's own statement that Eliza never joined the Presbyterian church in Chicago).

46. Sampling of moral cases in session minutes for September 14, 1835 (defrauding another church member); March 17, 1837 ("immoral and indecent conduct"); August 6, 1837 ("improprieties of conduct"); August 28, 1838 (absence from Sunday services); October 15, 1839 (frequenting the theater); December 2, 1839 (selling "spiritous liquors"); January 8, 1840 (attending public balls); May 4, 1840 (adultery); September 29, 1841 (falsehood and "unchristian conversation").

47. John Sanderson, *Sketches of Paris: In Familiar Letters to His Friends, by an American Gentleman* (Philadelphia: E. L. Carey & A. Hart, 1838), 169; see also Paul S. Boyer, *Urban Masses and Moral Order in America, 1820–1920* (Cambridge, MA: Harvard University Press, 1978), 11 (instancing a case, in 1822, of a poor family unable or unwilling to pay for a pew and therefore being refused membership in a Presbyterian church).

48. The 1840 *Manual for the Communicants of the First Presbyterian Church* states the form of admission, which consists of a profession of faith and commitments to the moral code, but there is no reference here to religious experience or to the session asking for testimonies about it. Evidence of those examinations is, however, preserved in the clerk's minutes of session meetings; for example, an entry for August 31, 1835, records the admission of two men

based on inquiry into their "religious experience," and another entry for September 7, 1838, refers to a married couple being "severally examined touching their religious experience" (Minutes of the Session, First Presbyterian Church of Chicago, 19, 43).

49. There is a parallel in her later effort, as a Methodist, to receive what Holiness divines called "entire sanctification," which was also thought to happen in a definite experience, with intense feelings and sometimes the same bodily signs that attended the moment of conversion. Years later Eliza attended church revivals in the hopes of having this experience, but it never came. She talks about her disappointment in a letter to Melinda Hamline (March 21, 1850). See chapter 7.

50. See the life sketch in Harold E. Raser, *Phoebe Palmer: Her Life and Thought* (Lewiston, NY: Edwin Mellon Press, 1987), 21–74.

51. Raser, *Phoebe Palmer*, 35–36 ("the psychologist"); Palmer, *Faith and Its Effects, or Fragments from My Portfolio* (New York: Joseph Looking, 1850), 63–64 ("state of extreme anguish" and self-doubts); Richard Wheatley, *The Life and Letters of Mrs. Phoebe Palmer* (New York: Palmer and Hughes, 1876), 19 ("exciting influences"); Raser, *Phoebe Palmer*, 34–35 (doubts about her conversion); Wheatley, *Life and Letters of Mrs. Phoebe Palmer*, 26 ("a treasure given"); Phoebe Palmer, *The Way of Holiness* (New York: printed for the author, 1854), 256 (chastened attitude); Wheatley, *Life and Letters of Mrs. Phoebe Palmer*, 31–32 (her response to the loss of her baby to the nursery fire). Phoebe hints at the same idea of the death of a child as divine chastening when she writes in a poem of "the parents' chastened, earthly love," which the death of the child redirects to heaven, its proper object. See Phoebe Palmer, *A Mother's Gift, or A Wreath for My Darlings* (New York: W. C. Palmer; London: F. E. Longley, 1875), 92 (in the poem "Our First-Born").

52. Eliza Garrett to Melinda Hamline, January 29, 1849 (spelling and punctuation corrected).

53. See Barbara L. Epstein, *The Politics of Domesticity: Women, Evangelism, and Temperance in Nineteenth-Century America* (Middleton, CT: Wesleyan University Press, 1981). Epstein interprets the women's anger at God as a cipher for women's hostility to men in an era when women were seeking greater freedom from patriarchy. Epstein may be correct, but she draws this inference without being able to adduce a single account where an antebellum woman makes the connection. In any case, the accounts show that women did experience anger at God as part of their spiritual struggle and that many had difficulty "submitting," as was expected of them, and attaining the sought-after experience.

54. E. Brooks Holifield, *A History of Pastoral Care in America: From Salvation to Self-Realization* (Nashville: Abingdon Press, 1983), 128–29 (mentioning an example of a minister exhorting a mourning woman), 130 ("affable and affective," etc.).

55. Abigail Price quoted in Karin E. Gedge, *Without the Benefit of Clergy: Women and the Pastoral Relationship in Nineteenth-Century American Culture* (Oxford: Oxford University Press, 2003), 164.

4. CRASH AND CONVERSION

1. Alfred T. Andreas, *History of Chicago: From the Earliest Period to the Present Time*, vol. 1: *Ending with the Year 1857* (Chicago: A. T. Andreas, 1884), 134 (quoting an address by Joseph Balestier to the Chicago Lyceum in 1840), 135 (Garrett's auction room was "the most popular resort of the speculating crowd"); Thomas Ford, *A History of Illinois: From Its Commencement as a State in 1814 to 1847* (Chicago: S. C. Griggs, 1854), 181 ("only one great town market"); Alvaro D. Field, *Worthies and Workers, Both Ministers and Laymen, of the Rock River Conference* (Cincinnati: Cranston & Curts, 1896), 314 (description of "Col. George"); Howard L. Conard, "Western Real Estate Speculation Fifty Years Ago: Chicago's Famous Auction House: Nathaniel J. Brown," *National Magazine* 15, no. 6 (April 1892): 667–77, 670 (description of Col. George); Harriet Martineau, *Society in America*, vol. 1 (New York: Saunders and Otley, 1837), 259–60 (description of an auctioneer crier in Chicago in 1836 in terms that clearly indicate she witnessed the work of Col. George).

2. Field, *Worthies and Workers*, 313–14 ("through the long winter evenings . . . 'Going, going, gone!'"), 129 (Borein and the handkerchief); John V. Farwell, *Some Recollections of John V. Farwell: A Brief Description of His Early Life and Business Reminiscences*, ed. John V. Farwell Jr. (Chicago: R. R. Donnelley & Sons, 1911), 52–53 (Garrett and the magician's trick).

3. Selah W. Cogshall, "Chicago in 1839: The Reverend Selah W. Cogshall's Early Remembrances of Methodism in Chicago—The Great Revival in the Winter of 1839—Conversion of Mr. Garrett, Etc.," *Chicago Daily Tribune*, November 24, 1873, 5.

4. Daniel Bluestone, *Constructing Chicago* (New Haven: Yale University Press, 1991), 64 (quoting Hallam regarding paper town plats on auction room walls in Chicago); Ford, *History of Illinois*, 181–82.

5. Conard, "Western Real Estate Speculation," 670 (quoting Brown regarding Garrett and their partnership).

6. Conard, "Western Real Estate Speculation," 670–71. According to Conard, relying on Brown's recollection, one buyer of an Ionia lot was an

Illinois state senator named W. L. D. Ewing, who, having purchased a lot that fall of 1835, used his influence the following winter to get the federal government to locate the Grand River district land office in Ionia. The idea was that this would stimulate population growth in the region, which in turn would benefit the sprouting Ionia. But when the land commissioners arrived, Conard says, they set up in another place, to which they gave the same name, Ionia. This recollection is somewhat imperfect. The county seat was indeed established, after a good deal of competition, in late 1835 or early 1836 at the place that later became the city of Ionia, but Brown's Ionia was never a contender. See E. E. Branch, ed., *History of Ionia County, Michigan*, vol. 1 (Indianapolis: B. F. Bowen, 1916), 201.

7. Conard, "Western Real Estate Speculation," 671; Andreas, *History of Chicago*, 527 (purchase of building at LaSalle and South Water), 528 (average amount of the firm's bank deposits); Alfred T. Andreas, *A History of Cook County* (Chicago: A. T. Andreas, 1884), 852 (Nathaniel's brother, Daniel B. Brown, included in partnership; see also the next note).

8. Conard, "Western Real Estate Speculation," 671 (the dealings and growth of the firm). Conard's biography does not specify the "other businesses," but the nature of the firm's business is clarified in an ad in the *Chicago American*, published January 30, 1836, but carrying the internal date of November 27, 1835. It announces the firm "Garrett, Thompson, Brown, and Co." as a partnership of Garrett, Nathaniel and Daniel Brown, and Oliver H. Thompson. The ad also references the "late firm of Garrett & Brown," which is evidently shorthand for Garrett, Brown & Brother, as that firm was named in ads for town lots (published in the *Chicago American*, October 17, 1835). It may be that "Garrett, Brown & Brother" remained the name of a land agency owned by the new corporation, inasmuch as ads in 1836 still refer to Garrett, Brown & Brother (e.g., *Chicago American*, February 27, 1836, in an ad for Juliet lots). The types of goods the firm sold are indicated in three ads that appeared in the *Chicago American* on January 23, 1836 (with internal dates of December 22, 1835).

9. Joseph N. Balestier, "The Annals of Chicago," in *The Annals of Chicago: A Lecture Read before the Chicago Lyceum, January 21, 1840; Republished from the Original Edition of 1840, with an Introduction Written by the Author in 1876, and Also a Review of the Lecture Published in the* Chicago Tribune *in 1872* (Chicago: Fergus, 1876), 29. The firm's ad in the *American*, January 30, 1836, mentions the following Garrett and Brown businesses: "buying and selling Real Estate," "conducting a General Land Agency Business," and a "General Auction, Commission, and Mercantile business."

10. Separate advertisements in the *Chicago American*, October 31, 1835, list towns in which Garrett was selling lots on certain days in October and November. An ad in February mentions an upcoming sale of Juliet lots (*Chicago American*, February 27, 1836; ad internal date of February 18). Regarding Ionia: *Chicago American*, April 30, 1836 (ad for the partnership of Garrett and Brown with Hugunin and Place); Conard, "Western Real Estate Speculation," 670–71 (federal land agents establishing their own Ionia). The history of the ill-fated Ionia/Prairie Creek is also given in Branch, ed., *History of Ionia County*, 111–13 (Prairie Creek). Kankakee must be Kankakee City on the canal route, since the Kankakee that did become a city in Illinois was not founded until 1853. Likewise, Dresden is almost certainly the Dresden paper town on the canal route and not the Dresden that was founded in Indiana. On these doomed paper towns, see Ann Durkin Keating, *Chicagoland: City and Suburbs in the Railroad Age* (Chicago: University of Chicago Press, 2005), 36 (with a map showing paper towns and developed towns along the Illinois–Michigan canal). The town of Romeo was eventually renamed Romeoville, and Juliet changed its name to Joliet. As for Enterprise, the plat for the town was vacated, effective March 3, 1845. See *Laws of the State of Illinois Passed by the Fourteenth General Assembly* (Springfield, IL: Walters and Weber, 1845), 266.

11. Garrett's business letters mention various types of currency, and Garrett and Brown received notes from an insurance company called the New York Safety Fund (*Chicago American*, March 12, 1836). For a history of money and credit in antebellum America, see Rowena Olegario, *The Engine of Enterprise: Credit in America* (Cambridge, MA: Harvard University Press, 2016), 44–78.

12. Garrett and Brown published their side of the conflict with the bank in two notices, both published in the *Chicago American*, March 12, 1836.

13. Andreas, *History of Chicago*, vol. 1, 527 (bank opened for business in February of 1836 in the "four-story block owned by Garrett, Brown, & Brother at the corner of LaSalle and South Water Streets"); Conard, "Western Real Estate Speculation," 673 (withdrawal of $20,000); *Chicago American*, March 12, 1836 ("if a check").

14. Conard, "Western Real Estate Speculation," 673 (Brown's later account, including the quotation).

15. *Chicago American*, March 12, 1836 (the notices of Garrett, Brown & Brother regarding the Chicago branch of the Bank of Illinois). On the Specie Circular, see below; Bessie Louise Pierce, *A History of Chicago*, vol. 1: *Beginning of a City, 1673–1848* (Chicago: University of Chicago Press, 1937), 154–155 (on Democratic criticism of the bank), 157 (quotation about the firm

as "agent of the bank of Washtenaw," summarizing information in the *Chicago American*, February 20, 1836).

16. This story is told in Howard L. Conard, *Nathaniel J. Brown: Biographical Sketch and Reminiscences of a Noted Pioneer* (Chicago: Byron S. Palmer, 1892), 14. This 1892 history of Brown is a slightly different version of Conard's *National Magazine* article on Brown. Canalport was later renamed Bridgeport.

17. Alasdair Roberts, *America's First Great Depression: Economic Crisis and Political Disorder after the Panic of 1837* (Ithaca, NY: Cornell University Press, 2012), 39; see also the summary in Nicholas Cox, "The Panic of 1837," in *The Early Republic and Antebellum America: An Encyclopedia of Social, Political, Cultural, and Economic History*, ed. Christopher G. Bates (2010; repr., London: Routledge, 2015), 787–90.

18. Peter L. Rousseau, "Jacksonian Monetary Policy, Specie Flows, and the Panic of 1837," *Journal of Economic History* 62 (2002): 457–88; Roberts, *America's First Great Depression*, 39–40.

19. Roberts, *America's First Great Depression*, 39–43; article in *New-Yorker*, October 19, 1839, 75 (as quoted in Roberts, 39–40); the same article published in the *Niles' Weekly Register*, October 26, 1839, 142ff. (sourced to the *Philadelphia American Sentinel*).

20. Balestier, "Annals of Chicago," 26 ("The farmer forsook" / "The mechanic laid aside"); Malcolm J. Rohrbough, *The Land Office Business: The Settlement and Administration of American Public Lands, 1789–1837* (New York: Oxford University Press, 1968), 240 ("Everywhere we went"), 75–76 (government selling land on time); Augustus Garrett to A. Boyer Jr., February 25, 1845 (AGLB I: 83) (regarding plummeting land/real estate values: "the Western country is not worth more than 50 cents on the dollar. The revolution is quite as bad as it was in 1837"); Conard, "Western Real Estate Speculation," 672 (collapse of real estate market and dissolution of Garrett, Brown & Brother). A repeated notice in the *Chicago American* announced the selling off of the firm's stock of goods at its Water Street store (*Chicago American*, March 12, 1836, with internal date of March 9, 1836, for the notice itself).

21. Conard, *Nathaniel J. Brown*, 7; *Chicago American*, February 27, 1836 (ad giving terms for sale of Juliet lots). In 1843 Garrett told Seaman that there was envy toward him because he was purchasing too much property. See Garrett to John Seaman, December 30, 1843 (AGLB I: 32).

22. Letter to A. Boyes Jr., February 25, 1845 (AGLB II: 83) (regarding 50 percent fall in land values in 1837 and 1845; "the Western country"); Augustus to Amy and Benoni Clark, Chicago, January 15, 1845 (AGLB II: 31)

("accumulated a large amount of property"). He also writes in this letter (which was just a month before the letter to Boyes) that he has "a place within three miles of this city that is worth at least $3000," for which he was recently offered $1,500, which is all he can get for it. In the same letter he mentions to his in-laws that he has no cash reserves and would be forced to sell land at a loss if he were to help them (which, in the end, he agrees to do).

23. Receiving Book of First Methodist Episcopal Church, Chicago (date of establishment of second congregation under John T. Mitchell; see further below); Field, *Worthies and Workers*, 124–25 (on the challenges the church faced in 1837); Grant Goodrich, "Peter Ruble Borein," in *Annals of the American Pulpit*, vol. 7: *Methodist*, ed. William Buell Sprague (New York: Robert Carter & Brothers, 1859), 784–86, 784 (moving the church in the summer of 1838); Ulrich Danckers and Jane Meredith, *A Compendium of the Early History of Chicago to the Year 1835 When the Indians Left* (River Forest, IL: Early Chicago, 2000), 48 (period map showing the original location of the Methodist church); Henry H. Hurlbut, *Chicago Antiquities* (Chicago: Fergus, 1881), 599 (moving and enlarging the church building).

A Methodist mission to Chicago was under way by at least October of 1831, when it appears for the first time in the minutes of the Annual Conference of the Methodist Episcopal Church. Jesse Walker had the post, which covered a wide geographical district and not just the little Chicago settlement. It was probably later that same year that Rev. S. R. Beggs was appointed to serve the Chicago mission. He organized the first Methodist class at Chicago. This ten-member church met at Fort Dearborn, grew a bit, then scattered when the Black Hawk War broke out. In fact, most residents of Chicago left, including Beggs and his family. Beggs accompanied his wife and child to Plainfield, sent them on to Washington, DC, then returned to the fort. He found Chicago "almost deserted." Those undaunted by the Black Hawk War had lately departed for fear of cholera. Beggs had no congregation. Although "we now had peace on all our borders," he would later write, "there was no hope now of my doing anything in my station." So he journeyed to Washington to join his family and subsequently received an appointment elsewhere. See *Minutes of the Annual Conferences of the Methodist Episcopal Church for the Years 1829–1839* (New York: T. Mason and G. Lane, 1840), 85 (Walker's appointment to the Chicago mission); James Leaton, *History of Methodism in Illinois, 1793–1832* (Cincinnati: Walden and Stowe, 1883), 376 (on Beggs); Stephen R. Beggs, *Pages from the Early History of the West and Northwest* (Cincinnati: Methodist Book Concern, 1868), 86, 94, 104–6 (including the quotations).

In 1832 Jesse Walker—an aging Methodist circuit rider of the North-West, who had been serving the Chicago mission prior to its organization into a church by Beggs—was named presiding elder of the Chicago district. This gave him responsibility for a region that included Chicago and other towns of northwestern Illinois. Whether any of the ten or twenty people who had been part of Beggs's Chicago congregation were in the city when Walker arrived, it is extremely doubtful that he discovered an organized church there. He likely started a new class, but since he had not been appointed the elder of any Chicago congregation, he was not its pastor. Where the class met is uncertain, but Alvaro Field was able to gather some information about Methodists' use of buildings from 1832 to 1834. He understood that, in 1834 and for some years prior (but not earlier than 1832), the Methodists had a log church and also used the Mark Noble house and Watkins's schoolhouse to accommodate the three sections of the city (the north, south, and west sections created by the river). The log church was on the west side, the frame house on the north, the Noble house on the south. Beggs mentions a school-house that was used by Jesse Walker as a parsonage. He says nothing about a log church building, but Jeremiah Porter recalled that when he arrived at Fort Dearborn by schooner on May 4, 1833, he found that the Methodist circuit minister came once a month to hold services in a log schoolhouse on the west side of the river. Another account says that by September of 1833, the Baptists, Presbyterians, and Methodists were all using a building at Franklin and South Water. We can trust Porter for the information that the meetings of the Methodists for preaching services were only occasional, dependent on the presence of a minister, and that no church had been organized with its own minister. In the summer of 1834, the Methodists were constructing a building on the north side to serve as their city church. The earliest entries of this church's receiving book date to November of that year and give John T. Mitchell as "pastor-in-charge." Since Mitchell was not given the receiving book of the short-lived congregation of Beggs, it is evident that, as far as the Illinois Annual Conference was concerned, this was a new church, not a continuation of the previous one. First Methodist Church of Chicago was founded, therefore, in November of 1834. See Leaton, *History of Methodism in Illinois*, 58 (Walker's appointment as presiding elder over Chicago district, his retirement); Field, *Worthies and Workers*, 99–100; Jeremiah Porter, "Sketches of a Pioneer Ministry" (1877), in *Pioneer Collections: Report of the Pioneer Society of the State of Michigan*, vol. 4 (*Michigan Historical Collections* 4, 1883; repr., Lansing, MI: Wynkoop Hallenbeck Crawford, 1906), 84–88, 87 (on the log church on the west side); Andreas, *History of Chicago*, vol. 1,

132 (Mr. Temple's building at Franklin and South Water); Hurlbut, *Chicago Antiquities*, 598 (use of Temple building at Franklin and South Water); Receiving Book of First United Methodist Church, Chicago (earliest entries). Grant Goodrich also dated the organization of the church to 1834, the year the building was constructed (Gordon A. Riegler, "Jeremiah Porter, a History of the First Presbyterian Church Chicago, and a Narrative of the Frontier" [unpublished typescript, 1932], 78, citing Goodrich). Hurlbut (*Chicago Antiquities* 598) refers to a Henry Whitehead as successor to Walker and as occasionally preaching in the building at Franklin and South Water, but this probably means only that when Whitehead was in town, he sometimes preached for the Methodists.

24. Goodrich, "Peter Ruble Borein," 781–83; Alvaro Field, *Worthies and Workers*, 125–31; Joseph C. Evers, *The History of the Southern Illinois Conference* (Nashville: Parthenon, 1964), 97 (tensions in southern Illinois over Borein's antislavery opinions). The name is spelled "Borin" in a recollection by Selah Cogshall, who knew Borein, thus showing how the name was pronounced (Cogshall, "Chicago in 1839," 5).

25. Field, *Worthies and Workers*, 128–31, 134 (descriptions of Borein the preacher); Goodrich, "Peter Ruble Borein," 784–86 (including references to him falling to his knees to pray during a sermon because he was so overcome by emotion, singing in the middle of his prayers). Field recalled "an eminent lawyer" of Clark Street Church—undoubtedly Grant Goodrich—becoming overcome with emotion by his recollections of Borein (*Worthies and Workers*, 129). The Receiving Book of First Methodist Church of Chicago shows the main converts who joined that church during the Borein revivals, but there were undoubtedly others who, converted in the evangelical sense under Borein, went into churches of the denominations of their upbringing (Baptist and Presbyterian). On the numbers of converts, see the following note.

26. Receiving Book of First Methodist Church of Chicago; Grant Goodrich, "An Address," printed in Grant Goodrich, *Garrett Biblical Institute of the Methodist Episcopal Church at Evanston (near Chicago)* (Chicago: Daily Democrat Print, 1856), 3 (both Garretts were "converted" in 1839); "Mrs. Grant Goodrich" is listed as a member in *Manual for the Communicants of the First Presbyterian Church of Chicago, compiled Jan. 1, 1840* (Chicago: Edward H. Rudd, 1840), 9; Field, *Worthies and Workers*, 314; also Alvaro Field, *Memorials of Methodism in the Bounds of the Rock River Conference* (Cincinnati: Cranston & Stowe, 1886), 123, 127 (Eliza was "converted" under Borein). In December of 2015, I examined the Receiving Book of First Methodist Church of Chicago, making notes about the first page, the entries for the Garretts,

and the number of converts during Borein's ministry. From November 13, 1837, to July 16, 1839, 106 people joined the church, the vast majority of them as a result of the revival held by Peter Borein from December of 1837 through April of 1839. The receiving book has entries for Augustus and Eliza, dated March 1839, and gives the usual notation that they were received "on trial." The book was unavailable when I returned to the church several weeks later to make a photographic record of it. It seems to have been misplaced.

27. On the Presbyterian requirements for church membership, see chapter 3.

28. *The Doctrines and Discipline of the Methodist Episcopal Church* (New York: Mason and Lane, 1836), 81 (ch. 2, sect. 2, Q. 3, A. 1–2). On the nature of the personal self-disclosures at a class, see Joseph Nightingale, *A Portraiture of Methodism* (London: Longman, Hurst, Rees, and Orme, 1807), 181–83. In 1840 an addition to the Methodist *Doctrines and Discipline* stipulated that the candidate for admission give "satisfactory assurances both of the correctness of their faith, and their willingness to observe and keep the rules of the church." See Robert Emory, *History of the Discipline of the Methodist Episcopal Church*, rev. by W. P. Strickland (New York: Carlton & Porter, 1857), 198 (the 1840 addition to requirements for admission to membership). This was not applied as part of a formal procedure until 1864, when the candidate was required to give an affirmative answer to the question, "Do you believe in the doctrines of the Holy Scripture, as set forth in the *Articles of Religion* of the Methodist Episcopal Church?" See Thomas C. Oden, *Doctrinal Standards in the Wesleyan Tradition*, rev. ed. (Nashville: Abingdon, 2008), 72 (citing the 1864 *Doctrines and Discipline*). Even this requirement did not entail inquiry into religious experiences.

29. Charles Elliott, "Receiving Persons into the Church," *Western Christian Advocate* 7, no. 2 (May 1, 1840): 6.

30. On the extension of probation in American Methodism at the time of Eliza's conversion, see Elliott, "Receiving Persons into the Church," 6 (speaking of an extension of a month or two if there be doubt about the person's sincerity in seeking to live rightly). The receiving book indicates that Augustus never completed his trial period.

31. John Dempster, "The Teacher's Parting Word: An Address to the First Graduating Class of Garrett Biblical Institute," in *Lectures and Addresses by Rev. John Dempster*, ed. Davis W. Clark (Cincinnati: Poe and Hitchcock, 1864), 199–206, 199–200; Alvaro Field, *Worthies and Workers*, 315 (raised "in one of the finest Presbyterian families"; after she joined the Methodist church in 1839, she "became a noble and consistent Christian"), 313 ("at one time a probationer in the Methodist Church at Newburgh"), 273 ("a quiet,

reliable, noble Christian woman"), 316 (died "in holy triumph"), 314 (Augustus "returned to the world").

32. Alvaro Field, "Western Methodism," in *The Children's Centennial Memorial, or Exhibition Book*, ed. Daniel Wise (New York: N. Tibbals, 1866), 72–79, 77 (describing the Garretts as "gay, worldly people"); *Doctrines and Discipline* (1836), 76–78 (ch. 2, sect. 1.4); William H. Williams, *The Garden of American Methodism: The Delmarva Peninsula, 1769–1820* (Lanham: Rowman and Littlefield, 1984), 150 ("came out in plain Methodist dress," etc.). On Matthew Simpson's wife, see Charles E. Jones, *Perfectionist Persuasion: The Holiness Movement and American Methodism, 1867–1936* (Lanham, MD: Scarecrow Press, 2002), 11 (drawing from an anecdote in Robert D. Clark, *The Life of Matthew Simpson* [New York: Macmillan, 1956], 276); "A Mother" [Mrs. Allen D. Campbell], *Why I Am a Presbyterian* (Philadelphia: William S. Martien, 1852), 61 (Methodists no longer enforcing their strict rules on dress).

33. The photograph is reproduced in chapter 7 along with an engraving by J. C. Buttre, the caption of which states that it is based on a photograph (a reversal of the image through printing would explain the difference in perspective between the two), and a posthumous painting by C. V. Bond, which looks to be based on the same photograph. Recollections of Eliza: Jeremiah Porter, "The Earliest Religious History of Chicago: An Address Read before the Chicago Historical Society in 1859," in *Fergus' Historical Series* no. 14 (Chicago: Fergus, n.d. and collected with other articles; pagination not consecutive), 76; Cogshall, "Chicago in 1839," 5 (statement about Eliza Garrett's character, emphasis added). Presbyterian churches did not enshrine their moral code in their congregational covenant, but session minutes show the cases of moral impropriety for which people were warned, disciplined, or dismissed. These include such things as intemperance, sexual misconduct, failure to attend church, profanity, dancing, attending the theater, gambling, and working on Sunday ("Sabbath-breaking"). See William D. Blanks, "Ideal and Practice: A Study of the Conception of the Christian Life Prevailing in the Presbyterian Churches of the Nineteenth Century" (ThD diss., Union Theological Seminary in Virginia, 1960). Blanks's data are summarized in James O. Farmer, *Metaphysical Confederacy: James Henley Thornwell and the Synthesis of Southern Values* (Macon, GA: Mercer University Press, 1986), 168–70. The disciplinary cases in the session books of First Presbyterian Church of Chicago reflect the same set of standards.

34. Field, *Memorials of Methodism*, 169 (quoting Frink about Augustus speaking with tears streaming down his cheeks). According to Cogshall ("Chicago in 1839," 5), the anecdote about Garrett auctioning a handkerchief

and telling the crowd they were going to need it if they went to hear Borein referred to something Garrett said in his auction house during the revivals that winter, 1838–1839.

35. These descriptions of Borein and Augustus are based on the recollection of Cogshall, who was present during the meetings, and the quotations are from his account ("Chicago in 1839," 5).

36. Cogshall, "Chicago in 1839," 5.

37. From the evidence that Eliza underwent a conversion at one of the highly emotional Borein revivals, one can infer that she had the typical experience, a moment in which she felt an overwhelming awareness of divine love. Period conversion stories reflect the emotional releases people felt. Indeed, they not only reflect but also show us the templates that socialized people to experience conversion in certain patterned ways. See Claudia Stokes, *The Altar at Home: Sentimental Literature and Nineteenth-Century American Religion* (Philadelphia: University of Pennsylvania Press, 2014), 46 ("In hearing the speaker recount his or her worldly ordeals and the relief engendered by conversion, the listener is encouraged to identify with the speaker's story to a degree that he or she undergoes the same emotional transformation from sorrow to joy at *the sudden consciousness of divine love and mercy*" [emphasis added]). See also Virginia L. Brereton, *From Sin to Salvation: Stories of Women's Conversions, 1800 to the Present* (Bloomington: Indiana University Press, 1991), 16, 28.

5. THE POLITICIAN

1. *Morning Democrat*, February 27, 1840, no longer extant; facsimile in Alfred T. Andreas, *History of Chicago. From the Earliest Period to the Present Time*, vol. 1: *Ending with the Year 1857* (Chicago: A. T. Andreas, 1884), 369, col. 1 (reference to Garrett as former Whig); *Chicago American*, November 5, 1836, as summarized in Bessie Louise Pierce, *A History of Chicago*, vol. 1: *The Beginning of a City, 1673–1848* (Chicago: University of Chicago Press, 1937), 375 (the Whig vigilance committee); Otis S. Eddy, "Index of *Chicago American* for 1836–1837," s.v. "Garrett, Augustus" (Garrett appointed to Whig "Committee of Vigilants"). The expression "committee of vigilantes/vigilants" was used by political parties for their local governing committees (alternatively, "committee of vigilance"), but Pierce, who apparently had access to a now-lost copy of the *American*, says that the primary purpose in this case was to watch for election fraud.

2. Mayors served one-year terms. The first mayor of the newly incorporated city was a Democrat (Wm. B. Ogden); two Whig mayors followed; but

from 1840 through 1854, every mayor was a Democrat (Andreas, *History of Chicago*, vol. 1, 614). The council usually had Democratic majorities as well. According to Pierce, "on the whole, the decade following 1840 belonged to the Democrats" (*History of Chicago*, vol. 1, 385).

3. Augustus Garrett to John Wentworth, November 17, 1844 (AGLB I: 248) (statement that he would never vote Whig again).

4. Garrett to Wentworth, December 9, 1844 (AGLB I: 253) (comment on the greatness of Jackson).

5. Neil Foley, *The White Scourge: Mexicans, Blacks, and Poor Whites in Texas Cotton Culture* (Berkeley: University of California Press, 1997), 20 (quotations from Buchanan and Woodbury).

6. *Chicago Democrat*, March 14, 1843 (Garrett expressing an antislavery sentiment in his inaugural address as mayor); Garrett to Seaman, November 6, 1844 (AGLB I: 223) (Garrett on Texas). The term "Texian" originally referred to all inhabitants of Mexican Texas and, subsequently, of the Republic of Texas. But given racial attitudes behind white support for the independence of Texas from Mexico, it is likely that most whites of the era, including the Garretts, thought of the Texians as being chiefly or exclusively the Anglo residents and not the ethnically diverse population as a whole.

7. The conflict over the matter of bridges is documented in the Chicago Common Council files held by Illinois Regional Archives Depository. A history of the bridge wars, based on these files, newspaper accounts, and a few other sources is given in Robin L. Einhorn, *Property Rules: Political Economy in Chicago, 1833–1872* (Chicago: University of Chicago Press, 1991), 57–60. I have reexamined all the original sources.

8. 1872 review of Joseph N. Balestier's 1840 lecture, "The Annals of Chicago," in *The Annals of Chicago: A Lecture Read before the Chicago Lyceum, January 21, 1840; Republished from the Original Edition of 1840, with an Introduction Written by the Author in 1876, and Also a Review of the Lecture Published in the* Chicago Tribune *in 1872* (Chicago: Fergus, 1876), 48 (warehouses schemes, "sarve 'em right"); retrospective letter to the *Chicago Times* quoted in Andreas, *History of Chicago*, vol. 1, 198 (as many as five hundred wagons of grain a night, opposition of south-side businessmen to the bridge in hopes of garnering grain market); *Chicago American*, May 20, 1837 (as cited in Pierce, *History of Chicago*, 340) (on the opposition of captains of river vessels to a bridge); Ogden to Arthur Bronson, December 18, 1839 (WOLB) (on Hoosier wagons).

9. CCCPF Doc. 779, February 4, 1839 (report of street commissioner favoring a proposal from a Mr. Vanosdel to place a draw on the old bridge at Dearborn or to build an entirely new float bridge on Wells, "which may

be realized by the City through voluntary contributions if one should be built at that point"); CCCPF Doc. 781, February 25, 1839 (authorization of construction of a bridge at Wells Street); CCCPF Doc. 818, March 13, 1839 (proposals of Calhoun and Morrison to remove Dearborn Street bridge, or to widen it); CCCPF Doc. 828, April 8, 1839 (proposal of Orsemus Morrison to remove Dearborn Street bridge); CCCPF Doc. 838, May 6, 1839 (report of street commissioner on cost of removing the Dearborn Street bridge); Andreas, *History of Chicago*, vol. 1, 198 ("gathered upon the river").

10. Report of Committee on Streets and Bridges, CCCPF Doc. 944, April 6, 1840 (referencing, retrospectively, the Wells Street bridge project's failure to get private subscribers); Andreas, *History of Chicago*, vol. 1, 198–99 (quoting letter to the *Chicago Times* regarding the Ogden and Newberry bribe of land donated to the Roman Catholic diocese, where the cathedral was subsequently constructed, and the mayor casting the deciding vote). Benjamin W. Raymond is listed as a ruling elder in *Manual for the Communicants of the First Presbyterian Church of Chicago, Compiled Jan. 1, 1840* (Chicago: Edward H. Rudd, 1840), 4; he joined the church on July 12, 1837 (Minutes of the Session, First Presbyterian Church of Chicago, 31).

11. CCCPF Doc. 944, April 6, 1840 (the council's ordinance of December 2, 1839, authorizing the Clark Street bridge, specified and summarized in the report of the Committee on Streets and Bridges); William Ogden to Walter Newberry, February 6, 1840 (WOLB) (the form of payment, in city scrip); Ogden to Arthur Bronson, December 18, 1839 (WOLB); Ogden to Bronson, December 18, 1839 (WOLB) (explaining that "the City Council have passed an order again appropriating $3000 to build a bridge on Clark Street provided City Stock can be sold at par bearing interest at 7% . . . interest payable ½ yearly & an offset for taxes & c."). Ogden had hoped to garner local subscribers, including civic-minded Ira Miltimore, but in the end only a few of Ogden's Chicago friends purchased stock, and he had to buy most of the bonds himself, using his own limited funds and the money entrusted to him by his eastern investors. See Ogden to Newberry, February 2, 1840 (WOLB) (I had to "take the whole burden upon myself"—probably meaning that Ogden assumed all the stock and tried to get others to buy shares from him; only Newberry and Jackson did so). Harpster discusses Ogden's role in getting the Clark Street bridge built and states that Ogden bought a third of the bonds and committed his eastern investors to the rest. See Jack Harpster, *The Railroad Tycoon Who Built Chicago: A Biography of William B. Ogden* (Carbondale: Southern Illinois University Press, 2009), 90–91 (Harpster incorrectly assumes that the council's decision in 1839 took

place during Ogden's term as alderman and that he was the persuasive voice on the council; in fact, Ogden did not become an aldermen until 1840).

12. CCCPF Docs. 940 (Fourth Ward petition, April 6, 1840, referring to "the bridge that is about to be constructed"), 941 (general petition, April 6, 1840, also referring to "the bridge that is about to be constructed"); 939 (Third Ward petition, April 6, 1840); 955 (Third Ward petition, April 13, 1840, referring to Garrett as the alderman who brought their original petition, preserved as CCCPF Doc. 939); 944 (report of Committee on Streets and Bridges, April 6, 1840, showing that contracts had been made for immediate construction of a bridge at Clark Street and that the committee, chaired by Miltimore, supported the Clark Street bridge as the best option); Ogden to Newberry, February 2, 1840 (WOLB II: 357–58) (showing that Ogden expected Miltimore to subscribe to the Clark Street bridge, which also indicates Miltimore's support for it).

13. CCCPF Docs. 940 (Fourth Ward petition, April 6, 1840), 941 (general petition, April 6, 1840), and 944 (report of Committee on Streets and Bridges, April 6, 1840). The general petition reads, "1st that it interferes with our interests to have the river obstructed as low down [east, toward the lake] as Clark Street. 2nd that it will be more out of the way of vesles [vessels] & would not require to be opened once on Wells where it would ten times on Clark, whereby the traveling community will also be better accommodated. 3rd if the change be made and half if not two thirds of the expense of building the bridge will be paid by individual subscription."

14. *Chicago American*, April 15, 1840 (Garrett's motions at April 13 council meeting that the bridge site be moved to Dearborn and that this proposal be referred to the Committee on Streets and Bridges); *Chicago American*, April 15, 1840, and CCCPF Doc. 955, April 13, 1840 (citizen's complaint to the council alleging unauthorized addition to Third Ward petition). The insertion in the Third Ward petition (Doc. 939) is not in Garrett's handwriting.

15. Report of Committee on Streets and Bridges, CCCPF Doc. 944, April 6, 1840.

16. *Chicago American*, April 18, 1840 ("The erection of the bridge has commenced today by the driving of piles"); CCCPF Doc. 961, April 20, 1840 (petition favoring changing the bridge site to the end of the piers); *Chicago American*, April 22, 1840 (report of council meeting, including information that Garrett brought the petition to move the bridge site to the end of the piers as protection against invasion and that the council referred the matter "to the President of the United States"). According to Einhorn, some several months earlier the *Chicago American* had reported "'that the Common

Council last night *again voted* to erect a bridge over the Chicago River at the foot of Clark street,' a compromise between the Wells and Dearborn locations. South-siders fought against it—Alderman Augustus Garrett even claimed it would jeopardize national defense in the event of a British attack on Canada" (Einhorn, *Property Rules*, 59, quoting the *Chicago American*, December 3, 1839). This issue of the *American* has not been preserved in microform; hence it is not clear where Einhorn found the article. She also cites December 5, 1839; April 1, 1840; and May 1, 1841. These are also not covered by microform, and I have not been able to locate any institution that retains copies or images of these issues. The piers ran along the north and south sides of the river where it extended beyond Michigan Avenue toward the harbor. See the 1843 survey of Lieutenant W. H. Warner, reproduced in Harpster, *Railroad Tycoon Who Built Chicago*, 158 (from CHM doc. IChi-18072).

17. *Chicago American*, April 11, 1840 (a widely published Washington correspondent who called himself "the Spy in Washington" on the boundary dispute with Britain); *Chicago American*, April 21, 1840 (excerpt from *Toronto Patriot* on the boundary dispute). In 1838 the *Niles' Weekly Register* reported news from London regarding Britain's intentions to increase its military strength in Canada in response to "the revolt in Canada" (March 10, 1838, 17). A report of the chancellor of the exchequer on July 5, 1839, in response to a question about the corn duty (during Committee on the Post Office Acts, House of Parliament), gives an idea of the British concerns respecting Canada (and specifies British increases in troop strength there in the years 1837–1839) in view of the boundary that had to be guarded and the threat of "attacks of external as well as of internal enemies." See John Henry Barlow, ed., *The Mirror of Parliament for the Second Session of the Fourteenth Parliament of Great Britain and Ireland [. . .] February 5 [. . .] till August 27. 1839*, vol. 5 (London: Longman et al., 1839), 3673/367. See further the *Congressional Record, Containing the Proceedings and Debates of the Fifty-Second Congress, Second Session* vol. 34, no. 2 (Washington, DC: Government Printing House, 1901), 1403ff. (a collection of correspondence of President Van Buren, the secretary of war, and others regarding Canadian military buildup on the northern or northeastern boundary in 1840).

18. Report of Committee on Streets and Bridges, CCCPF Doc. 944, April 6, 1840 (recommending that although the subscribers did not oppose a Dearborn location, the Clark Street bridge project should go forward). In a letter to Bronson, Ogden states that their corporation had recently approved the Wells location, meaning they were willing to subscribe for it (Ogden to Bronson, March 5, 1839, WOLB). Clearly, the subscribers themselves,

Ogden chief among them, preferred Clark but were amenable to the other locations. But Garrett may not have known this. Or, when he learned that Ogden would accept Wells, that may have been his reason for changing his views and arguing for a location at the end of the piers.

19. Pierce, *History of Chicago*, vol. 1, 341–42 (new south branch bridge; "the aldermen from the south and west sides"); *Chicago American*, May 1, 1841 (on the partisan nature of the dispute); 1839 Fergus directory (names and occupations of Merrill, Morgan, Prescott, and Peck). Robert Fergus, comp., *Fergus' Directory of the City of Chicago, 1839* (Chicago: Fergus, 1876).

20. Garrett to John Seaman, December 30, 1843 (AGLB I: 33) (out of chronological order in the letter-book; spelling corrected); Howard L. Conard, *Nathaniel J. Brown: Biographical Sketch and Reminiscences of a Noted Pioneer* (Chicago: Byron S. Palmer, 1892), 15–16, 16 (quotation). According to Brown, Ballingall prevailed over Ogden in the election, but lists of Illinois senators and representatives following the 1840 election do not include either Ballingall or Ogden. See *Journal of the Senate of the Twelfth General Assembly of the State of Illinois, Convened [...] Nov. 23, 1840* (Springfield: Wm. Walters, 1841), 4; *Journal of the House of Representatives of the Twelfth General Assembly of the State of Illinois, Convened [...] Nov. 23, 1840* (Springfield: Wm. Walters, 1840), 4. Since Ballingall was a Democrat like Ogden and neither one ever served in the legislature, Brown was confused about some of this history. It is clear, however, that Ogden was a candidate in the general election for the Illinois legislature that year. Eddy's newspaper index refers to an article or letter (August 8, 1840) stating that Ogden was a candidate for the legislature in 1840 (Otis S. Eddy, "Index of *Daily Chicago American* from Oct. 9th 1840 to April 9th 1841," s.v. Wm. B. Ogden). According to Pierce, Ogden ran for the Illinois House of Representatives against fellow Democrat Ebenezer Peck, both men apparently competing as Democrats during a period of party rifts. See Pierce, *History of Chicago*, vol. 1, 377). Peck won (see reference above to the Illinois Senate's journal).

21. *Daily Chicago American*, April 29, 1940, as referenced with annotation in Eddy, "Index of *Daily Chicago American*," s.v. "Garrett, Augustus" (Garrett as delegate to Democratic convention in Springfield); Garrett to Seaman, December 30, 1843 (AGLB I: 33) ("I done it out of pure motives"); Harpster, *Railroad Tycoon Who Built Chicago*, 19 (Ogden's dishonesty). On Garrett's political dishonesty, see below with reference to the election of 1844. A recollection of Garrett, quoted in chapter 4, shows him being explicit about the way he justified his own underhanded dealings: "I have thought of joining the Church and being a good and honest man, but I will be damned if I can do

business with you Hoosiers and do that too." Quoted in Selah W. Cogshall, "Chicago in 1839: The Reverend Selah W. Cogshall's Early Remembrances of Methodism in Chicago—The Great Revival in the Winter of 1839—Conversion of Mr. Garrett, Etc.," *Chicago Daily Tribune*, November 24, 1873, 5; Garrett to Seaman, January 3, 1845 (AGLB II: 2) ("I love to cheat a cheat").

22. Garrett to John Seaman, December 30, 1843 (AGLB I: 32, out of order; commas added).

23. Garrett to John Seaman, December 30, 1843 (AGLB I: 32) ("All the wealth"); John Denis Haeger, *The Investment Frontier: New York Businessmen and the Economic Development of the Old Northwest* (Albany: State University of New York Press, 1981), 182 (mentioning the Lake House as collateral for the Bronson loan to Kinzie, the diminishing value of the hotel), 194–201 (description of Bronson's opposition to the appraisal law, his payment negotiations with Kinzie, and his lawsuit), 194–95 ("provided that no real"—Haeger's summary of the relevant part of the 1841 appraisal law). In the end, Bronson challenged the constitutionality of the appraisal law in the Illinois Supreme Court, prevailed, and paid his lawyer Isaac Arnold (who started off his legal career in Chicago writing real estate contracts for Garrett) a $125 fee and a $500 bonus, the very amount Bronson had offered Garrett. See Bronson v. Kinzie, 42 U.S. 1 (1 Howard 311); Haeger, *Investment Frontier*, 201 (Arnold's fee and bonus); Andreas, *History of Chicago*, vol. 1, 435 (Arnold's legal work for Garrett).

24. Andreas, *History of Chicago*, vol. 1, 527 (listing the directors of the bank); Pierce, *History of Chicago*, vol. 1, 190 with n75 (the wealthy men of the north side); Andreas, *History of Chicago*, vol. 1, 504 (on the Ogden, Kinzie, and W. H. Brown houses); Harpster, *Railroad Tycoon Who Built Chicago*, 44–45 (Kinzie, Hubbard, Hamilton, and Dole as the Chicago businessmen who welcomed Ogden's brother-in-law Charles Butler and his partner Bronson to form a corporation to build the Illinois and Michigan canal), 70 (Ogden's house).

25. Andreas, *History of Chicago*, vol. 1, 184 (listing members of Common Council in the 1840s—Garrett was an alderman only in 1840); *Chicago Democrat*, March 14, 1843 ("In consequence of extreme sickness in his family, the melancholy termination of which can be seen by reference to another column, the popular and deserving nominee of the Democratic party, Thomas Dyer, Esq., declined a canvass for the office of Mayor and the party allied with unparalleled unanimity upon Augustus Garrett, Esq., the nominee of last year"); Garrett to Thomas Dyer, February 9, 1843 (AGLB I: 90–91, out of order) (commenting on Hiram Pearsons and other possible candidates, including himself and his decision to run).

26. Vote tallies in "Chicago Mayors, 1837–2007," in the online *Encyclopedia of Chicago*, http://www.encyclopedia.chicagohistory.org/pages/1443.html; Garrett's inaugural address, *Chicago Democrat*, March 14, 1843. The same newspaper also noted that Garrett gave the address that evening (March 13) to the Common Council, which was evidently the usual custom (*Chicago Democrat*, March 21, 1843). On Democratic use of the expression "the greatest good for (to) the greatest number," see *The People's Democratic Guide*, vol. 1 (New York: James Webster, 1842), 1, 32, 40, 135, 138, 151, 294, 370. An anecdote was told many years later that Garrett said the following in his address to the Common Council: "Boys, I want to say that there will be no stealing; but if there is any to be done, I propose to do it" (from a broadside advertising the *Chicago Evening Journal* in 1887); the same anecdote is attributed to an "Old Timer" in "Augustus Garrett," an unsigned, unpublished sketch of Garrett's career (typescript at CHM). The statement does not appear in the published version of the address. If Garrett said it, it was plainly a joke. More likely, the story is apocryphal.

27. Andreas, *History of Chicago*, vol. 1, 182 (the 1837 city charter put a ceiling of 0.5 percent ["one half of one per cent"] on real and personal property); Robert M. Haig, *A History of General Property Tax in Illinois* (PhD diss., Columbia University; published, Champaign: University of Illinois, 1914), 57 (taxes stated in cents per hundred dollars, hence twenty cents = 0.2 percent; state land tax of 0.2 percent was established by 1839, this rate restored in 1843; county rate ceiling of 0.5 percent remains unchanged). The land tax in Illinois was a joint state-county tax, the revenues being divided between the state and county by various proportions. See Haig, *History of General Property Tax in Illinois*, 80, 87. The effective tax rate under Garrett's predecessor, Benjamin Raymond, had been 6 percent, and only a small fraction of that had come from the municipal tax rate on property (which was only half a percent). The rest must have come from special assessments. The raw tax information for these years is given in George F. Harding, *Sixty-Third Annual Report of the Comptroller of the City of Chicago, Illinois for the Fiscal Year Ended December 31, 1919* (Chicago: John F. Higgins, [1920]), 237 (table showing "Assessed Valuation, Taxes Thereon, and Indebtedness of the City of Chicago by Years"). On special assessments, see further below.

28. Mayor Raymond's inaugural address quoted in Weston A. Goodspeed and Daniel D. Healy, eds., *History of Cook County, Illinois*, vol. 1 (Chicago: Goodspeed Historical Association, 1909), 159; John J. Wallis, "Constitutions, Corporations, and Corruption: American States and Constitutional Change, 1842–1852," *Journal of Economic History* 65 (2005): 211–56, 212 (dynamics of democracy and both enthusiasm and opposition to government projects such

as the Erie Canal), 228 (sectional opposition in Illinois to canal project), 227 (benefit taxation in New York to finance Erie Canal), 228 (benefit taxation in Illinois to finance canal). Despite the tax rate ceiling in the charter, the city collected 6 percent on assessments in 1841 and 1842 but only 0.6 percent in 1843. See James Langland, ed., *The Chicago Daily News Almanac and Year-Book for 1921* (Chicago: Chicago Daily News, 1920), 876–77. This almanac gives amounts of taxes collected and amounts of assessments for each year, from which one can calculate the effective rate; Einhorn gets the same result using tables in a different publication (Einhorn, *Property Rules*, 92n68). It is unclear why there was a dramatic drop in the effective tax rate from 1842 to 1843. Nor is it clear whether special assessments (which the city claimed was not a tax) were responsible for the 6 percent rate, which was far above the tax rate that the charter allowed.

29. Charles H. Taylor, ed., *History of the Board of Trade of the City of Chicago*, vol. 1, part 1 (Chicago: Robert O. Law, 1917), 108 (state debt, canal, railroads); Thomas Ford, *A History of Illinois from Its Commencement as a State in 1814 to 1847* (Chicago: Griggs, 1854), 222–27 (the debt crisis), 223 ("the good money"), and 294 ("Heavy taxation would have depopulated the country [i.e., Illinois], and the debt would never be paid").

30. Taylor, ed., *History of the Board of Trade*, vol. 1, part 1, 109–110; Haig, *History of General Property Tax in Illinois*, 87 (state banknotes outlawed for tax payments, specie required; people "scarcely able to pay"; suspension of interest fund tax and state rate set at twenty cents = 2 percent).

31. Harding, *Sixty-Third Annual Report of the Comptroller*, 237 (table showing city debt); Pierce, *History of Chicago*, vol. 1, 359 (on warrants as a form of currency).

32. Garrett's inaugural address; Lloyd F. Sunderman, "Chicago's Centennial of School Music," *Music Educators Journal* 28, no. 5 (1942): 28–30 and 63–64, 28. The history of the school fund is given in Einhorn, *Property Rules*, 44–49.

33. Garrett's inaugural address. By the end of 1843 there were four temperance societies in the city, to which 26 percent of the city population belonged (Pierce, *History of Chicago*, vol. 1, 261).

34. Garrett's inaugural address; speech of Rev. H. H. Kellogg in *Proceedings of the General Anti-Slavery Convention Called by the Committee of the British and Foreign Anti-Slavery Society and Held in London [. . .] 1843*, recorded by J. F. Johnson (London: British and Foreign Anti-Slavery Society, 1843), 265–74, 271. On nonenforcement of slave laws in Chicago, see note 36 below. The history of antislavery work and abolitionism in the nation and in

Illinois in this period is illuminatingly summarized in Sidney Blumenthal, *A Self-Made Man: The Political Life of Abraham Lincoln, 1809–1849* (New York: Simon and Schuster, 2016), 303–18.

35. Alfred T. Andreas, *History of Chicago from the Earliest Period to the Present Time*, vol. 2: *From 1857 until the Fire of 1871* (Chicago: A. T. Andreas, 1885), 454; George Manierre, "The Manierre Family in Early Chicago," *Journal of the Illinois State Historical Society* 8, no. 3 (1915): 448–58, 451; Harpster, *Railroad Tycoon Who Built Chicago*, 135 (on the Ogden family's antislavery sentiments, as illustrated by the Heathcock incident).

36. Margaret Garb cites articles by John Jones, published in the *Chicago Tribune* in 1864 and also printed as a separate pamphlet, as evidence of non-enforcement of slave laws in Illinois. See Margaret Garb, *Freedom's Ballot: African American Political Struggles in Chicago from Abolition to the Great Migration* (Chicago: University of Chicago Press, 2014), 23; John Jones, *The Black Laws of Illinois, and a Few Reasons Why They Should Be Repealed* (Chicago: Tribune Book and Job Office, 1864). The Black Code of Illinois concerned persons of color: those brought into the state as slaves, those otherwise in the state as indentured servants, and those who were free persons in the state. Jones pointed out which provisions were being enforced and which were dead letter. The latter included the laws requiring that law enforcement and the courts prosecute and return fugitive slaves, a law requiring free blacks to carry a certificate of freedom, laws protecting the rights of masters over their slaves in Illinois, provisions limiting freedom of movement by slaves (such as straying too far from their masters or assembling), whipping of a slave as punishment for infractions of these provisions, and a number of other provisions. The case of Edwin Heathcock shows that the law that free blacks must carry a certificate was enforced in Chicago, if pressed by a citizen. Eastman, who was an antislavery participant in the events, recorded the story of the auction of Heathcock. Different parts of his narrative were later excerpted in Andreas, *History of Chicago*, vol. 2, 605; and in Rufus Blanchard, *Discovery and Conquests of the North West with the History of Chicago*, vol. 2 (Chicago: R. Blanchard, 1900), 283–85. According to Blanchard, Eastman put together a scrapbook of information on the conflict over slavery, and Blanchard had access to this scrapbook when he wrote up his own account, quoting Eastman's material (Blanchard, 312n). Eastman referred to "the second section of the act of 1829, referring to free negroes, etc.," as the basis for the judge's disposition of the case (Blanchard, 284).

37. Eastman quoted in Blanchard, *Discovery and Conquests of the North West*, vol. 2, 283 (comma added); Brian Dolinar, ed., *The Negro in Illinois:*

WPA Papers (Urbana: University of Illinois Press, 2013), 17 (DeWolf and the organization of the local Anti-Slavery Society in Chicago).

38. Eastman as quoted in Blanchard, *Discovery and Conquests of the North West*, vol. 2, 284; Andreas notes the location of the auction (*History of Chicago*, vol. 2, 605). Mahlon Ogden was a probate judge in 1843, so when he called out from an upstairs window, as Eastman reports, it must have been from an upper floor of the courthouse.

39. On differences among abolitionists about whether it was morally right to purchase slaves in order to give them their freedom, see Larry Gara, *The Liberty Line: The Legend of the Underground Railroad* (Lexington: University of Kentucky Press, 1961), 71–73. As Gara points out, some abolitionists who opposed the practice also had pragmatic reasons for doing so.

40. Augustus Garrett to James R. Malony, March 3, 1845 (AGLB II: 93) (abolitionist support for him). The abolitionist support of Garrett was short-lived and merely expedient but would not have been given at all if the Democrat Garrett had not been publicly known to be antislavery in some general sense.

41. Blumenthal, *A Self-Made Man*, 44 (description of slave auctions in New Orleans, the quotation); *The Doctrines and Discipline of the Methodist Episcopal Church* (New York: Mason and Lane, 1836), 77 (ch. 2, sect. 1.4)

42. Harding, *Sixty-Third Annual Report of the Comptroller*, 237 (table showing assessed valuations, tax revenues, and floating indebtedness of the city by mayoral years); Sunderman, "Chicago's Centennial of School Music," 28 ("At the end of the six months, music instruction was discontinued"); a summary of the city finances for 1843 is given in Goodspeed and Healy, *History of Cook County*, vol. 1, 166. On taxes, see also note 27 above.

43. A list of the standing committees of the Common Council is in the minutes of the council published in the *Chicago Democrat*, April 10, 1844.

44. Various CCCPF documents for 1843 relating to sidewalks (e.g., Docs. 1526, 1527, 1571).

45. The booster's mentality is evident in Garrett. In his letters Garrett makes frequent mention of his hopes that the state will complete the canal. To maximize its practicality, the canal required a Chicago harbor and permanent excavation of the sandbar (Pierce, *History of Chicago*, vol. 1, 90–93). Garrett was also on the committee for the Chicago River and Harbor Convention of 1847, an event designed to encourage the Polk administration to invest in the Chicago harbor and complete the canal as works of national benefit, a booster philosophy. Chicago boosters used special assessments purely pragmatically as a means of financing that, in a time of strained municipal finances, was better than borrowing and increasing city debt. In the period from about

1845 to 1851, however, the concept of special assessments became a philosophy of government ("segmentation"). This is one of the main contentions of Einhorn's book, *Property Rules* (see, e.g., 76).

46. Garrett refers to expenditures for things ornamental in his inaugural addresses of 1843 and 1844, and the latter gives a more precise definition of what *ornamental* meant. City expenditures in these years are indicated in the handful of council minutes that survive by virtue of being published in the *Chicago Democrat*, in the finance reports preserved in the CCCPF and sometimes in the papers, and by other references in the CCCPF. See for example, Doc. 865, July 15, 1839 ("City Expenditures from Commencement Municipal Year 1839 to 15th July 1839").

47. CCCPF Doc. 1678 and Doc. 1684, the latter passed May 13, 1843 (dumping ordinance with amended language); merchandise on the sidewalks is mentioned in the *Chicago American*, September 1, 1841, as excerpted in Goodspeed and Healy, *History of Cook County, Illinois*, vol. 1, 152.

48. Balestier, "Annals of Chicago," 33.

49. *Chicago Democrat*, March 13, 1844 (information on city expenses in Garrett's second inaugural address); J. W. Norris, *General Directory and Business Advertiser of the City of Chicago for the Year 1844* (Chicago: Ellis and Fergus, 1844), 18 (mentioning Mayor Garrett's negotiation of a reduction of the interest on the largest loan debt of the city).

50. Pierce, *History of Chicago*, vol. 1, 328 (provision for mayoral salary eliminated in 1841); Einhorn, *Property Rules*, 19 (antebellum Chicago offered politicians almost no possibilities to exercise patronage); Garrett to Seaman, February 3, 1844 (AGLB I: 52) (the quotation); Pierce, *History of Chicago*, vol. 1, 264 (Mayor Raymond donating his mayoral salary to support the poor); *Chicago Democrat*, March 6, 1844, celebrating Garrett's reelection in 1844 and referring to his public and private charity to the poor); Garrett to Seaman, February 3, 1844 (AGLB I: 51–52) (complaining about the work, the cost to his health, and the duty of giving to paupers).

51. Garrett to Seaman, December 30, 1843 (AGLB I: 33) (out of order; spelling corrected and a missing word added).

52. Garrett to Seaman, December 28, 1843 (AGLB I: 38) (punctuation added and spelling corrected); Garrett to Seaman February 3, 1844 (AGLB I: 51–52, 59); Garrett to Col. James Mitchell, February 18, 1844 (AGLB I: 64).

53. Garrett to J. A. Noonan, February 6, 1844 (AGLB I: 31) ("They have all sorts of reports"; spelling corrected, punctuation added).

54. Garrett to J. A. Noonan, February 21, 1844 (AGLB I: 65) (second request to Noonan; spelling corrected); editorial from *Milwaukee Courier*

republished in *Chicago Democrat*, March 13, 1844 ("*Hon. Augustus Garrett*, of Chicago, has been most ungenerously"). Garrett sent other letters to Noonan about the matter, in which he solicited Noonan's help in getting letters from people in Milwaukee that would help clear him of any suspicion (letters of February 13 and 22, 1844). On George Wentworth's dislike of Garrett, see below.

55. *Chicago Democrat*, February 28, 1844 (two separate articles on Garrett's administration of the mayoralty).

56. *Chicago Democrat*, February 28, 1844.

57. *Chicago Democrat*, February 28, 1844 ("would carry out"; emphasis added); *Chicago Democrat*, March 13, 1844, ("federalism, in all its forms, is annihilated here").

58. Ford, *History of Illinois*, 309 ("that their political opponents"); *Chicago Democrat*, February 28, 1844 (editorials about how a defeat of Whigs in the city election would signal or even impede their success in state elections); *Chicago Democrat*, February 21, 1844 (quoting William S. Brown); *Chicago Democrat*, April 9, 1845 (praise for Garrett's administration). On Mayor Raymond's interest in reducing municipal debt, see note 28. Einhorn also notes the rhetoric of national politics in municipal elections and comments that much of it was not really relevant to Chicago but represented purely partisan sentiment (*Property Rules*, 32–33).

59. See below for Garrett's activities on election day; Augustus Garrett to the editor of the *Express*, March 2, 1844 (AGLB I: 115) (regarding the cemetery plots and fence, including his defense of Raymond). Names are variously spelled, including that of Grier, sometimes rendered Greer.

60. *Chicago Democrat*, March 13, 1844 (election results); CCCPF Doc. 1881 (Official Oath of Mayor Augustus Garrett); CCCPF Doc. 1867, March 5, 1844 (petition of George W. Dole, itemizing all the complaints discussed).

61. *Chicago Democrat*, March 13, 1844 (inaugural address of Augustus Garrett); CCCPF Doc. 1867 (Dole petition with charges against Garrett and his supporters); CCCPF Doc. 1888, Report of Committee on Elections of Validity of Certain Elections, March 11[–16] (depositions).

62. CCCPF Doc. 1867 (petition of Dole); CCCPF Doc. 1888: deposition of Henry W. Clarke; of John Sullivan (referring to setting his clock to Welsh's watch); of Thomas Welsh (referring to Sullivan's clock and Sherwood's time, which the deposition of George Kirk seems to imply is Sherwood's time, which makes sense since Sherwood was the first jeweler in Chicago); of Martin S. Wood (Tremont House regulated its time by the jeweler Speer); of John Sullivan (referring to Michael Kennedy's complaint and what Sullivan's clock said); of Thomas Welsh (passed by polls about 7:20 by his watch, saw no one

there, later compared his watch to Sherwood's time); of clerks Henry Clarke and George Brady, and inspectors/judges William Sammons, Andrew Nielsen, and John Campbell (all stating that the first votes were received after 8:00 and before 8:30); of Elihu Granger and his boarder George Kirk; of Thomas Joyce and Samuel Grier; and second deposition of Henry Clarke. The Fergus city directory for 1843 was used to identify certain persons mentioned in the depositions: Robert Fergus, comp., *Directory of the City of Chicago, Illinois, for 1843* (*Fergus' Historical Series* no. 28; Chicago: Fergus, 1896), 45 (for Henry W. Clarke), 85 (for Reynold, assuming Clarke meant E. J. Reynold the clerk), 90 (Smith J. Sherwood, jeweler).

63. Depositions in CCCPF Doc. 1888: of Joyce; of Joel Ellis (about Joyce buying meat from him and him going to Washington Coffee House); of Martin S. Wood (about when the Washington Coffee House bell was usually rung for the first table).

64. CCCPF Doc. 1893, March 14, 1844 (Report of Majority Judiciary Committee on legality of elections in Third and Fifth Wards); Doc. 1867 (Dole petition); Doc. 1888 (depositions of election judges).

65. CCCPF Doc. 1888 (deposition of election judge George Brady); Doc. 1867 (Dole petition claiming that there were ten or more illegal votes in the Fifth Ward, including those of McCarty and Driscoll); the issue was also examined for the Third Ward (deposition of William Heacock, A. S. Sherman, and others—CCCPF Doc. 1894); further depositions dealing with the election are preserved in CCCPF Doc. 1907.

66. Criminal Code, sect. 140 in *The Public and General Statutes of the State of Illinois* (Chicago: Gale, 1839), 225 (on bribery, treating, etc.); CCCPF Doc. 1867, March 5 (Dole's petition alleging bribery and fraud on Garrett's part); CCCPF Doc. 1880, March 11 depositions (questioning in deposition of Andrew Nielsen about keg of beer brought to Grier's; same question in George Brady's deposition; and in the deposition of Samuel Grier; see further below); CCCPF Doc. 1907 (deposition of Oren Overson).

67. CCCPF Doc. 1888 (interrogations of Goodrich, Dole, and Murphy under oath).

68. CCCPF Doc. 1888 (depositions of Brady, Grier, Granger, and Nielsen).

69. CCCPF Doc. 1893, March 14, 1844 (Report of Majority Judiciary Committee on Legality of Elections for Third and Fifth Wards, submitted to Common Council by Buckner S. Morris and Asher Rossiter); CCCPF Doc. 1859, 1844 (Minority Report of the Committee on the Judiciary in Relation to the Election in Fifth Ward, submitted to the Common Council by George Davis).

70. Garrett to J. R. Malony, March 16, 1844 (AGLB I: 103).

71. Garrett to J. R. Malony, March 16, 1844 (AGLB I: 103).

72. CCCPF Doc. 1893, March 14, 1844 (Report of Majority Judiciary Committee on Legality of Elections for Third and Fifth Wards) (pointing out that opening of ballots, if known to those yet to vote, could tend to suppress voting, whether that was intended or not).

73. Garrett to J. R. Malony, March 16, 1844 (AGLB I: 103) (spelling corrected and punctuation added for clarity). The special committee on the election submitted a report to the council in the form of a set of depositions on March 18 (CCCPF Doc. 1896). This did not include all the depositions, for additional depositions were submitted on March 20 and 23 (CCCPF Docs. 1907, 1908). Some later accounts say that the Common Council met in Mrs. Chapman's building from 1842–1848, but Garrett refers to the Saloon Building as the venue for the Common Council meeting following the contested election of 1844. In fact, the Common Council used more than one location for its meetings during these years. For the election meeting, the larger upstairs hall of the Saloon Building was required.

74. Garrett to J. R. Malony, March 16, 1844 (AGLB I: 103–4) (spelling corrected and punctuation added for clarity).

75. Garrett to Malony, March 16, 1844 (AGLB I: 104).

76. Garrett to John Wentworth, March 24, 1844 (AGLB I: 110) (summarizing the council proceedings); Garrett to Seaman, April 4, 1844 (AGLB I: 128–29) ("After I resigned they destroyed the election of 2 wards on account of one of the clerks being underage and the other having been a resident only 4½ instead of 6 months").

77. Augustus Garrett to John Wentworth, no date (sometime at the end of March 1844) (AGLB I: 112).

78. Garrett to Seaman, April 4, 1844 (AGLB I: 128–29) (Garrett's account of the special election that ensued); *Chicago Democrat*, April 10, 1844 (special election initial tallies); final vote tallies in "Chicago Mayors, 1837–2007," in the online *Encyclopedia of Chicago*, http://www.encyclopedia.chicagohistory.org/pages/1443.html.

79. *Chicago Democrat*, April 10, 1844 (postelection praise for Sherman); Garrett to Seaman, April 4, 1844 (AGLB I: 128–29) (claiming he had schemed to get the Democrats to support Sherman).

80. Garrett to Seaman, December 4, 1843 (AGLB I: 4) ("I am busy"; punctuation, etc., added); Garrett to Seaman, January 25, 1845 (AGLB II: 38) (his exhaustion; spelling and punctuation altered).

81. Augustus Garrett to J. R. Malony, March 3, 1845 (AGLB II: 93–94).

82. Vote tallies in "Chicago Mayors, 1837–2007," in the online *Encyclopedia of Chicago*, http://www.encyclopedia.chicagohistory.org/pages/1443.html; Augustus Garrett to George H. Hutchins, March 8, 1845 (AGLB II: 98); *Chicago Daily Democrat*, March 12, 1845 (inaugural address).

83. *Chicago Daily Democrat*, March 12, 1845, cited by Pierce, *History of Chicago*, vol. 1, 387 (makeup of the new council under Garrett); *Chicago Daily Journal*, April 21, 1845 (resigns mayoralty over conflict with Alderman Scammon), and April 25, 1845 (reconsiders resignation) (newspaper references in the annotated Otis index; the issues themselves are not preserved in microfilm).

84. *Chicago Democrat*, January 10, 1844 (reporting minutes of Common Council meeting on December 30, 1843, in Garrett's first term: a committee was appointed by the mayor to consider the building of a city high school); Johnston, "Historical Sketches of the Public School System" (report of Committee on Schools from May, 1844, outlining the proposed building use); Andreas, *History of Chicago*, vol. 1, 121–22 (a city faction called the "Kickers" referred to the building as "Miltimore's Folly").

85. *Chicago Daily Democrat*, March 12, 1845 (Garrett's third inaugural address to Common Council, March 10, outlining the demerits of the new high school); *Chicago Daily Journal* April 21, 1845 (cited above regarding conflict with Scammon). The *Chicago Daily Journal* reported that Garrett "resigned" over differences with Alderman Scammon (see note 83), and it stands to reason that the quarrel began with Garrett's own criticism of Scammon's pet project, the big schoolhouse.

86. [J. Young Scammon,] "Speech of J. Young Scammon," in *Early Chicago: Reception of the Settlers of Chicago Prior to 1840 by the Calumet Club of Chicago, Tuesday Evening, May, 27, 1879* (Chicago: Calumet Club, 1879), 65–70, 66, 69 (twice summarizing Garrett's remark and treating it as serious, not a joke); Edwin O. Gale, *Reminiscences of Early Chicago and Vicinity* (Fleming H. Revell, 1902), 384–85 (treating the joke as a narrow-minded proposal); Andreas, *History of Chicago*, vol. 1, 211 (treating the joke as serious and thus enshrining for future generations the idea that this was Garrett's policy proposal for the building); J. Seymour Currey, "Chicago's First Public School House," *Fort Dearborn Magazine* 3, no. 8 (November 1922): 23 (treating the joke as a serious proposal). The joke continues to be taken as a statement of policy; for example, see Bradley W. Rasch, *The Governors of Illinois and the Mayors of Chicago* (Bloomington, IN: iUniverse, 2012), 58 (stating incorrectly that "as mayor he converted a large elementary school into an insane asylum").

87. Shepherd Johnston, "Historical Sketches of the Public School System of the City of Chicago," an appendix to *Twenty-Fifth Annual Report of the*

Board of Education for the Year Ending July 31, 1879 (Chicago: Clark & Edwards, 1880; also separately printed), 1–79, 19–20, 21 (Committee on Schools report from June, 1845, about erection of school building in District 4; and from March 1846 about the inability of municipal power to tax); Andreas, *History of Chicago*, vol. 1, 212 ($4,000 for school at LaSalle and Ohio).

88. Canal Trustees v. City of Chicago, 12 Ill. 403 (on whether special assessments are taxes, decided in 1851). The municipal charter gave the city the power to tax personal and real property up to 0.5 percent of assessed value for "lighting the city streets, supporting a night watch, making and repairing streets and bridges, and paying the operating expenses" (1837 charter quoted in Andreas, *History of Chicago*, vol. 1, 182). The charter also required each male citizen to contribute three days' labor to construct and maintain streets, with refusers to pay the equivalent as a fine. An 1839 ordinance specified the fine as three dollars, applicable to males twenty-two through fifty-nine years of age (*Chicago American*, May 3, 1839, cited in Pierce, *History of Chicago*, vol. 1, 336n97). Garrett wanted this reduced but did not succeed (third inaugural address). The 1847 revision of the charter reduced it to fifty cents a day and made it applicable to a person only for streets in his own ward. See *Private and Special Laws of the State of Illinois Passed by the Fifteenth General Assembly* (Springfield, IL: Lanphier, 1847), 84–85.

89. CCCPF Doc. 2602 (May 23, 1845, communication to council regarding removal of sand from City Cemetery); CCCPF Doc. 2837 (December 9, 1845, ordinance governing the cutting of holes in the ice); James Langland, ed., *Chicago Daily News Almanac and Year-Book for the Year 1922* (Chicago: Chicago Daily News, 1921), 902 (first lake pumping station constructed at Chicago Avenue and Lake Michigan); CCCPF Docs. 2773 (October 10, 1845, report on constructing aqueducts), 2780 (bids for aqueducts), 2900 (ordinance regarding private lading from aqueducts, referred to special committee, December 23, 1845), 2901 (slight amendments to aqueduct ordinance, passed December 30, 1845). Einhorn believes the aqueducts were for drainage (*Property Rules*, 92), but Doc. 2773 refers to laying aqueducts *from* the river, and Doc. 2901 speaks expressly of citizens taking water from aqueducts for their private use.

90. *Chicago Daily Democrat*, March 12, 1845 (Garrett's inaugural address); Shirk v. City of Chicago, 195 Ill. 298 at 311 (citing records of Common Council on July 5, 1845, appointing citizens to take measures against encroachment of the lake); CCCPF Doc. 2648 (Committee on Streets and Bridges tasked to report on the construction of a breakwater, the committee's July 5th report giving specifications and describing the breakwater as "extremely necessary"; the August 15th city contract with Tibbits, signed by Garrett,

records payments to Tibbits); Andreas, *History of Chicago*, vol. 1, 154 (August 5, 1845, decision to construct breakwater on the lakeshore); CCCPF Doc. 2692 (August bids for breakwater); CCCPF Docs. 2799, 2813 (petitions protesting special assessments); Einhorn, *Property Rules*, 92–93 (citizen lawsuits contesting special assessments for lakeshore protection, which the city began refunding in 1846).

91. CCCPF Doc. 2798 (ordinance of October 25, 1845, regarding articles on streets, sidewalks, alleyways, etc.); *Chicago Daily Journal*, April 24, 1845 ("a City of pestiferous odour," quoted in Pierce, *History of Chicago*, vol. 1, 205); *Chicago Daily Journal*, March 18 and 21, 1845 (whether to fill Wabash Street slough, cited in Pierce, *History of Chicago*, vol. 1, 337n101); *Chicago Daily Journal*, March 31 and April 11, as well as *Chicago Democrat*, April 9, 1845 (ordinance about sidewalk slope; the latter is not evident in microform copy, perhaps cited incorrectly in Pierce, *History of Chicago*, vol. 1, 338).

92. Common Council minutes summarized in [Board of Health of the City of Chicago,] *Report of the Board of Health of the City of Chicago for 1867, 1868, and 1869 and a Sanitary History of Chicago from 1833 to 1870* (Chicago: Lakeside, 1871), 17 (demand that the board of health does its duty; order to build hospital, also called a pest house); CCCPF Doc. 2483, April 1, 1845 (receiving bids for "pest house" or "hospital"); CCCPF Doc. 2484, April 4, 1845 (report of committee on the pest house); CCCPF Doc. 2484, April 4, 1845 (report of committee on the pest house); CCCPF Docs. 2545, April 25, 1845 (construction of hospital completed), and 2567, May 9, 1845 (proposal for plastering the hospital).

93. *Chicago Democrat*, April 9, 1845 (small pox proclamation; also reference to activity of the board of health against small pox).

94. It appears that two cemeteries were in view, distinguished as the Old Burying Ground and City Cemetery. See Goodspeed and Healy, *History of Cook County*, vol. 1, 156, 166; *Chicago Democrat*, February 28, 1844 ("No act passed by the present Council reflects so much honor upon each of its members, separately, as the respect it has shown in its deliberations in regard to the burial of the dead. How the Mayor of our city in 1842 [Whig Benjamin Raymond] could look on and see the coffins of our citizens lying exposed on the top of the ground, and their bones bleaching on the Lakeshore, and make no efforts in regards to the matter is a mystery. The exertions which have been made on the part of our present Mayor, Mr. Garrett, to have our cemetery properly fenced, too, will, we trust, long be remembered by our citizens"); *Chicago Democrat*, March 13, 1844 (second inaugural address of Augustus Garrett touching on problem of disinterment in City Cemetery);

Chicago Daily Journal, March 31, 1845 (third inaugural address touching on erosion in the Old Burying Ground); Common Council minutes summarized *Report of the Board of Health*, 17 (demand that sexton notify mayor about exposure of graves); CCCPF Doc. 1691, May 13, 1843 (an ordinance banning further burial in the cemetery, apparently the Old Burying Ground); on the whole subject, see also the postscript.

95. CCCPF Doc. 2732 (petition and ordinance passed August 29, 1845).

96. John Wentworth, *Early Chicago: A Lecture Delivered before the Sunday Lecture Society, at McCormick Hall, on Sunday Afternoon, April 11, 1875* (Chicago: Fergus, 1875), 16–17 (mentioning the British invasion of Mackinaw and recollecting his speech to Congress in 1845 or 1846); excerpt from Wentworth speech to Congress, June 18, 1845 (quoted in Pierce, *History of Chicago*, vol. 1, 390n157).

97. Alfred T. Andreas, *History of Cook County, Illinois: The Earliest Period to the Present Time* (Chicago: A. T. Andreas, 1884), 210 ("a meeting at the court house" cancelled, Andreas says, because leading citizens were in Rockford that day; Wentworth's letter, received January 13, about a lack of troops from Chicago for Mexican War and a concern about defending the forts at Mackinac and Chicago, the latter perhaps connected with a sense of national vulnerability on the northern border with forces being sent to the southwest for the Mexican War).

98. Andreas, *History of Cook County*, 213 (Charles P. Holden's recollection of "barbaric scenes"), 211 (Garrett letter about raising troops, published in the *Daily Democrat*, June 30, 1846; Governor Ford's second request; Garrett's failure to get quite enough recruits for a third full company).

99. Augustus Garrett to John Seaman, November 6, 1844 (AGLB I: 223).

6. THEIR SEPARATE SPHERES

1. Augustus Garrett to John Seaman, December 28, 1843 (AGLB I: 46).

2. Garrett to Seaman, December 28, 1843 (AGLB: 45) (Eliza "determined to go to housekeeping in the spring"), 46 ("I am a going to take the Governor with Dyer in a carriage to make calls on N Year day"). In the same letter, he says, "my wife is making preparations to receive calls," implying that she would see friends on New Year's Day in their rooms at the Sauganash, but he makes no reference to Ford visiting them there.).

3. The economy was only just recovering from the Panic of 1837. In Chicago, a bottom in land values had been reached the year prior, in 1842, and prices were now beginning to rise. See Homer Hoyt, *One Hundred Years of Land Values in Chicago: The Relationship of the Growth of Chicago to the Rise*

of Its Land Values, 1830–1933 (Chicago: University of Chicago Press, 1933), 41. There were further dips, however, in the mid-1840s. In early 1845, for example, a downturn caused Augustus to tell a man from New York named Boyer that "the Western country is not worth more than 50 cents on the dollar" (Garrett to A. Boyer Jr., NY, February 25, 1845 [AGLB II: 83]).

4. Jack Harpster, *The Railroad Tycoon Who Built Chicago: A Biography of William B. Ogden* (Carbondale: Southern Illinois University Press, 2009), 54 (Ogden resides at the Sauganash in 1835), 70–71 (Ogden's house).

5. J. W. Norris, comp., *Norris' Business Directory and Statistics of the City of Chicago for 1846* (Chicago: Eastman & Davidson, 1846), s.v. Garrett, Augustus (giving the address as Fran [Franklin] east between Las and South Water— Las must be Lake Street since LaSalle makes no sense; so the address must be Franklin, east side of the street, between Lake Street and South Water); J. W. Norris, comp., *Norris' Chicago Directory for 1848–49* (Chicago: Norris & Taylor, 1848), s.v. Garrett, Augustus (giving an office address for him at 12 Franklin Street, which suggests he was working out of his house by then). One can see the triangular block in the Wright map shown in chapter 5.

6. Garrett to Seaman, December 28, 1843 (AGLB I: 45–46, out of order; punctuation added) (describing the house, asking for "fashionable railings," etc.); Garrett to Seaman, March 24, 1844 (AGLB I: 116) ("a set of silver plated castors"). The New York City directories for the 1840s show John Seaman's address in lower Manhattan at 120 Water Street.

7. Garrett to Seaman, March 24, 1844 (AGLB I: 116) ("perhaps the forks"); Garrett to Seaman, January 3, 1844 (AGLB II: 1) (mentioning "our hyacinths" in bloom, which, given the time of year, implies they had a greenhouse).

8. Augustus Garrett to Frederick Flaglor, March 16, 1844 (AGLB I: 100–101).

9. Augustus Garrett to John Seaman, December 28, 1843 (AGLB I: 46, out of order) (on wanting Aunt Drake to be his "financier"). On the Drake family and its relation to Augustus, see chapter 1.

10. Garrett to Mahony, April 8, 1844 (AGLB I: 126) and April 4, 1844 (AGLB II: 129) (going to housekeeping "next week"); Garrett to Seaman, October 13, 1844 (AGLB I: 200–201) (mentioning their wallpaper); Garrett to Seaman, October 10, 1844 (AGLB I: 200) (mentioning the "hair seating" of the sofa," which would have been horsehair, and the new wallpaper); April 4, 1844 (AGLB I: 129) (fixing up a guest room); Garrett to Seaman, July 26, 1844 (AGLB I: 176) (expecting the Seamans to be in Chicago soon); Garrett to Seaman, October 22, 1844 (AGLB I: 212) (the ottomans). A letter the following January implies that the Seamans had still not paid the Garretts a visit—that Seaman had visited "this country" (perhaps going to see his

brother in Dixon) but had not gone to Chicago to see Garrett; that Seaman had fallen ill, without notifying Garrett, and had then returned to New York; and that Garrett was annoyed by that, adding that Eliza wants them both to visit (January 2, 1845 [AGLB I: 278–79]).

11. Various letters in spring and summer imply Garrett's travels to New York; Augustus Garrett to John Seaman, October 13, 1844 (AGLB I: 200–201) (regarding Edward Francis Heath, the orphan).

12. Garrett to Seaman, October 13, 1844 (AGLB I: 200–201) (regarding Edward Heath; punctuation added and small orthographic corrections).

13. Augustus Garrett to John Seaman, January 3, 1845 (AGLB II: 6) (mentioning the hyacinths, doing so also in a letter of January 17 [AGLB II: 34], saying their scent fills the parlors). His January 3 letter also mentions that "both rooms" were full on New Year's Day. In another letter Augustus speaks of sitting by the fire in his "front room" (Garrett to Seaman, February 9, 1845 [AGLB II: 65]). Hence, the two rooms for receiving guests were probably a parlor and this front room. A January 5 letter (AGLB II: 10) mentions the gift of the birdcage and canaries, whom they named "Katie" and "Robe." Perhaps Robe was Maloney's middle name.

14. Augustus Garrett to John Seaman, January 3, 1845 (AGLB II: 1, 6) (teasing "St. John" about his many long letters).

15. The history of the Clarks and Garrett's farm was pieced together from the following letters (the second of which mentions the letter from Eliza's parents), which arrived on New Year's Day: Augustus Garrett to Jeremiah Clark, April 8, 1844 (AGLB I: 134) (implying that Samuel had purchased the farm from the Clarks in what turned out to be a bad idea); Augustus Garrett to Benoni and Amy Clark, January 15, 1845 (AGLB II: 29–32); August Garrett to Frederick Flaglor, March 16, 1844 (AGLB I: 100) (telling Frederick to let Benoni know that he would be sending Benoni "his interest" in the next few days).

16. Augustus Garrett to Jeremiah Clark, April 8, 1844 (AGLB I: 134).

17. Augustus Garrett to Benoni and Amy Clark, January 15, 1845 (AGLB II: 31–32) (some punctuation added to the quotations).

18. Augustus Garrett to Mrs. Latitia [sic] Flaglor (his sister), March 18, 1844 (AGLB I: 102) (helping his sister out of debt, his mother's pension); Garrett to Seaman, January 23, 1845 (AGLB II: 35–37) (this letter and the prior one suggesting that many businesses and banks were failing and that debts were not being paid, which was affecting Seaman and Garrett); Augustus Garrett to A. Boyer Jr., NY, February 25, 1845 (AGLB II: 83) (plummeting land and real estate values: "the Western country is not worth more than

50 cents on the dollar. The revolution is quite as bad as it was in 1837"); see below regarding the bad debts of creditors, such as Donaghue and Marshall, that hurt Garrett and Seaman in these months; Garrett to Seaman, October 5, 1844 (AGLB I: 184) (selling horse and buggy); Garrett to cashier, branch of the State Bank of Indiana, Michigan City, December 30, 1844 (AGLB I: 251–52) (seeking to get a lower interest rate).

19. Garrett to Benoni and Amy Clark, January 15, 1845 (AGLB II: 32) ("We are tired of housekeeping and think of going to New York to live").

20. Alasdair Roberts, *America's First Great Depression: Economic Crisis and Political Disorder after the Panic of 1837* (Ithaca, NY: Cornell University Press, 2012), 47 (almost 90 percent bank failure). On the length and severity of the depression, see Roberts, 19–20, 23, 46–47, passim. Roberts (19–20) cites Mentor Williams, "A Tour of Illinois in 1842," *Journal of the Illinois State Historical Society* 42, no. 3 (1949): 292–312 (for Paulding quotations); and Eleanor Atkinson and the Editorial Staff of the Little Chronicle Company, *The Story of Chicago and National Development, 1534–1910* (Chicago: Little Chronicle, 1909), 58 (on nearly empty hotels).

21. [Henry Strong,] "Speech of General Henry Strong," in *Early Chicago: Reception to the Settlers of Old Chicago prior to 1840 by the Calumet Club of Chicago, Tuesday Evening, May 27, 1879* (Chicago: Calumet Club, 1879), 31 (26–34) ("often short of change," sending shirts back). That Garrett borrowed money is clear from references to loans he took or sought. See, for example, Garrett to Seaman, December 30, 1843 (AGLB I: 33–34).

22. The 1839 city directory lists Augustus as an auctioneer; the 1843 directory does not and contains an advertisement announcing his new partnership with John Seaman (a New York cousin). Garrett & Seaman ads in the Chicago city directory for 1844 are dated December 1843, and the ad for their commission business gives a start date of May 1, 1844. The earliest letters in Garrett's letter-books, which are essentially his correspondence for the partnership, date to October of 1843; and in March of 1844, Augustus tells his sister that he and John have "gone into a large business together" (Augustus to Letitia Flaglor, March 18, 1844 [AGLB I: 102]).

23. On the rumors about his assets and the matter of the affidavit, see Garrett to Seaman, December 30, 1843 (AGLB I: 33–34) (mentioning Ogden and Bronson) and Garrett to Seaman, February 3, 1844 (AGLB I: 50). In the second of these letters, having heard that rumors continued to circulate about his solvency, Garrett told Seaman, "two years since I left a record in the office in the Supreme Court which I wrote you about before. I can assure you that I am worth more now than I was then" (spelling corrected).

24. Garrett to Seaman, December 4, 1843 (AGLB I: 4) (wants to be consulted); Garrett to Seaman, February 3, 1844 (AGLB I: 50) (teasing John about his long letters; punctuation added and orthography corrected).

25. See the next note.

26. For this and the preceding paragraph: Augustus Garrett to John Brower (sic), November 1, 1843 (AGLB I: 66); Augustus Garrett to John Brouwer, November 11, 1843, two separate letters on the same day (AGLB I: 68–70, 78–80); also Augustus Garrett to J. W. Savage, secretary, National Insurance Company, November 26, 1843 (AGLB I: 78–79) (same topics).

27. Augustus Garrett to John Seaman, December 22, 1843 (AGLB I: 15–16); Garrett letters to Garrett, Seaman & Stearns, Dixon, IL, January 3, 11, 22, 1844 (AGLB I: 21, 24) (showing that Garrett, Seaman & Stearns had been formed in Dixon and that this firm was a customer and probably also an agent of Garrett & Seaman); J. W. Norris, *General Directory and Business Advertiser of the City of Chicago for the Year 1844* (Chicago: Ellis and Fergus, 1844), s.v. Seaman, Willett (showing Willett Seaman as a clerk for Bracken & Tuller).

28. Garrett to John Seaman, November 12, 1844 (AGLB I: 236).

29. Garrett to Alfred Courtenius, November 8, 1844 (AGLB I: 224–25); Garrett to Seaman, January 3, 1845 (AGLB II: 3).

30. Garrett to Alfred Courtenius, November 8, 1844 (AGLB I: 224–25) (mentioning the three insurance companies and what they earn from them); Garrett to Seaman, January 23, 1845 (AGLB II: 35) ("It is singular").

31. Many letters in this period refer to notes that cannot be paid and imply that Garrett and Seaman are the creditors for the sellers they represent or the guarantors for the sellers' loans.

32. Garrett to Seaman, January 3, 1845 (AGLB II: 2); Garrett to Seaman, December 22, 1844 (AGLB I: 265).

33. Garrett to Seaman, January 11 and 25, 1845 (AGLB II: 19–21, 37); Garrett to Seaman, January 3, 1845 (AGLB II: 2); Garrett to Spears and Vanderhoof, February 3, 1845 (AGLB II: 53–54). "O'Donahue" is spelled variously in the correspondence.

34. Garrett to Seaman, January 3, 1845 (AGLB II: 5–6).

35. Garrett to John Wentworth, November 17, 1844 (AGLB I: 247); Garrett to Wentworth, December 9, 1844 (AGLB I: 252–53); Garrett to Seaman, February 22, 1845 (AGLB II: 81) (referring to his hope for a post under Polk doing Kinzie's job, register at the land office, which pays $3,000); Garrett to Malony, March 22, 1845 (AGLB II: 132).

36. Garrett to James K. Polk, April 8, 1845 (AGLB II: 175); Norris, *Norris' Business Directory and Statistics of the City of Chicago for 1846* (listing

appointments to receiver's and register's offices); J. Seymour Currey, *Chicago: Its History and Its Builders*, vol. 3 (Chicago: S. J. Clarke, 1918), 333, 358 (Hart L. Stewart appointed postmaster in 1845 and 1846). Polk's collected letters record Garrett's letter to Polk but no response. See *Correspondence of James K. Polk*, vol. 9: *January–June 1845*, ed. Wayne Cutler and Robert G. Hall (Knoxville: University of Tennessee Press, 1996), 527.

37. Garrett to Malony ("Robe"), March 21, 1845 (AGLB II: 128–29) (Robe has been sick; Augustus counsels him, encourages him); Garrett to Malony, March 22, 1845 (advice about rest and Sassaparilla [sarsaparilla]) (AGLB II: 131); Garrett to Seaman, April 3, 1845 (AGLB II: 156) (fears Robe is going to die; "there will be no one alive"); Garrett to George Wilde, April 7, 1845 (AGLB II: 160–61) (writes to Wilde about Robe, his "best friend").

38. Garrett to R. L. Malony (Robe's father?), April 28, 1845 (AGLB II: 185) (hears Robe has recovered). The last letters in the Garrett letter-books are for November 1845. This suggests that the correspondence for Garrett and Seaman's business concluded about that time, which corresponds with other evidence. Norris's 1846 directory shows new agents for the Atlantic and National Insurance Companies (*Norris' Business Directory and Statistics*, 44–45). It has no listing of any business for Garrett but shows him as mayor, which means that the directory was published in January or February of 1846, that is, before he left office. The last appearance of Seaman & Garrett in Doggett's New York City directory is 1845. See [John Doggett,] *Doggett's New-York City Directory for 1845 & 1846* (New York: John Doggett, 1845), 323 ("Seaman & Garrett, com. merch., 120 Water"). In subsequent directories, Seaman's name stands alone for the commercial merchant business at that address.

39. Garrett to Seaman, February 22, 1845 (AGLB II: 81) (governor and legislators to dine with the Garretts after passage of "the Revenue Bill"); John Moses, *Illinois, Historical and Statistical*, vol. 1 (Chicago: Fergus, 1889), 461 (summarizing the revenue bills of that session).

40. *Chicago Democrat*, June 25, 1845, in Bessie Louise Pierce, *A History of Chicago*, vol. 1: *The Beginning of a City, 1673–1848* (Chicago: University of Chicago Press, 1937), 207 (new racetrack, Gurnee treasurer), 212 (people of means went to dinners and balls).

41. Garrett to Seaman, December 28, 1843 (AGLB I: 46) (quotation; punctuation, etc., added).

42. On women's benevolent associations, see chapter 3. On the reform efforts and evangelistic missions of some of them, see Lisa J. Shaver, *Beyond the Pulpit: Women's Rhetorical Roles in the Antebellum Religious Press* (Pittsburgh:

University of Pittsburgh Press, 2012), 80–82; Catherine E. Kelly, *In the New England Fashion: Reshaping Women's Lives in the Nineteenth Century* (Ithaca, NY: Cornell University Press, 1999), 199–203. On Protestant doubts about whether Catholics were truly Christian, see Clifford S. Griffin, "Converting the Catholics: American Benevolent Societies and the Ante-bellum Crusade against the Church," *Catholic Historical Review* 47 (1961): 325–41. On Juliette Kinzie's attitude toward revivalist religion, see chapter 3. Augustus Garrett to Jeremiah Clark, April 8, 1844 (AGLB I: 133) ("Eliza was elected" and "the Methodists complain").

43. The *Norris' General Directory and Business Advertiser* for 1844 tells the story: Mrs. Adams (laundress), Mrs. G. Anderson (milliner and straw-hat maker), Mrs. Armstrong (milliner and mantua maker), Mrs. Atkinson (milliner and dressmaker), Miss Barnes (teacher), Mrs. Braise (dressmaker and tailor), Mrs. Brock (straw and tuscan milliner), Mrs. Brown (dress and cloak maker), Miss Maria Delap (milliner), Mrs. Duffie (laundress), Mrs. A. Gale (milliner), Mrs. Hadley (dress and cloak maker), Mrs. Hathaway (dressmaker), Miss McComber (milliner), Mrs. Post (operating a boardinghouse called "Mrs. Post's"), Miss Ellen Shaddle (teacher), Mrs. Wariner (schoolteacher), Mrs. Margaret Green (boardinghouse operator?), Mrs. E. Haight (boardinghouse).

44. Elias P. Fordham, *Personal Narrative of Travels in Virginia, Maryland, Pennsylvania, Ohio, Indiana, Kentucky; and of a Residence in the Illinois Territory, 1817–1818*, ed. Frederic A. Ogg (Cleveland: Arthur H. Clark, 1906), 192–93 ("Business and politics"); Eliza Garrett to Melinda Hamline, February 3, 1853 (EGLC).

45. Recent scholarly literature on the "two spheres" of nineteenth-century America has, with some justification, stressed that this was a white, chiefly New England ideal and that social reality was much less compartmentalized, varying from one social group or class to another. Yet the obstacles women faced in seeking to acquire higher education, break into the professions, win suffrage, or acquire property, etc., show that a good deal of compartmentalization was a pervasive reality, by both custom and law, whatever the variations across race, region, and class may have been.

46. Garrett to Seaman, December 22, 1844 (AGLB I: 263–64) (with some punctuation added); his mention of Bower refers to assertions of Joseph Bower in *Memoir of Joseph Bower* (Whitby, UK: W. Forth, 1838).

47. Garrett to Malony, February 22, 1845 (AGLB II: 74) (Garrett's temperance pledge; punctuation added); Alvaro Field, *Worthies and Workers, Both Ministers and Laymen, of the Rock River Conference* (Cincinnati: Cranston &

Curts, 1896), 314–15 (describing Garrett's second profession of religion and "childlike recitals in the church basement, which Eliza would have heard as well); Garrett to Seaman, February 3, 1844 (AGLB I: 57) ("Although I am not religious"); Garrett to Seaman, January 3, 1845 (AGLB II: 1) ("our Savior"). Field's recollection of Garrett's second conversion can be correlated with Grant Goodrich's information about the basement. The Methodists finished the basement and classrooms of their new brick church in November of 1845: in Stephen R. Beggs, *Pages from the Early History of the West and Northwest* (Cincinnati: Methodist Book Concern, 1868), 184–85.

48. *The Doctrines and Discipline of the Methodist Episcopal Church* (New York: Mason and Lane, 1836), 75–76 (defining a "class"); Field, *Worthies and Workers*, 273 (Eliza belonging to Bradley's class, her character); John H. Wigger, *Taking Heaven by Storm: Methodism and the Rise of Popular Christianity in America* (Oxford: Oxford University Press, 1988), 84 (the Methodist class meeting); Joseph Nightingale, *A Portraiture of Methodism* (London: Longman, Hurst, Rees, and Orme, 1807), 181–84 (the class meeting).

49. *Doctrines and Discipline*, 76–79 (requirements for class admission and moral behavior).

50. Field, *Worthies and Workers*, 315 (Augustus's matching gifts to the church).

51. Augustus Garrett to George Hutchins, April 10, 1842 (AGLB I: 86) (will go "South" if his health permits; letter out of chronological order); Garrett to Seaman, February 3, 1844 (AGLB I: 51) ("more than a person in my health"); Garrett to Seaman, April 10, 1844 (AGLB I: 142) (gaining a pound a day); Garrett to Seaman, February 9, 1845 (AGLB II: 68) (bleeding as a health measure).

52. Norris, *Norris' Chicago Directory for 1848–49*, s.v., Garrett, Augustus (giving an office address for Garrett at 12 Franklin Street, his house). In April of 1846 Augustus was in New York City when he received a letter from John Link, in which Link refers to a lawyer calling *at the house* and dropping off a lease (John Link to Augustus Garrett, April 16, 1846, Garrett Papers, CHM). The city directories for 1847–1848 carry no "card" for a Garrett commission store, but the reference in the Link letter points to continued business in real estate. His death notice in the *Chicago Weekly Democrat* states that he died at the Sherman House (week of December 1, 1848).

53. Eliza Garrett to Melinda Hamline, January 29, 1849 (EGLC) (Eliza's account of Augustus's death, with quotations).

54. *Chicago Weekly Democrat*, December 1, 1848 (internal notice dated December 2) ("We regret to announce the decease of Hon. Augustus Garrett,

at the Sherman House, in this city, on Thursday night last, at half past 10 o'clock, after a short illness, which terminated in congestion of the brain;" details of his career, praise of his generosity).

55. *Chicago Daily Democrat*, December 5, 1848 (the winter storm on the lake).

56. Eliza Garrett to Melinda Hamline, January 29, 1849 (Augustus's funeral wishes); *Chicago Daily Democrat*, December 5, 1848, p. 2 (funeral held at the Methodist church with the Methodist minister and the Episcopal priest both officiating); Grant Goodrich, *The Garrett Biblical Institute of the Methodist Episcopal Church, at Evanston, Illinois (near Chicago), Being a History of the Events Which Led to Its Organization and Endowment, with a Copy of Its Charter and the Will of the Late Mrs. Garrett* (Chicago: Daily Democrat, 1856), 7 (Eliza regarded John Link as a son). An obituary for John Link says that he was born about 1822 and served as Garrett's clerk (*Chicago Daily Tribune*, August 8, 1909, 6); correspondence shows that he was working for Augustus at least as early as April of 1846 and that the office was the Garrett house (see note 52). Link would have been about twenty-six at the time of Augustus's death. Eliza made him a sizable bequest in her will, which shows how fond she was of him.

57. Eliza Garrett to Melinda Hamline, January 29, 1849 (what Augustus said to Eliza, in her paraphrase: that he was "not afraid to die although he knew that he had not lived as he wished he had done"). Goodrich, Augustus's attorney, handled the will. The description of Augustus using the words "returned to the world" and "vicious habits" is that of the devout Methodist Alvaro Field, who knew the Garretts (*Worthies and Workers*, 314–15).

58. *Chicago Daily Democrat*, December 5, 1848, 2. The records of City Cemetery do not mention Augustus but do list "Garrett Biblical Institute" as the owner of two adjacent plots—441 and 442 in the oldest section (transcription of Common Council files by Pamela Bannos: http://hiddentruths. northwestern.edu), which must have been those of Augustus and Eliza, the ownership being passed on to the school as part of Eliza's will. The Garretts' remains were later moved to Rose Hill (later Rosehill) Cemetery.

59. Eliza Garrett to Mr. and Mrs. Hamline, January 29, 1849 (EGLC) (some spelling and punctuation corrected and modernized).

7. THE FOUNDER

1. Eliza Garrett to Mr. and Mrs. Hamline, January 29, 1849 (EGLC) (reference to living with a friend); Amy Clark's death date from her gravestone in Marlboro cemetery (First Presbyterian Church of Marlborough);

Eliza Garrett letter to Melinda Hamline, October 16, 1849 (EGLC) (death of Eliza's mother, the Hamlines' Chicago real estate).

2. *Northwestern Christian Advocate* 3, no. 48 (November 28, 1855): 191 (Eliza living with Walter S. Gurnee family since the death of Augustus). Eliza probably did not move in with the Gurnees immediately, for in her letter to the Hamlines two months after Augustus's death (see note 1), she said she had moved in with "a friend," not "friends" or "a family" as she described the Gurnees in a subsequent letter to Melinda Hamline, quoted below. On the presence of the Gurnees at the Sauganash, see chapter 3, note 37. The Gurnees may have named a son after Augustus (Augustus C. Gurnee, born March 11, 1855). See Robert Fergus, comp., *Fergus' Directory of the City of Chicago, 1839* (Chicago: Fergus, 1876). Chicago city directories for 1839, 1843, and 1844 mention the Gurnee store (partner with Matteson). See Robert Fergus, comp., *Fergus' Directory of the City of Chicago, 1839* (Chicago: Fergus, 1876); Robert Fergus, comp., *Directory of the City of Chicago, Illinois, for 1843* (*Fergus' Historical Series*, no. 28; Chicago: Fergus, 1896). The 1848 directory lists the store and the Gurnee tannery. See J. W. Norris, comp., *Norris' Chicago Directory for 1848–49* (Chicago: Norris & Taylor, 1848).

3. *Norris' Chicago Directory for 1848–49*, s.v. Gurnee, Walter (giving Gurnee's home address as 128 Michigan Ave.); Robert Fergus, comp., *The Chicago City Directory and Business Advertiser 1855–56* (Chicago: Fergus, 1855) ("Gurnee, Walter S. h128 Michigan Avenue"); 1850 federal census, listing the members of the household but misspelling Gurnee as "Green"). The house was a mansion and "stood on the site now occupied by the Chicago Club" ("Early Mayor Dead"). This site is the corner of Michigan and Van Buren, and the building once occupied by the Chicago Club still stands there. But better information is given in a *Chicago Tribune* notice of the sale of the house, which places it on Michigan near Adams and says that it was eighty-eight feet in front. *Chicago Tribune*, September 24, 1865, 4. A lithograph from the era shows four- and five-story dwellings on Michigan (Jevne and Almini, CHM).

4. Eliza Garrett to Melinda Hamline, March 21, 1850 (EGLC) (describing the family; spelling corrected, with some punctuation added).

5. Eliza Garrett to Melinda Hamline, March 21, 1850 (EGLC) ("a greate many correspondents"). The children and their ages are given in the 1860 federal census (name misspelled "Gurner" in Ancestry.com locator), and this record makes it possible to establish the abbreviated names in the 1850 census (see preceding note). Eliza named Delia and Mary Evelyn in her will. Eliza Garrett to Melinda Hamline, March 21, 1850 (EGLC) (describing the family, referring to her many correspondents; spelling corrected, with some punctuation added).

6. Eliza Garrett to Melinda Hamline, October 16, 1849 ("I feel the necessity"); Leonidas Hamline quoted in Freeborn G. Hibbard, *Biography of Rev. Leonidas L. Hamline* (Cincinnati: Walden & Stowe, 1881; New York: Phillips & Hunt, 1881), 261 ("I have not served " and "I have to remember").

7. The testimonies of Apess, Lee, Elaw, and Foote cited in Ted A. Campbell, "Spiritual Biography and Autobiography," in *The Cambridge Companion to American Methodism*, ed. Jason E. Vickers (Cambridge: Cambridge University Press, 2013), 243–60, 250; for Leonidas Hamline, see Walter C. Palmer, *Life and Letters of Leonidas L. Hamline* (New York: Carlton & Porter, 1866), 101 (reporting what Hamline had told him about his experience of entire sanctification), 94 (the date given by Leonidas Hamline for his experience).

8. Eliza Garrett to Melinda Hamline, October 16, 1849, and March 21, 1850 (spelling corrected; punctuation added).

9. On Palmer, Leonidas Hamline, and the debates about entire sanctification, see Timothy Smith, *Revivalism and Social Reform: American Protestantism on the Eve of the Civil War* (New York: Abingdon, 1957), 125–27. I wish to thank Jonathan Dodrill for pointing out to me that well-educated city Methodists looked down on the emotionalism and bodily antics of people at Holiness camp meetings. This made the Palmer method appealing to them.

10. [Melinda Hamline,] "Mrs. Bishop Hamline" [autobiography of her spiritual journey to entire sanctification] in *The Riches of Grace: or The Blessing of Perfected Love as Experienced, Enjoyed, and Recorded by Sixty-Two Living Witnesses* (Williamsburgh, NY: Henry J. Fox, 1854 [expansion of book by same title edited by Dexter S. King in 1847]), 287–90.

11. Eliza Garrett to Melinda Hamline, March 21, 1850 (describing the Clark Street Church revivals and her own disappointment, mentioning "the books you spoke of sending"). The books would have been practical guides to "holiness." For example, to help Frances Willard on the path to entire sanctification, Melinda Hamline recommended that Willard read certain books of the Holiness movement and copies of the Palmers' periodical, *Guide to Holiness*, when Willard was a student in Evanston. See Frances E. Willard, "X. Frances E. Willard (Methodist)," in *Forty Witnesses, Covering the Whole Range of Christian Experience*, ed. S. Olin Garrison (New York: Phillips & Hunt, 1888; Cincinnati: Cranston & Stowe, 1888), 90–99, 94.

12. In 1852 Eliza described her spiritual condition to Melinda without any reference to any lack of the "deeper work of grace": "In relation to myself I still feel to trust in my Savior. I know that he is able to keep me and sustain me under all circumstances. I bless his Holy name for the comforts that Religion affords, me, I feel like pressing my way on toward the land of rest,

Pray for me that I may be able to run the whole length of the Christian race, and with you receive a Crown that fadeth not away Eternal in Heaven." In the same letter she mentions more Clark Street Church revivals but says nothing about still hoping that she would finally experience "the blessing" or lamenting that she had not (Eliza Garrett to Melinda Hamline, February 21, 1852). Goodrich, after describing her as a model Christian from the time of his first acquaintance with her in Clark Street Church (following her conversion in 1839), nevertheless notes a deepening of her faith in her last years and implies that she spoke about it: "From some time before her death an increase in her piety was manifest *to herself* and others" Grant Goodrich, *The Garrett Biblical Institute of the Methodist Episcopal Church, at Evanston, Illinois (near Chicago), Being a History of the Events Which Led to Its Organization and Endowment, with a Copy of Its Charter and the Will of the Late Mrs. Garrett* (Chicago: Daily Democrat, 1856), 6, emphasis added.

13. Goodrich, *Garrett Biblical Institute*, 3. This passage from Goodrich is also quoted, imperfectly, in Davis W. Clark, "Mrs. Garrett: Founder of the Garrett Biblical Institute," *Ladies' Repository* 18 (July 1858): 427–30, 427.

14. Augustus Garrett to J. R. Malony, March 22, 1844 (AGLB I: 109) (some punctuation added).

15. The word *seminary* carried a wider meaning in the early nineteenth century than it does today and could refer to almost any kind of school for young people. Webster's dictionary of 1857 defines it as "a place of education; any school, academy, college, or university which young people are instructed in the several branches of learning." The Illinois Methodist Conference established Rock River Seminary on donated land in a place they decided to call Mt. Morris in dual honor of Bishop Morris and Mount Morris, New York, in accord with the wishes of one of the founders. The school replaced a local grammar school by upgrading and expanding the curriculum. Although it probably included some study of religion, it was not a theological institution. See Alvaro D. Field, *Worthies and Workers, Both Ministers and Laymen, of the Rock River Conference* (Cincinnati: Cranston & Curts, 1896), 256, 304, 306, passim; Harry G. Kable, *Mount Morris: Past and Present* (Mount Morris, MI: Kable Brothers, 1900); Royal B. Way, ed., *The Rock River Valley: Its History, Traditions, Legends, and Charms*, vol. 1 (Chicago: S. J. Clarke, 1926), 316–17, 589–90, 592. The Rock River Seminary taught young men and women (Kable, *Mount Morris*, 86). The professors included Hooper Crews (Field, *Worthies and Workers*, 230). On school subscriptions through stock owned by subscribers, with the income going to the institution, see, for example, Emily Noyes Vanderpoel, comp., *Chronicles of a Pioneer School from 1792–1833, Being*

the History of Miss Sarah Pierce and Her Litchfield School, ed. Elizabeth C. Barney Buel (Cambridge: [Harvard] University Press, 1903), 260 (referring to such an arrangement being made in 1827 for the Litchfield Female Academy).

16. Field, *Worthies and Workers*, 314–15 (describing Garrett's return to Clark Street Church and his efforts at raising money to finish the basement).

17. Only parts of Augustus Garrett's will have been preserved (through quotation). The archives department of the Clerk of the Court (Cook County, Illinois) has no record of any wills for Garrett. It is presumed that they were consumed by the Chicago fire of 1871, when almost all the county records kept in the city were destroyed. No other copy or transcription of the will was preserved from his estate or from other sources, but aspects of the will are described and parts are quoted in court opinions arising from a dispute among the descendants of certain beneficiaries. These opinions are part of the so-called Flaglor cases, which were eventually heard by the United States Supreme Court. The Supreme Court opinion included the following comment and quotation: "The first six sections of this will mention the beneficiaries of his bounty as regards the *income* of his estate until the death of his wife Eliza, Mary Banks and Letitia Flaglor. . . . The seventh provision, which provides for the final disposition of his property after their decease . . . reads as follows: 'Upon the death of my wife Eliza and of Mary Banks and Letitia Flaglor, I direct that the whole of my estate shall then be equally divided between Charles D. Flaglor, son of said Letitia, and if he or his legitimate children survive said Letitia, (in case he be dead, his legitimate children shall take as their father would if alive,) and the said James Crow, and the said Thomas G. Crow, each taking one-third of the whole.'" Guy v. Parpart, 106 U.S. 679 (1883), reprinted in *The Supreme Court Reporter*, vol. 1, ed. Robert Desty (St. Paul, MN: West Publishing, 1883), 463. The opinion further states that "On the death of Mr. Garrett his will was submitted to probate on the twenty-eighth day of February 1849, and his widow, Eliza Garrett, having renounced the benefits of its provisions, asserted her rights of dower, whereby she became entitled to one-half the estate" (463–64). The opinion goes on briefly to describe a partition agreement in 1851, which is also explained in an article from the *Monthly Western Jurist*, which summarizes the will as follows: "In December, 1848, one Augustus Garrett departed this life, leaving a will, by which he directed the income from his real estate, after the payment of his debts and legacies, to be divided between his wife, Eliza, his two sisters, Mary Banks and Letitia Flaglor, and his two nephews, James and Thomas G. Crowe, in certain specified proportions, and further directing, that on the death of his said wife and sisters, the real estate should be divided between

Charles D. Flaglor, son of Letitia, and said James and Thomas Crow, or if they should be dead, between their children *per stirpem*. The widow renounced the will and thereby became entitled to one half of the realty in fee. The parties interested, agreed to procure a partition without waiting for the death of the widow and sisters; and for that purpose Eliza Garrett, the widow, and the said James and Thomas Crow, filed a bill at the March term, 1851, of the Cook county circuit court." See "The Great Flaglor Suits," *Monthly Western Jurist* [bound under title *Weekly Jurist*] 1, no. 10 (February 1875): 433–34. This bill was later challenged by other descendants, giving rise to the Flaglor suits, but the challenge did not touch Eliza's portion.

18. Guy v. Parpart ("renounced the benefits" and "asserted her rights of dower"). On the legal provision for dower in Illinois at the time of Augustus's death, see ch. 34, sect. 15 of *Revised Statutes of the State of Illinois, Adopted by the General Assembly of Said State at Its Regular Session, Held in the Years A.D., 1844–'45* (Springfield, IL: William Walters, 1845), 220; also the same section in Norman H. Purple, comp., *A Compilation of the Statutes of the State of Illinois, of a General Nature, in Force January 1, 1856*, part 1(Chicago: Keen & Lee, 1856), 497–98. Eliza's inheritance from Augustus is correctly stated in an early capsule biography of her, although the particular legal provision that made it possible is not mentioned. Abel Stevens, *The Women of Methodism: Its Three Foundresses, Susanna Wesley, the Countess of Huntingdon, and Barbara Heck* (New York: Carlton & Porter, 1866), 284 ("she became possessed of *one half* his property absolutely and in fee"; emphasis added).

19. Robert D. Sheppard and Harvey B. Hurd, eds., *History of Northwestern University and Evanston* (Chicago: Munsell, 1906), 54–57 (organization of the school, charter, etc.); Eliza Garrett to Melinda Hamline, February 21, 1852 ("The committee of M. E. University are making an effort"; punctuation added and spelling corrected); Eliza Garrett to Melinda Hamline, February 3, 1853 (on the Hamlines' property in Chicago, her hope that the Hamlines will not sell it but will move to Chicago as planned); cf. Augustus Garrett to Melinda Hamline, November 10, 1848 (regarding a parcel of land in Chicago, which may be the one that the Hamlines later purchased); Eliza Garrett to Melinda Hamline, October 16, 1849 (regarding taxes she has paid on behalf of the Hamlines on their Chicago property). The Northwestern University Board minutes for June 14, 1851, speak of a plan to raise $20,000 to build a Preparatory Department, presumably as part of the university (NU archives). It is doubtful that the "primary department," as Eliza calls it, was also to be part of the university. The board minutes nowhere refer to it. Both the primary and preparatory schools were to be located in Chicago. In August of 1852 the

university bid $4,800 on a Chicago lot owned by the Universalist Church but shortly thereafter decided on a somewhat larger lot owned by P. F. W. Peck at LaSalle and Jackson, and the site was purchased in the name of John Evans for $8,000 (Sheppard and Hurd, *History of Northwestern University and Evanston*, 57). According to the board minutes for September 22, 1852, the board authorized buildings for the Preparatory Department "on the site of P. F. W. Peck" and also purchased the title from Evans. Further light is shed by an article on Lunt in the *Evanston Review*, January 18, 1951. According to Lunt, the organizers purchased this lot at LaSalle and Jackson but never built on it.

20. *Chicago Daily Journal*, March 4, 1851.

21. Goodrich, *Garrett Biblical Institute*, 4 ("for several years she would only accept four hundred dollars a year for her support, and near half of that she devoted to pious purposes"). Goodrich wrote this from the perspective of her death in later 1855, which implies that she had made this reduction in her income around 1851.

22. Excerpt of letter from Leonidas Hamline to Eliza Garrett, October 3, 1851, in Walter C. Palmer, *Life and Letters of Leonidas L. Hamline* (New York: Carlton & Porter, 1866), 392; Eliza's will (eighth provision, referring to "female college") reproduced in Goodrich, *Garrett Biblical Institute*, 12–16; Dwight F. Clark, "A Forgotten Evanston Institution: The Northwestern Female College," *Journal of the Illinois State Historical Society* 35, no. 2 (1942): 115–32, 125 (Melinda Hamline's work to bring about university education for women). Leonidas made quite a bit of money through western land speculation and eventually donated large tracts—worth $25,000—to help found a Methodist university in Minnesota, which the trustees named after him. *History of the Hamline University of Minnesota When Located at Redwing from 1854 to 1869* (n.p.: Alumni Association of the College of Liberal Arts of Hamline University, 1907), 9–10. On Link's sympathy toward women's higher education, see *Second Biennial Report of the Superintendent of Public Instruction of the State of Illinois for the Years 1857–58* (Springfield, IL: Bailhache & Baker, 1859), 283 (describing the N.W. Female College and mentioning a fire and the rebuilding: "Arduous toil, encouraged by liberal loans by Jas. Suppiger, esq. of Madison county, and John Link, esq. of Chicago, enabled the Messrs. Jones to replace the first building with the present structure").

23. Grant Goodrich, *Manual of Information Respecting the Garrett Biblical Institute* (Evanston, IL: Trustees, 1857), 7 (Goodrich mentioning his 1852 and 1853 conversations with Eliza; the use of the first person implies Goodrich as author of this part of the *Manual*, and Goodrich is referred to internally as author of the introductory sections about the school, at least pages 7–16,

which deal with its history); Goodrich, *Garrett Biblical Institute*, 3 (describing his 1853 conversation with Eliza); G. E. Strobridge, *Biography of the Rev. Daniel Parish Kidder* (New York: Hunt and Eaton, 1894), 218–19 (what he told Goodrich when they met in September 1853, mentioning his meeting with Eliza in Goodrich's office a few days later and recalling that he had communicated the same opinion by letter to Goodrich a year prior).

24. Goodrich, *Garrett Biblical Institute*, 3–4; Strobridge, *Biography of the Rev. Daniel Parish Kidder*, 218–19 (stating that Goodrich and Kidder met in September 1853 and that a few days later both men met with Eliza); Kidder's Sermon Record (Styberg Library) shows that he was in Chicago from September 17 to 25 or a bit longer. Frances E. Willard, *A Classic Town: The Story of Evanston by an "Old Timer"* (Chicago: Women's Temperance Publishing Association, 1891), 29 (Eliza was influenced by Stephen Vail's book advocating for education of ministers); Stephen M. Vail, *Ministerial Education in the Methodist Episcopal Church* (Boston: George C. Hand, 1853 [preface dated March]).

25. Strobridge, *Biography of the Rev. Daniel Parrish Kidder*, 219 (Kidder's account of his meeting with Eliza in Goodrich's office). That she was thinking of a female college and the men were trying to talk her out of it is clear from a letter Kidder wrote to Goodrich (October 23, 1853), where he mentioned the female college and stated his opinion that ministerial training was more urgent (quoted below).

26. Goodrich, *Manual of Information*, 8 ("tenor" of the will decided by early October); Kidder to Goodrich, October 23, 1853, quoted in Ila Alexander Fisher, "Eliza Garrett: To Follow a Vision," in *Spirituality & Social Responsibility: Vocational Vision of Women in the United Methodist Tradition*, ed. Rosemary Skinner Keller (Nashville: Abingdon, 1993), 41–60, 52. The whereabouts of this letter is no longer known. The biography of Kidder, written by his son-in-law G. E Strobridge, says nothing about Eliza's wish to endow a female college.

27. Goodrich, *Manual of Information*, 12–13.

28. The excerpt of the will is from the transcription in Goodrich, *Garrett Biblical Institute*, 14–15.

29. Charles M. Stuart, "Garrett Marching On," *Christian Student* 23, no. 4 (November, 1922): 161–64, 161; Willard, *Classic Town*, 404 (Eliza's will had already been made when Dempster arrived in Chicago); Charles J. Little, "Garrett Biblical Institute," in Sheppard and Hurd, *History of Northwestern University and Evanston*, 163–67, 163 (also noting that Dempster arrived after the will was made).

30. Charles J. Little, "Garrett Biblical Institute," 163; Goodrich, "Peter Ruble Borein," in *Annals of the American Pulpit*, vol. 7: *The Methodist*, ed. William B. Sprague (New York: Robert Carter and Brothers, 1859), 784–86 (describing Borein's education).

31. Willard, *Classic Town*, 57 ("no provision had been made for women in their far-reaching plans"); On July 11, 1866, a petition was presented to the Northwestern University Board of Trustees regarding the location of a "North Western Female College" (Willard, *Classic Town*, 64–65; minutes of the Board of Trustees of Northwestern University, July 11, 1866). This must have been the new female college that interested citizens were urging the board to incorporate into the university or at least host. The board minutes do not name the petitioners, but presumably they were the same women who two years later established the Evanston College for Ladies, which a year after that was incorporated into Northwestern University after at least one more petition (Willard, *Classic Town*, 63; minutes of the Board of Trustees of Northwestern University, June 22, 23, 1869). The board's response to the earlier petition of 1866 had been to refer it to "a special committee appointed to consider the subject of electing a president," the implication being that no move on a women's college would be made without the support of the next president. Charles H. Fowler was elected that same day (July 11 board minutes) but resigned before taking up the duties of the office. No further action was taken on women's university education until three years later with the arrival of Erastus Haven, who made it a condition of his acceptance of the presidency.

32. Fisher, "Eliza Garrett," 50 (noting that even in 1855, some references to the school in the *Northwestern Christian Advocate* call the school "Methodist Episcopal Biblical Institute" or "Northwestern Biblical Institution"); *Northwestern Christian Advocate*, January 3, 1855 (referring to the school as "North-Western Methodist Biblical Institute"); Strobridge, *Biography of the Rev. Daniel Parrish Kidder*, 220 (quoting letter from Goodrich to Kidder suggesting the name "The Garrett Theological Institute of the Methodist Episcopal Church"); Edward M. Ruttenber, "The King's Highway: Its Early Road Districts and the Residents or Owners of Lands Thereon," *Historical Papers* [of the Historical Society of Newburgh Bay and the Highlands] 10 (1903): 21–33, 28; account of Eliza's funeral, *Northwestern Christian Advocate* 3, no. 48 (November 28, 1855): 191 (finally getting the name right and its intention: the school "has been named in compliment to her").

33. Transcription of the will of Eliza Garrett in Goodrich, *Garrett Biblical Institute*, 12. Census records permit the ages of the children to be established.

34. Christopher A. Schnell, "Wives, Widows, and Will Makers: Women and the Law of Property," in *In Tender Consideration: Women, Family, and the Law in Abraham Lincoln's Illinois*, ed. Daniel W. Stowell (Urbana: University of Illinois, 2002), 129–60, 129.

35. Goodrich, *Garrett Biblical Institute*, 5; Willard, *Classic Town*, 31–32 (mentioning that Dempster spoke and stating explicitly that the meeting was held in "the old Clark Street church"); account of the Clark Street Church meeting of the "Friends of Biblical Learning," together with other particulars of the organization of the school, in C. H. Fowler, "The Northwestern University," *Lakeside Monthly* 9 (June 1, 1873): 431–43, 441; contract between the directors and John Dempster, dated December 29, 1853 (original held by the Styberg Library of Garrett-Evangelical Theological Seminary); "First Circular of the Trustees and Faculty of North Western University" (1856), copy of transcription in Northwestern University Archives (mentions purchase of land for the university made by Lunt in August of 1853).

36. Goodrich, *Manual of Information*, 12–13 (writing in 1857, mentioning the debts but implying that as soon as the estate was producing income again, perhaps five years hence, the income would be devoted to the Garrett Biblical Institute; he also mentions damage by fires, but it is not clear whether these fires predated or postdated the signing of the will).

37. Goodrich, *Garrett Biblical Institute*, 5 (the first building, first students); Goodrich, *Manual of Information*, 13 (the initial four students, etc.), 38 (student room furnishings, tuition and rent free, cost for board and books); "North-Western Methodist Biblical Institute," *Western Christian Advocate* 22 (January 3, 1855): 3 (free tuition and rent; student rooms still need furnishing).

38. Thomas M. Eddy, "Funeral Sermon, Preached on the Occasion of the Death of John Dempster," separately paginated appendix to John Dempster, *Lectures and Address*, ed. Davis W. Clark (Cincinnati: Hitchcock, 1864), 15 (dedication held on January 1, 1855; Eliza present); Willard, *Classic Town*, 32 ("The Chicago friends came over by sleigh"), 25–26 (recollection of Orrington Lunt that one had to go mostly along the shore of Lake Michigan to get from Chicago to Evanston; he mentions the impressive oaks at the chosen site); recollection of James Waugh in *Semi-centennial Celebration, Garrett Biblical Institute, May Fifth to Ninth, 1906* (Evanston, IL: Garrett Biblical Institute, 1906) (Waugh entered the school in 1857 and remembered the thick woods and the plain building with one coat of white paint); Sheppard and Hurd, *History of Northwestern University and Evanston*, 342 (Dempster Hall had a chapel).

John Dempster, "The Teacher's Parting Word: An Address to the First Graduating Class of Garrett Biblical Institute" (1858), in Dempster, *Lectures and Address*, 200 (his memory of Eliza's face, "mantled with blushes at our opening, when designated by the thrilling utterances of our lamented Watson").

39. Arthur H. Wilde, *Northwestern University, A History: 1855–1905*, vol. I (New York: University Publishing Society, 1905), 169–70 (description of the celebration of the institute's first term and the university's first building); *Chicago Daily Democrat*, June 14, 1855 (description of anniversary, quoted by Wilde); cf. *Northwestern Christian Advocate*, June 30, 1855; Goodrich, *Manual of Information*, 13 (by first term's end, sixteen students were enrolled).

40. Garrett Faculty Minutes, October 27, 1873 (letter from the female student inquiring about admission; this letter was the only business of the day, implying that the faculty gathered specifically to discuss her request). The catalog of 1874 lists two female students, one in the preparatory program and one in the diploma, or bachelor of divinity, program. In 1876 Boston University School of Theology, also a Methodist school, became the first theological school in the United States to grant a theological degree (a bachelor of sacred theology, or BST) to a woman (Anna Snowden, a.k.a. Ana Oliver). Three years later, Garrett Biblical Institute awarded Mary Adelia Philips a diploma in theology, the degree preliminary to a BD. Students who graduated with the diploma (having done all the same coursework as BD students) could receive the BD upon demonstration of "due intellectual work and proficiency in the ministry for a sufficient period after graduation" (1876 catalog under Admission of Students). Unfortunately, Mary died within a year of her graduation. Despite the seminary's willingness to educate women, church culture ensured that female students would remain a rarity until well into the twentieth century.

Garrett Biblical Institute became Garrett Theological Seminary in 1959, when the trustees deemed it time to adopt a more modern, twentieth-century name for the school. The denominational union of the Methodist Episcopal Church and the Evangelical United Brethren Church, which created the United Methodist Church in 1968, also led, in 1974, to the merger of Garrett with Evangelical Theological Seminary in Naperville, the latter school moving to the Garrett campus. This resulted in the current hyphenated name, Garrett-Evangelical Theological Seminary. Along the way, Garrett also incorporated the Chicago Training School, founded in 1885. CTS educated young women for local ministries and overseas missionary work, and it also established a variety of service organizations to aid the needy of Chicago. The school became part of Garrett in 1934. The estimate of the total number of graduates as of September 2019 (more than 9,500) is based on statistics held by the seminary and a report for the years from the founding through 1906 in *Semi-centennial Celebration*, 137, 215.

41. Goodrich to Daniel Kidder, November 26, 1855, quoted by Fisher, "Eliza Garrett" (the letter can no longer be located), 51 ("bilious colic which resulted in congestion of the bowels"); *Northwestern Christian Advocate*, November 28, 1855 ("obstruction of the bowels"). "Bilious colic" was a vague diagnosis associated in the nineteenth century with vomiting bile and severe constipation. These symptoms may have resulted from any number of causes—from acute disease of the gall bladder to lead poisoning. It was usually a chronic condition. Eliza had almost certainly experienced prior attacks.

42. Goodrich to Daniel Kidder, November 26, 1855 (reporting what he learned from John Link).

43. Goodrich to Daniel Kidder, November 26, 1855. Goodrich suggests that she lifted her hands, quoted the psalm, and immediately expired. That sounds a bit too scripted. No doubt she did quote the psalm and soon after drifted off into a coma until death ensued shortly afterward. In an address the following year, evidently when the governance of the school was reorganized after being granted its charter and the organizing committee turned the school over to its trustees, Goodrich referred to November 23 as the date of her death (*Manual of Information*, 6). In that case, she died not on Thursday but on Friday. But her grave monument gives the date as the 22nd.

POSTSCRIPT

1. Minutes of the Board of Trustees of Garrett Biblical Institute, October 28, 1871, book one, 199 (Lunt's note about saving institute records); *Edwards' Chicago Directory, Fire Edition, Containing the Names of all Persons in Business in the City Whose Location Could Be Ascertained up to Dec. 12, 1871, and a Business Directory* (Chicago: Richard Edwards, n.d.), 106 (entry for Orrington Lunt, showing his pre-fire and post-fire business addresses).

2. Minutes of the Board of Trustees of Garrett Biblical Institute, October 28, 1871, book one, 199 (what Lunt saved of institute records; the safe, which the fire eventually destroyed).

3. Estelle F. Ward, *The Story of Northwestern University* (New York: Dodd, Mead, 1924), 120 (mentioning that Lunt retrieved both the university and the institute records from his office vault and that he lost his office and his Michigan Avenue home to the fire); Minutes of the Board of Trustees of Garrett Biblical Institute, October 28, 1871, book one, 199 (the safe that the fire destroyed, removal of materials to his Michigan Avenue home, then to another place of safety); 204 (treasurer's report noting destruction of the buildings owned by the institute), 195 (treasurer's statement, June 29, 1871, that "during the year the Garrett Building has been erected at the cost of

$65,000"); Frank A. Randall and John D. Randall, *History of the Development of Building Construction in Chicago*, 2nd ed. (Urbana: University of Illinois Press, 1999), 245 (the "Garrett Building" was constructed in 1871 at Lake and Market: 140 feet on Lake and 240 on Market, four stories).

4. Craig Buettinger, "The Concept of Jacksonian Aristocracy: Chicago as a Test Case, 1833–1857" (PhD diss., Northwestern University, 1982), 50 (based on his examination of the Antefire Tract Book held by the Chicago Title and Trust Company), 95n1 (noting that many of the property owners listed in the tax rolls had properties outside the city limits as well); Minutes of the Board of Trustees of Garrett Biblical Institute, August 26, 1858, book one, 60 (showing real estate owned by the institute, including the property on Michigan Avenue, which is also represented in a frontispiece of the book), 40 (June 23, 1857, reporting the board's action of selling its interest in certain lands in Wisconsin purchased by Garrett and Nathaniel Brown, as well as lands in the name of Eliza Garrett in Will and LaSalle Counties).

5. Garrett's real estate holdings in the Chicago business district by various years in Buettinger, "Concept of Jacksonian Aristocracy," 90 (listing the properties, on the tax rolls, belonging to James Crow and Eliza Garrett in the early 1850s and the type of buildings on those tracts); *Chicago Daily Journal*, March 4, 1851, according to Otis index s.v. "Fire, destruction of Sauganash and other buildings."

6. Buettinger, "Concept of Jacksonian Aristocracy," 19 (revealing that his later reference to the 1849–1850 tax rolls means the 1849 rolls for the south side, which is where Garrett's properties were located), 72 (value of Garrett's estate according to the 1849–1850 tax rolls, cited from the Antefire Tract Book now held by CHM), 21 (assessments 40–50 percent of actual value). Calculation in today's dollars based on a formula of the Federal Reserve using a consumer price index (CPI): 1849 dollars × (2018 CPI ÷ 1849 CPI). See https://www.minneapolisfed.org/community/teaching-aids/cpi-calculator-information.

7. *Ladies' Repository* 16 (February 1856): 12 ($100,000); Grant Goodrich, "Address," in *The Garrett Biblical Institute of the Methodist Episcopal Church, at Evanston, Illinois (near Chicago), Being a History of the Events Which Led to Its Organization and Endowment, with a Copy of Its Charter and the Will of the Late Mrs. Garrett* (Chicago: Daily Democrat, 1856; published separately and later bound with *Manual of Information Respecting the Garrett Biblical Institute* [Trustees, Evanston, Illinois, 1857]), 4 (assigning a value of $300,000); *Chicago Daily Tribune*, April 25, 1856 ($300,000, probably reflecting information supplied by Goodrich); *Mid-centennial Celebration, Garrett Biblical*

Institute, May Fifth to Ninth, Nineteen Hundred Six (Evanston, IL: Garrett Biblical Institute, 1906), 1 ($300,000 at time of founding).

8. Minutes of the Board of Trustees of Garrett Biblical Institute, August 26 and December 7, 1858, book one, 59 and 64 (real estate valuation and income).

9. *Chicago Tribune*, November 14, 1869, 3 (history of the wigwam); Humphrey H. Hood, "The Chicago Convention," in *Reminiscences of Chicago during the Civil War* (Chicago: R. R. Donnelley, 1914), 41–50, 42–44; Bessie Louise Pierce, *A History of Chicago*, vol. 2: *From Town to City, 1848–1871* (Chicago: University of Chicago Press, 1940), 277n100 (referring to period sources using the word *wigwam* for a proposed Democratic convention building).

10. Alvaro D. Field, *Worthies and Workers, Both Ministers and Laymen, of the Rock River Conference* (Cincinnati: Cranston & Curts, 1896), 202 (in 1860 all but three ministers of the Rock River Conference were antislavery supporters of the Republican platform, etc.); Arthur H. Wilde, *Northwestern University, a History: 1855–1905*, vol. 1 (New York: University Publishing Society, 1905), 136 (Goodrich, a Lincoln supporter).

11. T. Harry Williams, "The Committee on the Conduct of the War: An Experiment in Civil Control," in *Civil-Military Relations*, ed. Peter Karsten (New York: Garland Publishing, 1998), 173–90, 173 (with note 4 documenting abolitionists' frustrations with Lincoln, citing, among others, Goodrich to Lyman Trumbull, December 6, 1861); *Chicago Tribune*, September 9, 1862 (text of the Chicago "Memorial on Emancipation"); *Chicago Tribune*, September 23, 1862 (Dempster and Patton's account of their visit with Lincoln); also *New York Times*, September 26, 1862, and other papers, reprinted in *The Collected Works of Abraham Lincoln*, vol. 5, ed. Roy Basler (New Brunswick, NJ: Rutgers University Press, 1953), 421–25.

12. Scott W. Dill, *John Evans, 1814–1897: An Appreciation* (Evanston IL: Lester J. Morris, 1939), 48–49 (Evans, an antislavery Republican organizer); Ned Blackhawk et al., *Report of the Northwestern University John Evans Study Committee: Northwestern University, May 2014* (Evanston, IL: Northwestern University, 2014), 18, 98–99n22 (Evans, an antislavery Whig who was a delegate to the Illinois Republican Convention of 1860); Field, *Worthies and Workers*, 320 (Lunt used to sing at abolition meetings); Alfred T. Andreas, *History of Chicago. From the Earliest Period to the Present Time*, vol. 1: *Ending with the Year 1857* (Chicago: A. T. Andreas, 1884), 333 (Lunt helped the African American Methodists in getting and keeping a chapel); *Evanston Review*, January 18, 1851 (Lunt and the African American Methodist chapel). The antislavery views of the Garrett and Northwestern founders do not mean that they all believed in racial equality, a rare belief among whites at the time.

13. Minutes of the Board of Trustees of Garrett Biblical Institute, December 2, 1861, book one, 88 (contract to purchase wigwam), 94 (lease of wigwam to Broughton & Young), 181, 183 (November 30, 1869, and January 8, 1870: plans to construct new buildings on fire-ravaged wigwam site), 185 (March 23, 1870, report on construction on wigwam lot, bids received), 200, 204 (December 22, 1871, and January 25, 1872, concerning destruction of Garrett buildings); *Chicago Tribune*, November 14, 1869, 3 (history of the wigwam, purchase by Garrett for commercial use, the fire).

14. Lots 441 and 442 in section OS. See Pamela Bannos's transcription of City Cemetery lot owners at http://hiddentruths.northwestern.edu/lots. html; section OS can be seen under "Mapping the Cemeteries" at http:// hiddentruths.northwestern.edu/surveys.html; Eliza's will.

15. On the earliest Chicago cemeteries, see Andreas, *History of Chicago*, vol. 1, 141; Alfred T. Andreas, *History of Chicago from the Earliest Period to the Present Time*, vol. 2: *From 1857 until the Fire of 1871* (Chicago: A. T. Andreas, 1885), 448; James R. Grossman et al., *The Encyclopedia of Chicago* (Chicago: University of Chicago Press, 2004), 123; Pamela Bannos, http://hiddentruths. northwestern.edu. On Native American burial grounds in the region, including land that is not part of the City of Chicago, see Melvin Holli and Peter D'Alroy Jones, eds., *Ethnic Chicago: A Multicultural Portrait*, 4th ed. (Grand Rapids, MI: Wm. B. Eerdmans, 1995), 620; CCCPF Doc. 1691, May 13, 1843 (a law banning any further burial in the "old cemetery").

16. *Chicago Democrat*, February 28, 1844 (fencing); *Chicago Democrat*, March 13, 1844 ("depredations").

17. The account and a copy of the Pinkerton report can be found at http:// hiddentruths.northwestern.edu; this site also presents the retrospective from *Chicago Tribune*, December 29, 1878.

18. Images of original maps of the old City Cemetery can be found at http://hiddentruths.northwestern.edu. Rauch wrote a paper on the subject in 1858. It is not clear whether this paper has been preserved, but Rauch expanded on it several years later in a small book. See [Board of Health of the City of Chicago,] *Report of the Board of Health of the City of Chicago for 1867, 1868, and 1869 and a Sanitary History of Chicago from 1833 to 1870* (Chicago: Lakeside, 1871), 95 (referring to the 1858 paper); John H. Rauch, *Intramural Interments in Populous Cities and Their Influence on Health and Epidemics* (Chicago: Tribune Company, 1866), 62–65 (health risks posed by cemetery; grave depth; order passed by Common Council ending interments in City Cemetery "as a burial place"; agreement between the city and with Rosehill Cemetery, order not carried out until 1865). In May of 1860, Rosehill

Cemetery announced that it was opening to the public (advertisement in *Chicago Press and Tribune*, May 8, 1860, 4). On the whole subject, see also Mark Rosenthal and Carol Tauber, *The Ark in the Park: The Story of Lincoln Park Zoo* (Urbana: University of Illinois Press, 2003), 15–18.

19. Rauch, *Intramural Interments in Populous Cities*, 22–23 (on decomposing bodies producing injurious gases, but also recognizing that contaminated water was injurious to health), 48 (on grave depth in City Cemetery), 49ff. (on contamination of city drinking water), 52 (bodies from Camp Douglas interred at City Cemetery), 64 (adjudication of lawsuit over Milliman tract); George Levy, *To Die in Chicago: Confederate Prisoners at Camp Douglas, 1862–1865*, 2nd ed. (Gretna, LA: Pelican Publishing, 1999), 349–58 (reburials of Confederate soldiers from Camp Douglas).

20. Minutes of the Board of Trustees of Garrett Biblical Institute, December 7, 1858, book one, 66 (death of student); February 14, 1860, book one, 82 (reduced rate on Rosehill Cemetery lots, discussion of purchasing lots in case of student deaths); October 27, 1864, book one, 124 (decision to purchase a lot for Dr. Dempster and to inquire of the Garretts' friends and family about moving their remains to Rosehill).

21. Minutes of the Board of Trustees of Garrett Biblical Institute, October 5, 1869 [marginal date incorrect], book one, 178 ("The secretary reported that the remains of Mr. and Mrs. Garrett would be removed tomorrow the 6th of Oct., 1869, from the Old Cemetery to Rose Hill;" the following day, Secretary Lunt added his notice of the transfer of the remains); a letter from Iulian Moldovan (Rosehill Cemetery) to Janine Protzman, November, 2014 (section and lot number; aside from the location, the cemetery knew only that these graves were "among the earliest burials at Rosehill").

22. The inscriptions on the monument are now very faded, but enough is legible that, together with information from other sources, the details and arrangement of the lettering can be reconstructed. Among the additional sources is a transcription made in 1888 of the Garrett family monument in Rufus Emery et al., *Newburgh: A Record of the Inscriptions in the Old Town Burying Ground of Newburgh, N.Y.* (Newburgh, NY: Historical Society of Newburgh Bay and the Highlands, 1898), 132.

23. As noted in chapter 1, according to a notice of Augustus Garrett's death in the *Chicago Weekly Democrat*, December 1, 1848, he was in his forty-seventh year when he died. According to the parlance of the time, this meant that he had passed his forty-sixth birthday. In that case, he was born in 1802. The last digit of the year of birth on the Rosehill Cemetery marker is not legible, but what is visible is consistent with a 2.

24. The month is very worn but looks like "APRIL." A transcription made of the Newburgh monument states that Charles was ten months old when he died on February 9, 1833. That would suggest a May birthday. But if ten months means "in his tenth month" (i.e., having passed the nine-month mark), then a birthday sometime between April 1 and 9 is conceivable.

25. This numeral is not legible, but spacing makes it clear that it is a single digit, probably a 7 or a 1.

26. The stone is currently so faded that some of the information is no longer decipherable, but most of it is known from other sources. The birthday is given as March 5 in D. W. Clark, "Mrs. Eliza Garrett," *Ladies' Repository* 18 (July 1858), 201–9, 201.

BIBLIOGRAPHY

JUDICIAL OPINIONS

Bronson v. Kinzie, 42 U.S. 1 (1 Howard 311).

Canal Trustees v. City of Chicago, 12 Ill. 403.

Guy v. Parpart, 106 U.S. 679 (1883).

Johnson v. McIntosh, 21 U.S. 543 (1823).

Shirk v. City of Chicago, 195 Ill. 298 (also 63 NE Reporter 193).

CITY DIRECTORIES

Doggett, John, comp. *Doggett's New-York City Directory for 1845 & 1846.* New York: John Doggett, 1845.

Edwards' Chicago Directory, Fire Edition, Containing the Names of All Persons in Business in the City Whose Location Could Be Ascertained up to Dec. 12, 1871, and a Business Directory. Chicago: Richard Edwards, n.d.

Fergus, Robert, comp. *The Chicago City Directory and Business Advertiser, 1855–56.* Chicago: Fergus, 1855.

——— [Fergus/Norris], comp. *Directory of the City of Chicago, Illinois, for 1843. Fergus' Historical Series,* no. 28. Chicago: Fergus, 1896. This directory incorporates and supplements information from J. W. Norris, *General Directory and Business Advertiser of the City of Chicago for the Year 1844.* Chicago: Ellis and Fergus, 1844.

———, comp. *Fergus' Directory of the City of Chicago, 1839.* Chicago: Fergus, 1876.

Norris, J. W., comp. *General Directory and Business Advertiser of the City of Chicago for the Year 1844.* Chicago: Ellis and Fergus, 1844.

———, comp. *Norris' Business Directory and Statistics of the City of Chicago for 1846.* Chicago: Eastman & Davidson, 1846.

———, comp. *Norris' Chicago Directory for 1848–49.* Chicago: Norris & Taylor, 1848.

Robinson, A. F., and D. W. Fairbank, comps. *The Cincinnati Directory for the Year 1831.* Cincinnati: Robinson & Fairbank, 1831.

MUNICIPAL ARCHIVES

Bannos, Pamela. "Transcription of Common Council Files." *Hidden Truths: The Chicago City Cemetery & Lincoln Park*. 2019. http://hiddentruths .northwestern.edu.

Chicago Common Council Files. Illinois Regional Archives Depository at Ronald Williams Library of Northeastern Illinois University.

The New York Genealogical and Biographical Record. Vol. 53. 1922.

New York State Archives (Albany, New York), *Tax Assessment Rolls of Real and Personal Estates*, series B0950, reel 15, box 36, folder 18 (assessment of Benoni Clark's property).

Petition of Augustus Garrett, Guardian of James Crow, filed 18 August 1830, Baltimore City Register of Wills (Petitions), MSA SC 4239–14–141 M11025. Schweninger Collection, Maryland State Archives.

CHURCH ARCHIVES

Church Record Book of the Sixth Presbyterian Church, 1831–1887. Cincinnati Historical Society.

Minutes of the Sixth Presbyterian Church. Cincinnati Historical Society.

Receiving Book of First Methodist Episcopal Church, Chicago.

ARCHIVES OF LIBRARIES, MUSEUMS, AND OTHER INSTITUTIONS

"Augustus Garrett, Mayor 1843–1844, 1845–1846." Unpublished typescript. Chicago History Museum.

Beers, F. W. Map of Newburgh. 1875. Newburgh Free Library.

Eddy, Otis S. "Index of *Chicago American* for 1836–1837" and "Index of *Daily Chicago American* from Oct. 9th 1840 to April 9th 1841." Chicago History Museum.

"First Circular of the Trustees and Faculty of North Western University." 1856. Copy of transcription. Northwestern University Archives.

Illinois Public Domain Land Tract Sales Database. Illinois State Archives Depository.

Kidder, Daniel. Sermon Record. Styberg Library of Garrett-Evangelical Theological Seminary.

Kinzie, Juliette Augusta Magill. [*The Dorcas Society*]. Unpublished, undated, handwritten manuscript, lacking title and first chapter. Chicago History Museum.

Ledger of the Sauganash Hotel. Chicago History Museum.

Manual for Communicants of the First Presbyterian Church in Chicago, Compiled Jan. 1, 1840. Chicago: Edward Rudd, 1840. Copies held by the Richard J. Daley Library of the University of Illinois at Chicago and by the Newberry Library.

Minutes (1850s–1870s). Board of Trustees of Northwestern University. Northwestern University Archives.

Minutes of the Board of Trustees of Garrett Biblical Institute. Garrett-Evangelical Theological Seminary.

Minutes of the Faculty of Garrett Biblical Institute. Garrett-Evangelical Theological Seminary.

Minutes of the Session, First Presbyterian Church of Chicago. Newberry Library.

Porter, Jeremiah. Unpublished journals. Chicago History Museum.

Riegler, Gordon A. "Jeremiah Porter, a History of the First Presbyterian Church Chicago, and a Narrative of the Frontier." Typescript, 1932. Newberry Library.

Widmer, Rachel. Diary of Rachel Widmer. Transcription. Collection 19428. New York State Library, Albany.

HISTORICAL NEWSPAPERS

American Farmer
American Gardner's Magazine
Chicago American
Chicago Daily Democrat
Chicago Daily Journal
Chicago Daily Tribune
Chicago Weekly Democrat
Cincinnati Chronicle and Literary Gazette
Cincinnati Daily Gazette
Liberty Hall & Cincinnati Gazette
Newburgh Gazette
Newburgh Telegraph
New York Farmer
Niles' Weekly Register
Northwestern Christian Advocate

MONUMENTS

Clark family graves in Marlboro cemetery.
Garrett family monument in Old Town Cemetery, Newburgh.
Garrett family monument in Rosehill Cemetery, Chicago.

BOOKS AND ARTICLES

Aaron, Daniel. *Cincinnati, Queen City of the West, 1819–1838.* Columbus: Ohio State University Press, 1992.

Abraham, William J., and James E. Kirby, eds., *The Oxford Handbook of Methodist Studies.* Oxford: Oxford University Press, 2009.

Aiken, Gayle. "The Medical History of New Orleans." In *Standard History of New Orleans, Louisiana,* edited by Henry Rightor, 203–25. Chicago: Lewis, 1900.

[American Unitarian Association.] *First Annual Report of the Executive Committee of the American Unitarian Association.* Boston: Isaac R. Butts, 1826.

Andreas, Alfred T. *History of Chicago: From the Earliest Period to the Present Time.* Vol. 1, *Ending with the Year 1857.* Chicago: A. T. Andreas, 1884.

———. *History of Chicago: From the Earliest Period to the Present Time.* Vol. 2, *From 1857 until the Fire of 1871.* Chicago: A. T. Andreas, 1885.

———. *History of Chicago: From the Earliest Period to the Present Time.* Vol. 3, *From the Fire of 1871 until 1885.* Chicago: A. T. Andreas, 1886.

———. *A History of Cook County.* Chicago: A. T. Andreas, 1884.

Angle, Paul M. *"Here I Lived": A History of Lincoln's Springfield, 1821–1865.* Springfield, IL: Abraham Lincoln Association, 1935.

Arfwedson, C. D. *The United States and Canada, in 1832, 1833, and 1834.* Vol. 2. London: Richard Bentley, 1834.

Atherton, Lewis E. "Auctions as a Threat to American Business in the Eighteen Twenties and Thirties." *Bulletin of the Business Historical Society* 11 (1937): 104–7.

Atkinson, Eleanor, and the Editorial Staff of the Little Chronicle Company. *The Story of Chicago and National Development, 1534–1910.* Chicago: Little Chronicle, 1909.

Bagur, Jacques D. *A History of Navigation on Cypress Bayou and the Lakes.* Denton: University of North Texas Press, 2001.

Balestier, Joseph N. "The Annals of Chicago." In *The Annals of Chicago: A Lecture Read before the Chicago Lyceum, January 21, 1840; Republished from the Original Edition of 1840, with an Introduction Written by the Author in 1876, and Also a Review of the Lecture Published in the* Chicago Tribune *in 1872.* Chicago: Fergus, 1876.

Barclay, David. "Balmville: From the First Settlement to 1860." *Historical Papers* [of the Historical Society of Newburgh Bay and the Highlands] 8 (1901): 45–58.

Barlow, John Henry, ed. *The Mirror of Parliament for the Second Session of the Fourteenth Parliament of Great Britain and Ireland [. . .] February 5 [. . .] till August 27. 1839.* Vol. 5. London: Longman et al., 1839.

Barnes, Robert W. *Marriages and Deaths from Baltimore Newspapers, 1796–1816*. Baltimore: Genealogical Publishing, 1978.

———. *Maryland Marriages, 1801–1820*. Baltimore: Genealogical Publishing, 1993.

Bawden, William T., ed. *The National Crisis in Education: An Appeal to the People*. Washington, DC: Government Printing Office, 1920.

Beecher, Catherine E. *A Treatise on Domestic Economy, for the Use of Young Ladies at Home and at School*. Rev. ed. Boston: Thomas H. Webb, 1843.

Beers, Frederick W. *County Atlas of Orange, New York*. Chicago: Andreas, Baskin & Burr, 1875.

Beggs, Stephen R. *Pages from the Early History of the West and Northwest*. Cincinnati: Methodist Book Concern, 1868.

Bennett, Fremont O. *Politics and Politicians of Chicago, Cook County, and Illinois*. Chicago: Blakely, 1886.

Bernard, Karl. *Travels through North America, during the Years 1825 and 1826*. Vol. 2. 2 vols. in 1. Philadelphia: Carey, Lee, and Carey, 1828.

Blackhawk, Ned, et al., *Report of the Northwestern University John Evans Study Committee: Northwestern University, May 2014*. Evanston, IL: Northwestern University, 2014.

Blanchard, Rufus. *Discovery and Conquests of the North West with the History of Chicago*. Vol. 2. Chicago: R. Blanchard, 1900.

Blanks, William D. "Ideal and Practice: A Study of the Conception of the Christian Life Prevailing in the Presbyterian Churches of the Nineteenth Century." ThD diss., Union Theological Seminary in Virginia, 1960.

Bluestone, Daniel. *Constructing Chicago*. New Haven, CT: Yale University Press, 1991.

Blumenthal, Sidney. *A Self-Made Man: The Political Life of Abraham Lincoln, 1809–1849*. New York: Simon & Schuster, 2016.

[Board of Health of the City of Chicago.] *Report of the Board of Health of the City of Chicago for 1867, 1868, and 1869 and a Sanitary History of Chicago from 1833 to 1870*. Chicago: Lakeside, 1871.

Bolton, Robert. *A History of the County of Westchester from Its First Settlement to the Present Time*. Vol. 2. New York: Alexander S. Gould, 1848.

———. *History of the Protestant Episcopal Church, in the County of Westchester*. New York: Stanford & Swords, 1855.

Bower, Joseph. *Memoir of Joseph Bower*. Whitby, UK: W. Forth, 1838.

Boyer, Paul S. *Urban Masses and Moral Order in America, 1820–1920*. Cambridge, MA: Harvard University Press, 1978.

Branch, E. E., ed. *History of Ionia County, Michigan*. Vol. 1. Indianapolis: B. F. Bowen, 1916.

Brereton, Virginia L. *From Sin to Salvation: Stories of Women's Conversions, 1800 to the Present*. Bloomington: Indiana University Press, 1991.

Buettinger, Craig. "The Concept of Jacksonian Aristocracy: Chicago as a Test Case, 1833–1857." PhD diss., Northwestern University, 1982.

Bullock, William. *Sketch of a Journey through the Western States of North America from New Orleans, by the Mississippi, Ohio, City of Cincinnati, and Falls of Niagara, to New York, in 1827*. London: John Miller, 1827. Reprinted as *Bullock's Journey from New Orleans to New York in 1827*. Carlisle, MA: Applewood Books, 2007.

[Campbell, Mrs. Allen D.] *Why I Am a Presbyterian*. Philadelphia: William S. Martien, 1852.

Campbell, Ted A. "Spiritual Biography and Autobiography." In *The Cambridge Companion to American Methodism*, edited by Jason E. Vickers, 243–60. Cambridge: Cambridge University Press, 2013.

Canine, Craig. *Dream Reaper: The Story of an Old-Fashioned Inventor in the High-Tech, High-Stakes World of Modern Agriculture*. Chicago: University of Chicago Press, 1995.

Carnahan, James, ed. *The Autobiography and Ministerial Life of the Rev. John Johnston*. New York: M. W. Dodd, 1856.

Carnes, Marc C. "From Merchant to Manufacturer: The Economics of Localism in Newburgh, 1845–1900." In *America's First River: The History and Culture of the Hudson River Valley*, edited by Thomas S. Wermuth, James M. Johnson, and Christopher Pryslopski, 113–31. Poughkeepsie, NY: Hudson River Valley Institute, 2009.

Carter, Ruth C. "Cincinnatians and Cholera: Attitudes toward the Epidemics of 1832 and 1849." *Queen City Heritage*, Fall 1992, 32–48.

Carter, Thomas, comp., and John C. Grant, ed. "An Historical Sketch." In *The Second Presbyterian Church: June 1st, 1842 to June 1st, 1892*, 19–151. Chicago: Knight, Leonard, 1892.

Caton, John D. "The Last of the Illinois and a Sketch of the Pottawatomies." 1870. In *Miscellanies*, edited by John D. Caton, 114–45. Boston: Houghton, Osgood, 1880.

Chaudhuri, Keya, and S. N. Chatterjee. *Cholera Toxins*. Berlin: Springer, 2009.

Cherry, Conrad. *Hurrying toward Zion: Universities, Divinity Schools, and American Protestantism*. Bloomington: Indiana University Press, 1995.

"Chicago Mayors, 1837–2007." In *Encyclopedia of Chicago*. Chicago History Museum, Newberry Library, and Northwestern University. http://www.encyclopedia.chicagohistory.org/pages/1443.html.

Cist, Charles. *Cincinnati in 1841: Its Early Annals and Future Prospects*. Cincinnati: by the author, 1841.

[City of Cincinnati.] *Charter and Code of Ordinances of the City of Cincinnati*. Cincinnati: Council of the City of Cincinnati, 1828.

Clark, Davis W. "Mrs. Eliza Garrett." In *Our Excellent Women of the Methodist Church in England and America*, 201–9. New York: J. C. Buttre, 1861. Originally published as "Mrs. Garrett: Founder of the Garrett Biblical Institute," *Ladies' Repository* 18 (July 1858): 427–30.

Clark, Dwight F. "A Forgotten Evanston Institution: The Northwestern Female College." *Journal of the Illinois State Historical Society* 35, no. 2 (1942): 115–32.

Clark, Edgar W. *History and Genealogy of Samuel Clark, Sr., and His Descendants*. 2nd ed. St. Louis: Nixon-Jones Printing, 1902.

Clark, Robert D. *The Life of Matthew Simpson*. New York: Macmillan, 1956.

Clifton, James A. *The Prairie People: Continuity and Change in Potawatomi Indian Culture, 1665–1965*. Expanded ed. Iowa City: University of Iowa Press, 1998.

Cochrane, Charles H. *The History of the Town of Marlborough, Ulster County, New York: From the First Settlement in 1712, by Capt. Wm. Bond, to 1887*. Poughkeepsie, NY: W. F. Boshart, 1887.

Coggeshall, William T. "The Advantages of Planting Grain with a Drill, Practically Considered." *New Jersey Farmer* 4, no. 6 (February 1859).

[Cogshall, Selah.] "Chicago in 1839: The Reverend Selah W. Cogshall's Early Remembrances of Methodism in Chicago—The Great Revival in the Winter of 1839—Conversion of Mr. Garrett, Etc." *Chicago Daily Tribune*, November 24, 1873, 5.

Colton, Calvin. *Manual for Emigrants to America*. London: F. Westley and A. H. Davis, 1932.

[A Committee of New York Merchants.] *An Examination of the Reasons Why the Present System of Auction Ought to Be Abolished*. Boston: Beals, Homer, 1828.

Conard, Howard L. *Nathaniel J. Brown: Biographical Sketch and Reminiscences of a Noted Pioneer*. Chicago: Bryon S. Palmer, 1892.

———. "Western Real Estate Speculation Fifty Years Ago: Chicago's Famous Auction House: Nathaniel J. Brown." *National Magazine* 15, no. 6 (April 1892): 667–77.

Congressional Record, Containing the Proceedings and Debates of the Fifty-Second Congress, Second Session. Vol. 34, no. 2. Washington, DC: Government Printing House, 1901.

Conkin, Paul K. *A Revolution Down on the Farm: The Transformation of American Agriculture since 1929.* Lexington: University Press of Kentucky, 2009.

Cox, Nicholas. "The Panic of 1837." In *The Early Republic and Antebellum America: An Encyclopedia of Social, Political, Cultural, and Economic History,* edited by Christopher G. Bates, 785–90. London: Routledge, [2010] 2015.

Cummings, Anson W. *The Early Schools of Methodism.* New York: Phillips & Hunt; Cincinnati: Cranston & Stowe, 1886.

Currey, J. Seymour. *Chicago: Its History and Its Builders.* Vol. 3. Chicago: S. J. Clarke, 1918.

———. "Chicago's First Public School House." *Fort Dearborn Magazine* 3, no. 8 (November 1922): 23, 29.

Cutler, H. G. "Chicago prior to 1840, V.: The Body of the Town." *Magazine of Western History* 13, no. 3 (1891): 338–43.

Cutler, Wayne, and Robert G. Hall, eds. *Correspondence of James K. Polk.* Vol. 9, *January–June 1845.* Knoxville: University of Tennessee Press, 1996.

Danckers, Ulrich, and Jane Meredith. *A Compendium of the Early History of Chicago to the Year 1835 When the Indians Left.* River Forest, IL: Early Chicago, 2000.

Darby, William, and Theodore Dwight. *A New Gazetteer of the United States of America.* Hartford, CT: Edward Hopkins, 1833.

David, Paul A. *Technical Choice, Innovation and Economic Growth: Essays on American and British Experience in the Nineteenth Century.* Cambridge: Cambridge University Press, 1975.

Dempster, John. "The Teacher's Parting Word: An Address to the First Graduating Class of Garrett Biblical Institute" 1858. In *Lectures and Addresses by Rev. John Dempster,* edited by Davis W. Clark, 199–206. Cincinnati: Poe and Hitchcock, 1864.

Dick, Everett N. *The Lure of the Land: A Social History of the Public Lands from the Articles of Confederation to the New Deal.* Lincoln: University of Nebraska Press, 1970.

Dill, Scott W. *John Evans, 1814–1897: An Appreciation.* Evanston, IL: Lester J. Morris, 1939.

The Doctrines and Discipline of the Methodist Episcopal Church. New York: Mason and Lane, 1836.

Dolinar, Brian, ed. *The Negro in Illinois: WPA Papers.* Urbana: University of Illinois Press, 2013.

[Dorcas Society of Boston.] *Constitution of the Dorcas Society Instituted in Boston, 1819*. Boston: n.p., 1829.

Drake, Benjamin, and E. D. Mansfield. *Cincinnati in 1826*. Cincinnati: Morgan, Lodge, and Fisher, 1927.

Eager, Samuel W. *An Outline History of Orange County*. Newburgh, NY: S. T. Callahan, 1846–1847.

Early Chicago: Reception to the Settlers of Chicago prior to 1840 by the Calumet Club of Chicago, Tuesday Evening, May, 27, 1879. Chicago: Calumet Club, 1879.

Eddy, Thomas M. "Funeral Sermon, Preached on the Occasion of the Death of John Dempster." In John Dempster, *Lectures and Addresses*, edited by Davis W. Clark, separately paginated appendix. Cincinnati: Hitchcock, 1864.

"Editorial Correspondence." *Public*, March 29, 1902, 805–8.

Einhorn, Robin L. *Property Rules: Political Economy in Chicago, 1833–1872*. Chicago: University of Chicago Press, 1991.

Elliott, Charles. "Receiving Persons into the Church." *Western Christian Advocate* 7, no. 2 (May 1, 1840).

Emery, Rufus, E. M. Ruttenber, William K. Hall, Charles H. Weygant, and Wm. Cook Belknap. *A Record of the Inscriptions of the Old Town Burying Ground*. Newburgh, NY: Historical Society of Newburgh Bay and the Highlands, 1898.

Emory, Robert. *History of the Discipline of the Methodist Episcopal Church*, revised by W. P. Strickland. New York: Carlton & Porter, [1857].

Epstein, Barbara L. *The Politics of Domesticity: Women, Evangelism, and Temperance in Nineteenth-Century America*. Middleton, CT: Wesleyan University Press, 1981.

Evers, Joseph C. *The History of the Southern Illinois Conference*. Nashville: Parthenon, 1964.

Farmer, James O. *Metaphysical Confederacy: James Henley Thornwell and the Synthesis of Southern Values*. Macon, GA: Mercer University Press, 1986.

Farwell, John V. *Some Recollections of John V. Farwell: A Brief Description of His Early Life and Business Reminiscences*, edited by John V. Farwell Jr. Chicago: R. R. Donnelley & Sons, 1911.

Fehrenbacher, Don E. *Chicago Giant: A Biography of Long John Wentworth*. Madison, WI: American History Research Center, 1957.

Field, Alvaro D. *Memorials of Methodism in the Bounds of the Rock River Conference*. Cincinnati: Cranston & Stowe, 1886.

———. "Western Methodism." In *The Children's Centenary Memorial, or Exhibition Book*, edited by Daniel Wise, 72–79. New York: N. Tibbals, 1866.

———. *Worthies and Workers, Both Ministers and Laymen, of the Rock River Conference*. Cincinnati: Cranston & Curts, 1896.

Fisher, Ila Alexander. "Eliza Garrett: To Follow a Vision." In *Spirituality & Social Responsibility: Vocational Vision of Women in the United Methodist Tradition*, edited by Rosemary Skinner Keller, 41–60. Nashville: Abingdon, 1993.

Foley, Neil. *The White Scourge: Mexicans, Blacks, and Poor Whites in Texas Cotton Culture*. Berkeley: University of California Press, 1997.

Ford, Thomas. *A History of Illinois from Its Commencement as a State in 1818 to 1847*. Chicago: S. C. Griggs, 1854.

Fordham, Elias P. *Personal Narrative of Travels in Virginia, Maryland, Pennsylvania, Ohio, Indiana, Kentucky; and of a Residence in the Illinois Territory, 1817–1818*, edited by Frederic A. Ogg. Cleveland: Arthur H. Clark, 1906.

Fowler, C. H. "The Northwestern University." *Lakeside Monthly* 9 (June 1, 1873): 431–43.

Frank, S. B. *Chicago: Memorable Events and the Mayors We've Had*. N.p., 1894. Copy in Chicago Public Library. SPE CCW 41/14.

Gale, Edwin O. *Reminiscences of Early Chicago and Vicinity*. Chicago: Fleming H. Revell, 1902.

Gara, Larry. *The Liberty Line: The Legend of the Underground Railroad*. Lexington: University of Kentucky Press, 1961.

Garb, Margaret. *Freedom's Ballot: African American Political Struggles in Chicago from Abolition to the Great Migration*. Chicago: University of Chicago Press, 2014.

Garrett, Augustus. "First Inaugural Mayoral Address to the Common Council of Chicago." *Chicago Democrat*, March 14, 1843.

———. "Second Inaugural Mayoral Address to the Common Council of Chicago." *Chicago Democrat*, March 13, 1844.

———. "Third Inaugural Mayoral Address to the Common Council of Chicago." *Chicago Daily Democrat*, March 12, 1845.

Gedge, Karin E. *Without the Benefit of Clergy: Women and the Pastoral Relationship in Nineteenth-Century American Culture*. Oxford: Oxford University Press, 2003.

Gellman, David N. *Emancipating New York: The Politics of Slavery and Freedom, 1777–1827*. Baton Rouge: Louisiana State University Press, 2006.

[General Assembly of the State of Ohio.] *Acts of a General Nature, Ordered to Be Re-printed, at the First Session of the Eighteenth General Assembly of the State of Ohio*. Vol. 18. Columbus, OH: P. H. Olsted, 1820.

Gillett, Ezra H. *History of the Presbyterian Church in the United States of America*. Vol. 2. Philadelphia: Presbyterian Publication Committee, 1864.

Goodrich, Grant. *The Garrett Biblical Institute of the Methodist Episcopal Church, at Evanston, Illinois (near Chicago), Being a History of the Events Which Led to Its Organization and Endowment, with a Copy of Its Charter and the Will of the Late Mrs. Garrett.* Chicago: Daily Democrat, 1856.

———. *Manual of Information respecting the Garrett Biblical Institute.* Evanston, IL: Trustees, 1857.

———. "Peter Ruble Borein." In *Annals of the American Pulpit.* Vol. 7, *The Methodist,* edited by William B. Sprague, 784–86. New York: Robert Carter and Brothers, 1859.

Goodspeed, Weston A., and Daniel D. Healy, eds. *History of Cook County, Illinois.* Vol. 1. Chicago: Goodspeed Historical Association, 1909.

Gordon, Thomas F. *Gazetteer of the State of New York.* Philadelphia: T. K. and P. G. Collins, 1836.

"The Great Flaglor Suits." *Monthly Western Jurist* [bound under title *Weekly Jurist*] 1, no. 10 (February 1875): 433–34.

Greve, Charles T. *Centennial History of Cincinnati and Representative Citizens.* Vol. 1. Chicago: Biographical Publishing, 1904.

Griffin, Clifford S. "Converting the Catholics: American Benevolent Societies and the Ante-bellum Crusade against the Church." *Catholic Historical Review* 47 (1961): 325–41.

Grigg, D. B. *The Agricultural Systems of the World: An Evolutionary Approach.* Cambridge: Cambridge University Press, 1974.

Groneman, Carol. "Working-Class Immigrant Women in Mid-Nineteenth-Century New York: The Irish Women's Experience." In *Industrial Wage Work,* edited by Nancy F. Cott, 145–63. Munich: K. G. Saur, 1993.

Grossman, James R., et al., *The Encyclopedia of Chicago.* Chicago: University of Chicago Press, 2004.

Haeger, John Denis. *The Investment Frontier: New York Businessmen and the Economic Development of the Old Northwest.* Albany: State University of New York Press, 1981.

Haig, Robert M. *A History of General Property Tax in Illinois.* PhD diss., Columbia University; Champaign: University of Illinois, 1914.

Hall, Frederick. *Letters from the East and from the West.* Washington, DC: F. Taylor and Wm. M. Morrison, 1840. Reprint, Carlisle, MA: Applewood Books.

Hall, W. W. "The Health of Farmers' Families." In *The Report of the Commissioner of Agriculture for the Year 1862,* 453–70. Washington, DC: Government Printing Office, 1863.

[Hamline, Melinda.] "Mrs. Bishop Hamline." In *The Riches of Grace: or The Blessing of Perfected Love as Experienced, Enjoyed, and Recorded by Sixty-Two Living Witnesses*, 287–90. Williamsburgh, NY: Henry J. Fox, 1854.

Harding, George F. *Sixty-Third Annual Report of the Comptroller of the City of Chicago, Illinois for the Fiscal Year Ended December 31, 1919*. Chicago: John F. Higgins, [1920].

Harper, Douglas. *Changing Works: Visions of a Lost Agriculture*. Chicago: University of Chicago Press, 2001.

Harpster, Jack. *The Railroad Tycoon Who Built Chicago: A Biography of William B. Ogden*. Carbondale: Southern Illinois University Press, 2009.

Hastings, Hugh, comp. and ed. *Military Minutes of the Council of Appointment of the State of New York, 1783–1821*. Vol. 1. Albany, NY: James B. Lyon, 1901.

Hayward, John. *Appendix to Hayward's New England Gazetteer and Specimens of the Northern Register*. [Boston]: W. White, 1841.

Hedrick, Joan D. *Harriet Beecher Stowe: A Life*. Oxford: Oxford University Press, 1994.

Henry, John F. "A Letter on the Cholera as It Occurred in Cincinnati, Ohio, in the Month of October, 1832." *Transylvania Journal of Medicine* 5, no. 4 (1832): 507–33.

Hibbard, Freeborn G. *Biography of Rev. Leonidas L. Hamline*. Cincinnati: Walden & Stowe, 1881; New York: Phillips & Hunt, 1881.

History of McHenry County, Together with Sketches of Its Cities, Villages, and Towns [. . .] Also a Condensed History of Illinois. Chicago: Inter-State Publishing, 1885.

History of the Hamline University of Minnesota When Located at Redwing from 1854 to 1869. N.p.: Alumni Association of the College of Liberal Arts of Hamline University, 1907.

Hodgson, Francis. *An Examination of the System of New Divinity; or, New School Theology*. New York: George Lane, 1839.

Hoffman, Charles F. *A Winter in the West: By a New-Yorker*. Vol. 1. New York: Harper & Bros., 1835.

Holifield, E. Brooks. *A History of Pastoral Care in America: From Salvation to Self-Realization*. Nashville: Abingdon Press, 1983.

Holli, Melvin G., and Peter d'Alroy Jones, eds. *Ethnic Chicago: A Multicultural Portrait*. 4th ed. Grand Rapids, MI: Eerdmans, 1995.

Hood, Humphrey H. "The Chicago Convention." In *Reminiscences of Chicago during the Civil War*, 41–50. Chicago: R. R. Donnelley, 1914.

[House of Representatives.] *Journal of the House of Representatives of the United States, Being the Second Session of the Eighteenth Congress, Begun and Held at the City of Washington, Dec. 6, 1924.* Washington, DC: Gales & Seaton, 1824.

Hoyt, Homer. *One Hundred Years of Land Values in Chicago: The Relationship of the Growth of Chicago to the Rise of Its Land Values, 1830–1933.* Chicago: University of Chicago Press, 1933.

Hurlbut, Henry H. *Chicago Antiquities.* Chicago: Fergus, 1881.

Hyde, James N. *Early Medical Chicago: An Historical Sketch of the First Practitioners of Medicine in Chicago.* Chicago: W. B. Keen, Cooke, 1876.

Inskeep, Steve. *Jacksonland: President Andrew Jackson, Cherokee Chief John Ross, and a Great American Land Grab.* New York: Penguin Books, 2015.

Jaher, Frederic C. *The Urban Establishment: Upper Strata in Boston, New York, Charleston, Chicago, and Los Angeles.* Urbana: University of Illinois Press, 1982.

Johnston, Shepherd. "Historical Sketches of the Public School System of the City of Chicago." Appendix to *Twenty-Fifth Annual Report of the Board of Education for the Year Ending July 31, 1879,* 1–79. Chicago: Clark & Edwards, 1880.

Jones, Charles E. *Perfectionist Persuasion: The Holiness Movement and American Methodism, 1867–1936.* Lanham, MD: Scarecrow Press, 2002.

Jones, John. *The Black Laws of Illinois, and a Few Reasons Why They Should Be Repealed.* Chicago: Tribune Book and Job Office, 1864.

Journal of the House of Representatives of the Twelfth General Assembly of the State of Illinois, Convened [. . .] Nov. 23, 1840. Springfield: Wm. Walters, 1840.

Journal of the Senate of the Twelfth General Assembly of the State of Illinois, Convened [. . .] Nov. 23, 1840. Springfield: Wm. Walters, 1841.

Kable, Harry G. *Mount Morris: Past and Present.* Mount Morris, MI: Kable Brothers, 1900.

Keating, Ann Durkin, ed. *Chicago Neighborhoods and Suburbs: A Historical Guide.* Chicago: University of Chicago Press, 2008.

———. *Chicagoland: City and Suburbs in the Railroad Age.* Chicago: University of Chicago Press, 2005.

———. *Rising Up from Indian Country: The Battle of Fort Dearborn and the Birth of Chicago.* Chicago: University of Chicago Press, 2012.

Kellogg, H. H. [Speech.] In *Proceedings of the General Anti-Slavery Convention Called by the Committee of the British and Foreign Anti-Slavery Society and Held in London [. . .] 1843,* 265–74. London: British and Foreign Anti-Slavery Society, 1843.

Kelly, Catherine E. *In the New England Fashion: Reshaping Women's Lives in the Nineteenth Century.* Ithaca, NY: Cornell University Press, 1999.

Kinzie, Juliette [Mrs. John H. Kinzie]. *Wau-Bun: The "Early Day" in the North-West*. New York: Derby & Jackson, 1856.

Koester, Nancy. *Harriet Beecher Stowe: A Spiritual Life*. Grand Rapids, MI: Eerdmans, 2014.

Kotar, S. L., and J. E. Gessler. *The Steamboat Era: A History of Fulton's Folly on America's Rivers, 1807–1860*. Jefferson, NC: McFarland, 2009.

Krauth, Charles P. *Infant Baptism and Infant Salvation in the Calvinist System: A Review of Dr. Hodge's Systematic Theology*. Philadelphia: Lutheran Book Store, 1874.

Kugler, J. Newton. *A Brief History of the First Presbyterian Church, Marlborough, New York, 1764–1914*. Newburgh, NY: News, ca. 1914.

Langland, James, ed. *The Chicago Daily News Almanac and Year-Book for 1921*. Chicago: Chicago Daily News, 1920.

———, ed. *The Chicago Daily News Almanac and Year-Book for the Year 1922*. Chicago: Chicago Daily News, 1921.

Lantz, Herman R., Margaret Britton, Raymond Schmitt, and Eloise C. Snyder. "Pre-industrial Patterns in the Colonial Family in America: A Content Analysis of Colonial Magazines." *American Sociological Review* 33 (1968): 413–26.

Larkin, Jack. *The Reshaping of Everyday Life, 1790–1840*. New York: Harper & Row, 1988.

Laws of the State of Illinois Passed by the Fourteenth General Assembly. Springfield, IL: Walters and Weber, 1845.

Leaton, James. *History of Methodism in Illinois, 1793–1832*. Cincinnati: Walden and Stowe, 1883.

Leslie, Augusta. "Record of Baptisms and Marriages Copied from and Compared with the Original Entries in Stewards' Book, Newburgh, N.Y., Circuit of the Methodist Episcopal Church," *Historical Papers* [of the Historical Society of Newburgh and the Highlands] 8 (1901): 7–30.

Levy, George. *To Die in Chicago: Confederate Prisoners at Camp Douglas, 1862–1865*. 2nd ed. Gretna, LA: Pelican Publishing, 1999.

Little, Charles J. "Garrett Biblical Institute." In *History of Northwestern University and Evanston*, edited by Robert D. Sheppard and Harvey B. Hurd, 163–67. Chicago: Munsell, 1906.

Littlefield, Daniel F., and James W. Parins, eds. *Encyclopedia of American Indian Removal*. Vol. 1. Santa Barbara, CA: Greenwood, 2011.

Louisiana Writers' Project. *Louisiana: A Guide to the State*. New York: Hastings House, 1941.

Lyford, W. G. *The Western Address Directory* [. . .] *Together with Historical, Topographical, and Statistical Sketches (for the Year 1837).* Baltimore: Jos. Robinson, 1837.

Lystra, Karen. *Searching the Heart: Women, Men, and Romantic Love in Nineteenth-Century America.* Oxford: Oxford University Press, 1989.

Mahan, MaryLou. *The First Hundred Years.* Lincoln, NE: Writers Club Press, 2002.

Mahoney, Timothy R. *Provincial Lives: Middle-Class Experience in the Antebellum Middle West.* Cambridge: Cambridge University Press, 1999.

Manierre, George. "The Manierre Family in Early Chicago History." *Journal of the Illinois State Historical Society* 8, no. 3 (1915): 448–58.

Martineau, Harriet. *Society in America.* Vol. 1. New York: Saunders and Otley, 1837.

———. *Society in America.* Vol. 2. Paris: Baudry's European Library, 1837.

McCarthy, Kathleen D. *Noblesse Oblige: Charity and Cultural Philanthropy in Chicago, 1849–1929.* Chicago: University of Chicago Press, 1982.

McCulloh, Gerald O. *Ministerial Education in the American Methodist Movement.* Nashville: United Methodist Board of Higher Education and Ministry, 1980.

McMahon, Sarah F. "Laying Foods By: Gender, Dietary Decisions, and the Technology of Food Preservation in New England Households, 1750–1850." In *Early American Technology: Making and Doing Things from the Colonial Era to 1850,* edited by Judith A. McGaw, 164–96. Chapel Hill: University of North Carolina Press, 1994.

Merrill, Estelle M. H. "By an Old-Time Fireside." *New England Kitchen Magazine* 1, no. 3 (1894): 131–36.

Miller, Donald L. *City of the Century: The Epic of Chicago and the Making of America.* New York: Simon & Schuster, 1996.

Miller, Glenn T. *Piety and Intellect. The Aims and Purposes of Ante-bellum Theological Education.* Atlanta: Scholars, 1990.

Miller, John C. *The First Frontier: Life in Colonial America.* New York: Dell, 1966.

Minutes of the Annual Conferences of the Methodist Episcopal Church for the Years 1829–1839. New York: T. Mason and G. Lane, 1840.

Moriarty, John D. "Newburgh Campmeeting." *Methodist Magazine* 8, no. 11 (November 1825): 440–41.

Moses, John. *Illinois, Historical and Statistical.* Vol. 1. Chicago: Fergus, 1889.

Moses, John, and Joseph Kirkland. *History of Chicago, Illinois.* Vol. 1. Chicago: Munsell, 1895.

Mosteller, Kelli. "Potawatomi Allotment in Kansas." In *Indigenous Communities and Settler Colonialism: Land Holding, Loss, and Survival in an Interconnected World*, edited by Zoë Laidlaw and Alan Lester, 214–32. Basingstoke, UK: Palgrave Macmillan, 2015.

[New York Manumission Society.] *Selections from the Revised Statutes of the State of New York, Containing All Laws of the State Relative to Slaves and the Law Relative to the Offences of Kidnapping, Which Several Laws Took Effect January 1, 1830.* New York: Vanderpool & Cole, 1830.

Nightingale, Joseph. *A Portraiture of Methodism.* London: Longman, Hurst, Rees, and Orme, 1807.

"North-Western Methodist Biblical Institute." *Western Christian Advocate* 22 (January 1855): 3.

Norwood, Frederick A. *From Dawn to Midday at Garrett.* Evanston, IL: Garrett-Evangelical Theological Seminary, 1978.

Oden, C. Thomas. *Doctrinal Standards in the Wesleyan Tradition.* Rev. ed. Nashville: Abingdon, 2008.

———, ed. *Phoebe Palmer: Selected Writings.* New York: Paulist, 1988.

Olegario, Rowena. *The Engine of Enterprise: Credit in America.* Cambridge, MA: Harvard University Press, 2016.

Otis, Philo A. *The First Presbyterian Church, 1833–1913.* Rev. ed. Chicago: Fleming H. Revell, 1913.

Palmer, Phoebe. *Faith and Its Effects, or Fragments from My Portfolio.* New York: Joseph Looking, 1850.

———. *A Mother's Gift, or A Wreath for My Darlings.* New York: W. C. Palmer; London: F. E. Longley, 1875.

———. *The Way of Holiness.* New York: printed for the author, 1854.

Palmer, Walter C. *Life and Letters of Leonidas L. Hamline.* New York: Carlton & Porter, 1866.

Parker, Amos A. *Trip to the West and Texas, Comprising a Journey of Eight Thousand Miles through New-York, Michigan, Illinois, Missouri, Louisiana and Texas, in the Autumn and Winter of 1834–5.* Concord, NH: White and Fisher, 1835.

The People's Democratic Guide. Vol. 1. New York: James Webster, 1842.

Pierce, Bessie Louise. *A History of Chicago.* Vol. 1, *The Beginning of a City, 1673–1848.* Chicago: University of Chicago Press, 1937.

———. *A History of Chicago.* Vol. 2, *From Town to City, 1848–1871.* Chicago: University of Chicago Press, 1940.

Pierson, George W. *Tocqueville and Beaumont in America.* Oxford: Oxford University Press, 1938.

Pittman, Grace M. "O My Son Benoni: A Personal Name as Marker of Family Circumstances." *NEXUS* 7 (1990): 17–21.

Porter, Jeremiah. "The Earliest Religious History of Chicago: An Address Read before the Chicago Historical Society in 1859." In *Fergus' Historical Series* no. 14. Chicago: Fergus, n.d.

———. "Sketches of a Pioneer Ministry" (1877). In *Pioneer Collections: Report of the Pioneer Society of the State of Michigan*. Vol. 4. of *Michigan Historical Collections*. 1883. Reprint, Lansing, MI: Wynkoop Hallenbeck Crawford, 1906.

Power, John C., and S. A. Power. *History of the Early Settlers of Sangamon County, Illinois*. Springfield, IL: Edwin A. Wilson, 1876.

Prentiss, George L. "Infant Salvation and Its Theological Bearings." *Presbyterian Review* 4 (1883): 548–80.

Private and Special Laws of the State of Illinois Passed by the Fifteenth General Assembly. Springfield, IL: Lanphier, 1847.

Proceedings of the National Convention for the Protection of American Interests in the City of New-York, April 5, 1841. New York: Greeley and McElrath, 1841.

The Public and General Statutes of the State of Illinois. Chicago: Gale, 1839.

Purple, Norman H., comp. *A Compilation of the Statutes of the State of Illinois, of a General Nature, in Force January 1, 1856*. Part 1. Chicago: Keen & Lee, 1856.

Quaife, Milo M. *Chicago and the Old Northwest, 1673–1835*. Chicago: University of Chicago Press, ca. 1913.

Randall, Frank A., and John D. Randall, *History of the Development of Building Construction in Chicago*. 2nd ed. Urbana: University of Illinois Press, 1999.

Rasch, Bradley W. *The Governors of Illinois and the Mayors of Chicago: People of Regional, National, and International Consequence*. Bloomington, IN: iUniverse, 2012.

Raser, Harold E. *Phoebe Palmer: Her Life and Thought*. Lewiston, NY: Edwin Mellon, 1987.

Rauch, John H. *Intramural Interments in Populous Cities and Their Influence on Health and Epidemics*. Chicago: Tribune, 1866.

Reed, Christopher R. *Black Chicago's First Century*. Vol. 1, *1833–1900*. Columbia: University of Missouri Press, 2005.

Register of Debates in Congress, Comprising the Leading Debates and Incidents of the First Session of the Twenty-First Congress. Vol. 6. Washington, DC: Gales and Seaton, 1830.

Revised Statutes of the State of Illinois Adopted by the General Assembly of the State of Illinois, at Its Regular Session Held in the Years, A.D., 1844–1845, prepared by M. Brayman. Springfield, IL: William Walters, 1845.

Rice, N. L. *God Sovereign and Man Free: On the Doctrine of Foreordination and Man's Free Agency*. Philadelphia: Presbyterian Board of Publication, 1850.

Richey, Russell E., Kenneth E. Rowe, and Jean Miller Schmidt. *The Methodist Experience in America*. Vol. 1, *A History*. Nashville: Abingdon, 2010.

Roberts, Alasdair. *America's First Great Depression: Economic Crisis and Political Disorder after the Panic of 1837*. Ithaca, NY: Cornell University Press, 2012.

Robertson, John E. L. *Paducah: 1830–1980, a Sesquicentennial History*. Paducah, KY: published by the author, [1980].

Rohrbough, Malcolm J. *The Land Office Business: The Settlement and Administration of American Public Lands, 1789–1837*. New York: Oxford University Press, 1968.

Rosenberg, Charles E. *The Cholera Years: The United States in 1832, 1849, and 1866*. Chicago: University of Chicago Press, 1962.

Rosenthal, Mark, and Carol Tauber. *The Ark in the Park: The Story of Lincoln Park Zoo*. Urbana: University of Illinois Press, 2003.

Rotundo, E. Anthony. *American Manhood: Transformations in Masculinity from the Revolution to the Modern Era*. New York: Basic Books, 1993.

Rousseau, Peter L. "Jacksonian Monetary Policy, Specie Flows, and the Panic of 1837." *Journal of Economic History* 62 (2002): 457–88.

Ruttenber, Edward, M. *History of the County of Orange, with a History of the Town of Newburgh*. Newburgh, NY: E. M. Ruttenber and Sons, 1875.

———. *History of the Town of Newburgh*. Newburgh, NY: E. M. Ruttenber, 1859.

———. "The King's Highway: Its Early Road Districts and the Residents or Owners of Lands Thereon." *Historical Papers* [of the Historical Society of Newburgh Bay and the Highlands] 10 (1903): 21–33.

S. [Sawyer, J. T.] "Salvation of Infants." *Christian Messenger* 1 (March 10, 1832): 149.

Sanderson, John. *Sketches of Paris: In Familiar Letters to His Friends, by an American Gentleman*. Philadelphia: Carey & Hart, 1838.

[Scammon, J. Young.] "Speech of J. Young Scammon." In *Early Chicago: Reception to the Settlers of Chicago prior to 1840 by the Calumet Club of Chicago, Tuesday Evening, May, 27, 1879*, 65–70. Chicago: Calumet Club, 1879.

Schnell, Christopher A. "Wives, Widows, and Will Makers: Women and the Law of Property." In *In Tender Consideration: Women, Family, and the Law in Abraham Lincoln's Illinois*, edited by Daniel W. Stowell, 129–60. Urbana: University of Illinois, 2002.

Schultz, Rima Lunin, and Adele Hast, eds., *Women Building Chicago, 1790–1990: A Biographical Dictionary*. Bloomington: Indiana University Press, 2001.

Seale, Richard. "The Town of Natchitoches." In *Natchitoches and Louisiana's Timeless Cane River*, edited by Philip Gould, Richard Seale, Robert DeBlieux, and Harlan M. Guidry, 6–49. Baton Rouge: Louisiana State University Press, 2002.

Second Biennial Report of the Superintendent of Public Instruction of the State of Illinois for the Years 1857–58. Springfield, IL: Bailhache & Baker, 1859.

Seeger, Eugen. *Chicago, the Wonder City*. Chicago: Geo. Gregory, 1893.

Semi-centennial Celebration, Garrett Biblical Institute, May Fifth to Ninth, 1906. Evanston, IL: Garrett Biblical Institute, 1906.

Sewall, Richard B. *The Life of Emily Dickinson*. 2 vols. in 1. Cambridge, MA: Harvard University Press, [1974], 1994.

Shaver, Lisa J. *Beyond the Pulpit: Women's Rhetorical Roles in the Antebellum Religious Press*. Pittsburgh: University of Pittsburgh Press, 2012.

Sheppard, Robert D., and Harvey B. Hurd, eds. *History of Northwestern University and Evanston*. Chicago: Munsell, 1906.

Simpson, Matthew, ed. *Cyclopedia of Methodism*. 5th ed. Philadelphia: Louis H. Everts, 1883.

Sisson, Richard, Christian K. Zacher, and Andrew R. L. Clayton, eds. *The American Midwest: An Interpretive Encyclopedia*. Bloomington: Indiana University Press, 2007.

Smith, Daniel B. "The Study of the Family in Early America: Trends, Problems, and Prospects." *William and Mary Quarterly* 39 (1982): 3–28.

Smith, Timothy. *Revivalism and Social Reform: American Protestantism on the Eve of the Civil War*. New York: Abingdon, 1957.

Spafford, Horatio G., ed. *A Gazetteer of the State of New York*. Albany, NY: B. D. Packard, 1824.

[State of New York.] *Laws of the State of New York Passed at the Fortieth Session of the Legislature*. Vol. 4. Albany, NY: Websters and Skinners, 1818.

———. *Laws of the State of New York Passed at the Twenty-Second Session, Second Meeting, of the Legislature*. Albany, NY: Loring Andrews, 1799.

"Steamboats in the West." *Hazard's Register of Pennsylvania* 5 (1830): 74–75.

Stevens, Abel. *The Women of Methodism: Its Three Foundresses, Susanna Wesley, the Countess of Huntingdon, and Barbara Heck*. New York: Carlton & Porter, 1866.

Stokes, Claudia. *The Altar at Home: Sentimental Literature and the Nineteenth Century America*. Philadelphia: University of Pennsylvania Press, 2014.

Strobridge, G. E. *Biography of the Rev. Daniel Parish Kidder*. New York: Hunt and Eaton, 1894.

[Strong, Henry.] "Speech of General Henry Strong." In *Early Chicago: Reception to the Settlers of Old Chicago prior to 1840 by the Calumet Club of Chicago, Tuesday Evening, May 27, 1879*, 26–34. Chicago: Calumet Club, 1879.

Stuart, Charles M. "Garrett Marching On." *Christian Student* 23, no. 4 (November 1922): 161–64.

Stufflebean, Debra Guiou(n). *A French Huguenot Legacy: A Biography of the Guion Huguenots*. Morrisville, NC: LuLu Enterprises, 2011.

Sunderman, Lloyd F. "Chicago's Centennial of School Music." *Music Educators Journal* 28, no. 5 (1942): 28–30, 63–64.

Sylvester, Bartlett N. *History of Ulster County, New York*. Philadelphia: Everts & Peck, 1860.

Taylor, Charles H., ed. *History of the Board of Trade of the City of Chicago*. Vol. 1, part 1. Chicago: Robert O. Law, 1917.

Terzian, Sevan G., and Nancy Beadie. "'Let the People Remember It': Academies and the Rise of Public High Schools, 1865–1890." In *Chartered Schools: Two Hundred Years of Independent Academies in the United States, 1727–1925*, edited by Nancy Beadie and Kim Tolley, 251–83. London: Routledge, [2002] 2013.

Thalheimer, M. E. "History of the Vine Street Congregational Church of Cincinnati." In *Papers of the Ohio Church History Society*. Vol. 9, edited by Delavan L. Leonard, 41–56. Oberlin, OH: Ohio Church History Society, 1898.

Thuesen, Peter J. *Predestination: The American Career of a Contentious Doctrine*. Oxford: Oxford University Press, 2009.

Tracy, Joseph. *The Great Awakening: A History of the Revival of Religion in the Time of Edwards and Whitefield*. Boston: Charles Tappan, 1845.

Trollope, Frances. *Domestic Manners of the Americans*. Vol. 1. London: Whittaker, Treacher, 1832.

United States Department of Agriculture. *Social and Labor Needs of Farm Women*. Report no. 103. Washington, DC: Government Printing Office, 1915.

United States Department of the Treasury. "Report from the Secretary of the Treasury in Compliance with a Resolution of the Senate, relative to Increase of the Salaries of Clerks, 24th Congress, 1st Session, S. Doc. 355." In *Public Documents Printed by Order of the Senate of the United States, First Session of the Twenty-Fourth Congress*. Vol. 5. Washington, DC: Gales & Seaton, 1836.

Vail, Stephen M. *Ministerial Education in the Methodist Episcopal Church.* Boston: George C. Hand, 1853.

Vanderpoel, Emily Noyes, comp. *Chronicles of a Pioneer School from 1792–1833, Being the History of Miss Sarah Pierce and Her Litchfield School,* edited by Elizabeth C. Barney Buel. Cambridge, MA: [Harvard] University Press, 1903.

Vickers, Jason E., ed. *The Cambridge Companion to American Methodism.* New York: Cambridge University Press, 2013.

Wallis, John J. "Constitutions, Corporations, and Corruption: American States and Constitutional Change, 1842–1852." *Journal of Economic History* 65, no. 1 (2005): 211–256.

Ward, Estelle F. *The Story of Northwestern University.* New York: Dodd, Mead, 1924.

War Department Annual Reports, 1913. Vol. 2, *Report of the Chief of Engineers, U.S. Army.* Part 1. Washington, DC: Government Printing Office, 1913.

Washington, Margaret. *Sojourner Truth's America.* Urbana: University of Illinois Press, 2009.

Way, Royal B., ed. *The Rock River Valley: Its History, Traditions, Legends, and Charms.* Vol. 1. Chicago: S. J. Clarke, 1926.

Wentworth, John. *Early Chicago: A Lecture Delivered before the Sunday Lecture Society, at McCormick Hall, on Sunday Afternoon, April 11, 1875.* Chicago: Fergus, 1875.

[Wentworth, John.] "Speech of Hon. John Wentworth." In *Early Chicago: Reception to the Settlers of Chicago prior to 1840 by the Calumet Club of Chicago, Tuesday Evening, May 27, 1879,* 45–62. Chicago: Calumet Club, 1879.

Wheatley, Richard. *The Life and Letters of Mrs. Phoebe Palmer.* New York: Palmer and Hughes, 1876.

Whittock, Nathaniel, J. Bennett, J. Badcock, C. Newton, et al. *The Complete Book of Trades.* London: Thomas Tegg, 1842.

Wigger, John H. *Taking Heaven by Storm: Methodism and the Rise of Popular Christianity in America.* New York: Oxford University Press, 1988.

Wilde, Arthur H. *Northwestern University, a History: 1855–1905.* Vol. 1. New York: University Publishing Society, 1905.

Willard, Frances E. *A Classic Town: The Story of Evanston by an "Old Timer."* Chicago: Women's Temperance Publishing Association, 1891.

———. "X. Frances E. Willard (Methodist)." In *Forty Witnesses, Covering the Whole Range of Christian Experience,* edited by S. Olin Garrison, 90–99. New York: Phillips & Hunt, 1888; Cincinnati: Cranston & Stowe, 1888.

Williams, Mentor L. "A Tour of Illinois in 1842." *Journal of the Illinois State Historical Society* 42, no. 3 (1949): 292–312.

Williams, T. Harry. "The Committee on the Conduct of the War: An Experiment in Civil Control." In *Civil-Military Relations*, ed. Peter Karsten, 173–90. New York: Garland Publishing, 1998.

Williams, Wellington. *The Traveller's and Tourist's Guide through the United States of America*. Philadelphia: Lippincott, Grambo, 1855.

Williams, William H. *The Garden of American Methodism: The Delmarva Peninsula, 1769–1820*. Lanham, MD: Rowman and Littlefield, 1984.

Woodson, Carter G. *Negro Makers of History*. Washington, DC: Associated Publishers, 1928.

Woolsey, C. M. *History of the Town of Marlborough, Ulster County, New York, from Its Earliest Discovery*. Albany, NY: J. B. Lyon, 1908.

Wright, John S. *Chicago: Past, Present, Future*. 2nd ed. Chicago: Horton & Leonard, 1870.

Yrigoyen, Charles, ed. *T & T Clark Companion to Methodism*. London: T & T Clark, 2010.

INDEX

Page numbers in *italics* refer to illustrations.

Texas, annexation or independence of,
32–33, 91–92, 130, 206n27
Texians, 92, 232n6
theater (Chicago), 56
Third Ward (Chicago), 95–96, 116, 118,
120, 123, 234n14, 244n65
Thompson, Oliver H., 73, 223n8
timekeeping and clocks, 117–18
Tocqueville, Alexis de, 30–31
travel times and distances, 24, 43,
45, 52, 174, 207n34, 209n50, 210n2,
214n19
Trollope, Frances, 25
Tyler, John, 91

Uncle Tom's Cabin (Stowe), 34
Underground Railway, 33, 106
United Methodist Church, creation
of, 267n40
United States Hotel (Chicago), 55, 56
U.S. Supreme Court, 57

vaccinations, small pox (Chicago),
127–28
Van Buren, Martin, 79, 90
View of Cincinnati (Wild), 25
"vigilance" committees, 90, 231n1
voting irregularities, charges of,
116–23, 244n65, 245n73

war dance of Potawatomi tribe, 57,
58–59
Watson, James, 174

Wentworth, Elijah, 82
Wentworth, George, 114, 123
Wentworth, John: arrival and early
days in Chicago, 43, 56; friendship
of Augustus with, 61, 90, 123; as
mayor and congressman, 1, 109, 129,
146–47
Western Christian Advocate, 85
western expansion as destiny, 25–27
Whig Party, 27, 90–91, 114–16, 118,
120, 123, 124
White, George, 70
Wild, John Caspar, 25, 30
Willard, Frances E., 169
Wilson, Joshua, 32, 33, 40
Wolf Point (Chicago), 45, 46, 135,
216n23
women in early 1800s: anger at God
as reaction of, 68, 221n53; education and, 2, 165, 167–70, 175, 189n3,
264nn25–26, 265n31, 267n40; in
1844 Chicago city directory, 149,
255n43; estate laws and, 162–63,
171, 261n17; farm life for, 7–8, 19, 31,
193n13, 199n38, 205n25; marriage,
lack of power in, 131, 132, 137, 148, 152,
171; opportunity, lack of, 149–50,
255n45; pastoral care, lack of, 38,
68–69; public viewpoints, lack of, 61;
recognition, lack of, 1–2, 149, 189n2
Wright, James S., 94, 135

yellow fever, 40, 41

CHARLES H. COSGROVE is a professor of early Christian literature and the director of the PhD program at Garrett-Evangelical
Theological Seminary, a union of schools descended from the
institution founded by Eliza Garrett in 1853 that is located on
the campus of Northwestern University. He is the author of
numerous books and articles in a wide range of fields, including
theology, ethics, ancient music, and legal history. A lifelong native
of the Chicago area, Cosgrove is an aficionado of the city's history
and makes the occasional appearance in area music venues as a
professional jazz trombonist.